SAP Query Reporting

Danielle Larocca Signorile

SAMS

800 East 96th Street
Indianapolis, Indiana 46240

CONTENTS AT A GLANCE

SAP Query Reporting

International Standard Book Number: 0-672-32902-6

Library of Congress Catalog Card Number: 752063329023

Printed in the United States of America

First Printing: July 2006

10   09   08   07   06   4   3   2   1

Trademarks

All terms mentioned in this book that are known to be trademarks or service marks have been appropriately capitalized. Sams Publishing cannot attest to the accuracy of this information. Use of a term in this book should not be regarded as affecting the validity of any trademark or service mark.

Warning and Disclaimer

Every effort has been made to make this book as complete and as accurate as possible, but no warranty or fitness is implied. The information provided is on an "as is" basis. The author and the publisher shall have neither liability nor responsibility to any person or entity with respect to any loss or damages arising from the information contained in this book.

Bulk Sales

Sams Publishing offers excellent discounts on this book when ordered in quantity for bulk purchases or special sales. For more information, please contact

U.S. Corporate and Government Sales
1-800-382-3419
corpsales@pearsontechgroup.com

For sales outside of the U.S., please contact

International Sales
international@pearsoned.com

Associate Publisher
Greg Wiegand

Acquisitions Editor
Loretta Yates

Development Editor
Kevin Howard

Managing Editor
Gina Kanouse

Project Editor
Christy Hackerd

Copy Editor
Kitty Jarrett

Indexer
Lisa Stumpf

Proofreader
Gayle Johnson

Technical Editor
A.J. Whalen

Publishing Coordinator
Sharry Lee Gregory

Interior Designer
Anne Jones

Cover Designer
Gary Adair

Page Layout
Nonie Ratcliff

TABLE OF CONTENTS

About the Author

Danielle Larocca Signorile, an independent executive SAP consultant, has written a handful of books on SAP technologies. Danielle is a featured speaker at many SAP conferences throughout the United States. Her articles have been published in multiple trade magazines, including *SAP Professional Journal*, *SAP Insider*, and *SAP HR Expert*, a publication on which she served as an advisor and columnist for the "Ask the Expert" section. Danielle has also been interviewed for *HR Executive Magazine*. She earned a bachelor of science degree in psychology and holds certificates and certifications for many areas of SAP, including Human Resources, ABAP Programming, and Basis Technologies. Danielle is an ABAP programmer as well as an expert on SAP query-based reporting and the Human Capital Management module. Danielle has documented and instructed people on multiple computer languages and applications, including ABAP, Visual Basic, Electronic Data Interchange (EDI), Oracle, PeopleSoft, and SAP. Danielle is also an avid technical and leisure reader. She is currently working for the 12th-largest employer in the world, Compass Group, as vice president of HR Information Systems for the Americas Division.

Danielle is originally from Massapequa, Long Island, New York. She and her husband James and their chocolate Labrador retriever, Casey, live in Weddington, North Carolina. They can be reached at jcsdl@prodigy.net.

Dedication

To my best friend, Jimmy

Acknowledgments

Quite some time ago, I thought it would be a great idea to write a book on SAP query reporting. After all, for years I have been storing hand-written notes on the topic in an overstuffed 5-inch binder. I had developed a habit of scribbling down information and tips on this subject almost religiously. One day it was a nugget of information I picked up while consulting for a company in need. The next day it was a piece of knowledge from a participant in a SAP conference where I was speaking. Yet another day it was a technique that reaped dividends for my department at work. Over the years, that binder has grown exponentially, as has my desire to publish a book that accurately reflects the sum of all my thoughts, knowledge, and work experience on SAP query reporting. This is that book.

For the past 10 years, I have spent more time on this subject than any other. The process of transforming the contents of my binder into chapter upon chapter of this book has been a truly rewarding experience. I care deeply about this book and hope that the information contained in it will be as useful to you as it has been to me.

In my previous books, I have declared my thanks and appreciation for the support of my family, friends, staff, and colleagues. I even dropped in a few friends' names, knowing they would get a kick out of it. This time around, I wish to extend a sincere thank-you to all I have met, spoken to, and interacted with at SAP conferences and training seminars, especially those who take the time to share their experiences with me. I am a richer person for it. Thank you to Bonnie Penzias and Wellesley Information Services (www.wispubs.com), UCG Technology, the publishers of *SAP Professional Journal*, and the hosts of the many informative SAP conferences for providing me the various opportunities that they have. Thanks also to my current employer, Compass Group, The Americas Division, and my boss, Bob Kovacs, for providing a wonderful work environment. Finally, thanks to my staff in the HR Information Systems department for their continued great work and successes.

Most importantly, thank you to the love of my life, my husband, Jim Signorile.

WE WANT TO HEAR FROM YOU!

As the reader of this book, you are our most important critic and commentator. We value your opinion and want to know what we're doing right, what we could do better, what areas you'd like to see us publish in, and any other words of wisdom you're willing to pass our way.

As an associate publisher for Sams Publishing, I welcome your comments. You can email or write me directly to let me know what you did or didn't like about this book—as well as what we can do to make our books better.

Please note that I cannot help you with technical problems related to the topic of this book. We do have a User Services group, however, where I will forward specific technical questions related to the book.

When you write, please be sure to include this book's title and author, as well as your name, email address, and phone number. I will carefully review your comments and share them with the author and editors who worked on the book.

Email: feedback@samspublishing.com

Mail: Greg Wiegand
            Associate Publisher
            Sams Publishing
            800 East 96th Street
            Indianapolis, IN 46240 USA

READER SERVICES

Visit our website and register this book at www.samspublishing.com/register for convenient access to any updates, downloads, or errata that might be available for this book.

CHAPTER

1

GETTING STARTED WITH THE SAP R/3 QUERY REPORTING TOOLS

In this chapter

The reporting attributes, objects, and tools discussed in this book apply equally to both the SAP R/3 and mySAP ERP solutions, which this book refers to collectively as the *SAP enterprise solution*. Your SAP enterprise solution is delivered with standard query reporting tools that end users can use to create their own reports, without needing any technical programming skills. These tools provide functionality that many SAP customers do not know is possible.

Having the ability to extract and report on data from the SAP enterprise solution is empowering for you as an end user because it means you will not have to rely on others to gain access to the information you need in order to make business decisions. A common complaint I hear from SAP enterprise solution users is about their inability to get access to the data they need and their reliance on others to provide it for them. This book explains everything you need to know to work with the SAP enterprise solution reporting tools so that you can have access to the information you need.

The challenge most SAP users face is the unavailability of training materials specific to end-user reporting. Many SAP customers are under the mistaken impression that R/3 reporting is accomplished via four main avenues:

- Standard SAP-delivered "canned" reports.
- Reports created by trained programmers via Advanced Business Application Programming (ABAP). (ABAP is a high-level programming language created by SAP.)
- A purchased SAP add-on solution such as Business Warehouse (BW), soon to be known as SAP NetWeaver Business Intelligence (or BI or BIW).
- A purchased non-SAP third-party add-on solution (such as Crystal Reports).

THE SAP R/3 QUERY REPORTING TOOLS

In addition to these four main avenues, SAP comes preinstalled with the following end-user reporting tools:

- SAP Query
- InfoSet (Ad Hoc) Query
- QuickViewer

The added bonus of these solutions is overwhelming. Instead of using standard canned reports, you can use these tools to create your own reports from scratch, selecting the fields, formatting, and so on. Unlike reports created via ABAP programming, reports created with these tools require no programming skills whatsoever. Many customers assume that BW (or BI or BIW) is the reporting solution designed for all reporting in SAP. BW is a great tool for customers who require it, but many people do not understand several facts about BW:

- You have to purchase, license, and install BW.
- BW is not part of your R/3 environment and therefore requires separate configuration.

- BW does not provide real-time reporting; rather, it reports from a storage warehouse of data.
- BW is designed primarily for SAP installations where reporting from multiple non-SAP solutions as well as SAP is required.

If the SAP R/3 Query tools are so useful, why aren't they more popular? Let's start with the history. The earliest versions of SAP offered a tool originally called the ABAP/4 Query tool. This tool was the first one designed to allow end users to create their own reports. It was rudimentary in its first deployment, and early on it received a bad reputation for being a resource hog on the SAP R/3 database. Nevertheless, over the years and following releases, SAP continued to work with the updated ABAP Query tool to improve its indexing, speed up its retrieval methods, and encourage the use of standard delivered logical databases as the data source behind the reporting engine. In SAP 4.6, the tool was drastically improved, and by then it was no longer considered a resource hog.

About the same time that the ABAP Query tool was improved, SAP stopped offering training classes on the query-based reporting tools, even though the SAP Query tool had just been enhanced and updated and the new query-based tools, including InfoSet Query and QuickViewer, had just been introduced. Some think that SAP wanted to encourage its SAP customers to purchase and install BW (a new revenue generator), and others believe that SAP simply wanted to make a commitment to its custom ABAP coding for reports, which is a popular class in the SAP training catalog. What the motivation was is unimportant; what is pressing is that reporting tools are available to end users for the creation of custom reports that require no advanced technical training or programming capabilities. Everything you need to know about how to configure and use these tools is included in this book.

NOTE

> The SAP R/3 Query tools are SAP Query, QuickViewer, and InfoSet (Ad Hoc) Query. When I refer to the SAP Query tool, I am referring to the individual SAP Query tool, and when I refer to all three of the tools, I use the term *SAP R/3 Query tools*. This may appear a bit confusing at first, but you will get the hang of it as you move along.

Detailed information, especially training materials, for the three SAP R/3 Query tools is hard to find. Even harder to find is a comprehensive comparison of what these tools offer, their configuration and usage considerations, and how they rank comparatively. The following sections introduce the three SAP R/3 Query reporting tools; later in the book, you will learn more about each tool so you can compare and contrast them yourself.

THE SAP QUERY TOOL

The SAP Query tool, known as the ABAP Query tool in earlier versions of SAP, is delivered with the SAP R/3 system. End users can use this tool to quickly and easily create reports from data stored in the SAP R/3 database. This tool can be used in any application module in SAP. Its easy-to-use format simplifies the report creation process. The SAP Query tool includes basic and advanced features for every level of end user. The SAP Query tool offers a broad range of ways to define output and create different types of reports, such as basic lists, statistics, and ranked lists. This tool can be used in a basic or graphical mode.

THE INFOSET (AD HOC) QUERY TOOL

Unlike the SAP Query tool, which is a complete reporting solution, the InfoSet Query tool is designed for basic users to retrieve simple, single-use lists of SAP R/3 data. In SAP 4.6, the Human Capital Management module reporting tool called the Ad Hoc Query tool was combined with the technology of the SAP Query tool and made available for all modules; its new name is the InfoSet Query tool (although it is still referred to as the Ad Hoc Query tool when executed for human resources reporting). This book refers to it as the InfoSet (Ad Hoc) Query tool.

Unlike with the SAP Query tool, all query information, including the selection criteria, for InfoSet Query tool reporting is available on a single screen. You can use the InfoSet (Ad Hoc) Query tool to quickly answer simple questions or to create a comprehensive report for printing or downloading to your PC. A user can use the InfoSet (Ad Hoc) Query tool to pose questions to the SAP system and receive real-time answers.

THE QUICKVIEWER TOOL

The QuickViewer tool that is delivered with a SAP 4.6 system is a WYSIWYG ("what you see is what you get") utility for quickly collecting data from an R/3 system. The QuickViewer tool is actually a variant of the robust SAP Query tool that is designed for new or occasional users or for single-use data inquiry reports. You can use this tool to create reports referred to as QuickViews. To define a report with the QuickViewer tool, you simply enter texts (titles) and select the fields and options that define the QuickView. QuickViews cannot be exchanged among users, but they can be converted to reports to be used with the SAP Query tool.

HOW THE SAP R/3 QUERY TOOLS WORK

Query tools are based on the foundation of the SAP R/3 database. Historically, the primary method of creating reports in SAP was by using the ABAP Workbench and writing code in the language of ABAP. Specially trained programmers could write a long series of lines of code in an ABAP editor to retrieve information from the database, compute relationships, configure security, design selection screens, and present data in a particular arrangement. The skill set for ABAP programming is challenging to learn and usually requires experience in each application area of SAP for which programming will occur. For example, an ABAP programmer with experience in the Financials module would require special training to change functions and create reports in the Sales and Distribution area. Because these programming skills are substantial, SAP created the Query family of tools so that end users could pick and choose the fields they want to include in their reports and, behind the scenes, SAP would handle all the technical details. Figure 1.1 is a diagram that shows the foundation of the SAP Query tools.

Figure 1.1
An overview of the technical aspects of the SAP R/3 Query tools.

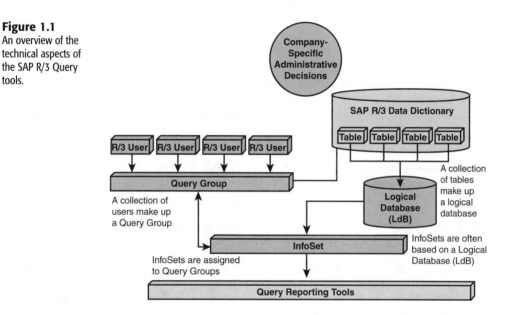

As described in the following sections, the SAP R/3 Query tools—SAP Query, InfoSet (Ad Hoc) Query, and QuickViewer—are built on the foundation of four main components:

- Query areas
- Query groups
- InfoSets
- Administrative decisions (which are company-specific)

Query Areas

Query areas (known as application areas in versions of SAP earlier than 4.6) contain SAP Query elements, queries, InfoSets, and query groups. SAP has two distinct query areas:

- **Standard**—Standard query areas are client-specific. That is, by default, they are available only within the client in which they were created. For example, if they were created in the live production client, they would exist only in the production client. Transport of query objects created in the standard area can be accomplished between multiple clients on the same application server.

- **Global**—Queries designed in the global query area are used throughout the entire system and are client-independent. In version 4.6, SAP delivers many of its standard reports in the SAP Query global query area. These queries are also intended for transport into other systems and are connected to the ABAP Workbench.

QUERY GROUPS

Query groups were known as user groups in versions of SAP prior to version 4.6. A query group is a collection of SAP users who are grouped. A user's assignment to a query group determines which queries he or she is allowed to execute or maintain. In addition, it designates which InfoSets (that is, data sources) the user has access to work with. Basically, query groups give a user access to create, modify, and execute reports in a certain area within R/3. For example, you could create a query group for the Finance department that would house your financial users, or you could create a query group for the Human Resources department that only members of the Human Resources department would belong to. Using query groups is an easy way to group and segregate reports and users.

Query groups, which are often maintained by a system administrator, are created on the User Groups: Initial screen, which you can find by using the transaction code /nSQ03.

Users can belong to multiple query groups and might, under certain circumstances, copy and execute queries from other query groups (if the permissions are the same). Any user within a query group has authority to execute queries that are assigned to it, but only users with the appropriate authorization can modify queries or define new ones. Users are not permitted to modify queries from other query groups.

INFOSETS

InfoSets, known as functional areas in earlier versions of SAP, are areas that provide special views of logical databases and determine which fields of a logical database or data source can be evaluated in queries. That is, an InfoSet is basically the data source, from which you get data to use in reports.

InfoSets can be built on a variety of different sources, but the most common is the use of an SAP logical database. Remember that writing reports without Query tools requires a programmer to write code that goes into the main R/3 database and retrieves the records it needs, and that is no easy skill. SAP delivers *logical databases*, which are rational prearranged groupings of data from multiple related indexed tables. SAP places all the fields you want to report from in a nice container from which you simply select the fields you want to include in your report.

ADMINISTRATIVE DECISIONS FOR QUERY TOOL USE

Using any new tool in an SAP R/3 system requires that you plan ahead and make sure you have all your administrative bases covered before you dive in and start creating reports. Because the SAP tools are so easy to configure and use, you might be tempted to skip ahead in this book and begin creating reports. Although that is possible, it is a best practice to first review and make some administrative decisions before proceeding, as described in this section.

From the get-go, deciding which departments will have ownership of and responsibility for the different areas of the Query tools is imperative. Again, because the tools are so easy to configure and use, it is possible to configure the tools and begin creating reports without ensuring that you are following the desired strategic direction of the organization. Making sure you review the different options and recommended best practices in this section is crucial to your successful deployment of query-based reporting at your organization. The following sections use the most popular and most robust query solution, the SAP query, instead of continually referring to each of the query tools individually.

ADMINISTRATIVE DECISIONS FOR QUERY AREAS

In Chapter 2, "One-Time Configuration for Query Tool Use," you will learn how to do the behind-the-scenes configuration for the SAP R/3 Query tools. This configuration is very easy to perform, and it is important that you first decide ownership and rules for the different query items.

One important administrative decision is how to use query areas. In version 4.6, SAP began to distribute its standard R/3 canned reports in the global query area. Those reports are now automatically available to every client on the application server because they exist in the global query area. A common best practice is to allow SAP to continue to deliver reports via the global area and for end users to use the standard query area to create all query-related reports. Reports created in this standard area are client-specific and by default exist only within the client in which they are created. However, they can be transported to other clients via the transport truck on the InfoSets screen (SQ02), bypassing the ABAP Workbench Organizer. The recommended best business practice is for SAP customers to use the standard query area to create their reports.

ADMINISTRATIVE DECISIONS FOR QUERY GROUPS

Another important administrative decision is where to keep and maintain the query groups and InfoSets. For example, will you keep them in your development environment or in your production environment? With custom-coded ABAP reports written by programmers, the traditional methodology for report creation was as follows: A programmer accessed a development environment, where the first draft of the custom report was coded and tested. Next, the report was transported to a testing or quality assurance client, where it was more thoroughly tested. If it passed the testing, it was then moved on to the production environment for use.

The Query tools were added to SAP to give end users with no technical skills the ability to create reports in real time. With this in mind, your organization has to make a decision regarding a transport strategy. Query objects can be created in any client. However, there are some best practices. For starters, end users who will be using the Query tools often only have user IDs in the live Production environment. Because of this, and because the Query tools are designed for real-time live access to information, the best practice is to maintain query groups live in the production client.

Helpful Hint

If your organization uses some version of a standard new SAP user request form, it would be ideal to add a section to that form where you specify which query groups the new user will belong to and assign the task of placing users in the appropriate query groups as part of the SAP ID creation process.

ADMINISTRATIVE DECISIONS FOR INFOSETS

Although InfoSets can be created in any client, best practice dictates that they be treated in line with normal programming methodology: InfoSets should be created in a development environment owned by a technical professional and transported to a testing quality assurance client, where they are tested and then moved on to production for use. InfoSets are treated differently from the other fundamental objects of the query tools, such as query areas, because a trained user can add special coding or programs to InfoSets that may have an impact on system resources or functioning, and testing them is required in those cases. So the best business practice is to create InfoSets in your development environment.

ADMINISTRATIVE DECISIONS FOR QUERIES

Finally, you need to make some administrative decisions regarding the reports (queries) themselves. Unlike custom-coded ABAP reports, query reports are designed to be made in real time in an ad hoc fashion, so the best practice is to create queries live in your production environment. Although the Query tools no longer have the resource hog reputation that existed in the early days, a user still needs to be trained before using queries in production.

As with all SAP-delivered canned reports and all of your organization's custom ABAP reports that are available to end users in your production client, if a user does not input the appropriate information on the report's selection screen, he or she runs the risk of pulling an incorrect amount of data from the database. This is also true of queries. The same training that new users of SAP receive to learn how to run standard reports must be extended to the Query tools as well. The best business practice is to allow trained end users to create queries live in your production environment.

COMPARING THE QUERY TOOLS TO DECIDE WHICH TO USE

As described earlier in this chapter, in version 4.6C and above of the SAP R/3 enterprise solution, SAP delivers the following Query tools: the SAP Query tool, the InfoSet (Ad Hoc) Query tool, and the QuickViewer. Each of these tools has a different purpose.

The best end user reporting solution is the SAP Query tool, because it has the broadest range of features, is very easy to use, and can be used to create complex reports with no programming skills whatsoever. Because this tool is the most robust, it is often used by power users, functional and business analysts, and savvy end users. The InfoSet (Ad Hoc) Query and QuickViewer tools are often used by a casual user performing a single lookup or inquiry.

You should select a tool for primary and exclusive use by your organization and train your end users on it. That way, you avoid any possible data inconsistencies due to the use of different or multiple tools. I always recommend the use of the SAP Query tool above all other tools because it has the most features and flexibility. The SAP Query tool has the most coverage in this book. Throughout this book, you will learn about each of the SAP R/3 Query tools and will be able to decide for yourself which is an appropriate fit for your organization.

THINGS TO REMEMBER

- The SAP Query family of reporting tools is available for free within all standard SAP installations.
- You should use the standard query area for your queries.
- You should create your query groups live in your production environment.
- You should create InfoSets in your development client and test them in a test or quality assurance client before making them available in your live production client.
- Trained users should create queries in your live production client.
- Use of all three Query tools at the same time may yield inconsistent data, so an organization should commit to a reporting tool and use it exclusively.

CHAPTER

2

ONE-TIME CONFIGURATION FOR QUERY TOOL USE

In this chapter

This chapter covers everything you need to know to make the SAP R/3 Query family of tools ready for use. The steps for the configuration are broken down in such a simple and easy-to-use format that anyone can perform them. However, the decision to use a particular tool or tools and the administrative methodology that will be put into place to use the tools requires deeper consideration.

Before you dive in and begin performing the one-time configuration that is necessary before you can use the SAP Query reporting tools, you should review Chapter 1, "Getting Started with the SAP R/3 Query Reporting Tools." As discussed in Chapter 1, the SAP R/3 Query tools (SAP Query, InfoSet (Ad Hoc) Query, and QuickViewer) are built on a foundation of four main components:

- Query areas
- Query groups
- InfoSets
- Administrative decisions (which are company-specific)

This chapter covers how to configure query groups and InfoSets so that you can begin using the Query family of tools.

STEPS IN CONFIGURING THE QUERY TOOLS

After you have made the administrative decisions described in Chapter 1, you can perform the one-time configuration of the Query tools in four quick and easy steps:

1. Create query groups.
2. Assign users to query groups.
3. Create InfoSets.
4. Assign each InfoSet to a query group.

STEP 1: CREATE QUERY GROUPS

A query group (known as a user group in versions of SAP prior to version 4.6) is a collection of SAP users who are grouped. The best way to think of query groups is to think of them along the lines of departments within an organization and the functional areas within those departments. For example, an organization's Finance department may have multiple functional areas, including Accounts Payable, Accounts Receivable, Payroll, and so on. Creating user groups allows an organization to group its reporting users (and subsequently their reports) into functional areas. A user's assignment to a query group determines which queries he or she can execute or maintain. Using query groups is an easy way to group and segregate your report users and reports.

To create a new query group, you perform the following steps:

1. Log in to your SAP client where your query groups will be maintained. (As noted in Chapter 1, best practice dictates that they be maintained in your live production client.)

2. Navigate to the User Groups: Initial screen by using the transaction code /nSQ03, as shown in Figure 2.1.

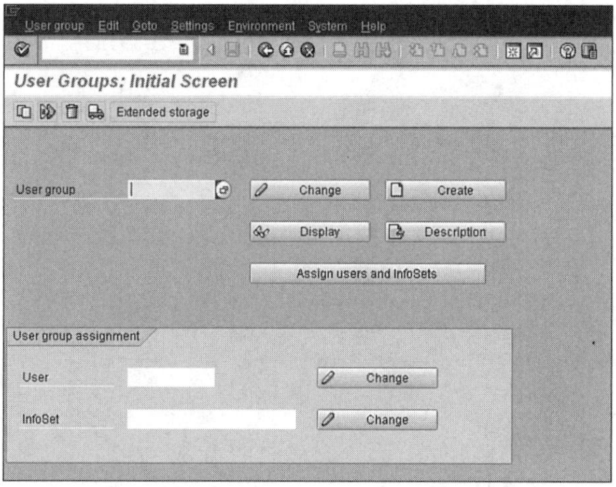

Figure 2.1
SAP query groups are created and modified using the User Groups: Initial screen.

3. Ensure that you are in the appropriate query area by following the menu path Environment, Query Areas and selecting Standard Area. (Best practice dictates that you maintain query areas in the standard area, as discussed in Chapter 1.)

4. Type in the name for your query group in the User Group field. (For purposes of this example, I'm naming mine **ZTEST**.) Then click the Create button.

5. When a dialog box appears, asking you to provide a description for your query group, type **Test Query Group 1** and then click the green checkmark Save button.

STEP 2: ASSIGN USERS TO YOUR QUERY GROUPS

To assign users to a query group, perform the following steps:

1. Click the Assign Users and InfoSets button.

2. Type in the SAP user IDs of any users you wish to include in your test group, making sure to include your own user ID (see Figure 2.2).

3. Click the Save button on the toolbar. A message appears in your SAPGUI status bar, saying "User group ZTEST saved."

Now that you have a query group created, the next step is to create an InfoSet.

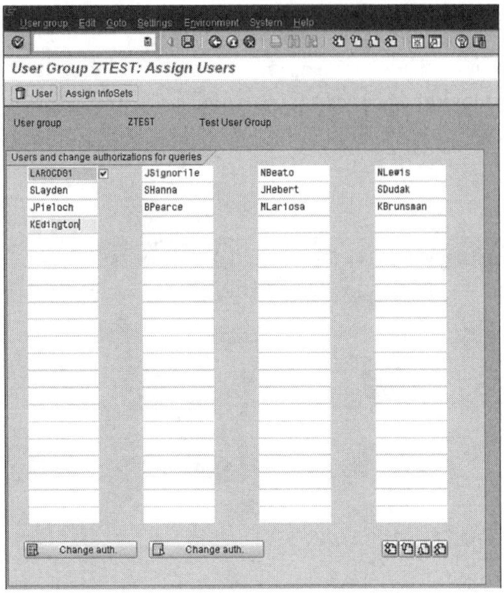

Figure 2.2
Input the SAP user IDs for any user you wish to belong to the query group.

STEP 3: CREATE INFOSETS

You create InfoSets (known as functional areas in versions of SAP prior to version 4.6) on the InfoSet: Initial screen, shown in Figure 2.3. As stated in Chapter 1, an InfoSet is basically the data source from which you get the data to use in your reports. You can picture an InfoSet as an organized container that holds all your stuff. InfoSets can be built on a variety of different sources, but the most common is the use of a logical database.

To create a new InfoSet, you perform the following steps:

1. Log in to your SAP client where your InfoSets will be maintained. (As noted in Chapter 1, best practice dictates that you maintain them in your development client.)

2. Navigate to the InfoSet: Initial screen by using the transaction code **/nSQ02** (see Figure 2.3).

3. Ensure that you are in the appropriate query area by selecting Environment, Query Areas and then selecting Standard Area. (Best practice dictates that you maintain query areas in the standard area, as covered in Chapter 1.)

4. Type in a name for your InfoSet. (For purposes of this example, I'm naming mine **ZTEST**.) Then click the Create button.

5. On the InfoSet: Title and Database screen, type an InfoSet description in the Name field. (For purposes of this example, I'm naming mine **Test InfoSet 1**.)

6. On the InfoSet: Title and Database screen, select the Logical Database radio button and select or input logical database **f1s** in the field to its right (see Figure 2.4), and then press Enter.

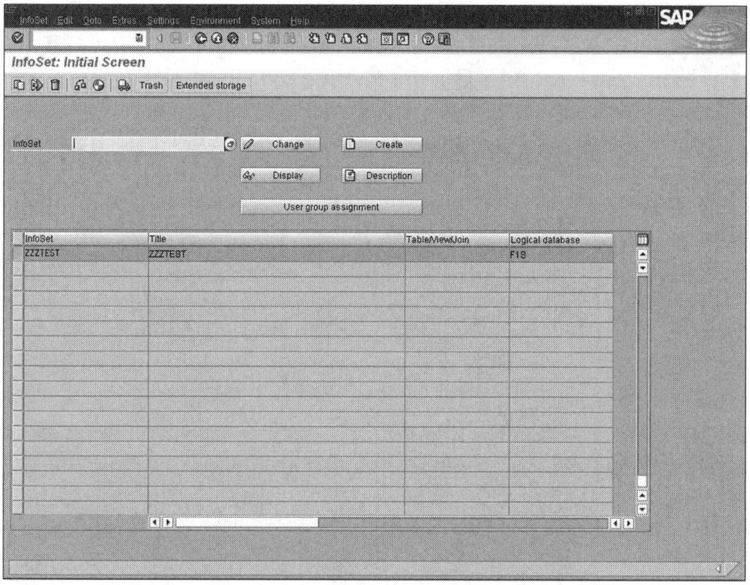

Figure 2.3
A list of all previously created InfoSets is displayed on the InfoSet: Initial screen.

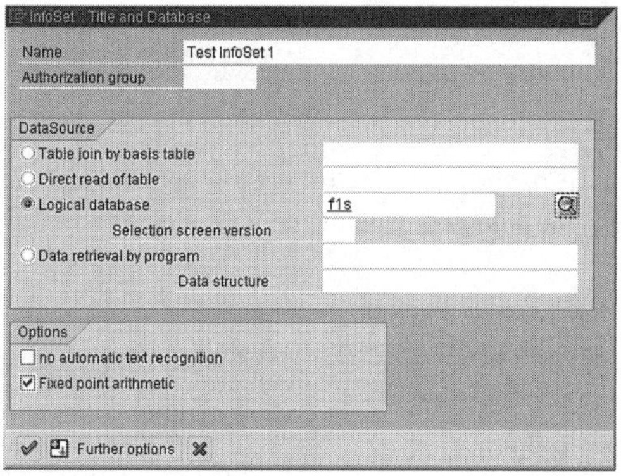

Figure 2.4
There are several hundred logical databases to choose from.

Helpful Hint

InfoSets can be created with various data sources, including logical databases, tables, table joins, and so on. The best business practice is to use the SAP-delivered logical databases as your data source. They have been created for this purpose, and at least one logical database is delivered with your system for each application area/module in SAP. The F1S logical database used in this example is the database that SAP uses in its training classes, which use a fictional airline scheduling system. It is best to use this for your test cases. If you have difficulty accessing this predelivered SAP test training solution, contact your system administrator, who can ensure that it was installed.

A Change InfoSet screen, similar to the one shown in Figure 2.5, appears. The Change InfoSet screen displays a list of all tables available in the selected logical database for your InfoSet. The logical database selected, F1S, contains three test tables, called

SPFLI, SBOOK, and SFLIGHT, which correspond to the three field groups listed at the top right. The field groups are what the end users see when they are creating reports using the SAP Query reporting tool.

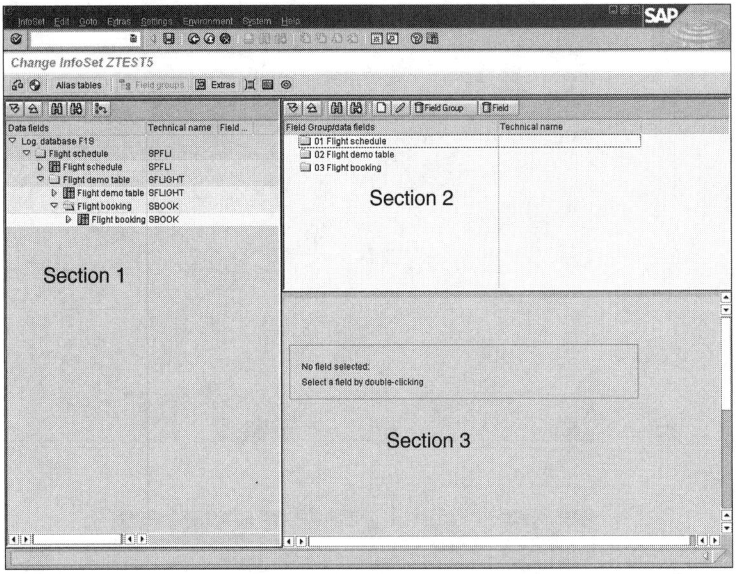

Figure 2.5
The Change InfoSet screen is divided into three sections.

7. To view the fields in each of the three tables, use the expand subtree button next to each table name. The table selected expands and displays the fields underneath, as shown in Figure 2.6.

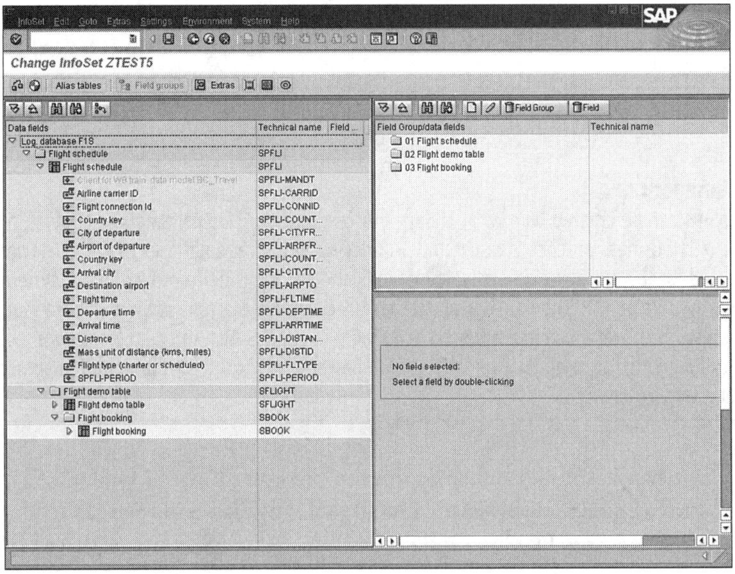

Figure 2.6
The left side of the screen lists the tables and fields, and the right displays the field groups.

8. Assign fields to the field groups (shown on the top right of the screen) within the InfoSet. These field groups will display in the SAP Query tool during reporting. Only the fields that you include in your field groups will be available for field selection in the SAP Query tool that uses this InfoSet as its data source. By default, these field groups are empty.

> **NOTE**
>
> For all modules in SAP, by default, your field groups will be empty, and you will need to manually insert fields into them. This is true for all modules except for the Human Capital Management module and the InfoSets that support it. For those, the field groups will already be created for you, with a default set of fields; you can add additional fields, if required, as discussed in Chapter 15, "HR and Payroll Reporting Options in the HCM Module."

9. Place your cursor on the first field group, Flight Schedule, and double-click to highlight that field group as the selected field group. Next, select fields from the left side of the screen from the Flight Schedule table and add them to the Flight Schedule field group by placing your cursor on a field on the left side of the screen, right-clicking, and selecting the option Add Field to Field Group (see Figure 2.7).

Figure 2.7
You should only add fields to their corresponding field groups (for example, Flight Schedule table to Flight Schedule field group).

10. When the field you just added to the Flight Schedule field group appears at the top right of the screen, add fields to your selected functional group by following the procedure outlined in step 9. Be sure to add fields to the appropriate field groups. For example, fields in the Flight Schedule table should be added to the Flight Schedule field

group, and fields from the Flight Booking table should be added to the Flight Booking field group.

11. After you have added a series of fields to your field groups, click the Save button on the toolbar. A message appears in the status bar, saying that your InfoSet was saved.

12. Generate the InfoSet by clicking the Generate button (the red beach ball) on the Application toolbar. A message appears in the status bar, saying that the InfoSet was generated.

> **NOTE**
>
> Clicking the Generate button for your InfoSet causes SAP to check whether any errors are present in the logic of the configuration of the InfoSet.

13. Exit the Change InfoSet screen by clicking the green back arrow.

STEP 4: ASSIGN EACH INFOSET TO A QUERY GROUP

You have now created a Query group, assigned users to it, and created an InfoSet. The last step before you begin creating reports is to assign your InfoSet to your Query group. This is an easy task:

1. On the InfoSet: Initial screen (which you reach by entering transaction code /nSQ02), make sure your InfoSet name (in my example, ZTEST) is present in the InfoSet text box, and click the User Group Assignment button.

2. In the InfoSet: Assign to User Groups screen that appears, highlight your query group (in my example, ZTEST) by selecting the gray button to the left of it, and then click the Save button. A message appears in the status bar, saying that the assignment of InfoSet has been saved.

3. Exit the InfoSet: Assign to User Groups screen by clicking the green Back arrow.

You are now ready to begin creating reports with the SAP R/3 Query reporting tools. Chapter 3, "Creating Basic Reports with the SAP Query Tool," describes how to do so using SAP Query.

PERFORMING MAINTENANCE ON INFOSETS

The following sections provide details on maintenance functions that are available for InfoSets. These sections are designed to assist users who are responsible for the maintenance of InfoSets. Users who are being trained on the concepts of InfoSets need not review these maintenance functions. As recommended in Chapter 1, those designated personnel who will be responsible for the InfoSets can read on to see how to perform the different maintenance functions.

RETURNING TO AN INFOSET TO ADD FIELDS

After an InfoSet is created, you can return to it at any time to make changes. It is a best business practice to maintain an InfoSet in your development environment so any changes can be tested before the InfoSet is transported to your live production client. (See Chapter 1 for more information.)

To add an additional field to your InfoSet, follow these steps:

1. Log in to the SAP client where your InfoSets are maintained.
2. Navigate to the InfoSet: Initial Screen by using the transaction code /nSQ02.
3. Ensure that you are in the appropriate query area by selecting Environment, Query Areas and then selecting Standard Area.
4. Type in the name of the InfoSet that you want to make changes to, and then click the Change button.
5. Review the fields that are currently present in the field groups (shown on the top right of your screen) in your InfoSet.
6. When you initially created the InfoSet, it is likely that you did not add all fields in the logical database to your field groups. Determine which field group is the appropriate one to add a field to. Place your cursor on that field group, and double-click it to highlight it as the selected field group. Then select fields from the left side of the screen from the corresponding table and add them to the highlighted field group by placing your cursor on a field on the left side of the screen, right-clicking, and selecting the option Add Field to Field Group Remember to ensure that you add fields to the appropriate field group. Your newly added fields now appear in your selected field group.
7. When you have finished adding additional fields, click the Save button on the toolbar. A message appears in the status bar, saying that the InfoSet was saved.
8. Generate the InfoSet by clicking the Generate button on the Application toolbar. A message appears in the status bar, saying that the InfoSet has been generated.

RETURNING TO AN INFOSET TO DELETE FIELDS

After an InfoSet is created, you can return to it any time to remove fields. As mentioned earlier, it is a best business practice to maintain your InfoSet in your development environment so any changes can be tested before the InfoSet is transported to your live production client.

To delete a field from your InfoSet, follow these steps:

1. Log in to the SAP client where your InfoSets are maintained.
2. Navigate to the InfoSet: Initial screen by using the transaction code /nSQ02.
3. Ensure that you are in the appropriate query area by following the menu path Environment, Query Areas and selecting Standard Area.

4. Type in the InfoSet name and then click the Change button. The Change InfoSet screen appears, displaying a list of all the tables available in your InfoSet. The logical database F1S that is selected contains three test tables, called SPFLI, SBOOK, and SFLIGHT, which correspond to the three field groups listed at the top right.

5. To view the fields in each of the three tables, use the expand subtree button next to each table name. The table selected expands and displays the fields underneath.

6. Review the fields that are currently present in the field groups (shown on the top right of your screen) in your InfoSet.

7. Determine which field group you wish to delete fields from, and place your cursor on it. Double-click the field group to highlight it as the selected field group. Next, place your cursor on a field in the field group on the top-right side of the screen, right-click, and select the option Delete Field from Field Group. The deleted fields no longer appear in your selected field group.

8. When you have finished deleting fields, click the Save button on the toolbar. A message appears in the status bar, saying that InfoSet was saved.

9. Generate the InfoSet by clicking the Generate button on the Application toolbar. A message appears in the status bar, saying that the InfoSet has been generated.

NOTE

If you selected to remove fields that are already used in existing queries, you will receive an error message saying "Field used in existing query." A best practice is to first determine whether the field is in use. You do so by placing your cursor on the field, right-clicking, and selecting the Queries for Field option. SAP then displays a list containing any existing queries that use that field. You need to access that query and remove the field from its output before you can save the changes to your InfoSet.

CHANGING THE NAME OF A FIELD OR COLUMN HEADER

Many users will be looking for a field name that corresponds to a field name on an SAP screen, so it is important to be very careful when renaming fields and column headers. However, there are rare situations in which you may need to do so. You can alter the name of a field and its column heading when it appears in a query-based report by simply following these steps:

1. Select a field by double-clicking it in the top-right side of the screen. The details of that field appear on the bottom-right side of the screen, as shown in Figure 2.8.

2. Alter the field name by editing the text in the Long Text field, and edit the column heading of the field as it will appear in reports by editing the text in the second line of the Header field at the bottom right, as highlighted in Figure 2.8.

3. Click the Save button on the toolbar. A message appears in the status bar, saying that the InfoSet was saved.

4. Generate the InfoSet by clicking the Generate button from the Application toolbar. A message appears in the status bar, saying that the InfoSet has been generated.

Figure 2.8
It is not a best practice to rename fields.

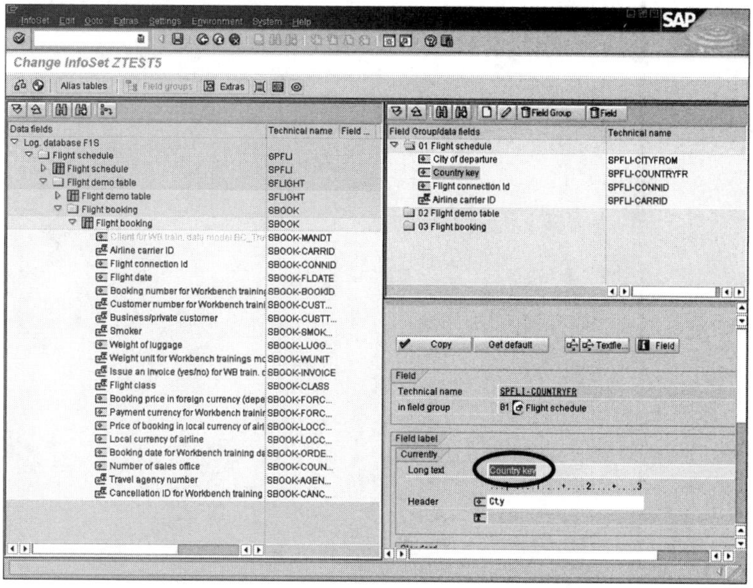

REVERTING THE NAME OF A FIELD OR COLUMN HEADER TO ITS ORIGINAL NAME

If you have altered the name of a field or column heading, you can revert it to the SAP standard delivered text by following these steps:

1. Select a field by double-clicking it in the top-right side of the screen. The details of that field appear on the bottom-right side of the screen.

2. Click the Get Default button. The field and column names revert to their original names.

3. Click the Save button on the toolbar. A message appears in the status bar, saying that the InfoSet was saved.

4. Generate the InfoSet by clicking the Generate button on the Application toolbar. A message appears in the status bar, saying that the InfoSet has been generated.

THINGS TO REMEMBER

- Configuring the SAP Query tools is very easy.
- You should use your company's standard naming convention when you perform this configuration at your organization.
- Be sure to add your own user ID to your newly created query group.
- You should add fields to corresponding field groups when building an InfoSet.
- Use caution when renaming fields or column headings to ensure that your end users will be able to recognize the fields.

CHAPTER 3

CREATING BASIC REPORTS WITH THE SAP QUERY TOOL

In this chapter

This chapter describes how to create basic list SAP reports by using the SAP Query tool. It introduces everything you need to know to create basic list type reports in any application module of SAP. The step-by-step setup of this chapter makes it easy for any user, regardless of technical skill level, to create custom reports by using the SAP Query tool.

Helpful Hint

Although it is recommended that you create SAP query reports live in your production environment, while you are learning how to use SAP, it is important that you practice in your test quality assurance client so you do not cause any problems in your production environment.

THE SAP QUERY TOOL

The SAP Query tool, in its standard form, is designed so that an end user with no technical skills can create a report from scratch. It has five basic screens that an end user can go through to create a report. Each of the screens performs a function, and the end user can navigate between the screens by using navigational arrows on the Application toolbar. These are the five basic screens:

- **Title, Format (Screen 1)**—You use this screen to give a report a name.
- **Select Field Group (Screen 2)**—You use this screen to select the field groups that contain fields you want to include in your report.
- **Select Field (Screen 3)**—You use this screen to select the fields from the field groups you want to include in your report.
- **Selections (Screen 4)**—You use this screen to add any additional fields to your report's selection screen to further specify your report output upon execution.
- **Basic List Line Structure (Screen 5)**—You use this screen to define what you want the report to look like.

CREATING A BASIC LIST QUERY BY USING THE SAP QUERY TOOL

The most frequent comment I hear from fellow SAP customers is that they want the ability to extract their own information. It is empowering to know that you can go into SAP and select the data you want and have it come out formatted and sorted in the manner you choose. This section walks you through how to create a basic list report by using the SAP Query tool. The following sections explain all the options on the screens used to create the query report.

To create a basic list query by using the SAP Query tool, follow these steps:

1. Log in to your SAP client where your query reports will be created. (Best practice dictates that they be maintained in your live Production client.)

2. Navigate to the Maintain Queries Initial screen by using the transaction code /**nSQ01**. Beginning with R/3 release 4.6A, SAP offers a graphical version of the SAP Query tool, called the Graphical Query Painter; if you have not used the SAP Query tool, the Graphical Query Painter is set as your default. To turn off the Graphical Query Painter and learn to create easy step-by-step reports by using the SAP Query tool, select Settings, Settings and then deselect the Graphical Query Painter check box.

3. The title bar lists the query group you are currently in. For example, your title bar might read Query from User Group ZTEST: Initial Screen. If you are assigned to multiple query groups, press F7 to see a list of all of them.

4. As discussed in Chapter 1, "Getting Started with the SAP R/3 Query Reporting Tools," it is recommended that you create your queries in the standard query area. Ensure that you are in the standard query area by selecting Environment, Query Areas and then selecting Standard Area.

5. In the Query field, type **DLS_QUERY_01** where **DLS** is your initials) as the name for the query you are creating, and then click the Create button (see Figure 3.1).

Figure 3.1
The main screen of the SAP Query tool lists all the queries available in the designated query group.

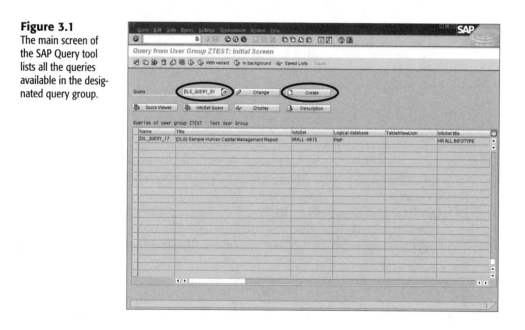

6. The InfoSets of User Group ZTEST window appears, listing all the available InfoSets (that is, data sources) for your query group. Because you created only one (in my example, I called it ZTEST), in Chapter 2, "One-Time Configuration for Query Tool Use," it will be the only one listed. Select the InfoSet you created (ZTEST, in my example) and then click the green check mark button.

7. The Create Query Title Format screen appears. This screen allows you to save the basic formatting specifications for your query, including the name (title) and any notes

you want to store for the query. The only required field is the Title (long report description). For this example, fill in only the Title field, as shown in Figure 3.2, and then click Save. (For my example, I used the title (DLS) SAP Query Exercise #01.)

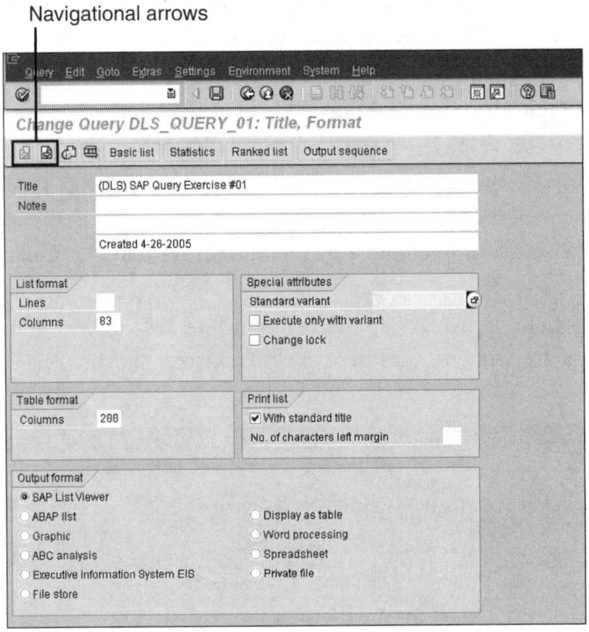

Navigational arrows

Figure 3.2
The Application tool-bar for the SAP Query tool contains naviga-tional arrows that permit you to navi-gate between the screens of the query.

8. Navigate to the next screen in the SAP query creation process by selecting the Next Screen (white navigational arrow) button from the Application toolbar. (You can use the navigational arrows to navigate between the different screens of the SAP Query tool.) The Select Field Group screen appears, listing all the Field groups available within your InfoSet. Figure 3.3 shows this screen with the field groups Flight Schedule [SPFLI], Flight Demo Table [SFLIGHT], and Flight Booking [SBOOK] listed.

9. Place a check mark next to each field group from which you want to include fields in your report. Navigate to the next screen in the SAP query creation process by selecting the Next Screen (white navigational arrow) button on the Application toolbar. The Select Field screen appears, showing a list of all the available fields in the selected field groups.

10. Place a check mark next to each field that you want to include in your report. You can use the Page Up and Page Down keys to navigate between all the fields (see Figure 3.4). Select the Next Screen (white navigational arrow) button from the Application toolbar to open the Selections screen, which lists all the fields you have selected.

Figure 3.3
All the field groups listed at the top right of the InfoSet screen during configuration of the InfoSet are listed on this screen.

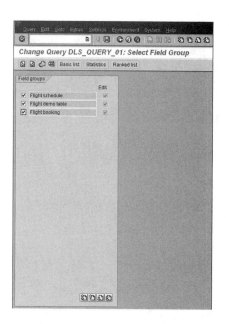

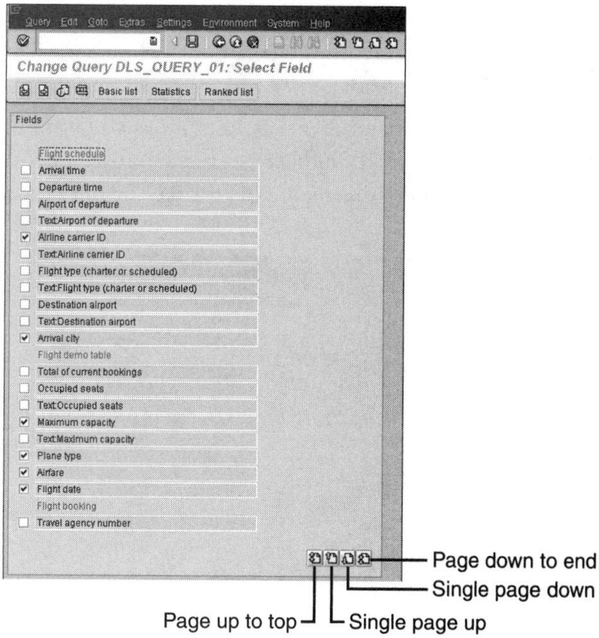

Figure 3.4
All the fields listed in the field groups at the top right of the InfoSet screen during configuration are listed here.

11. If desired, add any of the fields to the selection screen that will be presented when you execute your report. You can add a field to the Selections screen by placing a check mark next to each one (see Figure 3.5).

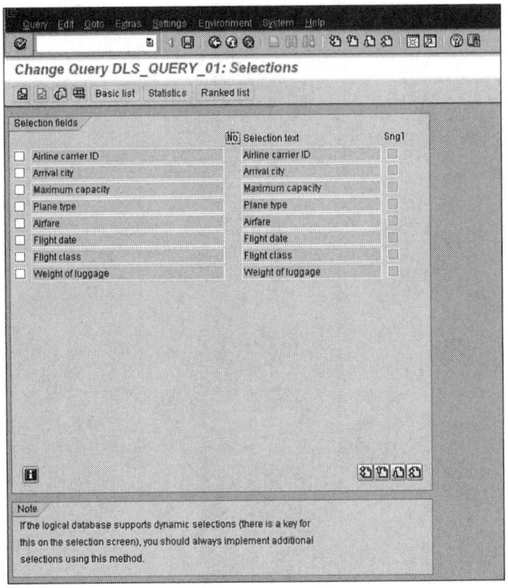

Figure 3.5
Having fields available on the report's selection screen gives you the ability to specify your report output upon execution.

12. Click the Basic List button from the Application toolbar to create an SAP basic list query. The Basic List Line Structure screen appears, showing a list of the fields you selected to include in your report.

13. For each field, specify the line and sequence number as you want them to appear on your report. Also use this screen to indicate sort order, totals, and counts, if needed. Start by entering the line and sequence numbers, like the ones shown in Figure 3.6.

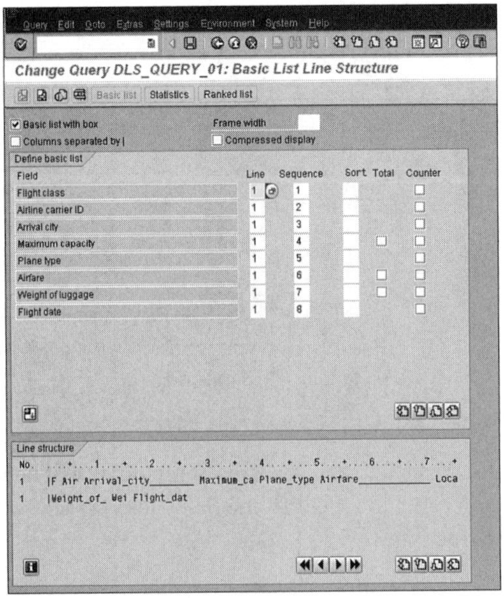

Figure 3.6
Basic output options are defined on the SAP Query tool Basic List Line Structure screen.

NOTE

You can use Figure 3.6 as follows:

- **Line column**—The values in this column correspond to the line numbers the fields will appear on in the report.
- **Sequence column**—The numbers in this column determine the order of the fields for the line.
- **Sort column**—This column dictates the order in which the data will be sorted.
- **Line Structure box**—After you click the Save button, a preview of the format appears in the Line Structure box at the bottom of the screen.

14. For this example, proceed directly to the report by pressing F8, which causes the report to execute.

15. As with almost all other reports in SAP, when you execute this report, you see the report's selection screen. Specify any criteria for the output of your report. Notice that any fields indicated on the Selections screen are included on your selection screen, under the heading Program Selections (see Figure 3.7).

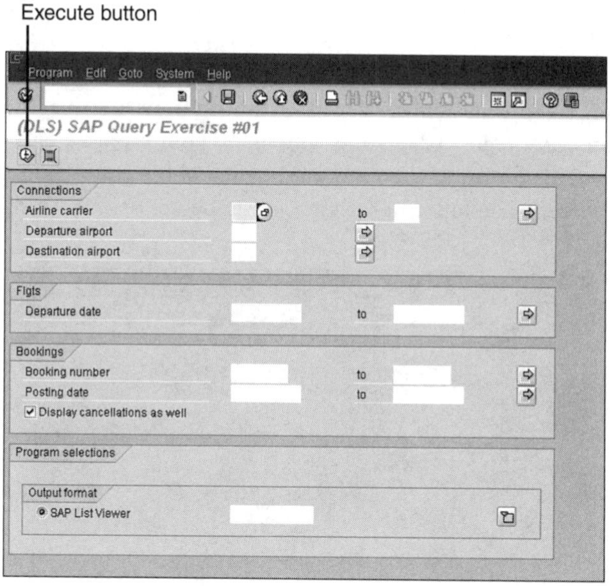

Execute button

Figure 3.7
Selection screens enable you to further specify report output.

16. Select the F8 Execute button on your Application toolbar (it looks like a clock) to display your finished report. Your report output appears; it should look similar to what is shown in Figure 3.8. (Keep in mind that the actual values vary by organization: The output of the report corresponds to the specification entered on the Basic List Line Structure screen.)

Class	ID	Arrival city	Capacity	Plane	FlgtPrice	Curr.	Wt	In	Flgt date
C	LH	NEW YORK	350	A319	899.00	DEM	20	KG	02/28/1995
F	LH	NEW YORK	350	A319	899.00	DEM	20	KG	02/28/1995
Y	LH	NEW YORK	350	A319	899.00	DEM	30	KG	02/28/1995
Y	LH	SAN FRANCISCO	350	A319	1,499.00	DEM	20	KG	11/17/1995
C	LH	SAN FRANCISCO	350	A319	1,499.00	DEM	20	KG	11/17/1995
C	LH	FRANKFURT	220	A319	1,090.00	USD	20	KG	06/06/1995
Y	LH	FRANKFURT	220	A319	6,000.00	LIT	20	KG	04/28/1995
F	SQ	NEW YORK	380	DC-10-10	849.00	DEM	20	KG	02/28/1995
C	SQ	NEW YORK	380	DC-10-10	849.00	DEM	20	KG	02/28/1995

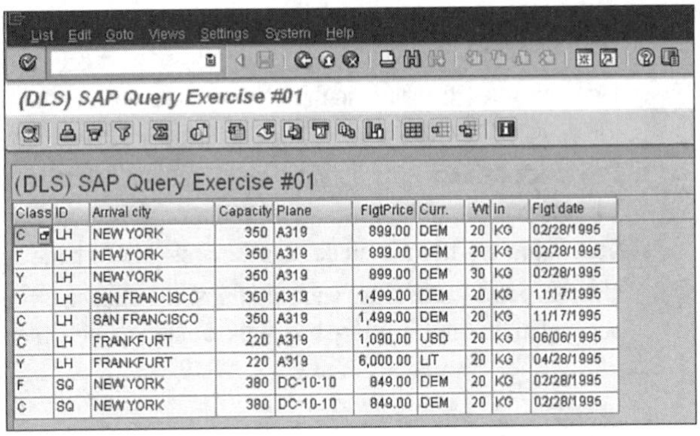

Figure 3.8
In SAP 4.6 and higher, by default, your report displays in the SAP List Viewer.

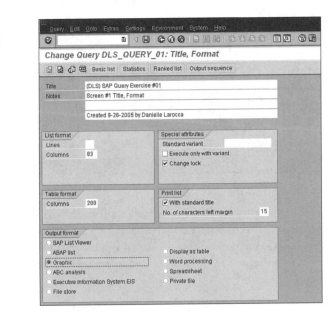

REVIEWING THE OPTIONS ON EACH OF THE FIVE BASIC SCREENS

The following sections serve as a reference of what options are available on each of the five basic screens of the SAP Query tool.

THE TITLE, FORMAT SCREEN

The Title, Format screen, shown in Figure 3.9, is where you insert the basic data about your report, including its title and the format in which you want it displayed. The Title, Format screen stores the basic report processing options for your report. For organizational purposes, it is a good idea to enter the name of the user who created the report in the Notes section of this screen. The following sections describe the options available on this screen.

Figure 3.9
The Title, Format screen.

LIST FORMAT

By default, on execution, a report is displayed in the SAP List Viewer (refer to Figure 3.8). The options listed in the List Format section apply only if you change the output format to appear in a text file or ABAP list. List Format options available on the Title, Format screen allow you to designate the line and column width of your report.

You use the Lines field to specify the number of lines to be output on one page for a list generated by the query. The default is blank, which outputs a continuous list on a single page. You can use the Lines field to enter the number of lines to be output on a single page. If you do not want page breaks, you should leave this field empty. The Columns field stores the number of columns per line. This field determines the maximum number of characters that can be displayed on one line of the list created by the query. Lines exceeding this length are broken. The maximum number permitted is 255. The number entered in the Columns field should be the closet estimation possible, because it helps determine the printed layout of the report. For example, if you set all reports to be the maximum of 255 so that all your columns fit on a single line, your printed report may contain very small text to accommodate all 255 columns. Again, these settings are required only if the output format is a text file or an ABAP list. (See the section "Output Format" on the next page.)

SPECIAL ATTRIBUTES

The Special Attributes section allows you to specify whether the report should run with a variant. (Variants are introduced in Chapter 6, "Using Reporting Selection Screens: Advanced Skills.") You use the Change Lock check box to indicate whether you want other users to be able to make changes to your query. By default, this check box is unmarked, indicating that any other user in your query group who has the appropriate authorizations can make changes to your report. To prevent this, select this check box for each new query you create.

TABLE FORMAT

You use the options listed in the Table Format section only if you change the output format to appear in a table. (See the section "Output Format.") You use the Columns field in the Table Format box to indicate the maximum number of characters for the width of a table view control if you select your data to be viewed as a table. You can use table view controls to display the data of single-line basic lists, statistics, and rankings in a special format. This specification affects only the visible width, and the table control may contain more data columns than are visible in a single R/3 window.

PRINT LIST

The Print List box includes the With Standard Title check box, which you use to indicate whether you want your output to include the standard title that you specified at top of the screen, in the Title field. By default, this box is selected. You use the No. of Characters Left Margin box to specify how many characters to save room for at the left side of the page in the printed report, in case you want to have room for binding or punched holes.

OUTPUT FORMAT

Upon report execution, your report is displayed in the SAP List Viewer format (refer to Figure 3.8). The Output Format options allow you to have a report's data output in different formats. The default setting is SAP List Viewer, which is a screen that appears very similar to a Microsoft Excel worksheet and is the standard for all reports in SAP version 4.6C and higher. The options available in this box are described in Table 3.1.

Specifying an output option on the Title, Format screen of the SAP Query tool ensures that when the report is executed, it will be displayed in the selected format. When you select an option on the Title, Format screen, it is set as a default parameter for the selection screen of that report only.

TABLE 3.1 SAP QUERY TOOL TITLE, FORMAT SCREEN OUTPUT FORMAT OPTIONS

Option	Description
SAP List Viewer	When you select this option, your list will not be displayed onscreen in the normal form when the query is processed. Instead, the first sublist is transferred to the SAP List Viewer directly, as shown in Figure 3.8. You must be able to transfer this first sublist (it must be either a single-line basic list, a statistic, or a ranked list). This is the default selection.
ABAP List	When you select this option, the report will appear in SAP as a basic list, without any formatting or fancy Microsoft Excel–looking features. This was the format of all standard SAP Query tool reports in versions earlier than SAP 4.6C.
Graphic	This function allows you to display the information from your list by using SAP Business Graphics. In contrast to the other functions described in this table, the Graphic function can only handle an extract from one column of your sublist, and the column must contain numeric values. In addition, your SAP system has to have Business Graphics enabled.
ABC Analysis	You can use the ABC Analysis function for any single-line basic list, all statistics, and any ranked list that contains at least one numeric field.
Executive Information System EIS	This function provides a link to the Executive Information System (EIS). It transfers the data in your query to the EIS database via an interface so that you can perform further analyses. When you activate this function, you specify various options for storing the data in a dialog box.
File Store	When you select this option, the list is not displayed onscreen when you execute the query, but the first sublist is passed directly to the download interface and stored as a file. The first sublist must be a single-line basic list, a statistic, or ranked list. When you select the field, a parameter is predefined on the selection screen.
Display as Table	When you select this option, your report output is displayed in an SAP Table Control object that looks similar to the SAP List Viewer but offers less functionality. The first sublist must be a one-line basic list, a statistic, or ranked list. When you select this option, a parameter is predefined on the selection screen.

Option	Description
Word Processing	When you select this option, the word processing functions can be called from the list display and from the table display. You can use this option to create Microsoft Word form letters.
Spreadsheet	When you select this option, the spreadsheet functions can be called from the list display and from the table display. You can use this option to create Microsoft Excel spreadsheets.
Private File	When you select this option, the list is not displayed onscreen when you execute the query, but the sublist is passed directly to a function module. This is an SAP enhancement and must be implemented by the customer.

THE SELECT FIELD GROUP SCREEN

In the Select Field Group screen, shown in Figure 3.10, a list of all the available field groups is populated during the creation of the InfoSet. (See Chapter 2 for more information.) This example has only three field groups; however, some logical databases contain hundreds. You place a check mark next to any field group that contains fields you want to include in your SAP query.

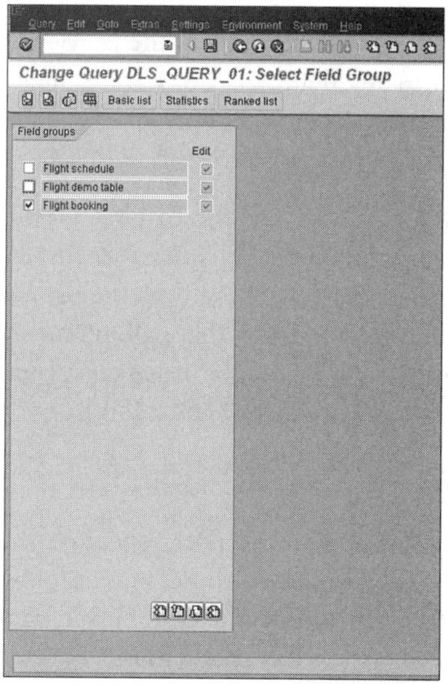

Figure 3.10
All the field groups listed at the top right of your InfoSet screen during configuration of the InfoSet are listed on this screen.

THE SELECT FIELD SCREEN

In the Select Field screen, shown in Figure 3.11, a list of all the available field groups populated during the creation of the InfoSet is expanded to display all the fields contained within them. You place a check mark next to any field you want to include in your SAP query.

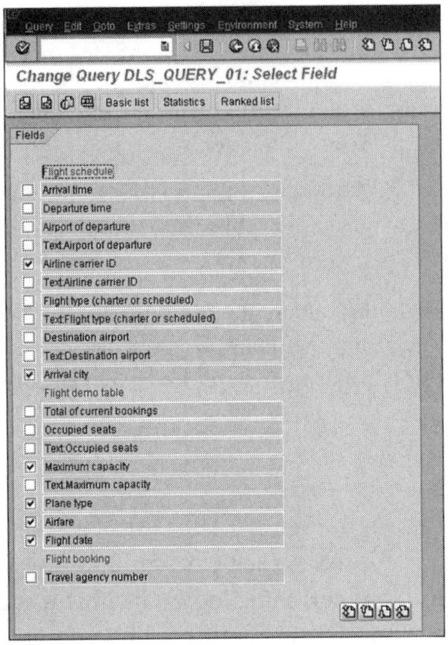

Figure 3.11
All the fields listed in the field groups at the top right of your InfoSet screen during configuration are listed here. This screen is also used for advanced functions covered later in this book.

THE SELECTIONS SCREEN

In the Selections screen, shown in Figure 3.12, a list of all the previously selected fields appears. You place a check mark next to any field that you want to include on the Selections screen that appears upon report execution. This gives you the option to specify particular data.

For example, in Figure 3.12, I selected that I wanted the Airfare, Maximum Capacity, and Weight of Luggage fields to appear on my report's Selections screen. This means that when I execute my report and see the Selections screen, those three fields will be listed there, under the heading Program Selections. Having them there allows me to run the report based on specific airfares, maximum capacity, or weight of luggage. (For example, I could run a report that contains a list of flights between $50 and $200.)

THE BASIC LIST LINE STRUCTURE SCREEN

By default, only the first few selected fields of your report appear on the Basic List Line Structure screen, shown in Figure 3.13. They are all there, but with the default view, they are not all visible. You can use the Page Up and Page Down buttons on the right side of the screen to navigate between them, or you can select the Without Explanation button (at the bottom left of the screen) to view more fields on a single screen. The Basic List Line Structure screen lists all the fields you want to include in your output. You can have fields listed here for sorting purposes but not included in the output by simply leaving the Line and Sequence fields blank.

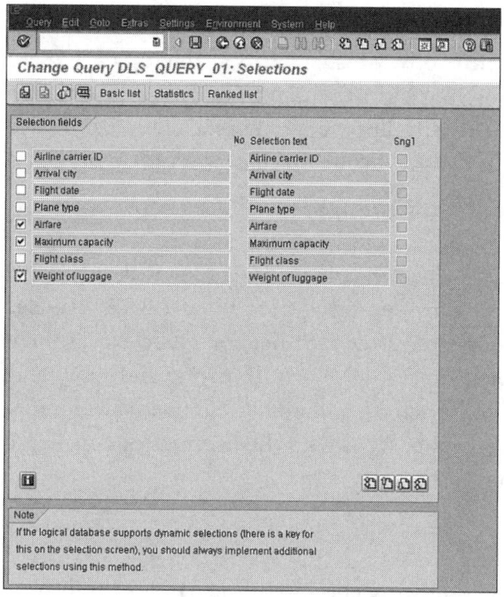

Figure 3.12
Having fields available on your report's selection screen gives you the ability to specify your report output by varying your input prior to report execution.

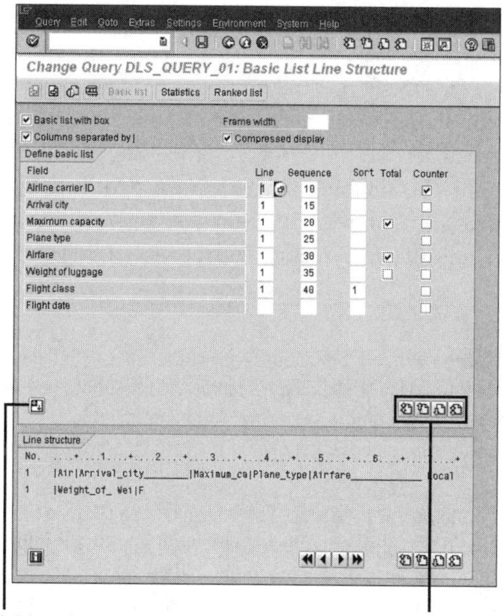

Figure 3.13
This is the screen where you dictate how you want your report to appear, including sequence and sorting specifications.

Used to show more fields, where available   Page up and down buttons

The following sections describe the various options available in the Basic List Line Structure screen.

BASIC LIST WITH BOX

The Basic List with Box check box, which appears at the top of the screen, is used for basic ABAP lists. If you select for your report output to be an ABAP list, selecting this check box causes the basic list to display with lines separating the columns. It is used as a formatting preference only. The box is designed so that it encloses only the filled part of the basic list.

COLUMNS SEPARATED BY |

The Columns Separated by | check box is available only if the Basic List with Box check box is selected. If you select for your report output to be an ABAP list, selecting this check box causes a vertical bar to be inserted after each field on a line except the last. An underscore is output before and after each control-level text (if sorting and subtotaling are used) and is inserted before and after each total. In addition, the individual columns in the standard header are separated by vertical bars. As with the previous option, this one is used as a formatting preference only.

COMPRESSED DISPLAY

If you select the Compressed Display check box, the basic list is displayed in compressed format, provided that compressed display is possible.

LINE

The Line column is where you specify the line number on which you want your output to appear. Specifying Line 1 for all fields will make them all appear as columns next to each other in the form of a standard report. Indicating multiple line numbers usually works only if you set your report output to be anything other than the SAP List Viewer or the table display. Multiple-line indicators are used most often for creating mailing labels or addressing envelopes, where the data output is on three or four sequential lines.

Helpful Hint

When entering the line numbers, keep in mind the database structure. Lines with fields from hierarchically superior tables must be output before lines with fields from hierarchically subordinate tables. Fields from hierarchically parallel tables may not be output on the same line. You might need help from your technical staff if your report does not output the way you hoped; it may be correctable by adjusting the line assignments on this screen.

The terms *hierarchically superior* and *parallel* are really fancy terms that just mean where the data resides in the database. Picture how a standard purchase order looks: At the top it has basic information (purchase order number, vendor name, account number, and so on), and in the middle are the line item details for each item ordered (for example, Qty 24 widgets blue $4.00, Qty 3 widgets green $5.00, Qty 134 widgets white $2.00). If you were to try to run a report off this data, you would not want it all along one line. Rather, you would want information from the top of the purchase order (the hierarchically superior fields for purchase order number, vendor name, and so on) to appear along one line and the information from the middle of the purchase order (the hierarchically inferior fields, such as the line item detail for each item ordered) to appear as individual (or parallel) lines in your report. If you are working with complex data such as financial purchase orders, invoices, or human capital management organizational charts, you need to be sure you understand the data before including it in your reports.

SEQUENCE

You use the Sequence column to identify the order in which you want your data to appear in the line. For example, if all of your fields are on Line 1, you can specify that you want the Booking Number field to appear first, followed by the Airline Carrier ID, and so on. It is a best business practice to list your sequence of fields in increments, as shown in Figure 3.13. That way, if you need to modify the report output, add a field, or delete a field, you do not need to renumber the entire sequence in the report. A popular way to do this is to use increments of 5, as shown in Figure 3.13.

SORT

When you have set up the way you want your fields displayed with the Line and Sequence settings, you can specify the sort order for the fields by using the Sort column. You can assign sequence numbers between 1 and 10 to sort on up to 10 different fields.

Helpful Hint
The fields do not have to be sorted in the same order in which they are presented onscreen. For example, even if the Flight Class field were set to output as the last column in the report, you could still indicate it as the data you want to sort on, as shown in Figure 3.13.

TOTAL

Check boxes for the Total column appear only for numeric fields that can be totaled. You can place a check mark for each numeric field for which you want to output the total at the end of the basic list and, if sort criteria exist, subtotals at the end of each control level. Chapter 7, "Creating Advanced Reports with the SAP Query Tool," talks more about control levels and subtotaling.

COUNTER

You can select check boxes in the Counter column for each field you want to count. The total is then displayed at the end of the list.

Helpful Hint
It has been my experience that, depending on your SAP GUI version and your installed version of Microsoft Office and its related settings, sorts and counts may appear only if your report is viewed as an ABAP list and not via the SAP List Viewer.

MODIFYING AN SAP QUERY

After you have created a query, you might want to navigate between the various screens to make changes and modifications. You can use the Next Screen and Previous Screen white arrow buttons on the Application toolbar in the first four screens of the SAP Query tool.

You can also click the Basic List button to jump to the Basic List Line Structure screen or press the F8 key to navigate to the selection screen or finished report output from the selection screen. Clicking the green Back button on the Application toolbar from the finished report output screen brings you to the report's selection screen. You can also navigate between screens by using the toolbar menus.

SAVING A QUERY

From any screen in the SAP Query tool except the Selections screen or the finished report output screen, you can click the Save button on the Application toolbar to save your query. This makes sense: If you click the Save button on the selection screen, the system thinks you want to save the entries as a variant, and if you click the Save button on the list screen, the system thinks you want to save your output as a list.

MAINTAINING QUERIES

You can maintain and execute queries from the main SAP Query tool screen, which you access by using the transaction code **SQ01**. By using the buttons at the top of this screen, you can execute, change, create new, or view descriptions of queries in R/3. By using the Application toolbar, you can also copy, delete, or rename your queries (see Figure 3.14).

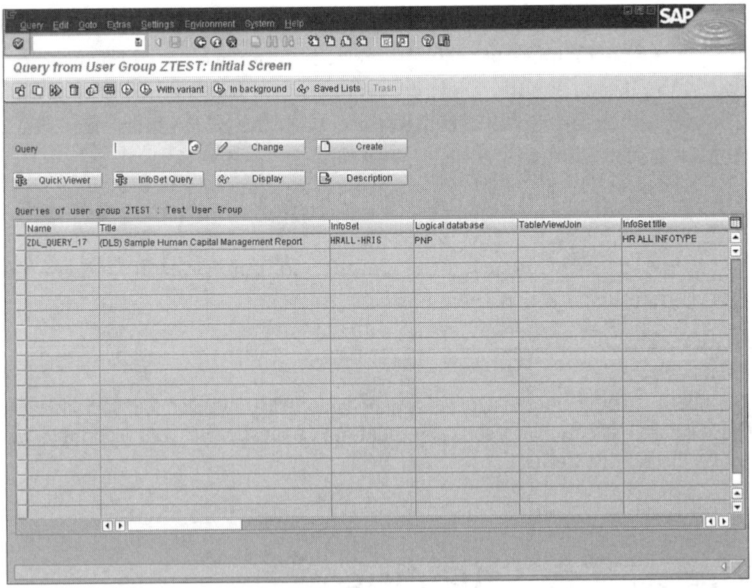

Figure 3.14
The main screen of the SAP Query tool contains functions on the menu bar for maintaining queries.

THINGS TO REMEMBER

- Creating a query report using the SAP Query tool is very easy.
- You can navigate between the basic screens of the SAP Query tool by using the navigational arrows on the Application toolbar.
- Whenever you want to execute your report, you can do so by pressing F8 on your keyboard.
- When you execute a report, you always see a selection screen that gives you the opportunity to further specify your selections.
- When creating reports, it is a good idea to format your output on the Basic List Line Structure screen in increments to make it easier to edit your report in the future.

3

CHAPTER **4**

THE FUNDAMENTALS OF REPORTING WITH THE SAP QUERY TOOL

In this chapter

Now that you have completed the one-time configuration and have begun creating basic SAP queries, it is important to practice navigating within the SAP Query tool to edit and work with your queries. This chapter covers everything you need to know to excel at SAP query report writing and, more importantly, how to start off on the right foot.

SAP QUERY REPORTING IN THE REAL WORLD

Chapter 3, "Creating Basic Reports with the SAP Query Tool," details how to create a basic SAP query report by using the five screens of the SAP Query tool. Before you proceed to more advanced topics, it is crucial that you understand how the maintenance of queries works, because you will spend a great deal of time manipulating and changing existing queries. This chapter builds on what you learned in Chapter 3.

Requests for information from the SAP database are generally received in this format: "How many widgets do we have in stock in our database?" or "Please give me a list of all associates in Texas and their annual salaries." The following sections present a real-world example of the types of reports you will be creating using the SAP Query tool.

YOUR FIRST OFFICIAL REPORT REQUEST

For this example, you need to prepare a report that answers the question, "In your SAP solution, how many flights with Plane Type A319 are scheduled for arrival in the city of Frankfurt on the flight date June 1995?" (Although your SAP system may contain different information than this example, the report format should be the same.) This type of request is common in the sense that it asks for an answer based on multiple criteria.

Most often, reports are created to answer a specific question and not to simply review long lists of data. Producing a list of all active cost centers in the SAP database would waste a lot of paper. But you can use a basic report such as a list of all active cost centers to produce a list of which active cost centers are in Mexico. A simple change to an entry on a selection screen can make a simple report of all cost centers into a myriad of different types of useful reports, each of which can then be used to answer a business-specific challenge or question.

The example presented in this chapter shows how you can use a single report multiple times to satisfy multiple needs without having to change the core report. To answer the question posed earlier, you execute a basic list SAP query report (which you should call *DLS_Query_02*, where *DLS* is your initials) that includes the fields you need for output in addition to some other fields. Figure 4.1 shows the output of this report.

When you review the report output, you can easily answer the question posed earlier. The answer in this example is 1. (Your answer may be different, depending on your system output.)

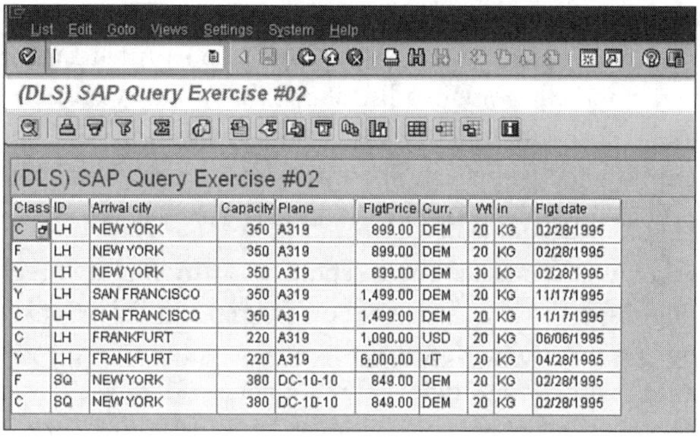

Figure 4.1
The report output screen of the SAP Query tool, listing the fields used in the report to answer the question in this example.

Class	ID	Arrival city	Capacity	Plane	FlgtPrice	Curr.	Wt	in	Flgt date
C	LH	NEW YORK	350	A319	899.00	DEM	20	KG	02/28/1995
F	LH	NEW YORK	350	A319	899.00	DEM	20	KG	02/28/1995
Y	LH	NEW YORK	350	A319	899.00	DEM	30	KG	02/28/1995
Y	LH	SAN FRANCISCO	350	A319	1,499.00	DEM	20	KG	11/17/1995
C	LH	SAN FRANCISCO	350	A319	1,499.00	DEM	20	KG	11/17/1995
C	LH	FRANKFURT	220	A319	1,090.00	USD	20	KG	06/06/1995
Y	LH	FRANKFURT	220	A319	6,000.00	LIT	20	KG	04/28/1995
F	SQ	NEW YORK	380	DC-10-10	849.00	DEM	20	KG	02/28/1995
C	SQ	NEW YORK	380	DC-10-10	849.00	DEM	20	KG	02/28/1995

Report Naming

As you can see from the previous example and Chapter 3, it is very easy to quickly create SAP query reports. Because of this, many organizations start off small, but after a few months they have thousands of reports. Using the naming convention *DLS_ReportName* (replacing *DLS* with your initials) used in the previous example is a great start. At the very least, if you follow this convention, each user's reports will be segregated by user to make it easier to locate users.

BEST NAMING CONVENTIONS FOR SAP QUERY REPORTING

Because it is so easy to create reports, many companies end up with a library of thousands of reports, many of which are duplicates. To ensure that your organization is utilizing the reporting functionality in the most efficient manner possible, it is a good idea to set some guidelines. Following three rules will ensure a clean library and SAP environment, assist you in custom report identification, and help with upgrades, where applicable, because you can easily identify key reports and report creators:

1. When you create custom reports that you intend to reuse for yourself, use a naming convention such as *DLS_ReportName*, replacing *DLS* with your initials.

2. When you create custom reports that you do not intend to reuse (designed for single-inquiry lookup), use a naming convention such as DELETE_*DLS*01, replacing *DLS* with your initials. Routinely delete reports whose names have the prefix DELETE_ to ensure that your library remains clean and efficient.

3. When you create custom reports that are standards for your organization (and that will be used by multiple users), use a common prefix to identify them as major reports that can be used by anyone. For example, you could follow the convention *ABC*_Report04, where *ABC* is an abbreviation of your company's name.

Organizations that begin using the SAP Query tool often have several users creating reports. They use the proper report naming convention, but, as discussed in Chapter 3, a SAP query also has a long description of the report (for example, List of Open Invoices by Cost Center). Although it is a good idea to use a long title that is descriptive, it is also important to keep in mind that other users may stumble upon your report and think that it is just what they are looking for, based purely on the title. But a report titled List of Open Invoices by Cost Center may not actually contain a list of open invoices by cost center. Unless instructed formally otherwise, you should follow Rule 1 and identify your SAP queries by your initials in the short description and be generic about the report data contained within the report in the report's long description, because then it is clear what the reports really are.

As mentioned earlier, you can use a single report to satisfy multiple reporting requirements by simply changing the information entered on the report's Selections screen. The long description of your report should describe what those columns are—for example, invoices sorted by cost center, without specifying which invoices—because a user can vary the selection such that only open invoices or closed invoices are included upon report execution.

If you are creating a report just to look something up, and you will likely use the report only one time, it is best to follow Rule 2 and name the report using the convention DELETE_Report01. This way, you can be certain that others will not trust the report and misuse it. More importantly, the DELETE_ prefix is a flag for the report to be deleted during regular maintenance.

You and others will create at least a dozen reports that will become staples in your organization. As mentioned earlier in this chapter, you can create a single report, and simply by varying your entries on the selection screen, you can use the report to satisfy a multitude of different reporting requirements. Major reports should be collectively agreed upon and locked against changes, as described in the section "Special Attributes" in Chapter 3. You should also follow Rule 3 and use an abbreviation of your company's name as a prefix in the name of any such report. Here is a real-world example: In my organization we use the SAP Query tool for approximately 85% of the company's human resources and payroll reporting (with the remaining 15% handled in ABAP). We have a standard SAP query called *ABC_EELIST* (where *ABC* is my company's initials). This SAP query of the Human Capital Management module simply contains a list of associate names, addresses, and phone numbers. Table 4.1 shows a snapshot of the output of five fictional associate records from this report. This basic SAP query outputs the fields associate first name, last name, street address 1, street address 2, city, state, postal code, and telephone number.

TABLE 4.1 SNAPSHOT OF FIELDS AND DATA FROM SAP QUERY *ABC_EELIST*

First Name	Last Name	Street 1	Street 2	City	State	Postal Code	Telephone
Grace	MacFarland	1 Smith St	Apt 15	Brooklyn	NY	11209	212-555-1212
Will	Adler	2 Milky Way		Charlotte	NC	28217	704-555-1212
Jack	Walker	3 Oak Ct	Suite JCS	Wantagh	NY	11793	516-555-1212
Karen	Truman	4 Red Ave		Garden City	NY	11530	516-799-1212
Anastasia	Behausen	5 Bell Ln		Weddington	NC	28173	704-555-1213

You could execute this single report or produce hundreds of different reports simply by altering the text on the selection screen when you execute the report. For example, this single SAP query could be used to create the following reports and more:

- A list of all associates and their addresses
- Mailing address labels for all active associates in North Carolina
- A list of all retired associates and their phone numbers
- A list of union associates in benefits plan A
- A mailing list of associates over the age of 75

You will notice that some of the sample reports listed here contain data that is not displayed in the report output. As mentioned in Chapter 3, you can include data in your selection criteria but not in your report output.

You do not need a dozen different reports; you can simply create the one main SAP query and vary the output on the selection screen to ensure that you get just the data you need. This type of report is an ideal candidate for Rule 3.

DO YOU WANT FRIES WITH THAT?

Inevitably, all organizations run into the same problem: which measurements to use to classify major items. My department calls this the "Do you want fries with that? syndrome" because we always need to ask an additional question of people asking for report data. For example, in my day-to-day job, I am often asked, "How many associates do we have?" It seems like an easy enough question, but I need to ask about a number of details: "Do you mean active headcount? Do you want me to include associates on paid leave? Do you want me to count full-time associates or all associates, regardless of status (student, temporary, and so on)? Should I include union associates?" Without the follow-up questions, I could provide dozens of different answers. As you can see, standards are key to reporting.

SAP QUERY REPORTING STANDARDS

Regardless of which application area you will be reporting on (Materials Management, Sales & Distribution, Finance, and so on), you need to identify reporting standards. You then need to publish and distribute these standards so that anyone creating or receiving reports knows what they are.

At my workplace, we have a published document that we update and redistribute monthly. It includes all the standards needed to understand creating and receiving reports. It is often easiest to use the Human Capital Management (HCM) module as an example, because unlike the other functional areas, all readers are familiar with the workings of human resources. Table 4.2 shows an example of reporting standards for HCM module reporting.

TABLE 4.2   SAMPLE FICTIONAL SAP QUERY REPORTING STANDARDS FOR THE HCM MODULE

Data	Sample Fictional Company Reporting Standard
Active associates	Employee Group 1 + 7 on infotype 0001
Terminated associates	Employee Group 3, 5, and 9 use infotype 41 to get term date
Associates on leave	Employee group = 7
EE status	To pull all salaried ee's (S*), all hourly ee's (H*), etc. Please note all temporary (T*) and on-call (O*) are excluded from our scheduled management level reports and are not included in the LTO numbers we report.
Home address	Use Infotype 0006 Address Record Type 1 Permanent address
Union associates	Employee Sub Groups beginning in U are considered union (e.g. to pull all union ee's use U*)
Gender	Infotype 02, text gender key
Race	Infotype 77, text ethnic origin

In Chapter 3 you learned how easy it is to create reports. In this chapter, it is critical that you understand that reports created without reporting standards are not meaningful, because you will continually be comparing apples to oranges.

SAP QUERY MAINTENANCE FUNCTIONS

Performing maintenance—including locking your queries against changes, transporting them between clients, and so on—is a task you will likely perform on a regular basis as you work with SAP Query. Having a good understanding of these maintenance functions is the key to properly administering the reporting solution in your organization.

LOCKING YOUR SAP QUERIES

Earlier in this chapter, I encouraged the use of the SAP Query tool's locking feature. The locking feature, described in the "Special Attributes" section in Chapter 3, allows a user to lock an SAP query. A locked query can be executed, copied, and transported (to the standard or global application area), but it cannot be altered or deleted by anyone other than the person who locked it (not the person who created it). Note that any user who opens an SAP Query (via the Change or Create button) and selects the Change Lock check box has his or her SAP user ID locking that query.

Best practice dictates that if you are creating queries associated with Rule 1, it is a good practice to lock your own queries during the creation process. In line with Rule 2, you should never select the lock indicator for queries that you intend to delete (those starting with a DELETE_ prefix). Finally, for those queries that will be used by multiple users and will become company staples (refer to Rule 3), you should ask your system administrator/ owner to lock these individual company reports. This way, you can rest assured that queries cannot accidentally be modified or deleted.

Helpful Hint
Keep in mind that when a user locks a query and then is no longer a user, the only way the query can be unlocked is for the system administrator to reset that user's password and log in as that user to unmark the query. Another workaround is to simply make a copy of the query and then make changes to the copied version.

COPYING EXISTING SAP QUERIES (SAME CLIENT, SAME QUERY GROUP)

Although it is a great idea not to duplicate one report over and over, there are instances in which a standard report contains everything you need but is missing only a field or two. Because of Rule 3, you cannot change a company query. However, you can simply make a quick copy of the report (and its variant, if it has one; this is covered in Chapter 6, "Using Reporting Selection Screens: Advanced Skills," in the section "Variants") and than make the change you need to the copied version.

Follow these steps to copy a query:

1. Navigate to the main screen of the SAP Query tool by using transaction code **SQ01** and select from the list the query you want to copy (or type the query's name in the Query box at the top of the screen).

2. Click the white copy button on the Application toolbar. A dialog box like the one shown in Figure 4.2 appears.

Copy button

Figure 4.2
The Copy a Query dialog box allows you to enter a new name for your copied query.

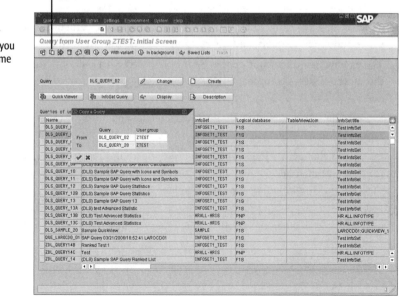

3. Type in a new name for your copied SAP query in the To Query Name box and then press Enter. Be sure to follow the naming rules discussed earlier in this chapter when naming the copied query.

4. When your copied SAP query appears in the same user group as the original, change the long report title (description) of the copied query to distinguish it from the original.

COPYING OR MOVING EXISTING SAP QUERIES (SAME CLIENT, DIFFERENT QUERY GROUP)

In some cases, you might want to copy or move an existing query from one query group on the client to another. At any time, if you want to see a list of valid query groups on the client, you can navigate to the SAP Query tool main screen (by using transaction code **SQ01**) and press Shift+F7, to get a list. This list will appear only if you are currently assigned to multiple query groups (or if you have an administrator or SAP_ALL login type of security access). Although it is a great idea not to duplicate reports between query groups, in some cases, there is a business case for moving or copying a query to a different query group.

Follow these steps to copy a query to a new query group:

1. Navigate to the main screen of the SAP Query tool by using transaction code **SQ01** and select from the list the query you want to copy (or type the query's name in the Query box at the top of the screen).

2. On a scrap of paper, write the name of the query and the name of the query group in which it currently resides.

3. Press Shift+F7 to view a list of all query groups to which you are assigned.

4. Double-click the query group you want to move the query to. You are now on the main screen of the SAP Query tool, and the query group is listed on the top left of the screen.

5. Click the white Copy button on the Application toolbar.

6. When a dialog box like the one shown in Figure 4.2 appears, take a look at your scrap of paper and type the query and query group names into the form.

7. Type a new name for your copied SAP query in the To Query Name box, ensuring that the Query (User) Group lists the new query group name to which you are moving the query.

8. Press Enter. Your copied SAP query, with its new name, appears in the new query group, along with the original query group.

9. Be sure to change the long report title (description) of the copied query to distinguish it from the original (as needed), and be sure to follow the naming rules discussed earlier in this chapter when naming the copied query

10. If you want to move and not copy a query, return to the original query group by pressing Shift+F7 and then delete the copied query as described in the following section.

Deleting SAP Queries

To delete an SAP query, follow these steps:

1. Navigate to the main screen of the SAP Query tool by using transaction code **SQ01** and select from the list the query you want to delete (or type the query's name in the Query box at the top of the screen).

2. Select the trash can Delete button on the Application toolbar (see Figure 4.3).

Delete

Figure 4.3
The Delete Query dialog box allows you to delete existing queries.

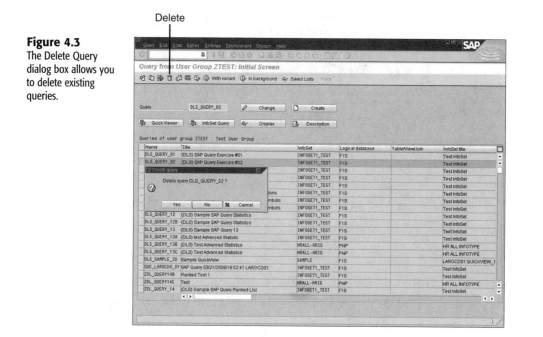

3. When a Delete Query dialog box like the one shown in Figure 4.3 appears, confirm that you want to delete the query by pressing Enter. A message appears in the bottom left of the screen, letting you know that the query has been successfully deleted.

Helpful Hint

Keep in mind the following guidelines when deleting reports:

■ Never delete another user's report.

■ Never delete a report that has the prefix *ABC_* (where *ABC* is an abbreviation of your company's name).

■ If you are unsure whether to delete a report, ask first. (It's better to be safe than sorry!)

Working on Your Existing SAP Queries

Now that you have learned how easy it is to create queries, copy them, and delete them, you need some real-world practice with editing and making changes to a query that already exists. Here is your opportunity to practice receiving report requests, performing maintenance, and editing them.

As your first exercise, create an SAP query from scratch and name it *DLS*_Query_03 (replacing *DLS* with your initials). The query should contain the following output: flight class, airline carrier ID, arrival city, maximum capacity, plane type, and airfare. Your finished output should be similar to what is shown in Figure 4.4.

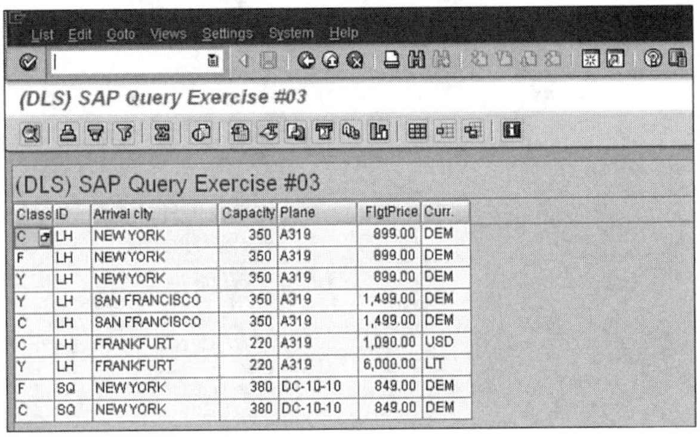

Class	ID	Arrival city	Capacity	Plane	FlgtPrice	Curr.
C	LH	NEW YORK	350	A319	899.00	DEM
F	LH	NEW YORK	350	A319	899.00	DEM
Y	LH	NEW YORK	350	A319	899.00	DEM
Y	LH	SAN FRANCISCO	350	A319	1,499.00	DEM
C	LH	SAN FRANCISCO	350	A319	1,499.00	DEM
C	LH	FRANKFURT	220	A319	1,090.00	USD
Y	LH	FRANKFURT	220	A319	6,000.00	LIT
F	SQ	NEW YORK	380	DC-10-10	849.00	DEM
C	SQ	NEW YORK	380	DC-10-10	849.00	DEM

Figure 4.4
Your report output will vary from what is shown here, based on your system's data, but the column format should appear the same.

Navigating Through an Existing SAP Query

After a query is created, quite often you need to return to it and make modifications. You have a couple options for editing existing queries and the related navigation:

- You can navigate to the main screen of the SAP Query tool by using transaction code **SQ01** and select from the list the query you want to copy (or type the query's name in the Query box at the top of the screen).
- You can click the Change button to open your existing SAP query for editing. You are then presented with the first of the five basic screens of the SAP Query tool.
- You can navigate between the screens of the SAP Query tool by using the directional arrows at the top left of the screen and by clicking the Basic List button on the Application toolbar to get to the last screen.
- You can navigate between the five basic screens of the SAP Query tool by using menu paths. From any screen in the SAP Query tool, you can select Goto, Field Selection, and then select one of the first four screens to jump directly to it. You can access the last screen, the Basic List screen, by selecting Goto, Basic List, Structure.

MODIFYING AN EXISTING QUERY: ADDING FIELDS

Now that you have mastered navigating an existing query, you can move on to the next exercise: Modify the SAP query you created in the preceding exercise (refer to Figure 4.4) by implementing the following changes: Add a Weight of Luggage field between the Plane Type and Airfare fields. Also add the Flight Date and Destination Airport fields at the end of the report. Your finished output should appear similar to Figure 4.5.

Names of Fields in SAP

You may have noticed the field I have been referencing called Airfare (see Figure 4.6, which has a column heading of Flgtprice, and Figure 4.7). In most cases within SAP logical databases, the field name (as it appears within query tool creation screens) and the column header (as it appears in the finished report output) are the same. However, in the SAP Flight Scheduling System logical database, it is different for this particular field and may cause confusion. Be aware of these types of differences. If you want to alter a column heading for a field, you can do so by accessing the InfoSet as described in Chapter 2, "One-Time Configuration for Query Tool Use," in the section "Changing the Name of a Field or Column Header."

Figure 4.5
Your revised report output will vary from what is shown here, based on your system's data.

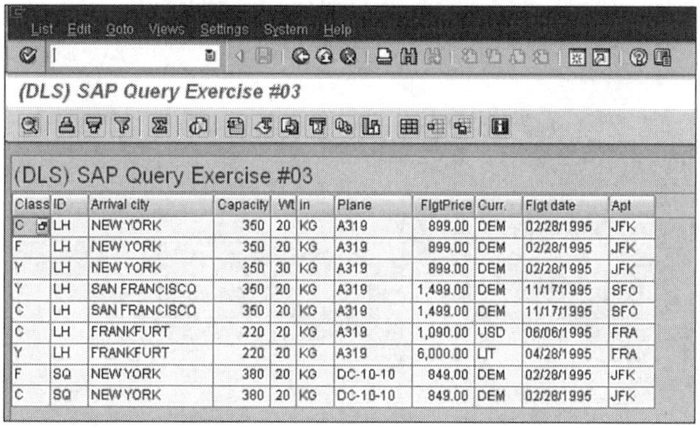

(DLS) SAP Query Exercise #03

Class	ID	Arrival city	Capacity	Wt	in	Plane	FlgtPrice	Curr.	Flgt date	Apt
C	LH	NEW YORK	350	20	KG	A319	899.00	DEM	02/28/1995	JFK
F	LH	NEW YORK	350	20	KG	A319	899.00	DEM	02/28/1995	JFK
Y	LH	NEW YORK	350	30	KG	A319	899.00	DEM	02/28/1995	JFK
Y	LH	SAN FRANCISCO	350	20	KG	A319	1,499.00	DEM	11/17/1995	SFO
C	LH	SAN FRANCISCO	350	20	KG	A319	1,499.00	DEM	11/17/1995	SFO
C	LH	FRANKFURT	220	20	KG	A319	1,090.00	USD	06/06/1995	FRA
Y	LH	FRANKFURT	220	20	KG	A319	6,000.00	LIT	04/28/1995	FRA
F	SQ	NEW YORK	380	20	KG	DC-10-10	849.00	DEM	02/28/1995	JFK
C	SQ	NEW YORK	380	20	KG	DC-10-10	849.00	DEM	02/28/1995	JFK

Helpful Hint

Recall from Chapter 3 that it is a best business practice to list your sequence of fields on the Basic List screen in increments (refer to Figure 3.13 in Chapter 3). That way, if you need to modify the report output, add a field, or delete a field, you do not need to renumber the entire sequence in the report. A popular way to do this is to use increments of 5.

MODIFYING AN EXISTING QUERY: REMOVING FIELDS AND MODIFYING THE SORT

Now that you have finished editing your query, you can move on to your next exercise: Modify your query by removing the output of the Flight Class, Airline Carrier ID, and Arrival City fields, but continue to indicate that you want to sort on the Flight Class field (see Figure 4.6). Your finished output should look similar to what is shown in Figure 4.7.

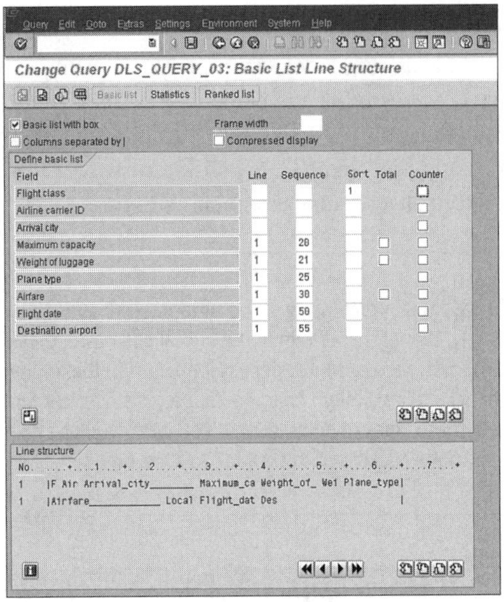

Figure 4.6
You use the Basic List screen of the SAP Query tool to define the report output.

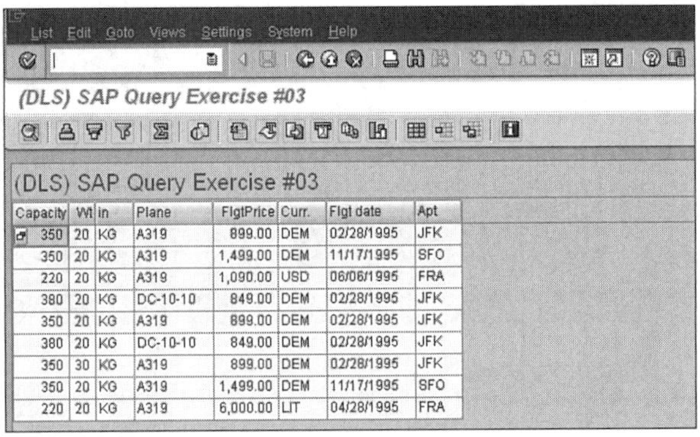

Figure 4.7
My sample report output when displayed in the SAP List Viewer auto-sizes each column to fit its contents.

To test all the skills you have learned in this chapter, you can try one final exercise: Make a copy of your existing SAP query and name it *DLS_Query_04* (replacing *DLS* with your initials). Change the title of the query on the first screen of the SAP Query tool to reflect that it is SAP Query 4. In this copied version, add the following fields: Text:Maximum Capacity (as the first field in the report output), Text:Flight Class (to the right of the Flight Date field), and Smoker and Text:Smoker (as the last two fields in the report). Add totals to appear in the report for the Maximum Capacity and Weight of Luggage fields. Your finished output should look similar to what is shown in Figure 4.8.

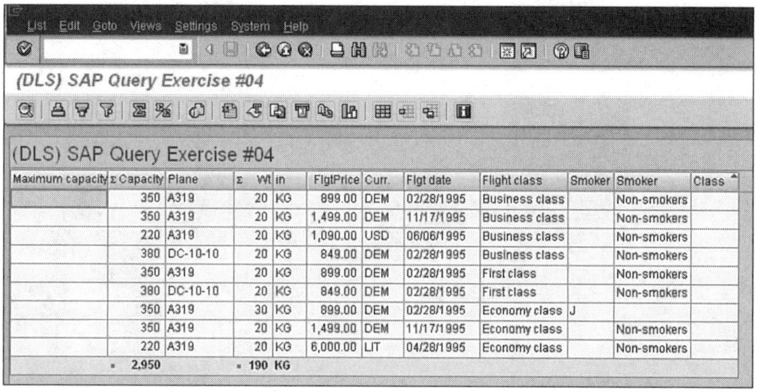

Figure 4.8
In this example, some of my column data is blank; this will vary based on what is stored in the database.

(DLS) SAP Query Exercise #04

Maximum capacity	Σ Capacity	Plane	Σ Wt	in	FlgtPrice	Curr.	Flgt date	Flight class	Smoker	Smoker	Class
	350	A319	20	KG	899.00	DEM	02/28/1995	Business class		Non-smokers	
	350	A319	20	KG	1,499.00	DEM	11/17/1995	Business class		Non-smokers	
	220	A319	20	KG	1,090.00	USD	06/06/1995	Business class		Non-smokers	
	380	DC-10-10	20	KG	849.00	DEM	02/28/1995	Business class		Non-smokers	
	350	A319	20	KG	899.00	DEM	02/28/1995	First class		Non-smokers	
	380	DC-10-10	20	KG	849.00	DEM	02/28/1995	First class		Non-smokers	
	350	A319	30	KG	899.00	DEM	02/28/1995	Economy class	J		
	350	A319	20	KG	1,499.00	DEM	11/17/1995	Economy class		Non-smokers	
	220	A319	20	KG	6,000.00	LIT	04/28/1995	Economy class		Non-smokers	
	• 2,950		• 190	KG							

THINGS TO REMEMBER

- The best way to ensure that your organization is utilizing the SAP reporting functionality in the most efficient manner is to utilize the three best practices described in this chapter.

- Identifying which measurements you use to classify major items and documenting them is the key to accurate, consistent reporting measures.

- You can execute a single SAP query report to produce hundreds of different reports simply by altering the text on the selection screen. When you execute a report, you almost always see a selection screen that gives you an opportunity to further specify your selections.

- You should never delete another user's report.

- It is easy to navigate between the five basic screens of the SAP Query tool by using menu paths. From any screen in the SAP Query tool, you can select Goto, Field Selection, and then select one of the basic screens to jump directly to it. You can access the Basic List Line Structure screen by selecting Goto, Basic List, Structure.

4

CHAPTER **5**

BASICS OF USING REPORTING SELECTION SCREENS

In this chapter

Now that you have created several test reports and learned about the fundamentals of reporting with the SAP Query tool, it important to leverage your knowledge of how to correctly use reporting selection screens. This chapter covers everything you need to know to maximize the reporting potential in SAP via the use of reporting selection screens.

THE REPORTING SELECTION SCREENS

When you execute virtually any report in the SAP R/3 environment—whether it is a system-delivered canned report, a query, or a custom-coded ABAP report—you are likely to see a selection screen that gives you the opportunity to specify exactly what you want.

Selection screens in SAP contain data relevant to the report being executed. For example, if you were running a report based on a SAP test flight scheduling system (as used in earlier chapters), your selection screen would automatically contain values relevant to that application (see Figure 5.1).

Figure 5.1
The standard selection screen used with all reports created using the flight scheduling system application is based on the F1S logical database.

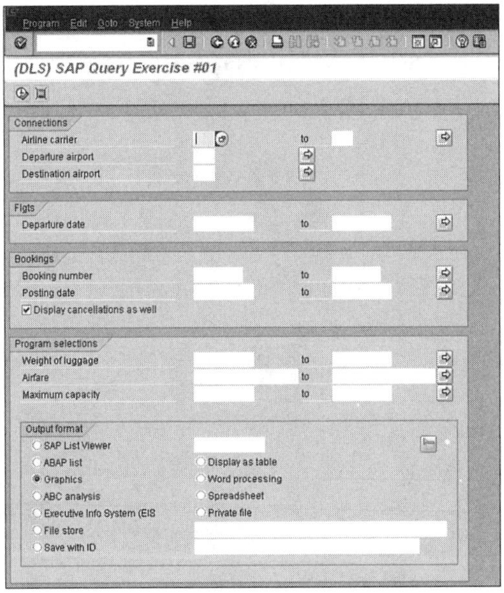

Recall from Chapter 2, "One-Time Configuration for Query Tool Use," that logical databases were used to build the InfoSets that you use for SAP query reporting. Remember that an InfoSet is the data source that houses the data you use in reports. If you look back to Figure 1.2 in Chapter 1, "Getting Started with the SAP R/3 Query Reporting Tools," you'll see that the logical databases are part of the InfoSet. A logical database is a prearranged grouping of data where fields from a similar application or module area are grouped hierarchically to allow for reporting.

How the Selection Screens Work

I love Italian food, and my husband and I often eat at a local Italian place, Mama Tricarico's, whose menus come with crayons. Instead of just selecting a dish from the menu, I can create a dish exactly the way I want it by writing on the menu and selecting the items I want. The menu lists each of the different types of pastas, sauces, and add-ins, from which I simply select what I want (see Figure 5.2).

Figure 5.2
The menu from my favorite Italian restaurant, which gives diners the option to choose precisely what they want.

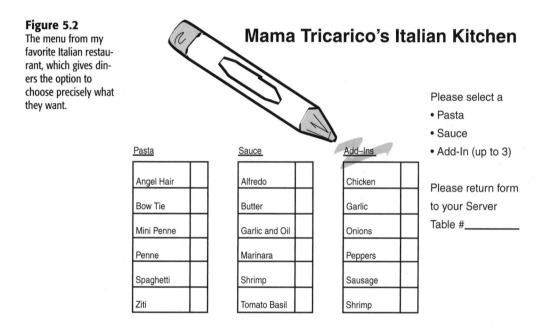

Mama Tricarico's Italian Kitchen

Please select a
• Pasta
• Sauce
• Add-In (up to 3)

Please return form
to your Server

Table #_____

Pasta		Sauce		Add–Ins	
Angel Hair		Alfredo		Chicken	
Bow Tie		Butter		Garlic	
Mini Penne		Garlic and Oil		Onions	
Penne		Marinara		Peppers	
Spaghetti		Shrimp		Sausage	
Ziti		Tomato Basil		Shrimp	

The reason I like the restaurant so much, besides the food, is that it allows for flexibility for every individual diner. If you are at all like me, you are hungry by now, but we're really here to talk about reporting selection screens. As you learned in Chapter 3, "Creating Basic Reports with the SAP Query Tool," reporting selection screens allow you to specify what you want in your report—similar to the way Mama Tricarico's lets you specify what you want in your meal. Table 5.1 shows an example of a basic SAP query report. By using a selection screen, you can simply pick and choose the data you want to include in your finished report output. For example, in Chapter 4, "The Fundamentals of Reporting with the SAP Query Tool," if I wanted to run a report of flights from the SAP test flight scheduling system where the flight date was June 1995, I could do so just by indicating June 1995 on the report's selection screen prior to executing the final report output.

5

TABLE 5.1   ALL ASSOCIATES OF MAMA TRICARICO'S IN THE SAP HCM MODULE IN A BASIC REPORT LIST

Last Name	First Name	Employee Group	Employee Group Text	Position Title	Rate	Shift	Per- sonnel Area
Smith	Nicholas	1	Active	Menu Designer	$ 8.50	1	3640
Stone	Michelle	1	Active	Chef	$14.50	1	3011
Black	Nicole	2	Leave	Waitress	$ 4.25	1	3640
Murphy	Janeen	1	Active	Hostess	$ 6.50	2	3866
Lancer	Patricia	1	Active	Waitress	$ 5.65	1	3640
Cane	Casey	2	Leave	Pot Washer	$ 5.00	1	3640
Whalen	Irene	1	Active	Waitress	$ 5.65	1	3640
Yankee	Kevin	1	Active	Waiter	$ 4.25	2	3591
Lawrence	William	1	Leave	Chef	$16.50	2	3841
Caldwell	Cindy	3	Terminated	Waitress	$ 4.25	2	3011
Count = 10				Total	$75.05		

Creating a basic SAP query report to display the Table 5.1 data from SAP is easy, using the basic instructions outlined in Chapter 3. (Note that it is not required for you to have the HCM module installed in order to proceed with this chapter, because you will not be creating any actual reports.) The fictional Table 5.1 is helpful in providing an overview of all the associates in the organization. However, as mentioned before, virtually any time a report is run in SAP, a selection screen is shown, giving you an opportunity to further specify your selections. The selection screen often comes from the logical database used in the data source (that is, the InfoSet). In this particular example, the SAP logical database PnP is used. PnP is one of the SAP standard logical databases used in the Human Capital Management (HCM) module. (You will learn more about human resources reporting in Chapter 15, "HR and Payroll Reporting Options in the HCM Module.") The standard PnP selection screen is shown in Figure 5.3.

The specifics of the Period section of the selection screen are covered in Chapter 15. For now, let's look at the Selection section, which contains fields specific to reporting in the HCM module. You may recognize two of the fields as ones that are included in the HCM sample report output displayed in Table 5.1 (Employee Group and Personnel Area). Having those fields allows you to use the selection screen to modify your criteria. For example, if you were to run the report shown in Table 5.1 and input **NOTHING** on the selection screen, that is what you would get. However, if you wanted to create a list of all "active" associates, you could easily do so by placing the appropriate value that designates an associate as active in the appropriate Employee Group field, as shown in Figure 5.4. The resulting report is shown in Table 5.2.

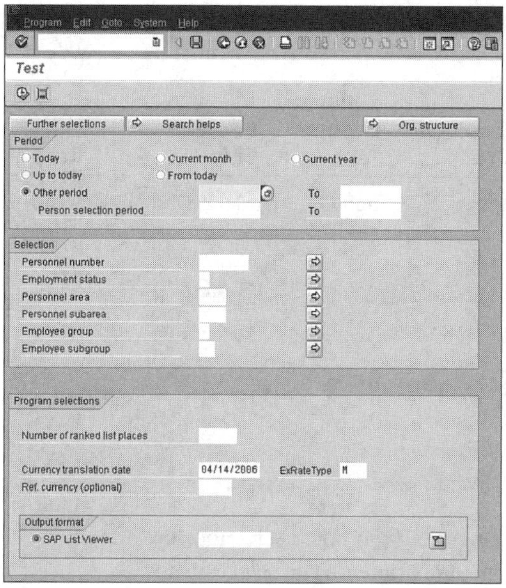

Figure 5.3
The fields included in the Period and Selection sections are specific to the Personnel Administration section of the HCM module.

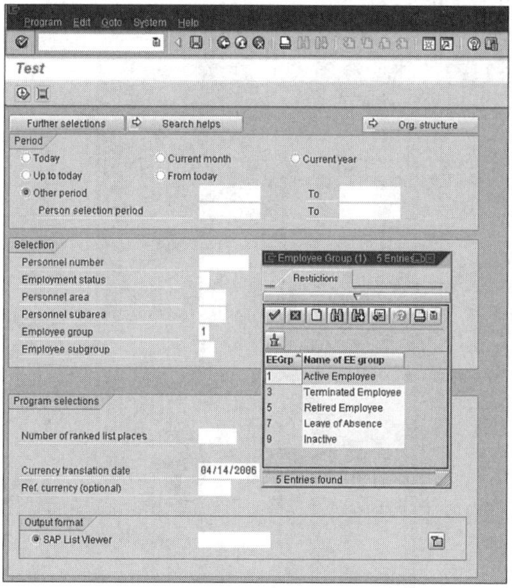

Figure 5.4
The selection screen from a basic SAP Query HCM report, showing the value options for the Employee Group field with the value selected.

5

TABLE 5.2   ALL ACTIVE ASSOCIATES OF MAMA TRICARICO'S IN THE SAP HR MODULE IN THE BASIC REPORT LIST

Last Name	First Name	Employee Group	Emloyee Group Text	Position Title	Rate	Shift	Personnel Area
Smith	Nicholas	1	Active	Menu Designer	$8.50	1	3640
Stone	Michelle	1	Active	Chef	$14.50	1	3011
Murphy	Janeen	1	Active	Hostess	$6.50	2	3866
Lancer	Patricia	1	Active	Waitress	$5.65	1	3640
Whalen	Irene	1	Active	Waitress	$5.65	1	3640
Yankee	Kevin	1	Active	Waiter	$4.25	2	3591
Count =	6			Total	$45.05		

By making one simple change to the report's selection screen, you can change the report. Let's view another example. This time on the selection screen, I specified that I wanted to include all associates who are on leave in Personnel Area 3640, as shown in Figure 5.5. The resulting report is shown in Table 5.3.

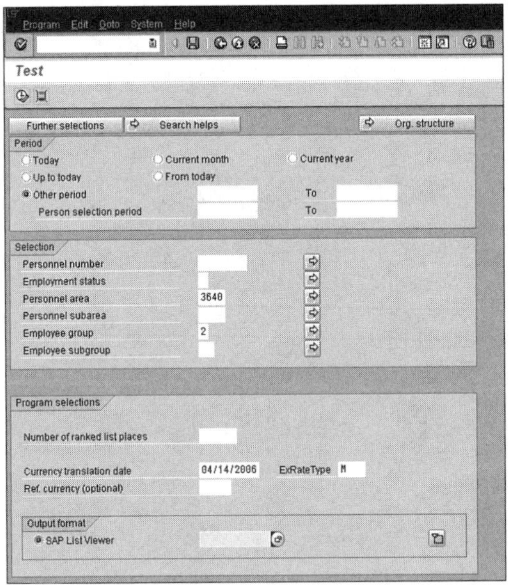

Figure 5.5
The selection screen from a basic SAP Query HCM report showing specifications in two fields.

TABLE 5.3 ALL ASSOCIATES OF MAMA TRICARICO'S WHO ARE IN PERSONNEL AREA 3640 AND WHO ARE CLASSIFIED AS ON LEAVE IN THE SAP HR MODULE IN THE BASIC REPORT LIST

Last Name	First Name	Employee Group	Emloyee Group Text	Position Title	Rate	Shift	Personnel Area
Black	Nicole	2	Leave	Waitress	$4.25	1	3640
Cane	Casey	2	Leave	Pot Washer	$5.00	1	3640
Count =	2			Total	$9.25		

As with the Mama Tricarico's menu, you can simply select what you want from a SAP report's selection screen.

MAXIMIZING THE USE OF SELECTION SCREENS IN SAP QUERY

As mentioned in Chapter 4 and shown in the examples in the preceding section, a user can create a single report and use it for multiple purposes. It is important to note that the use of selection screens is not a concept that is unique to query reporting. Selection screens appear for almost any type of report executed in SAP. With the SAP Query tool, customizing selection screens is easy. Recall from Chapter 3 that the SAP Query tool has five basic screens:

- Title, Format
- Select Field Group
- Select Field
- Selections
- Basic List Line Structure

Of these five screens, the Selections screen, shown in Figure 3.5 in Chapter 3, is the one that provides the most leverage for maximizing the use of selection screens. This is where things get confusing. The Selections screen in the SAP Query tool is where you add additional fields to appear on your report's selection screen that you will see when your report is executed. To make this confusing concept a little less so, let's take a look. The Selections screen is shown in Figure 5.6, and the corresponding selection screen for that report is shown in Figure 5.7.

The Selections screen of the SAP Query tool gives you the opportunity to add to your report's selection screen any field that you selected on the Select Field screen of the SAP Query tool. You can therefore add any relevant field to appear on the selection screen so that you can further specify your output, whether or not you wish to actually output data from that field in your report.

5

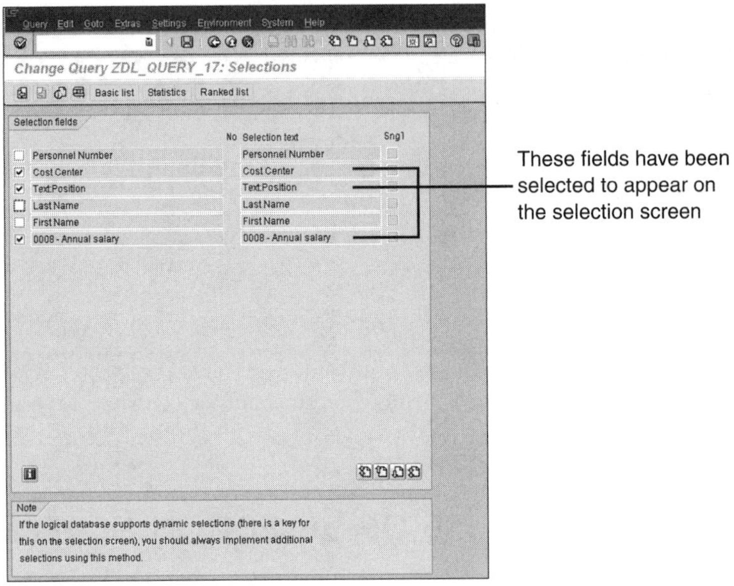

Figure 5.6
Any field indicated on the Selections screen of the SAP Query tool shows up on the report's selection screen when the report is executed.

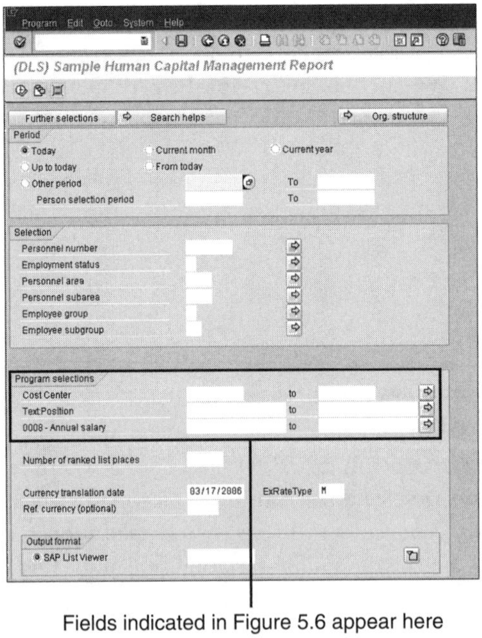

These fields have been selected to appear on the selection screen

Figure 5.7
Fields listed under the Program Selections heading on the report's selection screen were designated on the Selections screen of the SAP Query tool.

Fields indicated in Figure 5.6 appear here

UNDERSTANDING OUTPUT OPTIONS ON THE SELECTION SCREEN

As mentioned earlier in this chapter, the values on your selection screen vary, based on the logical database selected in your report's InfoSet. However, one item is standard on all selection screens: the Output Format section (see Figure 5.8).

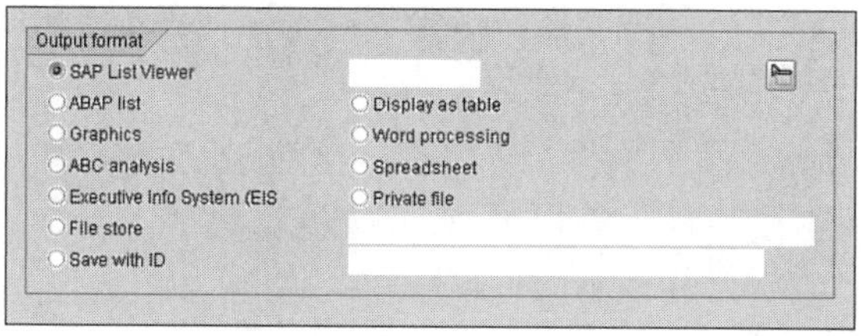

Figure 5.8
The Output Format section of the screen is where you identify the desired format you prefer for the specified report.

By default, in version 4.6C of SAP and higher, SAP List Viewer is the selected option for almost all reports. The SAP List Viewer was introduced in version SAP GUI 4.6C as an easier way to review and work with reports in a table view (similar to Microsoft Excel). In releases prior to 4.6C, the SAP List Viewer was called the ABAP List Viewer (ALV). Figure 5.9 shows an example of an SAP test flight scheduling system report displayed in the SAP List Viewer.

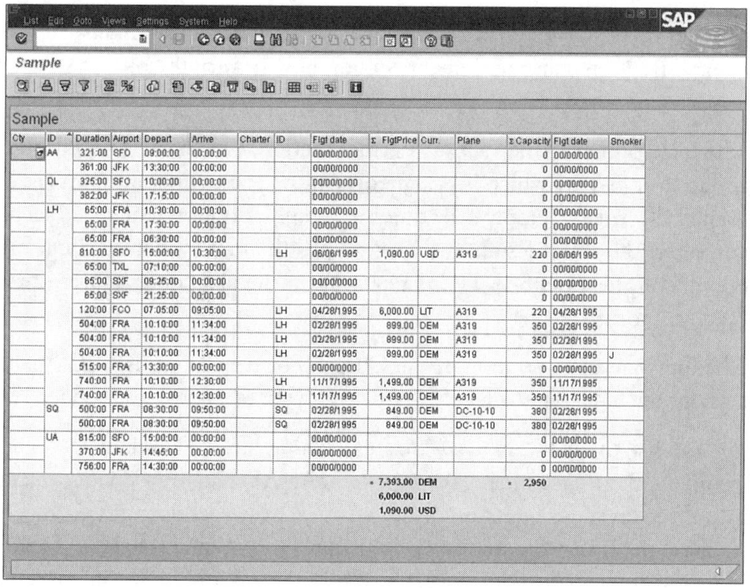

Figure 5.9
In versions of SAP earlier than 4.5, the standard display was in an ABAP list, without the table view.

5

In versions of SAP earlier than version 4.5, the second option in the Output Format list, ABAP List, was the default view. Figure 5.10 shows an example of the same SAP test flight scheduling system report shown in Figure 5.9, but this time displayed in ABAP list view.

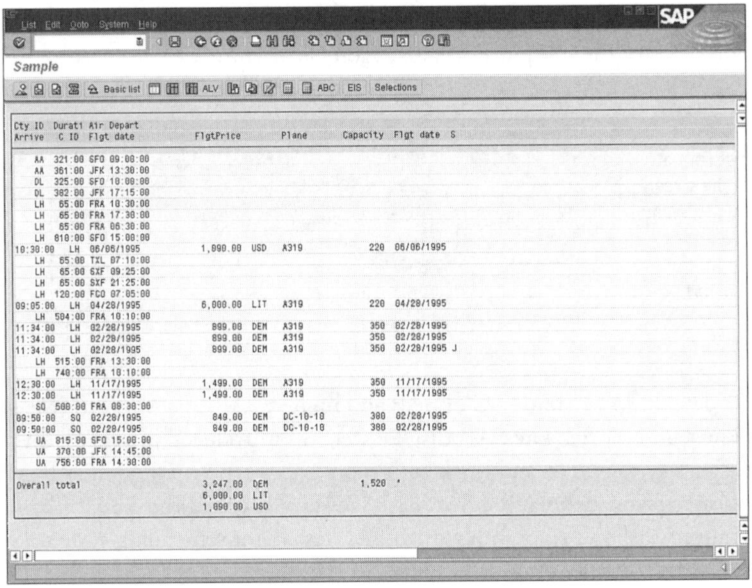

Figure 5.10
Without previously indicating any special formatting, the report text is likely to wrap to the next line at 80 characters.

Chapter 6, "Using Reporting Selection Screens: Advanced Skills," discusses advanced query-based reporting options, including how to vary the output of your data when it is displayed in a basic list.

The third option in the Output Format section, Graphics, is tied to the Business Graphics application in SAP, which is designed to allow you to create reports in a variety of different graphical formats. Simply selecting the Graphics option launches Business Graphics. When you select the Graphics option, SAP graphs the first numeric listing. Figure 5.11 shows an example of the same SAP HCM report from the preceding figures, this time displayed in graphical format.

The fourth available option in the Output Format section is ABC Analysis. When you select this option, a dialog box labeled ABC Analysis: Strategy appears (see Figure 5.12).

You can use the ABC Analysis: Strategy dialog box to stipulate how many data records a group (A, B, or C segment) is to contain. An ABC analysis divides the records of a dataset into three distinct segments (A, B, and C). These records must each contain a key figure (a numeric field) and any number of attributes (nonnumeric fields). The dataset is first sorted in descending or ascending order, using the key figure. This function can be used for any single-line basic lists, statistical lists, and any ranked lists that contain at least one numeric field. ABC analysis is most popular in financial-type analysis.

Figure 5.11
There are multiple options for graphical reporting, including pie charts and polar diagrams.

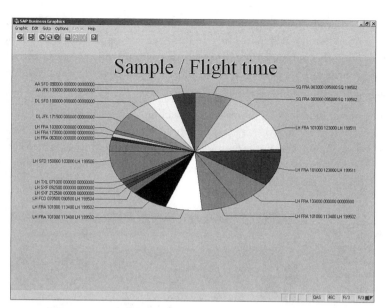

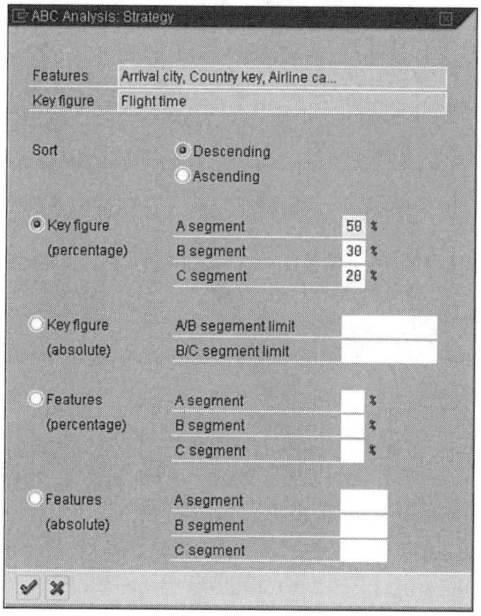

Figure 5.12
ABC Analysis can also be performed on SAP data in Microsoft Excel.

5

Helpful Hint

With the key figure strategy of ABC analysis, the percentage proportion of the key figure total must correspond to the overall total in this specification.

With the attribute strategy, the percentage proportion of the number of data records must correspond to the total number of data records in this specification. For example, if the specifications are A = 50%, B = 30%, and C = 20%, the transition from the A segment to the B segment applies when the percentage proportion exceeds 50. The transition from the B segment to the C segment applies when the percentage proportion exceeds 80 (50+30).

The next available output option is Executive Info System (EIS). This option is not utilized very often because it requires that an interface and separate database structure be in place. Indicating this output format in your SAP query provides a link to the EIS and, via an interface, transfers the report data to the EIS database for further analysis. Upon activation, a dialog box offers additional selections for formatting, sending, and storing the data.

The next option in the Output Format section is Display as Table. This option displays your report output in an SAP table control. It does not have the advanced functionality that the SAP List Viewer has, but it presents the data in a table format, which makes it easy to read. Figure 5.13 shows the same SAP HCM report shown earlier, this time displayed after the Display as Table option is selected.

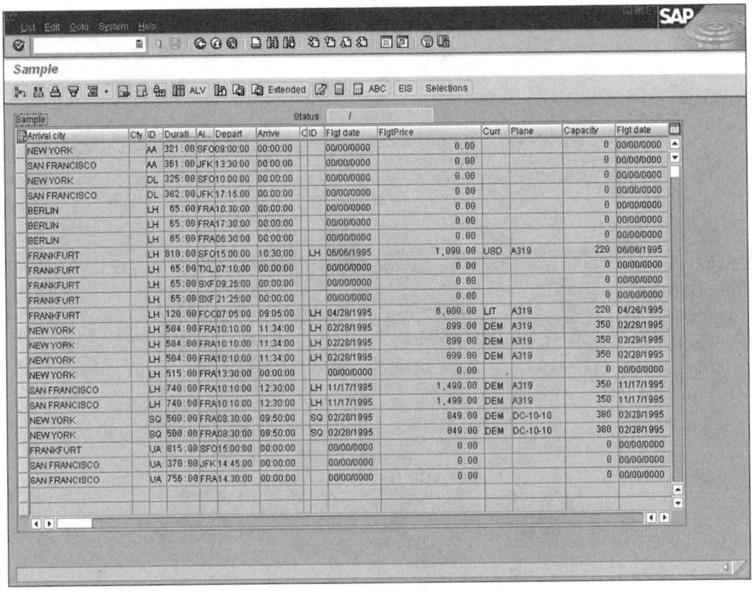

Figure 5.13
The application tool-bar contains various options but not as many as with the SAP List Viewer option.

You use the next available option in the Output Format section, Word Processing, to create a Microsoft Word form letter with the data from your SAP query. Creating form letters using your SAP data and Microsoft Word is discussed at length in Chapter 22, "SAP Query Reporting with Microsoft Word and Outlook." Chapter 21, "SAP Reporting with Microsoft Excel," provides an overview of using SAP with Microsoft Excel.

When you select the Spreadsheet option in the Output Format section, a dialog box appears, asking which of the following formats you want to use for the spreadsheet:

- **Store as PC File**—This option allows you to save the report in a spreadsheet format in a designated location.
- **Excel SAP Macros**—This option launches the Microsoft Excel <> SAP Communication window, which displays the report output in SAP Excel List Viewer format, with active macros in place.

- **Table > Excel**—This option launches a dialog box that lists a single option, Microsoft Excel. When you select this option, Microsoft Excel opens and displays your report data in a Microsoft Excel window in a basic datasheet view.

- **Pivot Table**—This option launches a dialog box that lists a single option, Microsoft Excel. When you select this option, Microsoft Excel opens and displays your report data in a Microsoft Excel window in a formatted PivotTable view.

Helpful Hint

If you ever experience a problem getting your SAP and Microsoft Excel applications to work in harmony, be sure to confirm that your Excel security is set to Medium. To do so in Microsoft Excel 2003, follow these steps:

1. Open the Excel document.

2. Select Tools, Macro, Security.

3. Set the Security to Medium.

4. Select the Trusted Sources tab.

5. Check the Trust All Installed Add-ins and Templates and Trust Access to Visual Basic Project check boxes.

6. Click OK.

7. Close Excel.

Figure 5.14 shows an example of the same SAP test flight scheduling system report as before, this time displayed in spreadsheet (PivotTable) format.

Figure 5.14
PivotTables in Microsoft Excel allow for instant analysis of the report data, and the raw, unformatted data can be found on a separate sheet in the existing workbook.

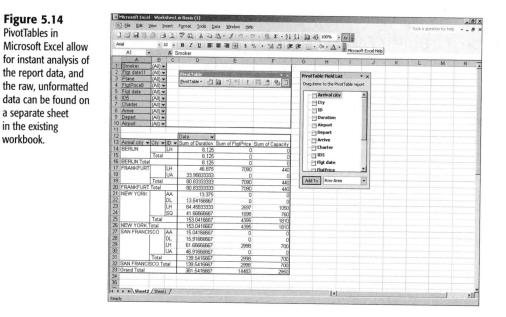

The Private File option in the Output Format section passes the report directly to a function module upon report execution instead of displaying it onscreen. This SAP enhancement is virtually obsolete. SAP continues to support this option for compatibility, but SAP recommends that you not use it and that you redefine any private files currently in use to other formats. (Please see the SAP Help if you require more information.)

The File Store option in the Output Format section allows you to select a destination and filename for your report output to be sent to. This option is popular for scheduled reports that are run in the background. To use this function, you simply type a destination address (for example, c:*filename*.asc) in the blank input field next to File Store. Files can be stored in the following formats:

- .asc (ASCII)
- .bin (binary)
- .dat (ACSII data table with column tab)
- .dbf (DBASE)
- .ibm (ASCII with IBM code page conversion)
- .wk1 (Lotus spreadsheet format)

The last available option in the Output Format section is Save with ID. To use this option, you type a user ID in the blank field next to File Store, and the list is then saved under that designated ID.

In the Output Format section, often by default all the options with the exception of the default are hidden. To see the full list, select the expand arrow to the far right of the SAP List Viewer radio button.

WHY DO THE OUTPUT FORMAT OPTIONS LOOK FAMILIAR?

The options in the Output Format section look familiar because they are the same as the options that are available in the Output Format section on the Title, Format screen of the SAP Query tool (see Figure 5.15).

The Output Format options are available in two places. Which section works better—the Title, Format screen of the SAP Query tool or the report's selection screen? If no variant is set (variants are discussed in Chapter 6), the report output value indicated on the Title, Format screen is automatically used in the Output Format section on the report's selection screen when the report is executed. However, you can override those settings on the selection screen before final execution and display of the report output.

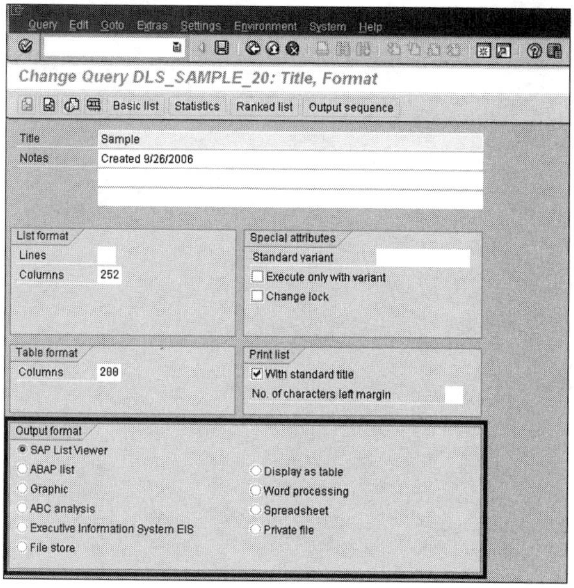

Figure 5.15
The Output Format options for a SAP query are available in at least two places in the SAP Query tool: on the Title, Format screen and on the report's selection screen, which is visible upon report execution.

THINGS TO REMEMBER

- You need to have a thorough understanding of the use of selection screens in order to produce valid report output.
- The data that appears on a selection screen varies, based on the data available in the logical database used in the report's InfoSet.
- You have multiple output options for a report, including Microsoft Excel, a data file, or a Microsoft Word merge file.
- When reporting in the SAP Query tool, you can set the output option on the Title, Format screen of the SAP Query tool or on the report's selection screen, which is displayed when the report is executed.

5

CHAPTER

6

USING REPORTING SELECTION SCREENS: ADVANCED SKILLS

In this chapter

Now that you understand how important selection screens are and how you can use them to produce multiple types of reports from a single query, you can take them a step further. This chapter covers the advanced usage of selection screens and how you can use them in query-based reporting.

Module-Specific Options on a Selection Screen

Depending on the data source (InfoSet) selected and the module for which it is designated—Human Capital Management (HCM), Accounts Payable, Sales and Distribution, and so on—different options may be available. This book covers many of them, but to best familiarize yourself with the items specific to the reporting area you are interested in, you should begin with a basic list report from within your area of interest and vary your selections to view the result on your selection screen and on your report output.

USING MULTIPLE SELECTION BUTTONS

Next to many of the fields on a selection screen is a multiple selection button (see Figure 6.1).

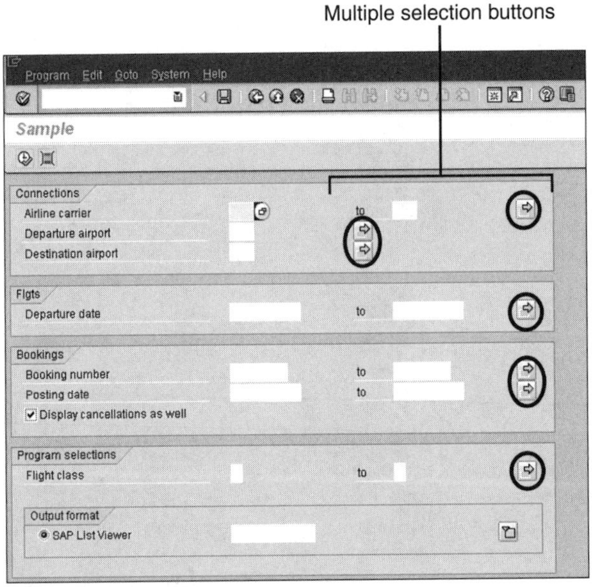

Figure 6.1
Each multiple selection button is a right-pointing arrow.

This button, located immediately to the right of the input field, allows you to specify multiple selections. In an example in Chapter 5, "Basics of Using Reporting Selection Screens" (refer to Figure 5.4 and Table 5.2), you input a value of 1 in the Employee Group field so that the report output would contain only associates (that have a number 1 designation in the Employee Group field) on their records. The multiple selection button gives you even more options.

SINGLE-VALUE INCLUSIONS

The first tab available in the Multiple Selection dialog box is Single Vals (indicated by two green circles), which gives you the ability to designate more than one single (nonsequential) entry. For example, if I select the multiple selection button to the right of the Employee Group field on the HCM report example from Chapter 5, I am indicating that I want to include associates from Employee Groups 1, 2, and 5 in the report, as shown in Figure 6.2.

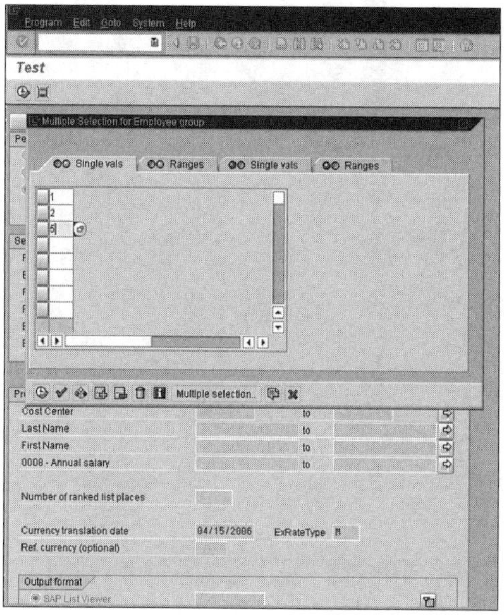

Figure 6.2
By indicating Employee Groups 1, 2, and 5, I ensured that associates classified in those categories are included and that all others are excluded.

RANGE INCLUSIONS

The second tab available in the Multiple Selection dialog box is Ranges (indicated by two green circles), which gives you the ability to designate a consecutive range of data by indicating start and end values. This data can be numeric or alphabetical; in either case, you enter the lower value in the first box (for example, A) and the higher value in the second box (for example, C). For example, if I selected the multiple selection button to the right of the Employee Group field on the HCM report example and then selected the Ranges tab, I could then indicate that I want to include associates from Employee Groups 1 through 7 in the report, as shown in Figure 6.3.

SINGLE-VALUE EXCLUSIONS

The third tab available in the Multiple Selection dialog box is Single Vals (indicated by two red circles), which gives you the ability to designate more than a single entry to be excluded from your report output. For example, when I click the multiple selection button to the right of the Employee Group field on the HCM report example and select the Ranges tab, I can indicate that I want to include associates from Employee Groups 1 through 5, as shown in Figure 6.3. If I then select the Single Vals (indicated by two red circles) tab and input value **3**, I would be including in the report output associates in Employee Groups 1, 2, 4, and 5 and excluding Employee Group 3, as shown in Figure 6.4.

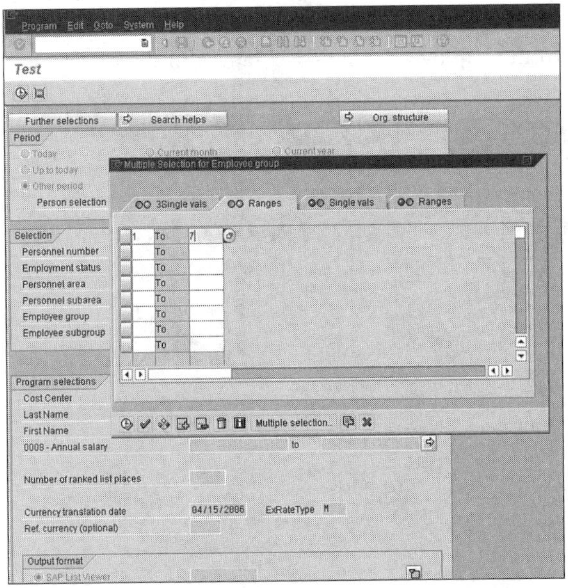

Figure 6.3
By indicating a consecutive range for the Multiple Selection option for the employee group, I ensured that associates classified in any of the Employee Groups 1, 2, 3, 4, 5, 6, and 7 are included in the report output.

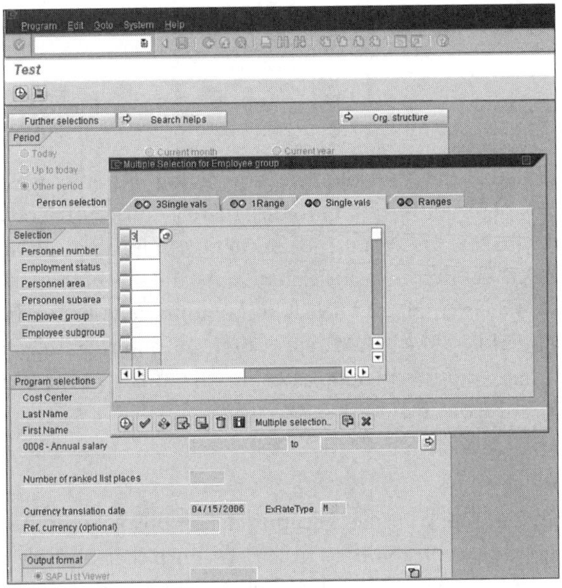

Figure 6.4
By indicating any values on the Single Vals tab (indicated by two red circles), I ensure that I will output all values except those where an employee group equals 3.

RANGE EXCLUSIONS

The fourth tab available in the Multiple Selection dialog box is Ranges (indicated by two red circles), which gives you the ability to designate a consecutive range of data to exclude by indicating start and end values. This data can be numeric or alphabetical, and again, you enter the lower value in the first box (for example, 1) and the higher value in the second box (for example, 3). For example, when I click the multiple selection button to the right of the Employee Group field on the sample HCM report and then select the fourth tab, I can indicate that I want to exclude associates from Employee Groups 1 through 5 in the report by indicating a starting value of 1 and an ending value of 5.

Helpful Hint

You can tell if multiple selections have been input for a field because the multiple selection button (to the right of the field) includes a green box under the existing yellow arrow. This signifies that values are input somewhere on the Multiple Selection dialog box for that field. (See the Personnel Number multiple selection button in Figure 6.7 later in this chapter.)

THE MULTIPLE SELECTION DIALOG BOX TOOLBAR

By now you have noticed that the Multiple Selection dialog box has a toolbar at the bottom (see Figure 6.5). The following sections describe each of these toolbar buttons.

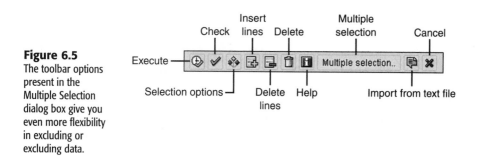

Figure 6.5
The toolbar options present in the Multiple Selection dialog box give you even more flexibility in excluding or excluding data.

EXECUTE

The first button on the Multiple Selection dialog box toolbar is the Execute button. This button functions the same as the Enter key: When you click it, any selections on the dialog box are transferred to the selection screen.

CHECK

The second button on the Multiple Selection dialog box toolbar is the Check button. This button functions as the validation key that checks your selections for validity and applicability.

6

SELECTION OPTIONS

The third button on the Multiple Selection dialog box toolbar is the Selection Options button. This button gives you even greater flexibility in selection, including options for equal to, greater than or equal to, less than, not equal to, and so on. This button was available in earlier versions of SAP, before the multiple selection button was enhanced.

INSERT LINES AND DELETE LINES

Two buttons, Insert Lines and Delete Lines, allow you to insert and delete lines in a dialog box so you can insert or remove indicated values.

DELETE

The sixth button on the Multiple Selection dialog box toolbar is the Delete button. This button deletes any entry or selections in any area of the dialog box—not just the displayed tab.

HELP

The next button on the Multiple Selection dialog box toolbar is the Help on Screen button. This button is available on almost all dialog boxes, and it serves as a specific item help reference.

MULTIPLE SELECTION

The Multiple Selection button serves the same function as the multiple selection arrow button that appears next to a field. Clicking this button brings up a list of all available options that are valid for the selected field.

IMPORT FROM TEXT FILE

The Import from Text File button on the Multiple Selection dialog box toolbar allows you to restrict your report output based on a pasted-in or imported set of values. This button is covered in the next section.

RESTRICTING VALUES IN A REPORT BASED ON AN EXISTING LIST OF VALUES

The Import from Text File button on the Multiple Selection dialog box toolbar is the button you are likely to use most often when reporting. It serves a couple different purposes. This button allows you to specify the precise list of data you want in your report output by using a pasted-in or imported list of values from any source.

For example, in my job, I am often provided with data from third-party solutions, such as a large Excel file that contains a list of associates' Social Security numbers. Let's pretend that this list of associates is from my benefits vendor, which is alerting me that the list of associates contains associates who can expect to have a benefits coverage change. I would like to easily identify these associates so that I can send each of them a personalized letter, informing them of the change. In the old days, I could use a Microsoft Access database to compare data from two sources and merge similar data (which is discussed in Chapter 23,

"SAP Reporting with Microsoft Access"), or I could use Excel's VLook-Up function to compare two data sources. However, by clicking the Import from Text File button, I can paste or upload the data I want directly into the selection screen to restrict my SAP query report output to contain only the records that match those included in the third-party file. For example, if my SAP HCM database contained 15,000 associate records, and my vendor sent me a list of 1,000 Social Security numbers, I could look up each one manually to find the correct name and address, use a Microsoft solution, or leverage the functionality of the Import from Text File button and simply reference the third-party values in one of the two ways described in the following sections.

Pasting in Third-Party Values

The first way to restrict values in a report is by pasting third-party values. To reference third-party values, you can either design a new SAP query report or use an existing one. In my third-party values example, upon execution of the query, when the selection screen is presented, I can go to the field that contains a value from the third party. In my list of Social Security numbers, I would simply make sure that the Social Security Number field is available on the selection screen. (For a quick refresher on how to add fields in a query to a selection screen, see the section "The Selections Screen" in Chapter 3, "Creating Basic Reports with the SAP Query Tool.") When I am viewing the query's selection screen, I minimize the SAP environment and navigate to the third-party file. Its format is relatively unimportant, so it is best to open it in a known application, such as Notepad or Excel. Then I select the data—in this example, all 1,000 Social Security numbers contained in the file—and then press Ctrl+C to copy this list to the Windows Clipboard. Next, I navigate to the SAP query report and the selection screen for the report and click the multiple selection button followed by the Import from Text File button. A second dialog box appears. When I click the Paste button, the list of 1,000 Social Security numbers is pasted from the Windows Clipboard memory to the value selection for the dialog box. When the SAP Query tool is executed, it will not contain all 15,000 records in the database; instead, it will contain detailed data for only the 1,000 values specified on the selection screen.

Transferring Text from a Text File

Instead of copying and pasting, you can restrict values in a report by transferring data directly from a file by clicking the Transfer button instead of the Paste button in the Import from a Local file dialog box and indicating the navigation path where the source file can be found (for example, c:\My Documents*source file*.txt). When I use this methodology when the SAP Query tool is executed, the report will not contain all 15,000 records in the database; instead, it will contain detailed data from SAP for only the 1,000 values specified in the source file that have been transferred to the selection screen.

Using Variants

As mentioned throughout this chapter and Chapter 5, you can use a single SAP query report to satisfy multiple reporting needs simply by changing the values entered on the report's selection screen. To spare a user from having to enter the values each time a report is executed, you can save entries on a selection screen as a variant. A report can have an unlimited number of variants associated with it.

As discussed in Chapter 5, which introduces the concept of selection screens, one basic report (for example, a list of all associates at Mama Tricarico's Restaurant) can be run with three different variations on the selection screen to produce three different reports. The following sections describe how to make a saved version of a selection screen for an SAP query report.

HOW TO CREATE A VARIANT FOR AN SAP QUERY

You can create a variant in several different ways. The following instructions work for any version of SAP, beginning with version 4.0:

1. Begin at the main screen of the SAP Query tool, which you reach by using transaction code **SQ01**. Select the query for which you would like to create a variant by selecting (highlighting) the gray bar to the left of the table or by typing the query name in the box at the top of the screen. (The example used here uses a test HCM query. To follow along, you can use an existing query of your own from any application module.)

2. Select Goto, Maintain Variants. The screen ABAP Variants - Initial Screen, shown in Figure 6.6, appears.

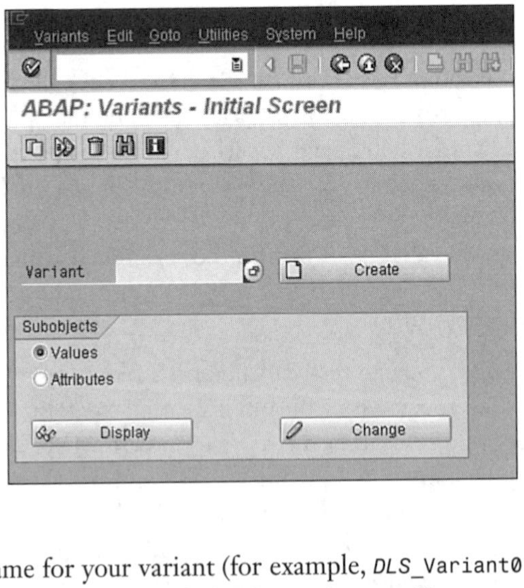

Figure 6.6
You use the screen ABAP Variants - Initial Screen to create variants for SAP queries.

3. Type a name for your variant (for example, DLS_Variant01, where you replace *DLS* with your initials) and then click the Create button. You are presented with the selection screen for the report for which you decided to create a variant in step 1. This screen gives you the opportunity to input selections that will be saved as a variant (see Figure 6.7).

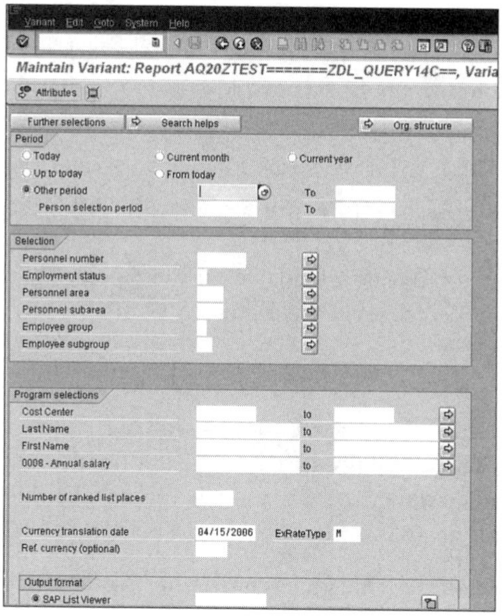

Figure 6.7
This selection screen lets you input selections that will be saved as a variant.

4. Input values on the selection screen that you want to save. Which specific values you input for the example are unimportant, but for the sake of this example, input the Period field as of today and enter the value **1** in the Employee Group field. After inputting any values you want to save, click the Save button on the Application toolbar. The first time you save the variant, the Save Attributes screen, shown in Figure 6.8, appears. When you modify an existing variant, you can click the Variant Attributes button to access this screen.

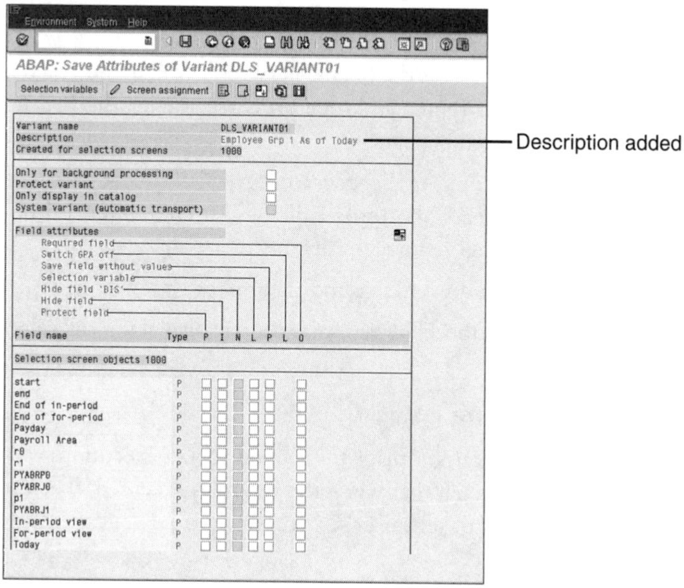

Figure 6.8
The Save Attributes screen looks the same for all reporting variants.

Description added

5. The only required field for entry on the Save Attributes screen is the Description field. Enter a description for your variant in this field and then click the Save button to complete the variant creation process. It is a good idea to use a description that describes the variant (refer to Figure 6.8).

6. Click the green Back button to return to the Maintain Variants screen.

7. Click the green Back button again to return to the main SAP Query tool screen.

To see that the variant you created is now available for the report, you need to execute the report that has the variant, as described in the following section.

EXECUTING A REPORT WITH A VARIANT (EXECUTE WITH VARIANT)

Upon report execution, you can select a variant for use in your report. By using variants, you can use a single report for multiple things, based on the information entered on the selection screen. Multiple variants can exist for a report, and you can decide which one to use prior to report execution by following these steps:

1. Begin at the main screen of the SAP Query tool, which you reach by using transaction code **SQ01**. Select your report and then click the Execute with Variant button on the Application toolbar. A dialog box that contains a drop-down field of all the variants for the selected report appears.

2. Select the variant you want to use and then press Enter.

3. Click the Execute button. The report executes, displaying the saved variant.

EXECUTING A REPORT WITH A VARIANT (EXECUTE)

You call also select the variant of your choice from a report's selection screen. Multiple variants can exist for a report, and you can decide which one to use upon report execution by following these steps:

1. Begin at the main screen of the SAP Query tool, which you reach by using transaction code **SQ01**. Select your report and then press F8 or click the Execute button. The report's selection screen appears.

2. On the Selection screen's Application toolbar, click the Get Variant button (immediately to the right of the Execute button). A dialog box containing a drop-down field of all variants for the selected report appears.

3. Select the variant you want to use and then press Enter.

4. Click the Execute button. The report executes, displaying the selected variant.

SAVING AN SAP QUERY WITH A VARIANT

In addition to selecting a variant prior to or upon report execution, you can save a variant with a query as a default, such that when the report is executed, that variant is automatically used to populate the report's selection screen.

1. Begin at the main screen of the SAP Query tool, which you reach by using transaction code **SQ01**. Select your report and then click the Change button. The Title, Format screen of the SAP Query tool appears.

2. In the Special Attributes section of the Title, Format screen, select the Variant drop-down box to see a list of all variants that exist for the selected report.

3. Select the variant you want to use and then press Enter.

4. Check the Execute Only with Variant check box.

5. Click the Save button and then press F8 or click Execute.

6. Click the Execute button. The report executes, displaying the saved variant. Because it was saved with the query, every time it is executed, the saved default variant will be used. The variant can be overwritten with new values, or a new variant can be selected after execution; however, it will always be presented as the default.

EDITING A VARIANT FOR SAP QUERY (DIRECTLY ON THE SELECTION SCREEN)

After a variant is created, you can modify it on the selection screen by following these steps:

1. On the selection screen, change the values as desired and then click the Save button on the Application toolbar. A confirmation box appears, asking if you want to overwrite the existing variant.

2. Click Yes. The changes to your variant are saved.

EDITING A VARIANT FOR SAP QUERY (ON THE MAINTAIN VARIANTS SCREEN)

After a variant is created, you can modify it on the Maintain Variants screen by following these steps:

1. Begin at the main screen of the SAP Query tool, which you reach by using transaction code **SQ01**. Select the query for which you would like to modify the variant by selecting (highlighting) the gray bar to the left of the table or by typing the query name in the box at the top of the screen.

2. Select Goto, Maintain Variants. The screen ABAP Variants - Initial Screen appears.

3. Select your variant from the drop-down box and then click the Change button. You are presented with the selection screen for the report.

4. Modify the values on the selection screen as you like and then click the Save button on the Application toolbar.

5. To modify the attributes, click the Variant Attributes button and make the desired changes.

6. Make any other modifications desired on this screen and then click the Save button to complete the variant modification process.

6

ADVANCED FUNCTIONS FOR VARIANTS

To see what options are available on the Variant Attributes screen, follow these steps:

1. Begin at the main screen of the SAP Query tool, which you reach by using transaction code **SQ01**. Select the query for which you would like to modify the variant by selecting (highlighting) the gray bar to the left of the table or by typing the query name in the box at the top of the screen.

2. Select Goto, Maintain Variants. The screen ABAP Variants - Initial Screen appears.

3. Select your variant from the drop-down box and then click the Change button. You are presented with the selection screen for the report.

4. Click the Variant Attributes button to view the available options on the Save Attributes screen (refer to Figure 6.8).

The Save Attributes screen has dozens of available options. Table 6.1 describes the general options available.

TABLE 6.1 GENERAL FUNCTIONS AVAILABLE ON THE SAVE ATTRIBUTES SCREEN

Option	Description
Variant Name	This field contains the name of the variant that is input on the Maintain Variants screen during the creation process.
Description	This field contains the required description field that users must populate with a description of the variant.
Created for Selection Screens	This field displays the number of the R/3 dynpro (screen) that is displayed at runtime. It may also be recorded in trace or logging information.
Only for Background Processing	If you select this check box, the variant can be executed only in the background. If you do not select it, it can be run both in the background and online.
Protect Variant	If you select this check box, the variant can only be changed by the person who created it or who last changed it.
Only Display in Catalog	If you select this check box, the variant name appears in the directory but not in the general input help.
System Variant (Automatic Transport)	This system variant is transported automatically.

The Field Attribute options listed in Table 6.2 can be indicated for any of the fields by placing a check mark in the bog next to each.

TABLE 6.2   FIELD ATTRIBUTES AVAILABLE ON THE SAVE ATTRIBUTES SCREEN

Option	Description
Required Field	This attribute indicates that the designated field requires entry on the selection screen prior to report execution.
Switch GPA Off	The field contents are ignored when the variant is imported.
Save Field Without Values	If you select this field, the value of the corresponding field on the selection screen is not affected when you start the program by using a variant.
Selection Variable	If you select this field, the field on the selection screen is assigned a value from a variant variable.
Hide Field 'BIS'	If you are using BIS, if you select this option, the corresponding field is not displayed when the user starts the program using this variant. However, you can still assign a value to the field in the variant.
Hide Field	If you select this option, the corresponding field is not displayed when the user starts the program using this variant. However, you can still assign a value to the field in the variant.
Protect Field	If you select this option, the user cannot overwrite the value in the field on the selection screen.

Note that the bottom section of the Save Attributes screen lists every field available on the selection screen. Each is classified with a type. The field type indicates whether the field is a parameter (P) or selection option (S).

Helpful Hint

The selection screens designated for the program are displayed one after the other. Because a parameter or selection option can occur on more than one screen, the attribute fields for that field accept input only the first time they appear.

THINGS TO REMEMBER

- The Multiple Selection dialog box has four key tabs.
- The Import from Text File button allows you to restrict your report output to data contained in a third-party list or data source.
- You can create a virtually unlimited number of variants for a single SAP query report.
- You have multiple options when executing a report with a variant, including saving the variant in the SAP Query tool as a default for a specific query.
- You can prevent users from modifying entries on a report's selection screen by using the Protect option.

CHAPTER 7

CREATING ADVANCED REPORTS WITH THE SAP QUERY TOOL

In this chapter

In Chapter 3, "Creating Basic Reports with the SAP Query Tool," you learned how to create basic list reports by using the SAP Query tool. This chapter describes how to use the additional screens of the SAP Query tool to perform more advanced functions in SAP query reporting.

Helpful Hint

Although it is recommended that you create SAP query reports live in your production environment, while you are learning, it is important that you practice in your test/quality assurance client so as to not have any impact on your live production environment.

AN OVERVIEW OF THE SAP QUERY TOOL'S ADVANCED SCREENS

The SAP Query tool, in its standard form, is designed so that an end user who has no technical skills can create a report from scratch. It has five basic screens that you can utilize to create a report. In addition to the five basic screens, seven advanced screens give you more options and functionality when creating reports with the SAP Query tool:

- **Control Levels**—You use this screen to add subtotals to a report. SAP uses the term *control level* to indicate subtotals.
- **Control Level Texts**—You use this screen to change subtotal texts.
- **List Line Output Options**—You use this screen to format the list line.
- **Field Output Options**—You use this screen to alter the column widths, add colors, hide leading zeros, and create templates.
- **Field Templates**—You use this screen to insert text to appear before output for each line.
- **Basic List Header**—You use this screen to create custom headers and footers.
- **Graphics**—You use this screen to create graphics (such as charts and diagrams).

USING THE ADVANCED SCREENS OF THE SAP QUERY TOOL

This section explains the functionality available on each of the advanced screens in the SAP Query tool. I'll use an SAP Human Capital Management (HCM) query report, DLS_Query_07, to display the impact that each of these advanced screens can have on an SAP query report. If you want to follow along on your own system, you can do so by selecting any existing SAP query from your list or creating one from scratch. You will want to have at least a half dozen fields in your output, including a combination of text fields and number fields (for example, Last Name and Age of Employee; see Figure 7.1).

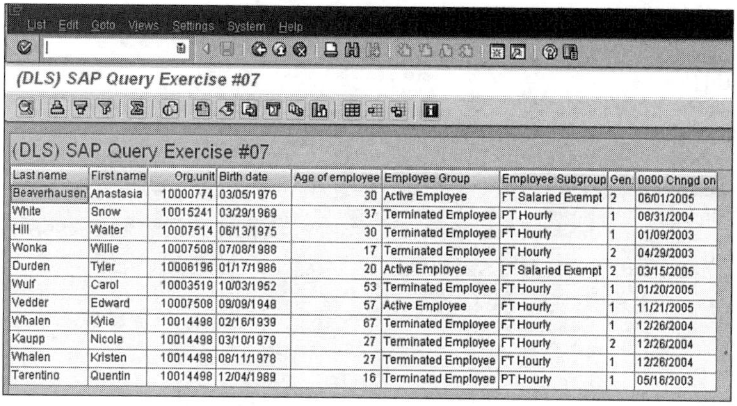

Last name	First name	Org.unit	Birth date	Age of employee	Employee Group	Employee Subgroup	Gen.	0000 Chngd on
Beaverhausen	Anastasia	10000774	03/05/1976	30	Active Employee	FT Salaried Exempt	2	06/01/2005
White	Snow	10015241	03/29/1969	37	Terminated Employee	PT Hourly	1	08/31/2004
Hill	Walter	10007514	06/13/1975	30	Terminated Employee	FT Hourly	1	01/09/2003
Wonka	Willie	10007508	07/08/1988	17	Terminated Employee	FT Hourly	2	04/29/2003
Durden	Tyler	10006196	01/17/1986	20	Active Employee	FT Salaried Exempt	2	03/15/2005
Wulf	Carol	10003519	10/03/1952	53	Terminated Employee	FT Hourly	1	01/20/2005
Vedder	Edward	10007508	09/09/1948	57	Active Employee	FT Hourly	1	11/21/2005
Whalen	Kylie	10014498	02/16/1939	67	Terminated Employee	FT Hourly	1	12/26/2004
Kaupp	Nicole	10014498	03/10/1979	27	Terminated Employee	FT Hourly	2	12/26/2004
Whalen	Kristen	10014498	08/11/1978	27	Terminated Employee	FT Hourly	1	12/26/2004
Tarentino	Quentin	10014498	12/04/1989	16	Terminated Employee	PT Hourly	1	05/16/2003

Figure 7.1
A sample SAP query report created in the HCM module of the SAP Query tool.

To navigate to the advanced screens of the SAP Query tool, you begin by navigating to the Queries from User Group: Initial screen by using the transaction code **`/nSQ01`**. You select one of your existing queries by selecting the gray tab to the left of the query or by typing the query name into the top of the screen in the SAP Query entry box (for example, `DLS_Query_07`). Then you click the Change button to get to the first screen of the SAP Query tool (that is, the Title, Format screen). To navigate to the advanced screens, you have a couple of options:

- Click the Basic List button on the Application toolbar and then click the Next Screen button (that is, the white navigational arrow) on the Application toolbar.
- Use the toolbar menu Goto, Basic List and then select one of seven advanced screens to jump directly to it.

NOTE

> In SAP terms, there is no real distinction between basic and advanced screens. I have coined these terms to make it easier for you to implement, teach, and use the SAP Query tool at your organization. After years of teaching the SAP Query tool, I found that it was helpful for users to first learn and master the five basic screens before moving on to these screens.

THE CONTROL LEVELS SCREEN

The Control Levels screen appears only if you indicated sorting information in the Sort column on the Basic List Line Structure screen for your field output, as shown in Figure 7.2.

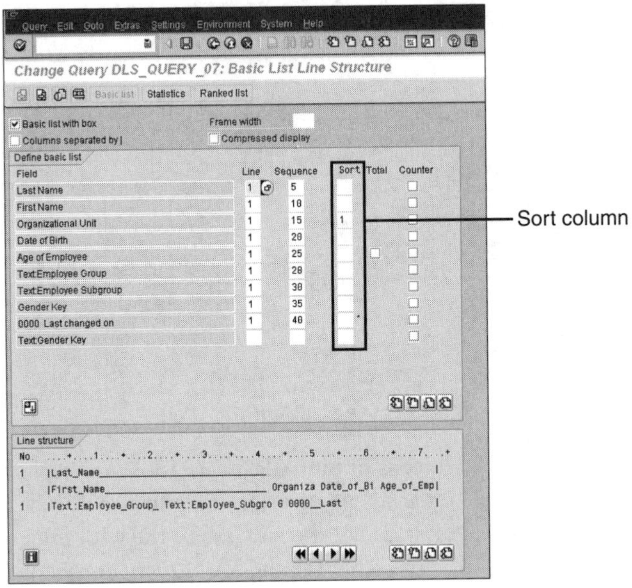

Figure 7.2
The Sort column on the Basic List Line Structure screen requires the input of at least one sort in order for the Control Levels screen to appear.

To use the Control Levels screen, follow these steps:

1. Navigate to the Queries from User: Group Initial screen by using the transaction code /nSQ01. Identify an existing query that you want to work with and then click the Change button.

2. Click the Basic List button on the Application toolbar to navigate to the Basic List Line Structure screen. On this screen, make sure a value is present somewhere in the Sort column (most appropriately on a field that you want to sort or group on). For example, Figure 7.2 shows a sort based on the Organizational Unit field. Click the Save button on the Application toolbar.

3. On the Basic List Line Structure screen, you click the Next Screen button on the Application toolbar. As shown in Figure 7.3, the Control Levels screen indicates any field that was specified as a sort on the Basic List Line Structure screen. For example, Figure 7.3 displays the Organizational Unit field. (Note that if more than one field was indicated as a sort, they would all be listed on this screen.)

4. The Control Levels screen provides options for formatting subtotals. Using Table 7.1 as a reference, vary the input on your screen (in my example, I selected the Desc, Total, Cnt, and Box check boxes).

5. To execute the report and view the selection screen, press F8. To see the finished report, click the Execute button on the Application toolbar (or press F8). Figure 7.4 shows the impact of these changes to a sample report.

7

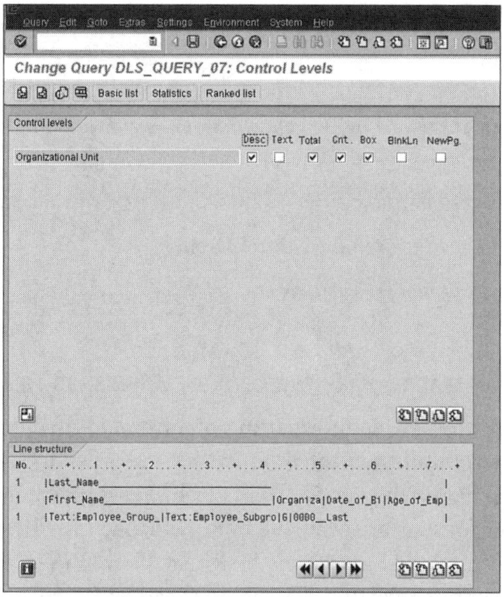

Figure 7.3
This advanced screen provides subtotaling and formatting options for any fields indicated on the previous screen as sorting criteria.

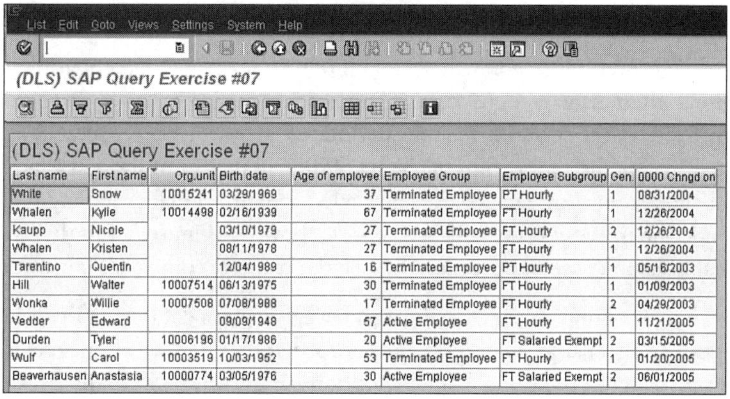

Last name	First name	Org.unit	Birth date	Age of employee	Employee Group	Employee Subgroup	Gen.	0000 Chngd on
White	Snow	10015241	03/29/1969	37	Terminated Employee	PT Hourly	1	08/31/2004
Whalen	Kylie	10014498	02/16/1939	67	Terminated Employee	FT Hourly	1	12/26/2004
Kaupp	Nicole		03/10/1979	27	Terminated Employee	FT Hourly	2	12/26/2004
Whalen	Kristen		08/11/1978	27	Terminated Employee	FT Hourly	1	12/26/2004
Tarentino	Quentin		12/04/1989	16	Terminated Employee	PT Hourly	1	05/16/2003
Hill	Walter	10007514	06/13/1975	30	Terminated Employee	FT Hourly	1	01/09/2003
Wonka	Willie	10007508	07/08/1988	17	Terminated Employee	FT Hourly	2	04/29/2003
Vedder	Edward		09/09/1948	57	Active Employee	FT Hourly	1	11/21/2005
Durden	Tyler	10006196	01/17/1986	20	Active Employee	FT Salaried Exempt	2	03/15/2005
Wulf	Carol	10003519	10/03/1952	53	Terminated Employee	FT Hourly	1	01/20/2005
Beaverhausen	Anastasia	10000774	03/05/1976	30	Active Employee	FT Salaried Exempt	2	06/01/2005

Figure 7.4
Based on the selections used in my example, the report output appears sorted.

The Control Levels screen has the seven options described in Table 7.1.

TABLE 7.1 OPTIONS ON THE CONTROL LEVELS SCREEN

Option	Description
Desc	Sorts in descending order. (When not indicated, the sort is automatically in ascending order.)
Text	Outputs a text description (the contents of the selected field) at the start of each control level.
Total	Outputs subtotals of the sums at the end of each control level. Any field indicated on the Basic List Line Structure screen is subtotaled here.

continues

7

TABLE 7.1   CONTINUED

Option	Description
Cnt.	Outputs a count at the end of each control level. Any field indicated on the Basic List Line Structure screen is counted here.
Box	Outputs a bracketed box around each of the indicated control levels.
BlnkLn	Outputs a blank line between the control levels.
NewPg.	Inserts a page break before each new control level.

MODIFYING THE OUTPUT FORMAT TO VARY THE LOOK OF A FINISHED REPORT

It is important to note that the look and formatting of a finished SAP query report varies based on the type of selected output indicated on the report's selection screen. That might sound confusing, but recall from Chapter 5, "Basics of Using Reporting Selection Screens," that multiple report output formats are available to select from. The default output format listed on the selection screen for SAP queries is SAP List Viewer. (See the section "Understanding Output Options on the Selection Screen" in Chapter 5 for more information.) What is important to note is that your finished report output format may vary based on the output format you selected on the report's selection screen.

To make it even more confusing, not all output formats are compatible with each of the options when displayed onscreen. Here is a real-world example: If you compare Figure 7.3 (which shows the selections I indicated on the Control Levels screen) against Figure 7.4 (which shows the report output), you will notice that even though I indicated that I wanted a total and a count for each of the subtotaled organizational units, my finished report did not include them. Rather, the finished report, shown in Figure 7.4, only groups the organizational units in descending order. (To see the change, compare Figure 7.1 against Figure 7.4.)

The default output format, SAP List Viewer, displays data in a spreadsheet format. However, you can easily change the report output format on your selection screen from SAP List Viewer to any of the other available options. Figure 7.5 shows the list of options.

In addition to the output format options having an impact on the report output, another field on the Basic List Line Structure screen has an impact on the look of the finished report: Total. For my example, I will navigate to the Basic List Line Structure screen and indicate that I want to have a total for my Age of Employee field (see Figure 7.6). Indicating the Total box to the right of the Age of Employee field (as it is the only truly numeric field in the report) will change my report output from what was displayed in Figure 7.4 to appear like the formatted sample shown in Figure 7.7.

Figure 7.5
If the output format options are not displayed on the selection screen, you can click the small arrow button to the right of the SAP List Viewer option.

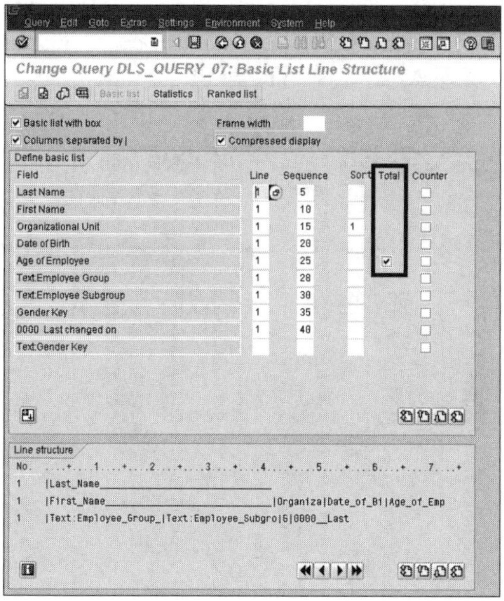

Output format options

Show/hide option button

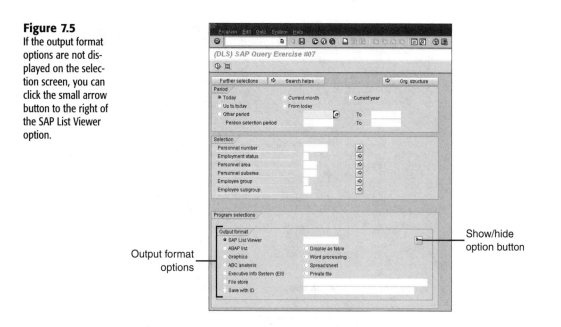

Figure 7.6
The Total field will only appear for any numeric field that can be mathematically totaled.

7

Figure 7.7
The indication to include a total in the report changes the format of the report output dramatically.

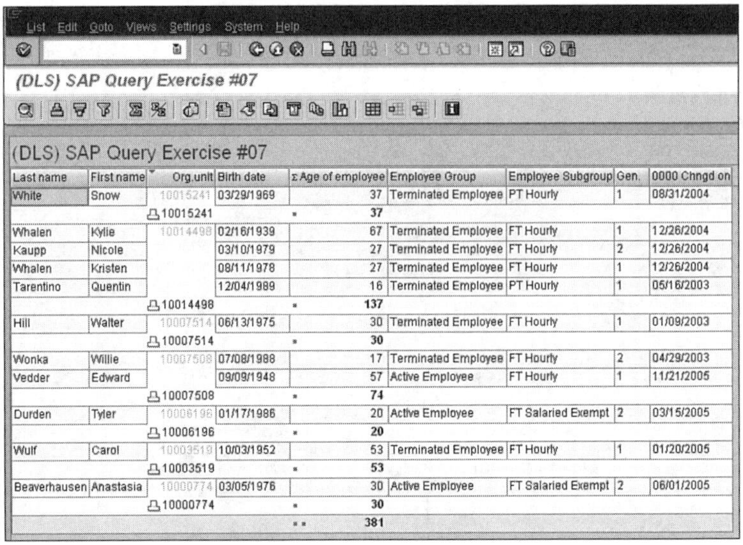

Now is a good time to vary the input on the Control Levels screen and change the output format selections on your selection screen to see the impact each modification makes when the report is viewed in different outputs. For example, you can change the report Output format from SAP List Viewer to ABAP List. The resulting report data appears in Figure 7.8.

Figure 7.8
The ABAP List view removes any special table or Excel-like formatting from the report.

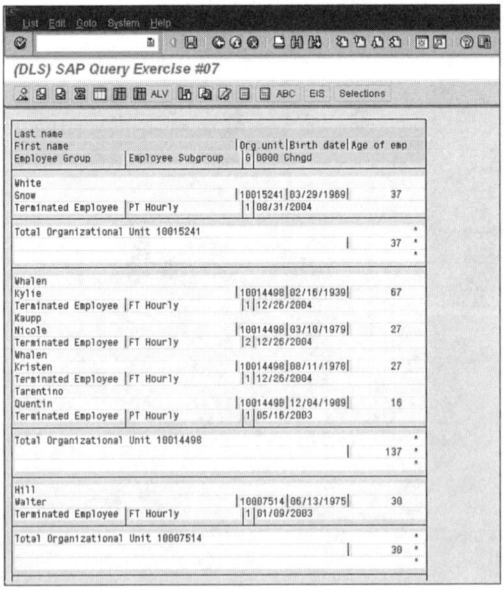

When you view this report in ABAP List view, you see that additional functions appear, including the counts and the control level texts. However, the text wraps on to the second line, and the report appears garbled. When a report is displayed onscreen in the ABAP List Output format, it often wraps the characters across lines based on the default paper size for printing in SAP. The most common is letter-size paper, and with that, the default column width setting is 83. (In other words, it will only display 83 characters of the first line before it wraps it to the second line.) If you want to expand that setting, you can go to the Title Format screen and vary the default width of the report by using the Column field, which drives the number of characters across the page. Figure 7.9 shows what the screen looks like if you change this setting from the default of 83 to 255 (the maximum for letter-size printing).

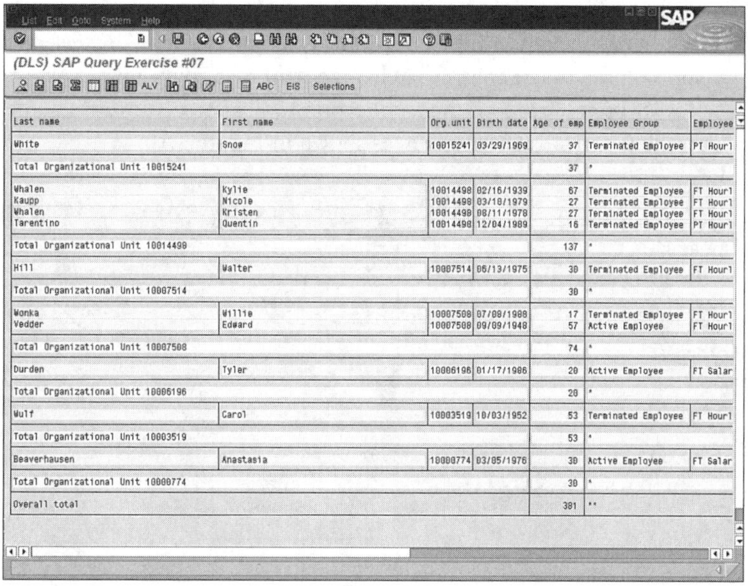
List Edit Goto System Help
SAP
(DLS) SAP Query Exercise #07
ALV ABC EIS Selections
Last name First name Org.unit Birth date Age of emp Employee Group Employee
White Snow 10015241 03/29/1969 37 Terminated Employee PT Hourl
Total Organizational Unit 10015241 37 *
Whalen Kylie 10014498 02/16/1939 67 Terminated Employee FT Hourl
Kaupp Nicole 10014498 03/10/1979 27 Terminated Employee FT Hourl
Whalen Kristen 10014498 08/11/1978 27 Terminated Employee FT Hourl
Tarentino Quentin 10014498 12/04/1989 16 Terminated Employee PT Hourl
Total Organizational Unit 10014498 137 *
Hill Walter 10007514 06/13/1975 30 Terminated Employee FT Hourl
Total Organizational Unit 10007514 30 *
Wonka Willie 10007508 07/08/1988 17 Terminated Employee FT Hourl
Vedder Edward 10007508 09/09/1948 57 Active Employee FT Hourl
Total Organizational Unit 10007508 74 *
Durden Tyler 10006196 01/17/1986 20 Active Employee FT Salar
Total Organizational Unit 10006196 20 *
Wulf Carol 10003519 10/03/1952 53 Terminated Employee FT Hourl
Total Organizational Unit 10003519 53 *
Beaverhausen Anastasia 10000774 03/05/1976 30 Active Employee FT Salar
Total Organizational Unit 10000774 30 *
Overall total 381 **

Figure 7.9
Altering the column width for the report and then changing the output format to ABAP List makes your special indicated formatting appear.

Helpful Hint
When displaying a format in the ABAP List view, it is a good idea to return to the Basic List Line Structure screen and select the check box Columns Separated by |. Doing so makes your report output appear more formatted, with boxes around each column of data.

THE CONTROL LEVEL TEXTS SCREEN

The Control Level Texts screen appears only if you indicated sorting information in the Control Level screen because this advanced screen gives you the opportunity to modify any of your subtotal heading, which SAP refers to as *control levels*.

To navigate to the second of the advanced screens, the Control Level Texts screen, you click the Basic List button on the Application toolbar and indicate at least one sort option (for example, Text:Gender Key). On the Basic List screen, you click the Next Screen button on the Application toolbar two times to navigate to the Control Level Texts screen. The

7

Control Levels screen, as shown in Figure 7.3, indicates any field that is specified as a sort on the Basic List Line Structure screen. The Control Level Texts screen appears only if you indicate sorting information in the Sort column on the Basic List Line Structure screen, and if you indicate selections on the Control Levels screen. The Control Level Texts screen allows you to vary the text that appears at each control level (see Figure 7.7).

To use the Control Levels screen, follow these steps:

1. Navigate to the Queries from User: Group Initial screen by using the transaction code /nSQ01. Identify an existing query that you want to work with and then click the Change button.

2. Click the Basic List button on the Application toolbar to navigate to the Basic List Line Structure screen. On this screen, make sure that a value is present somewhere in the Sort column (most appropriately on a field that you want to sort or group on). Click the Next Screen button on the Application toolbar to confirm that at least one entry exists on the Control Levels screen, as shown in Figure 7.10.

Figure 7.10
The section labeled Standard Texts at the top of the screen shows the subtotal texts as they appear before changes.

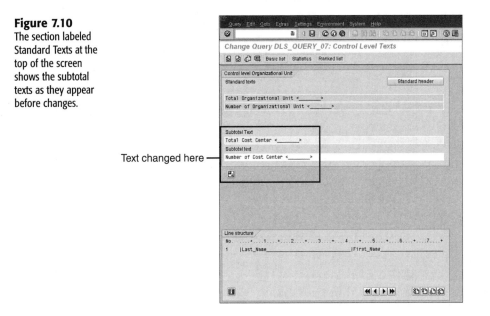

Text changed here

3. Vary how the subtotals appear by changing the text on this screen from the default (which is shown at the top). For example you could replace the words on the bottom half of the screen under the heading Subtotal Text from Organizational Unit to Cost Center. You should leave the field placeholders (<_____>) intact so that SAP knows where the data should be output.

4. To execute the report and view the selection screen, press F8. To see the finished report, click the Execute button on the Application toolbar (or press F8). Figure 7.11

shows the impact of these changes to a sample report; you can compare it to Figure 7.9 to see the changes.

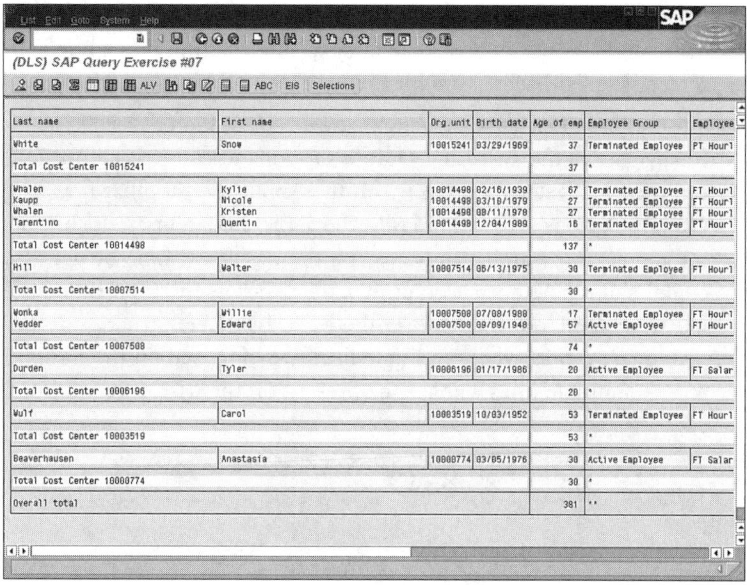

Figure 7.11
For this example, the report is output in the ABAP List view, and the text for each control level is different than it was in Figure 7.9.

At any time, you can return to the Control Level Texts screen and click the Standard Header button to return the control level texts to their original state.

NOTE

It is important that you not type over the placeholders on the Control Level Texts screen. For example, note that Figure 7.10 shows only the text to the left of the placeholder (indicated as <_____>) replaced. Overwriting that placeholder would interfere with the report output. It is import that when you use this screen, you toggle between Insert and Overwrite modes by pressing the Insert key on your keyboard. If you accidentally overwrite the placeholder, you can simply click the Standard Header button and then press the Insert key and try it again.

THE LIST LINE OUTPUT OPTIONS SCREEN

The List Line Output Options screen provides options for varying the output of the entire report list. In the examples included in this book so far, only a single list has been produced for each report. (*List*, in this case, is a collective term to describe the entire report output.) In Chapter 14, "Creating Ranked Lists with the SAP Query Tool," you will learn how to create multiple-line lists. To use the List Line Output Options screen, follow these steps:

7

1. Navigate to the Queries from User: Group Initial screen by using the transaction code /nSQ01. Identify an existing query that you want to work with and then click the Change button.

2. Click the Basic List button on the Application toolbar to navigate to the Basic List Line Structure screen. On this screen, make sure that the check box at the top-left side of the screen, labeled Basic List with Box, is checked.

3. On the Basic List Line Structure screen, select Goto, Basic List, Line Output Options to navigate to the List Line Output Options screen (see Figure 7.12). Alternatively, you can use the Next screen arrows on the Application toolbar for navigation. The List Line Output Options screen applies to the actual line items; a list line appears on this screen for any list line number indicated on the Basic List Line Structure screen. Most reports contain all report output on only one line across the top of the page because the Line box next to each of the fields in the Basic List Line Structure screen contains 1. For any SAP query report where multiple lines are indicated on the Basic List Line Structure screen, multiple lines will also be present on the List Line Output Options screen.

Figure 7.12
The List Line Output Options screen applies to the actual line items—lines in the report that are not headers or control-level text.

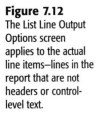

4. Using Table 7.2 as a reference, vary the input on your screen.

5. To execute the report and view the selection screen, press F8. To see the finished report, click the Execute button on the Application toolbar (or press F8). Figure 7.13 shows the impact of these changes to a sample report.

Figure 7.13
The report appears with a single space between lines, and the line color has been changed to deep green (PosThreshold).

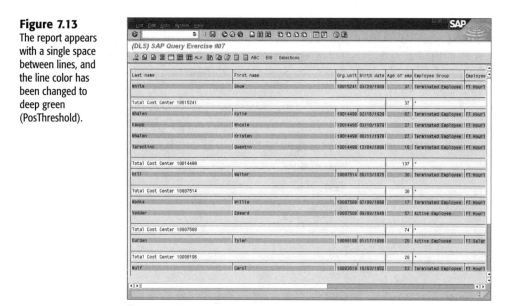

The List Line Output Options screen has the ten options outlined in Table 7.2.

TABLE 7.2 OPTIONS ON THE LIST LINE OUTPUT OPTIONS SCREEN

Option	Description
Line No.	Displays the line number specified on the Basic List Line Structure screen.
Gr	Indicates line numbers between 1 and 90.
Color	Modifies the color of the report's output; 15 different colors are available for selection.
Header Line	Presents column headers for the fields on the line.
Ref.	Specifies dependencies between different list lines. If the number of another line is entered here, the line is output only if the line entered is also displayed.
Slash Bef / To	Inserts a slash before or after the output line.
Blank Line Bef / Aft	Determines the number of blank lines to insert before and after each list line.
Columns With	Separates the individual fields of a line with a vertical line. This is available only if the Columns Separated by a I check box is selected on the Basic List Line Structure screen.
Page Header	Outputs the line in the page header when the line contents extend to a new page.
New Page	Begins a new page before the line is output in the report.

7

In my example, I indicated the color deep green for my report list, which has the technical name PosThreshold. Within SAP, each color is referred to by its standard placement within the system. For example, headers are usually displayed in aqua blue. So if you are looking to select a color in SAP for any reason, you need to select the color by using its technical name. Table 7.3 provides a reference of the technical names and the colors that they represent in SAP.

TABLE 7.3   AVAILABLE COLORS IN THE SAP QUERY TOOL

Color Name	Description
Header	Aqua blue
List Line 2	Sky blue
Overall Total	Bright yellow
Hier. Header	Orange
Neg Threshold	Red
Pos Threshold	Deep green
Key	SAP blue
Header 2	Medium blue
List Line	Gray
Sub-total	Yellow
Hier Info	Pale pink
Free	Pink
Indent	Light green
Highlight	Pale blue

THE FIELD OUTPUT OPTIONS SCREEN

The Field Output Options screen provides options for varying the output of individual columns within a report. Unlike the List Line Output Options screen, which provides options for the entire list line, the Field Output Options screen provides options to vary each individual field in the report output. To use the Field Output Options screen, follow these steps:

1. Navigate to the Queries from User: Group Initial screen by using the transaction code **/nSQ01**. Identify an existing query that you want to work with and then click the Change button.

2. On the Basic List Line Structure screen, select Goto, Basic List, Line Output Options to navigate to the Field Output Options screen. (Alternatively, you can use the Next screen arrows on the Application toolbar for navigation.) The Field Line Output Options screen applies to the individual columns within the report. The screen should appear similar to the Basic List Line Structure screen.

3. Using Table 7.4 as a reference, vary the input on your screen. (See Figure 7.14.) Click the Save button on the toolbar.

Figure 7.14
Unlike the List Line Output Options screen, which provides options for the entire list line, this screen provides options to vary each individual field in the report.

Column width changed

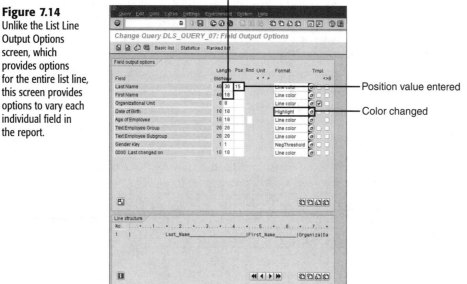

Position value entered

Color changed

4. To execute the report and view the selection screen, press F8. To see the finished report, click the Execute button on the Application toolbar (or press F8). Figure 7.15 shows the impact of these changes to a sample report.

The Field Output Options screen provides the seven options described in Table 7.4.

TABLE 7.4   OPTIONS ON THE FIELD OUTPUT OPTIONS SCREEN

Option	Description
Length Std/New	Indicates the standard width of the field in the ABAP database and a new larger or smaller number for that output.
Pos	Determines the exact position of the field in the output line of the report. The first character in the report has the position 1. If this option is not input for any fields, the first field is always 1, and the rest follow, based on the length indicated in the Length column. Clicking the Expand button at the bottom of the screen brings up a ruler you can use to specify the exact position for the field. (You will learn more about this ruler in Chapter 8, "Creating Extract Files and Interfaces with the SAP Query Tool.")
Rnd	Specifies the number of decimal places to use when rounding. For example, if you specify 3, the resulting amounts have three places before the decimal point (that is, rounding to the nearest thousand).

7

continues

TABLE 7.4   CONTINUED

Option	Description
Unit < * >	Provides three option buttons (for any field tied to a unit) that provide options for how to display the unit information. An example of a unit could be Currency ($) or Weight (pounds). You use the three option buttons as follows:
	■ Output the relevant unit description before the unit amount or quantity (for example, USD 1500.00).
	■ Do not output the relevant unit description (for example, 1500.00).
	■ Output the relevant unit description after the unit amount or quantity (for example, 1500.00 USD).
Format	Modifies the color of any of the fields (columns), using the color options identified in Table 7.3.
Tmpl.	Enables you to define a special output template on a subsequent screen. Output templates can be created only for nonnumeric fields.
<> 0	Performs two functions: If selected for a numerical field, it either hides the leading zeros so they do not display in your report output, or it keeps zero values from appearing in the selected numeric field.

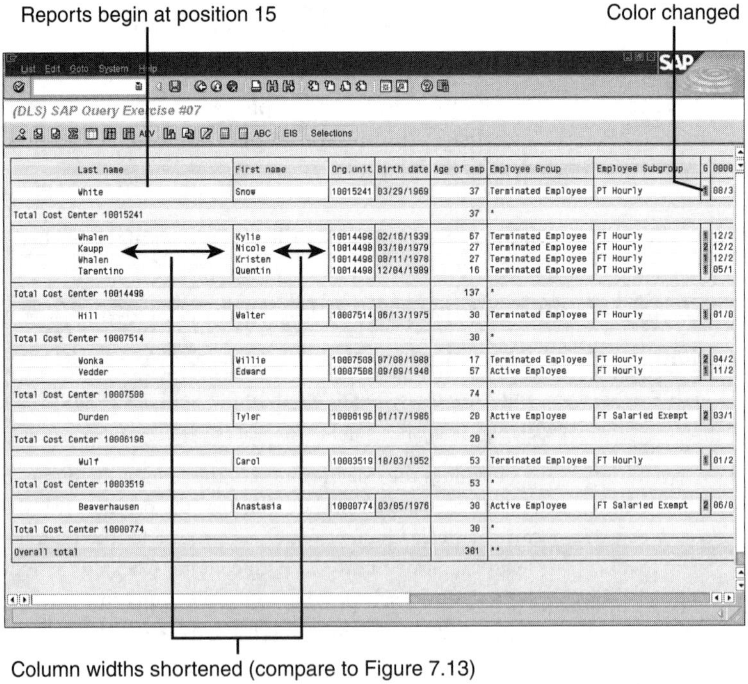

Reports begin at position 15   Color changed

Figure 7.15
Varying the column widths by using the length function allows you to fit more information on a report.

Column widths shortened (compare to Figure 7.13)

Keep in mind that the output of the selections on the executed report may vary based on the type of output selected on the report's selection screen. For the example shown in Figure 7.15, Figure 7.12 shows the impact on the executed SAP query report output in ABAP List Output view. (It is also important to note that if you are cumulatively working on these advanced screens using the same SAP query report, changes from previous screens also appear.)

Helpful Hint

Setting a field as a template includes formatting characters in a field. (For example, you can insert the word *UNIT* before a unit description is output.) You set the template specifications on the Field Templates screen.

It is important to note that the length of the field (column) is automatically increased according to the number of formatted characters introduced. For example, specifying that the word *UNIT* should appear in the column with the unit description would increase the Length New column by 4. However, a best business practice is to also insert a space after such text, so the value increases by 5. Otherwise, the output appears as UNIT12345 Unitname instead of UNIT 12345 Unitname.

The Field Templates Screen

The Field Templates screen works similarly to the Control Level Texts screen in that you can insert data to appear before report output. To use the Field Templates screen, follow these steps:

1. Navigate to the Queries from User: Group Initial screen by using the transaction code /nSQ01. Identify an existing query that you want to work with and then click the Change button.

2. On the Basic List Line Structure screen, select Goto, Basic List, Line Output Options to navigate to the Field Output Options screen. (Alternatively, you can use the Next screen arrows on the Application toolbar for navigation.)

3. On the Field Output Options screen, you need to mark the Template check box for at least one field in order for the Field Templates screen to be available. In my example, I have indicated that the Organizational unit field will have a template (see Figure 7.14).

4. Use the forward arrow navigational button to proceed to the Field Templates screen. You can insert text to appear before or after the field indicated as a template. In my example, the Organizational Unit field is the template field, and I inserted the text **Org Unit** to appear before the output of each organizational unit number. I left the < placeholder in place, and I typed my template wording into the space between it and the > (see Figure 7.16).

5. To execute the report and view the selection screen, press F8. To see the finished report, click the Execute button on the Application toolbar (or press F8). Figure 7.17 shows the impact of these changes to a sample report.

7

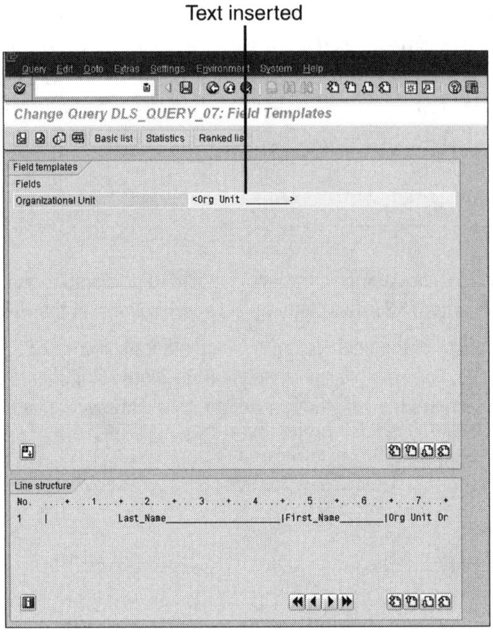

Text inserted

Figure 7.16
The Field Templates
screen works similarly
to the Control Level
Texts screen in that
you can insert data to
appear before report
output.

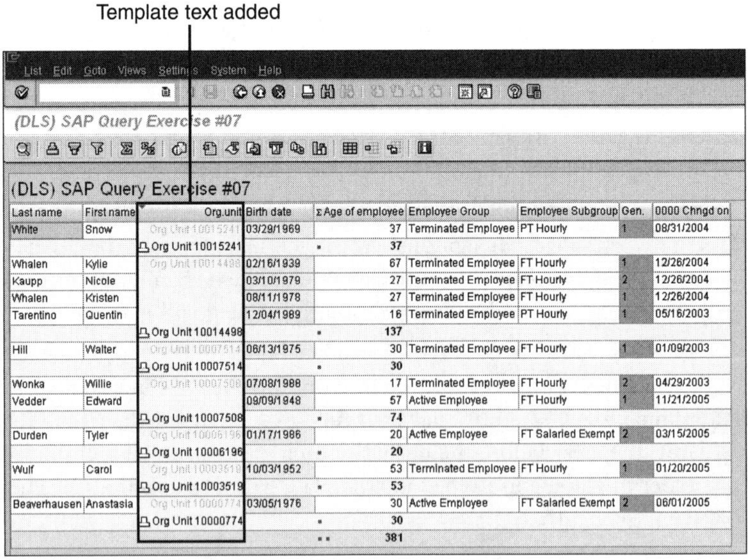

Template text added

Figure 7.17
The text Org Unit
appears before the
output of each
organizational unit
number in the report.

The difference between the Field Templates screen and the Control Level Texts screen is that on the Field Templates screen, you can insert data to appear before any column in the report, and on the Control Level Texts screen, you can vary only the subtotal and grand total (control levels) texts.

NOTE

It is important that you not type over the placeholders on the Field Templates screen. For example, note that Figure 7.16 shows text inserted only to the left of the placeholder, with no tying over the existing spaces (indicated as _____>). Overwriting those spaces would interfere with the report output.

The width of the placeholder is determined by the ABAP Data Dictionary and matches the Std Length column on the Field Output Options screen. For example, Figure 7.16 shows *Org Unit* so that this exact text appears in the report output.

THE BASIC LIST HEADER SCREEN

The Basic List Header screen allows you to insert custom headers and footers in a SAP query report. To use the Basic List Header screen, follow these steps:

1. Navigate to the Queries from User: Group Initial screen by using the transaction code **/nSQ01**. Identify an existing query that you want to work with and then click the Change button.

2. On the Basic List Line Structure screen, select Goto, Basic List, Line Output Options to navigate to the Field Output Options screen (see Figure 7.18). (Alternatively, you can use the Next screen arrows on the Application toolbar for navigation.)

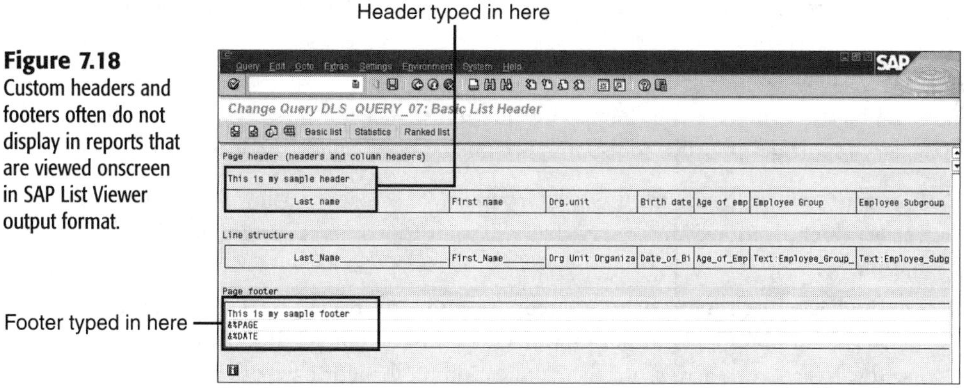

Header typed in here

Figure 7.18
Custom headers and footers often do not display in reports that are viewed onscreen in SAP List Viewer output format.

Footer typed in here

3. The Basic List Header screen allows you to insert custom headers and footers. Using Figure 7.18 as a reference, vary the input on your screen by simply typing text into the provided fields. To insert an additional line under the current line of the header or footer, double-click the line. In my example, I added both a custom header and footer.

4. To execute the report and view the selection screen, press F8. To see the finished report, click the Execute button on the Application toolbar (or press F8). Figure 7.19 shows the impact of these changes to a sample report.

7

Figure 7.19
Custom headers and footers appear on any hard copy printouts of the report as well as onscreen.

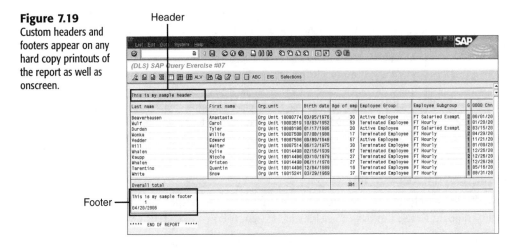

You can also use SAP ABAP code to indicate custom system fields so that the report automatically inserts the current date, time, page number, and so on. To do so, you simply input **&%DATE**, **&%USER**, and so on, and when the report is executed, it updates with the correct information (refer to Figure 7.19).

Again, it is important to note that the output of the selections on the executed or printed report may vary based on the type of output that is selected on the report's selection screen.

THE GRAPHICS SCREEN

The Graphics screen gives you the opportunity to use SAP Business Graphics to display a SAP query report graphically. To use the Graphics screen, follow these steps:

1. Navigate to the Queries from User: Group Initial screen by using the transaction code **/nSQ01**. Identify an existing query that you want to work with and then click the Change button.

2. On the Basic List Line Structure screen, select Goto, Basic List, Line Output Options to navigate to the Field Output Options screen (see Figure 7.20). (Alternatively, you can use the Next screen arrows on the Application toolbar for navigation.)

3. Select a graphic format (for example, perspective pie chart) and then click the Execute button.

4. On the report's selection screen, change the report output format to Graphics at the bottom of the screen in order to display your report graphically. Then click the Execute button on the Application toolbar (or press F8).

5. A Graphical Display dialog box appears. Click the green checkmark Enter key. Your finished graphical report appears onscreen, charting the figures interpreted by the SAP system (see Figure 7.21).

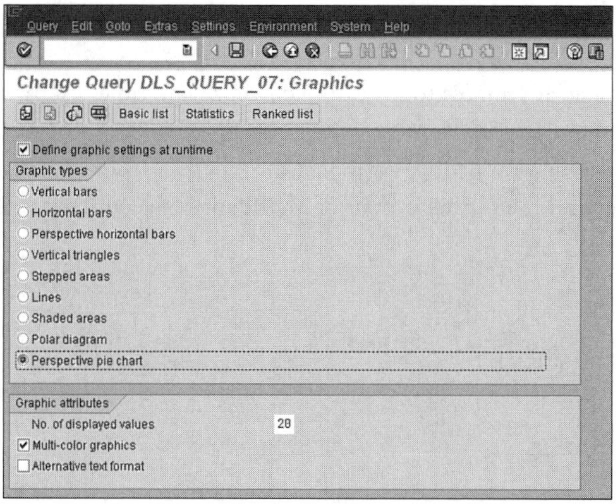

Figure 7.20
You can use SAP
Business Graphics to
display appropriate
numeric SAP queries
in a graphical format.

Figure 7.21
Pie charts, columnar
graphs, and other
graphical formats are
available on the
Graphics screen.

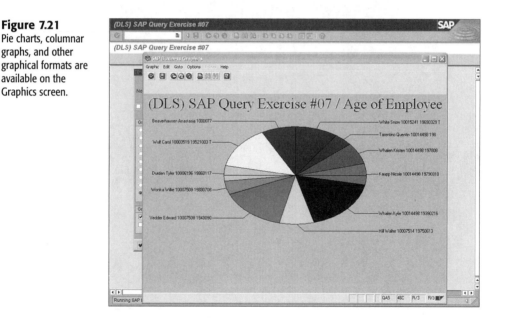

THINGS TO REMEMBER

- The look of the advanced screen report varies depending on the output format selected on the report's selection screen.
- The Control Level screen allows you to do sorting and subtotaling, and it also lets you do special formatting in a SAP query report for any field that you indicate to sort on the Basic List Line Structure screen.

7

- By using the advanced screens, you can manipulate the colors and texts of list lines or individual fields in a report.

- You can use special symbols to insert the current date, time, username, and page number in custom headers and footers.

- Graphical reporting is possible via the advanced screen, but you need to be sure to indicate Graphics and the format output on the report's selection screen.

CHAPTER 8

CREATING EXTRACT FILES AND INTERFACES WITH THE SAP QUERY TOOL

In this chapter

8

You may have a business need to create what are often referred to as *extract*, or *interface*, *files*. These types of files are often position- or character-location-specific files that are transmitted from one system or solution to another in a prearranged format. It is not common knowledge that the SAP Query tool can be used to create these files, so users often wait for programming staff to custom-code an extract file for them in ABAP. The benefit of using the SAP Query tool to produce these files is that it does not require any technical programming skills and is easy for an end user to do. You should read through the following section of this chapter, and if you determine that you will not be using the SAP Query tool to produce positional files, you can skip this chapter and proceed to Chapter 9, "Creating Basic Calculated Fields with the SAP Query Tool."

OVERVIEW OF INTERFACE/EXTRACT FILES

Many computer systems talk to each other through the sharing of files. Transmissions between SAP and third-party vendor computer systems are common. For instance, in my day-to-day job, I manage dozens of interfaces. An example is a file I send weekly to the unemployment office. My company uses a third-party vendor to handle unemployment processing. The file I transmit weekly contains a list of all associates who terminated and the date and reason why each one terminated. The third-party vendor uses this information to review and process potential claims for unemployment. Just emailing the vendor a printed list would require the vendor to manually look up a person each time a claim came in. To avoid all that work, the vendor demands that we send a file in a precise format so that it can be easily imported into the vendor's computer system.

When working with a vendor (as in the case of my company working with a third-party vendor on unemployment claims), the vendor provides what is referred to as a specification, or *spec*. The spec provides the precise details of how the file is supposed to look in its finished form. A very simple spec could look like the one shown in Table 8.1.

TABLE 8.1 BASIC SAMPLE SPEC LAYOUT FOR A TERMINATION REPORT TO AN UNEMPLOYMENT VENDOR

Position	Description of Data	Example
1–10	Company account number	1111112345
11–18	Date of termination	01012006
19–24	Personnel number of terminated associate	222111
25–26	Reason code for termination	65
27–27	Unemployment approval designator	X

This spec tells the developer creating the extract file exactly where each piece of data should reside in the file, based on the positional number. (By *positional*, I mean by reading through the spec, I know that the file requires the output of the company account number in positions 1–10 of the file. In other words, the first 10 characters of the report output would contain the company account number.) An example of what a single line of this extract would look like is 1111112345010120062221165X. If you were to count the position of each item in the extract, you would find that the position of each item matches exactly to the designation listed in the Position column. The following sections look at how you can use the SAP Query tool to create a positional report.

CREATING A FIXED POSITIONAL EXTRACT FILE BY USING THE SAP QUERY TOOL

As discussed in Chapter 3, "Creating Basic Reports with the SAP Query Tool," the SAP Query tool, in its standard form, is designed so that an end user who has no technical skills can create a report from scratch. Chapter 7, "Creating Advanced Reports with the SAP Query Tool," describes how the SAP Query tool's advanced screens give you even more advanced options and functionality. These are the seven advanced screens of the SAP Query tool:

- Control Levels
- Control Level Texts
- List Line Output Options
- Field Output Options
- Field Templates
- Basic List Header
- Graphics

The following sections explain how to use the SAP Query tool to create a fixed positional formatted file based on a specification, using the sample SAP flight scheduling IDES system that has been used in other examples in this book so far. The spec shown in Table 8.2 details the expected format of an SAP extract file, using the data in the SAP flight scheduling IDES system. The table explains which data should be in which positions in the file. For example, by reading through the table, you can expect that the first 10 characters of the extract file will contain the flight date.

TABLE 8.2 A SAMPLE SPEC LAYOUT FOR A REPORT OF DATA FROM THE IDES TEST DATABASE

Position	Description of Data	Example
1–10	Flight date	01/01/2006
11–21	Plane type	ABCDEFGHIJKLMNOPQRST
22–42	Airfare	100,000,000,000,000.00
43–54	Company-specific name designator	ABCDEFGHIJK
55–75	Flight class text	ABCDEFGHIJKLMNOPQRST
76–81	End-of-line filler, XXXXX	XXXXX

This spec tells you where each piece of data should reside in the file, based on the positional number. An example of what a single line of this extract would look like is 01/01/2006ABCDEFGHIJKLMNOPQRST100,000,000,000,000.00ABCDEFGHIJK ABCDEFGHIJKLMNOPQRSTXXXXX. In the following sections, you will follow three main steps to build an extract based on this specification:

1. Create a basic SAP query list report.

2. Perform the additional configuration needed to meet the specification.

3. Download the extract file.

STEP 1: CREATING THE BASIC SAP QUERY LIST REPORT

As discussed in Chapter 3, you can create a basic list report by using the five main screens of the SAP Query tool. (For details on how to create a basic list report with the SAP Query tool, see Chapter 3.) Your first step is to create an SAP query basic list report that outputs the fields listed in Table 8.2 in the order in which they are listed in the table. For my example, I called my new SAP query report DLS_QUERY_08. Your finished report will output the Flight Date, Plane Type, Airfare, and Flight Class text fields.

However, simply creating this report does not satisfy the specification requirement. For example, the report is not positionally spaced according the spec and does not contain the two additional fields listed in Table 8.2 as Company-Specific Name Designator and End-of-Line Filler. The purpose of a positional extract file is to be interpretable by another computer system that takes each piece of information in the positional location and loads it to the computer system. It is therefore required that each piece of data reside exactly where the specification says it should reside.

For example, you can download your current SAP query report (for example, DLS_QUERY_08) to see how much it differs from the output request in the specification. A quick and easy way to download report data to a text file from the displayed report output screen is to select List, Export, Local File (or press Ctrl+Shift+F9) and then select the Unconverted Text option. You can then specify a location for your saved text file. For my example, I entered **c:\step1.txt** and clicked the Transfer button. The report output is then downloaded to a text file in the designated location.

Helpful Hint

You can use several different types of software solutions to check that a positional text file has each of the characters in the appropriate place. These include the DOS editor (or the DOS command prompt, which you can get to by selecting Start, Run and typing **CMD**) and the Microsoft Excel import text file function. However, because you may not have either of these tools on hand, this chapter simply uses the Microsoft standard Notepad to count the characters to ensure that they are correct for this example.

After you download your SAP query report data, you can follow these steps to open your report data with Microsoft Notepad to see if your data is in the correct positions compared to the spec:

1. Launch Notepad by selecting Start, Run and then typing **notepad** and pressing Enter.

2. Select the file you saved earlier by selecting File, Open and indicating the path where you saved the text file (for example, c:\step1.txt).

3. Press Enter. The resulting file should look similar to the one displayed in Figure 8.1. (Keep in mind that your report output may appear different based on the data you have stored in your SAP test IDES solution.)

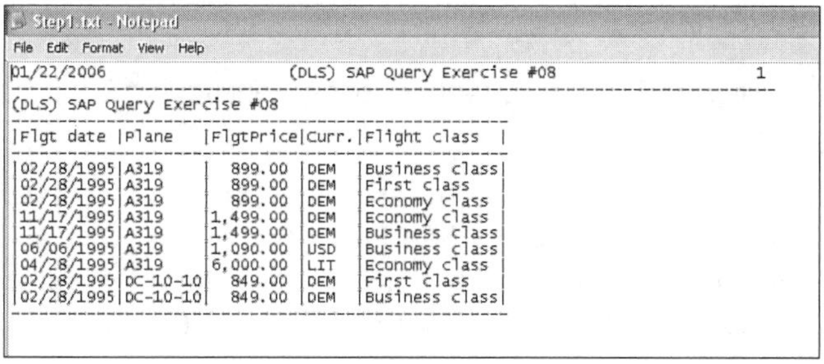

Figure 8.1
Viewing the file data in Notepad allows you to view what the file output would look like.

As mentioned earlier, in order to be interpreted by a third-party computer system, the expected report output should appear in a fixed positional format. For the example we're using, the expected output should appear in the format of the sample output shown in Figure 8.2.

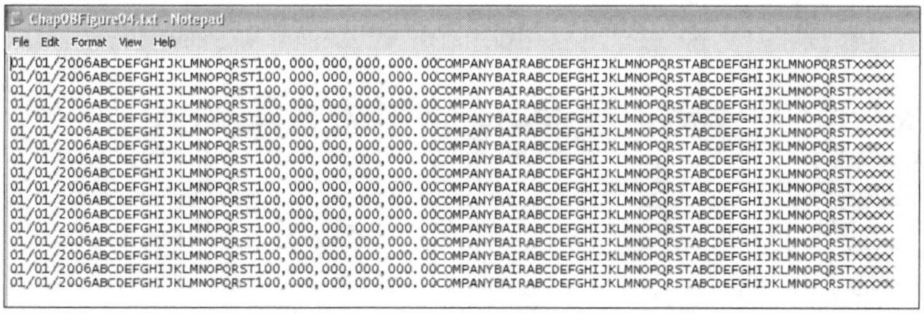

Figure 8.2
The expected positional output based on the spec shown in Table 8.2.

If you compare Figures 8.1 and 8.2, you can see why the third-party system would easily recognize the data in Figure 8.2 and why the system would likely reject the data in Figure 8.1. The data in Figure 8.1 has the following problems:

- The report has three header lines preceding the actual report data.
- The report has field separators in the - or | format, designating section or column breaks.
- The report has column headers.
- The report has an additional column for currency designation.
- The report is not the positional format requested.
- The report does not contain the filler values designated in positions 43–54 and 116–120.

The following section describes how to overcome these problems and how you can use the SAP Query tool to create an extract file based on a spec.

Step 2: Performing the Additional Configuration to Meet the Specification

You use the advanced screens covered in Chapter 7 to make the fixed-width positional extract file meet the specification. The following sections describe the steps you need to take.

Removing the Header Lines, Column Headers, Formatting Lines, and Field Separators

The first change you need to make to your report is to remove the header lines from the report. In this example, by default the SAP Query tool inserts three header lines that identify, among other things, the current date, query name, and page number. You also need to remove the column headers and field separators. To make these changes, you follow these steps:

1. In your existing SAP query, navigate to the Basic List Line Structure screen by clicking the Basic List button on the Application toolbar. Deselect the Basic List with Box check box at the top left of the screen to remove the box that appears around the displayed report, which may interfere with the extract download.

2. Navigate to the List Line Output Options screen by selecting Goto, Basic List, Line Output Options. As shown in Figure 8.3, the List Line Output Options screen provides options for varying the output of the entire report list.

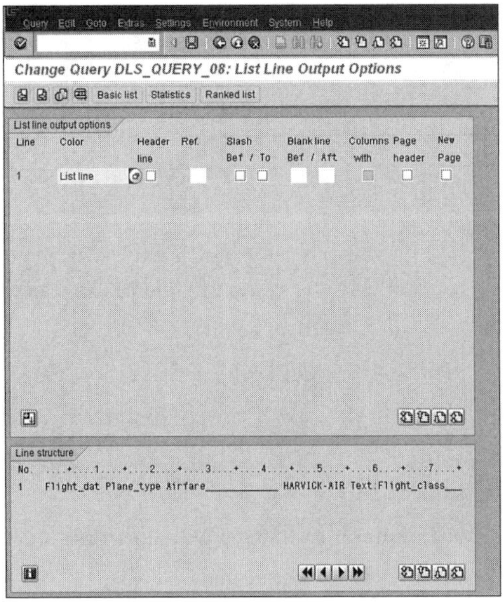

Figure 8.3
The List Line Output Options screen applies to the actual line items in the report. Most basic list reports contain only one line, so all fields are designated as appearing on line 1 on the basic List Line Structure screen.

3. Deselect the Header Line check box (which is selected by default) to remove the header line from your SAP query report.

4. Select Goto, Field Selection, Title Format to access the first screen of the SAP Query tool (the Title, Format screen) and make three adjustments:

- Change the Output Format designator at the bottom of the screen from SAP List Viewer to ABAP List. This change enables you to see the formatting changes directly on the report's output screen because the report will no longer be formatted in the pretty table view.

- Change Columns Option from its default setting of 83 to a setting of 255. The 83 setting designates that in ABAP List view, the number of characters across a single line will wrap after 83 characters. Changing this from 83 to 255 causes the wrap to not occur until character 256.

- Deselect the Print List, With Standard Title check box, which prevents the report title from displaying in the report.

5. Click the Save button and then press the F8 key to execute the report and to view the report's standard selection screen. Notice that the format output on the selection screen is listed as ABAP List because that is what is indicated on the Title, Format screen. Press the F8 key again to execute the report. Your report should now appear similar to the report shown in Figure 8.4.

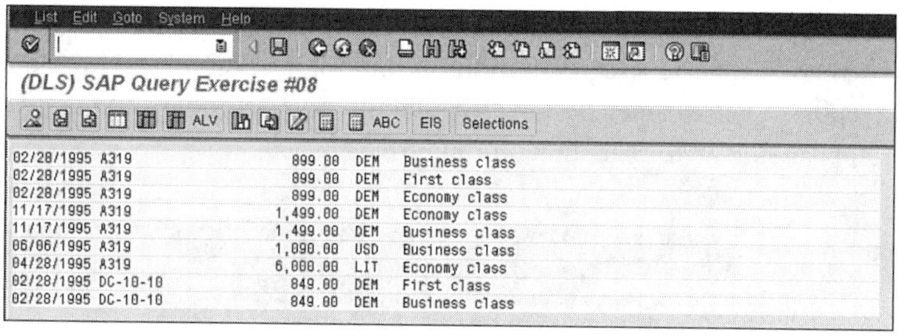

Figure 8.4
Viewing your SAP report data in ABAP List view is very similar to viewing it in the Notepad editor, and it saves you the extra step of downloading your report to view each small change.

The quick changes you have made so far have resolved the first three listed problems with the report, so you're now ready to tackle the last three.

REMOVING THE MEASUREMENT DESIGNATION (WHERE APPLICABLE)

Not all reports contain some form of measurement classification, such as currency (for example, U.S. dollars) or weight (for example, 123 lb.), so this step is applicable only if you have a measurement classification that requires removal. Removing the measurement designation is easy. To remove the measurement classification (in this case, Currency) from your existing SAP query, you follow these steps:

1. Navigate to the Field Output Options by clicking the Basic List button on the Application toolbar and then selecting Goto, Basic List, Field Output Options. As shown in Figure 8.5, the Field Output Options screen provides options for varying the output of specific fields in a report.

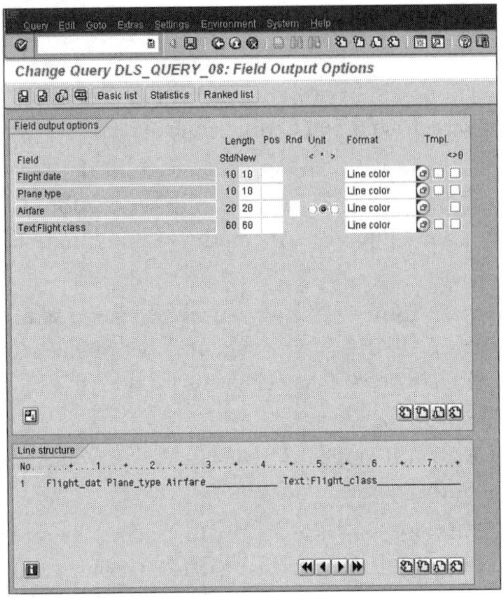

Figure 8.5
This screen provides options to vary each field in a report.

2. In the Unit field, select the second option button to remove the currency column from your report. (Chapter 7 describes the three Unit field option buttons.)

3. Click the Save button and then press F8 to execute the report and view its selection screen. Click the Execute button on the Application toolbar to see the changes to your report. The currency designations should now be gone, and your report output should appear similar to that shown in Figure 8.6.

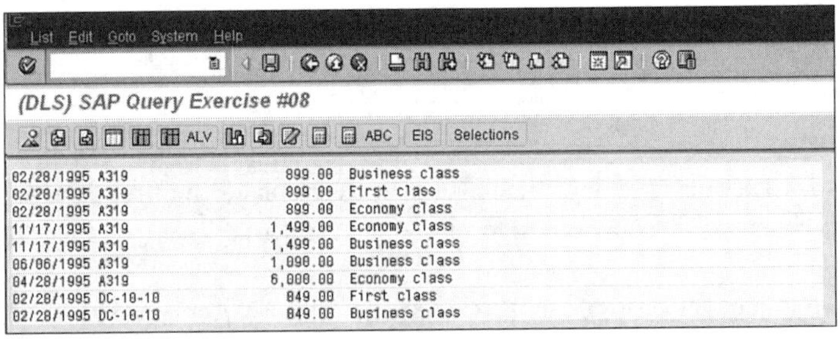

Figure 8.6
You have three options with regard to displaying units of measurement for a field.

If you compare Figure 8.4 with Figure 8.6, you can see that the entire Currency column has been removed. This quick change has resolved the fourth of the six problems with the report. You now need to fix only two more problems.

MAKING THE CORRECT POSITIONAL DESIGNATIONS

At this point, you need to see if your column widths match up to those listed in the specification shown in Table 8.2, earlier in this chapter.

As discussed in Chapter 7, the column width designations are on the Field Output Options screen. To vary the column widths of your SAP query report to match the specification, follow these steps:

1. Navigate to the Field Output Options by clicking the Basic List button on the Application toolbar and then selecting Goto, Basic List, Field Output Options.

2. View the Length Std/New column on this screen, which indicates the standard width of the field in the ABAP database. Compare the values listed here with the values listed in your specification for the designated field widths listed in the Position column. The New field allows you to input a longer or shorter number for the width of that field. By default, the Std and New columns contain the same numbers. If you find any that require modification, insert the appropriate value into the New column. In my example, all fields were the appropriate width except for the Text: Flight Class field, which I changed to 20 characters to match the spec (see Figure 8.7).

Changed width

Figure 8.7
When making fields shorter, be sure to consider whether you have any report output in that field that is larger than the designated number.

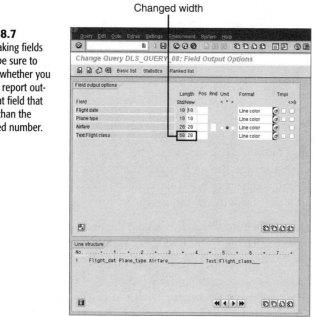

Helpful Hint
Editing the width of basic text fields is permitted. However, before modifying a field's width, you should check the database to learn whether there is a list of acceptable values that are tied to that field; this will assist you in determining the maximum and minimum widths you can set for the field. For example, the Flight Class field has three acceptable fixed values: First Class, Business Class, and Economy Class. The longest width of those three acceptable values is 14 characters. Modifying that column width is easy because the field can have only a limited number of values. A more challenging field would be something like Company Name, which could, for example, be set at 60 characters; most company names will fit within that width, but there could be a company name that is greater than 60 characters. You therefore need to use caution when varying a field's width.

The specification includes the starting and ending position numbers of each field in the Position column. To determine the width, you can subtract the starting value from the ending value of the Position column. For example, if the Position column in the spec says that the Text: Flight Class field goes from Position 55 to Position 75, you can subtract 55 from 75 to get a width of 20. By using basic math, you can translate that into column start and end values to compare. By looking at Figure 8.7, you can see the column widths, and you can extrapolate the start and end values, as shown in Table 8.3.

TABLE 8.3 THE DEFAULT LAYOUT FOR THE TEST SAP QUERY OF DATA FROM THE IDES TEST DATABASE COMPARED TO THE SPEC

Column STD	Description of Data	As-Is (Current) Position	To-Be-Modified Position
10	Flight date	1–10	1–10
10	Plane type	11–21	11–21
20	Airfare	22–42	22–42
	Company-specific name designator		43–54
60	Flight class text	43–103	55–75
	End of line filler, XXXXX		76–81

INSERTING FILLER DATA

Now you need to address the fields that are not included in your report, which I refer to as *filler fields*. When you examine Table 8.3, you see that the first three fields do not require any modification because they currently meet the spec. However, after the Airfare field and before the Flight Class text field, you need to insert the company-specific name designator in Positions 43–54. To insert a filler field, follow these steps:

1. Navigate to the Field Output Options screen by clicking the Basic List button on the Application toolbar and then selecting Goto, Basic List, Field Output Options.

2. The filler text you want to add appears both before and after the Text: Flight Class field. Recall from Chapter 7 that you can use the template indicator on this field to create templates. Templates give you the opportunity to insert text before and/or after the output of the field data. The only limitation with templates is that they cannot be longer than 46 characters in total width.

3. Indicate that you want to create a template for the Flight Class field by selecting the Template check box next to the field name.

4. Click the forward arrow button on the Application toolbar to navigate to the Field Templates screen, which you use to insert text before or after the output of a field that has been designated as a template. Type the appropriate filler values, as indicated in the spec—the company-specific name designator and the end-of-line filler XXXXX—without overwriting the 20-character placeholder for the output of the field (see Figure 8.8).

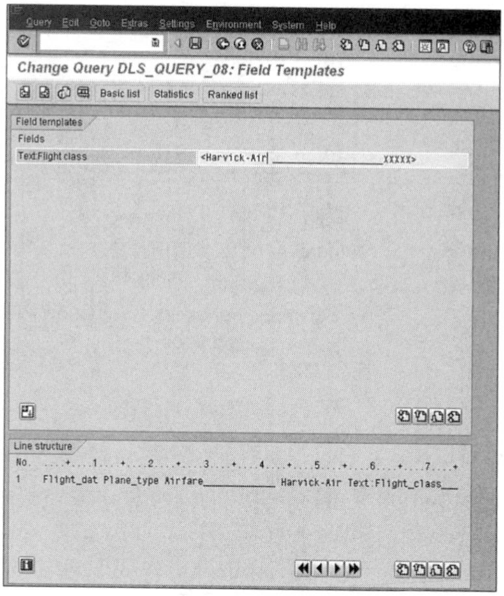

Figure 8.8
There is a space after the company name because the field width is designated as 12 characters, and the fictional company name HARVICK-AIR is only 11 characters.

5. Click the Save button and then press F8 to see the report's standard selection screen. Click the Execute button to see the changes to your report, which appear similar to the ones shown in Figure 8.9.

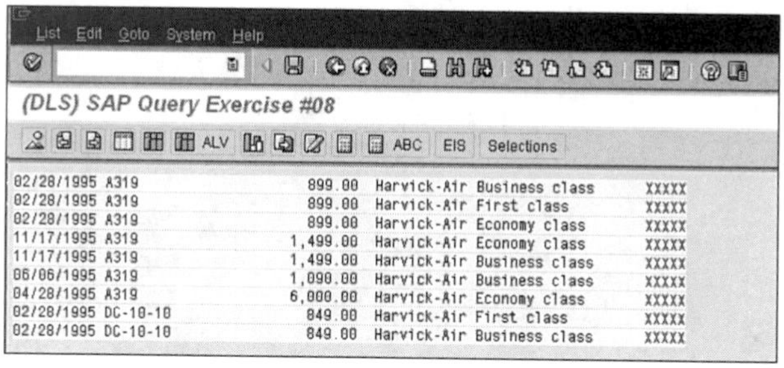

Figure 8.9
The report output now matches the specification.

STEP 3: DOWNLOADING THE EXTRACT FILE

The final step you need to take in creating a fixed positional extract file by using the SAP Query tool is to download the file. To complete this process, you follow these steps:

1. On your report's output screen, select List, Export, Local File (or press Ctrl+Shift+F9) and then select the Unconverted Text option. Then specify a location for your saved text file (for example, **c:\SPEC_SAMPLE.txt**) and then click the Transfer button. Your report output is then downloaded to a text file in the designated location.

2. Launch Notepad and open the file you saved earlier by selecting File, Open and indicating the path where the text file was saved (for example, c:\SPEC_SAMPLE.txt). The final specification file appears; it should look like the one shown in Figure 8.10.

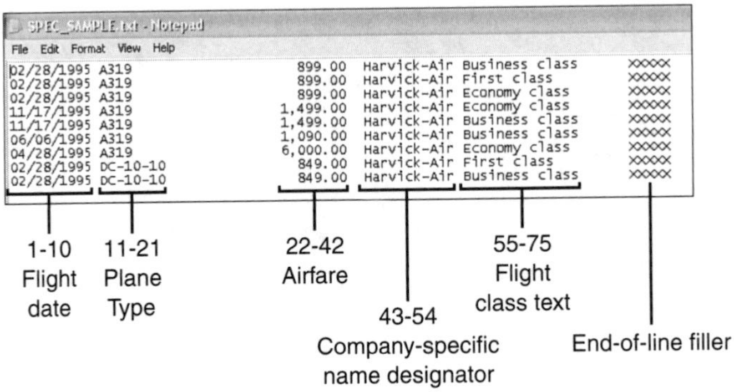

Figure 8.10
The report output
matches the
specification.

THINGS TO REMEMBER

- You can prepare fixed-width positional text files, often known as extracts, by using the SAP Query tool.

- Before creating any extracts, you need to be sure that you have a formal spec to work against.

- You should always change the format and column width on the Title Format screen when creating extract files.

- You can never change the width of a currency, date, or time field.

- Microsoft Notepad is a good tool to use when checking to make sure you have properly created positional extract files.

CHAPTER 9

CREATING BASIC CALCULATED FIELDS WITH THE SAP QUERY TOOL

In this chapter

In earlier chapters, you used the SAP Query tool to create reports. This chapter teaches you how to create basic calculated fields within those reports by using the SAP Query tool. A regular end user can perform the calculations explained in this chapter by using the SAP Query tool; no special ABAP training or security provisions are required.

As discussed in earlier chapters, you can use the SAP Query tool to create robust reports of your SAP data from any application module within SAP R/3. In addition to creating detailed reports, there may be times when you want to perform calculations on your data. A popular method many users use is to take advantage of the built-in integration with the Microsoft applications. A user can download a SAP R/3 report into Microsoft Excel and perform the calculations there, using Excel's easy-to-use formula tool. However, a more efficient and easy-to-learn method of performing calculations in reports is to use the SAP Query tool to do basic calculations.

The following are examples of calculations you might want to perform by using the SAP Query tool:

- **HR/payroll**—You could analyze how much it would cost for an employee on the third shift to work on a holiday by calculating the cost of increasing the hourly rate from straight time to time and a half.

- **Finance**—You could subtract the invoice date from the current date to determine the number of days that payment is past due.

- **Logistics**—You could subtract the inventory item count from the on-order item count to assist with determining restocking order amounts.

You can use calculated fields to perform if…then statements. For example, you might want to say that if the order value is greater than $100.00, enter the value $0.00 in the Shipping Cost column. You could also use a field that inserts a fixed value, such as the current date, in a column of your report output.

The ability to perform calculations on SAP data is a remarkable function because it means you are no longer required to extract your data into a third-party application such as Microsoft Excel to perform the calculations. In this chapter you will learn how to create a very basic mathematical calculation within an SAP query. You will also learn how to perform calculations when certain conditions are met (for example, "If X = 100, then multiply Y by 29"). Finally, this chapter shows you how to create a field for output based on real-time, dynamically decided input.

CREATING A BASIC SAP QUERY FOR THIS CHAPTER

For the examples in this chapter, you need to follow along in your own SAP system. To do so, you need to create a basic SAP query, using the instructions outlined in Chapter 3, "Creating Basic Reports with the SAP Query Tool," that contains the fields shown in Table 9.1. For my example, I named my report DLS_QUERY_09, where DLS is my initials.

TABLE 9.1   SAMPLE SAP QUERY IDES REPORT FOR USE IN CHAPTER 9 EXERCISES

Field Name	Line	Sequence
Airline carrier ID	1	1
Departure time	1	2
Arrival time	1	3
Airfare	1	4
Flight class	1	5
Text:Flight class	1	6

Figure 9.1 shows an example of the report output of this report.

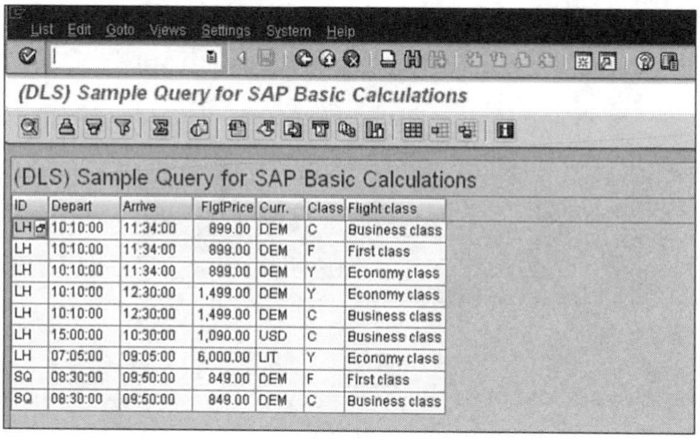

Figure 9.1
Your report output
may vary from what
is shown here based
on your system's
data.

When your SAP query is completed and your report output appears in the same format as
the example shown in Figure 9.1, you are ready to insert a basic mathematical formula into
the report.

USING A SIMPLE MATHEMATICAL FORMULA TO CREATE A BASIC CALCULATED FIELD

In this section you will insert a calculated field to perform a basic mathematical equation
within the query you created in the preceding section. You will create a calculated field that
subtracts 100 from the existing Airfare field and then shows the result as output. There are
several real-world applications for this type of calculation, including the following:

- **Human capital management**—You could perform an analysis for an increase in
  salaries to assist with budgeting and forecasting.
- **Finance**—You could monitor the incoming and outgoing cash flows.
- **Logistics**—You could calculate the number of days a plant maintenance order has been
  open.

You insert all basic calculations on the Select Field screen of the SAP Query tool. This screen, shown in Figure 9.2, lists the fields selected to be included in your SAP query. To add a basic mathematical calculation to your SAP query, you follow these steps:

Figure 9.2
The Select Field screen lists all the fields available within the InfoSet.

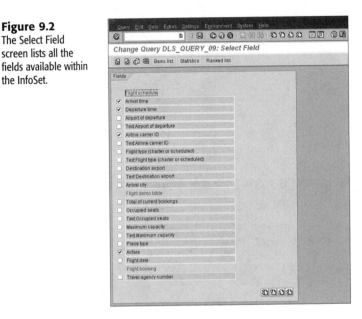

1. Navigate to the main screen of the SAP Query tool by using transaction code **SQ01**, select the query you want to work with (for example, DLS_QUERY_09), and click the Change button.

2. Navigate to the Select Field screen by clicking the Next Screen button on the Application toolbar twice. The screen should appear similar to the one shown in Figure 9.2.

3. Select Edit, Short Names, Switch On/Off. This allows you to create short names for your existing query fields so that you can easily refer to them in calculations. For example, enter TIXCOST as the short name for the Airfare field (see the background of Figure 9.3).

4. Position your cursor in the Airfare field to base your calculated field on it.

5. From the Select Field screen of the SAP Query tool, select Edit, Local Field, Create. Because your cursor was on the Airfare field, your custom-calculated field will be added to its field group (Flight Demo Table).

6. When the Field Definition dialog box appears, input a short name for your newly created local field (DISCOUNT) and input a field description (Airfare Discount), which will be the heading for the column in the report (refer to Figure 9.3).

Figure 9.3
The Field Definition dialog box displays all the attributes of your newly created calculated field in the SAP Query tool.

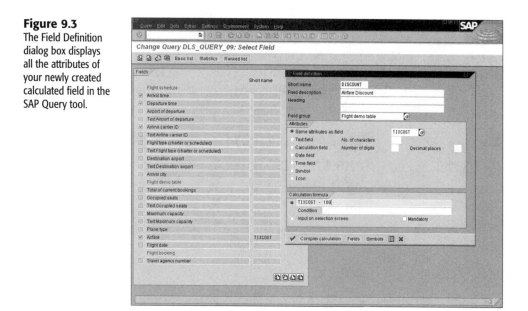

7. Define what kind of field your newly added custom field will be; the available options are listed in Table 9.2. Select the attributes for the field (refer to Figure 9.3) by indicating that the field is similar to the existing field that you created a short name for. That is, indicate that the field has the same attributes as the TIXCOST field. (Both are currency fields.)

TABLE 9.2   THE AVAILABLE FIELD ATTRIBUTES

Attribute	Description
Same attributes as field	Allows the user to select from a list of any fields in the SAP query that have been given a short name. This selection indicates that the new local field will have the same technical characteristics as the selected field.
Text field	Formats the field to be text and specifies the number of characters for the field (that is, the column width).
Calculation field	Formats the field to be numeric and specifies the number of digits and decimal places for the field (that is, the column width).
Date field	Formats the field to be a calendar-based date field in line with the system's calendar settings.
Time field	Formats the field to be a calendar-based time field in line with the system's calendar settings.
Symbol	Formats the field to be a black-and-white symbol from the list of hundreds available within SAP.
Icon	Formats the field to be a color icon from the list of hundreds available within SAP.

8. If it is not already selected, select the option button next to the Calculation Formula box at the bottom of the Field Definition dialog box and then enter your basic mathematical formula into the designated box to the right of it (refer to Figure 9.3). In this case, enter **TIXCOST-100**, which translates to an output in the Airfare Discount field of the calculation: Airfare minus 100. Several different types of basic mathematical symbols are available, as shown in Table 9.3. Press Enter to proceed.

TABLE 9.3   VALID OPERATORS AND OPERANDS FOR MATHEMATICAL FORMULAS

Operator	Description
*	Multiplication
/	Division
DIV	Whole-number division, where the result is an integer
MOD	Remainder
+	Addition
-	Subtraction
%NAME	The user's name
%DATE	The system date
%TIME	The system time
Numeric constants	A constant numeric value you input (for example, 10 or 28173.29)
Character strings	A constant alphabetic (nonnumeric) value you input (for example, THISISMYTEXT or ABC)
Symbols and icons	A black-and-white or color picture

9. To add the newly created field to your report output, confirm that the field is selected on the Select Fields screen by ensuring that the small box next to the Airfare Discount field at the bottom of the Flight Demo Table field group is selected.

10. Navigate to the Basic List Line Structure screen by clicking the Basic List button on the Application toolbar. You see your newly created field listed there, under the name you gave it in step 6. Add the new local field to your report output on the Basic List screen of the SAP query report by indicating a line and sequence number. (I listed mine as Line 1 and Sequence 7.) Click the Save button.

11. Execute your report by pressing F8. You are presented with the report's selection screen. Press F8 again to see your updated SAP query, which now contains your newly added calculated field (see Figure 9.4).

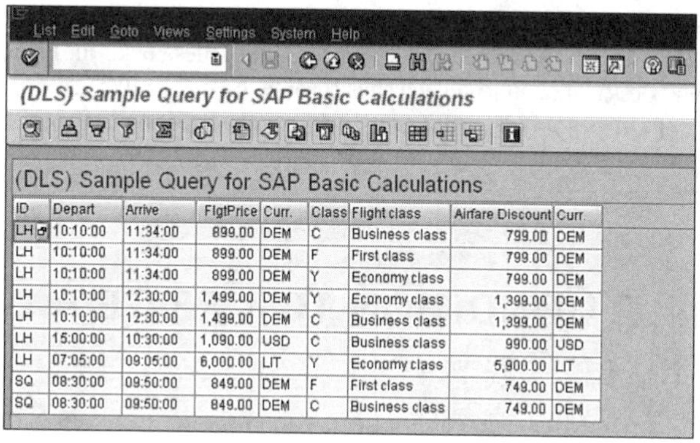

Figure 9.4
The newly added column that contains the value of the Airfare field minus 100 is now shown on the report.

ID	Depart	Arrive	FlgtPrice	Curr.	Class	Flight class	Airfare Discount	Curr
LH	10:10:00	11:34:00	899.00	DEM	C	Business class	799.00	DEM
LH	10:10:00	11:34:00	899.00	DEM	F	First class	799.00	DEM
LH	10:10:00	11:34:00	899.00	DEM	Y	Economy class	799.00	DEM
LH	10:10:00	12:30:00	1,499.00	DEM	Y	Economy class	1,399.00	DEM
LH	10:10:00	12:30:00	1,499.00	DEM	C	Business class	1,399.00	DEM
LH	15:00:00	10:30:00	1,090.00	USD	C	Business class	990.00	USD
LH	07:05:00	09:05:00	6,000.00	LIT	Y	Economy class	5,900.00	LIT
SQ	08:30:00	09:50:00	849.00	DEM	F	First class	749.00	DEM
SQ	08:30:00	09:50:00	849.00	DEM	C	Business class	749.00	DEM

Technical Details of SAP Query Calculations

When inserting mathematical formulas into an SAP query report, you structure formulas based on standard math procedures, using operands (values) and operators (operand links), which are described in Table 9.3. In case you are like me and remember nothing from college math classes, I have included some specific clarifications on calculations for your reference:

- The operators + and - can also be one-character operators. In this case, they do not link two operands but refer to subsequent operands.

- The processing sequence follows the usual rules, where the operators + or - take priority over characters *, /, DIV, and MOD, which in turn take priority over the operators + and - . However, you can change the processing sequence to suit your own requirements by using parentheses.

- In some cases, you may need to output the fields used in the calculation sequentially on the Basic List Line Structure screen in order for a detailed calculation to function as it is designed to function. For example, if the calculation formula is A + B and the local field is C, you may need to output A and B prior to C in your report output.

- Table 9.3 lists some operands, including %NAME, %DATE, and %TIME, which are special fields that the system automatically provides. %NAME is a 12-character text field that contains the name of the user entered when logging on to the SAP R/3 system. %DATE is a date field that contains today's date. %TIME is a time field that contains the current time. If the character ' appears within a character string, you must precede it with a ' so that it is correctly interpreted. Also, the following special notation is possible for field names and the special fields %NAME, %DATE, and %TIME:

  - **field[n1:n2]**—This field must have its attributes set as a text field. In addition, both n1 and n2 must be whole-number numeric constants (without decimal points), and n1 < n2. field[n1:n2] is the part of the text field that extends from the character at n1 to the character at n2. The first character of a text field appears at Position 1.

  - **field[YEAR], field[MONTH], field[DAY]**—This field must have its attributes set as a date field. The year, the month, and the day can then be provided (in number form).

  - **field[HOUR], field[MINUTE], field[SECOND]**—This field must have its attributes set as a time field. Hours, minutes, and seconds can then be provided.

- Formulas can extend over one or several lines in free format. For example, the individual operands and operators can appear one immediately after the other in a consecutive sequence, or there may be a number of spaces between them. However, there can be no spaces within field names, and field names and character strings cannot extend over more than one line.

- If the fields specified on the screen for the formula and the condition are sufficient to allow full specification of the calculation formula for the local field, you can use these fields for input. Otherwise, you need to use the Complex calculation function, which is covered in Chapter 10, "Creating Advanced Calculated Fields with the SAP Query Tool." This takes you to an editor where you can enter all the necessary calculations.

USING A SIMPLE CONDITION TO CREATE A BASIC CALCULATED FIELD

Now that you have created a basic calculation, you can take it a step further by using a condition to determine a calculation. In some cases, you might want to perform a calculation or output a value only if a certain condition exists. For example, in the SAP query you have been working with in this chapter, you could create a calculated field to specify that the discount field should have the 100 discount only if the passenger is listed as flying in first class. There are several real-world applications for this type of conditional calculation, including the following:

- **HR/payroll**—You could forecast how much it would cost to increase all associates' salaries by three percent within a department to assist in salary or budgeting projections.

- **Finance**—For fixed-asset management, you could determine which purchase requisitions are not assigned to an account.

- **Logistics**—You could calculate invoice payments based on the delivery dates and down payments.

For this example, you will continue working with the exercise query you created earlier in this chapter. To create a calculated field that is based on a condition, you follow these steps:

1. Navigate to the main screen of the SAP Query tool by using transaction code SQ01, select the query you want to work with (for example, DLS_QUERY_09), and click the Change button.

2. Navigate to the Select Fields screen by clicking the Next Screen button on the Application toolbar twice. If the short names are not already displayed, select Edit, Short Names, Switch On/Off to turn them on. Enter a short name for the Flight Class field (CLASS) in the Flight Booking Field group so that you can easily refer to it in your calculation.

3. Position your cursor in the Flight Class field, which you will base your calculated field on.

4. Select Edit, Local Field, Create. Because your cursor is in the Flight Class field, a custom field is added to its field group (Flight Booking Table).

5. When the Field Definition dialog box appears, input a short name for your newly created local field (FDISCOUNT) and input a Field description (First Class Airfare Discount), which will be the heading for the column in the report (see Figure 9.5).

CAUTION

The calculated field you created in the first example for airfare discount had the short description DISCOUNT. The calculated field you are now creating for this example is for first-class airfare discount, with the short name FDISCOUNT. Be sure not to get the two confused.

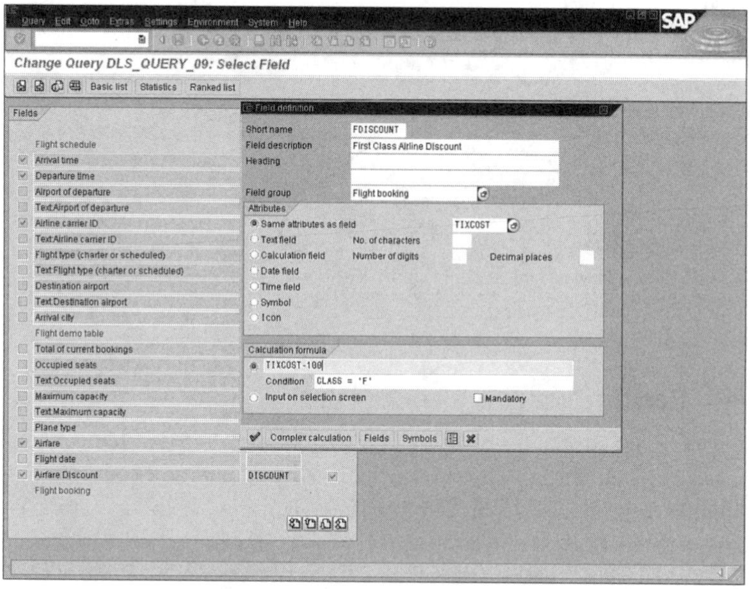

Figure 9.5
For this example, you input a short name and a field description, and you indicate for attributes that you want the field to be in the same format as the TIXCOST field.

6. Define the attributes for the field (refer to Table 9.2) by indicating that the field has the same attributes as the TIXCOST field. (Both are currency fields.)

7. If it is not already selected, select the option button next to the Calculation Formula box at the bottom of the Field Definition dialog box and then enter your basic mathematical formula into the designated box to the right of it (refer to Figure 9.5). In this case, enter **TIXCOST-100**. Because this formula is based on a condition, also input **CLASS = 'F'** into the Condition line under the formula. This translates to an output in the new First Class Airline Discount field of the value of the Airfare field minus 100 only if the flight class is listed as F. Press Enter to proceed.

8. To add the newly created field to your report output, confirm that the field is selected on the Select Fields screen by ensuring that the small box next to the First Class Airline Discount field at the bottom of the Flight Demo Table field group is selected.

9. Navigate to the Basic List Line Structure screen by clicking the Basic List button on the Application toolbar. You see your newly created field listed there, under the name you gave it in step 5. Add the new local field to your report output on the Basic List screen of the SAP query report by indicating a line and sequence number. (I listed mine as Line 1 and Sequence 7.) Click the Save button.

10. Execute your report by pressing F8. You are presented with the report's selection screen. Press F8 again to see your updated SAP query, which should now contain your newly added calculated field (see Figure 9.6).

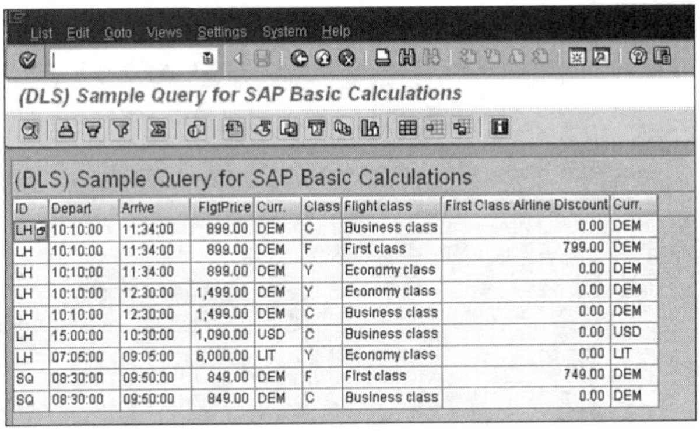

Figure 9.6
The report now shows the newly added column that contains the value of the Airfare field minus 100 only if the flight is first class.

DEFINING CONDITIONS FOR A LOCAL FIELD

Conditions are special formulas that always evaluate to true (that is, the condition is satisfied) or false (that is, the condition is not satisfied). A condition consists of a single comparison, although it is possible to link comparisons by using logical operators. A *comparison* consists of two operands linked by a valid operator, as shown in Table 9.4.

Valid operands are used in the SAP Query tool just as they are used in basic math. The processing sequence conforms to the usual rules—that is, negations (NOT operations) take priority over AND operations, which in turn take priority over OR operations. However, you can override this sequence by using parentheses. For more information on SAP calculation conditions, please refer to the SAP online help at http://help.sap.com and then select SAP Library, Cross Application Components, CA - Drilldown Reporting, How to Process Report Lists, Defining Display Conditions.

TABLE 9.4   VALID OPERATORS FOR LINKING OPERANDS AND COMPARISONS

Operator	Description
Operators for Linking Operands	
=	Equal to
<>,><	Not equal to
<	Less than

Operator	Description
<=,=<	Less than or equal to
>	Greater than
>=,=>	Greater than or equal to

Operators for Linking Comparisons	
NOT	Negation of the result of a subsequent comparison
AND	AND link of two comparisons
OR	OR link of two comparisons

9

USING AN INPUT VALUE TO CREATE A BASIC CALCULATED FIELD

Now that you have created a basic calculation and a simple conditional calculation, you can try something more dynamic. In some cases, you might want to perform a calculation or output a value based on a value that you may know only at report execution time (that is, a dynamic value). For example, you can use the same SAP query you have worked with throughout this chapter to create a calculated field to specify that the Discount field should subtract 100 or 200 or 500, with the actual numerical amount input at runtime. There are several real-world applications for this type of conditional calculation, including the following:

■ **HR/payroll**—You could analyze how much it would cost for an employee on the third shift to work on a holiday by calculating the cost of increasing the hourly rate by $1, $2, and so on.

■ **Finance**—You could monitor the impacts of accounts payable reports if an invoice were paid in 30 days, 60 days, and so on.

■ **Logistics**—You could calculate the number of days a plant maintenance order has been open as of today, as of next week, and so on.

To create a calculated field that is based on dynamic selection screen input, you follow these steps:

1. Navigate to the main screen of the SAP Query tool by using transaction code **SQ01**, select the query you want to work with (for example, DLS_QUERY_09), and click the Change button.

2. Navigate to the Select Fields screen by clicking the Next Screen button on the Application toolbar twice. If the short names are not already displayed, select Edit, Short Names, Switch On/Off to turn them on. You will reuse the local field you created in the first example, Airfare Discount, which has the short name DISCOUNT.

3. Position your cursor in the Airfare Discount field and select Edit, Local Field, Change to change your existing calculated field rather than create a new one.

4. When the Field Definition dialog box appears, delete TIXCOST-100 from the Calculation formula box and select the radio button Input on Selection Screen. Doing so includes the Airfare Discount field on the report's selection screen so that you can input a value at report runtime.

5. Create a calculated field that shows the value of the amount entered in the Airfare field minus the amount entered on the selection screen in the Airfare Discount field. In this case, you can reuse the First Class Airline Discount field that you used in the previous example. To modify this existing field, position your cursor in the First Class Airline Discount field and select Edit, Local Field, Change.

6. When the Field Definition dialog box appears, modify the formula TIXCOST-100 to say TIXCOST-DISCOUNT and leave the Condition line as is (see Figure 9.7). Press Enter to proceed.

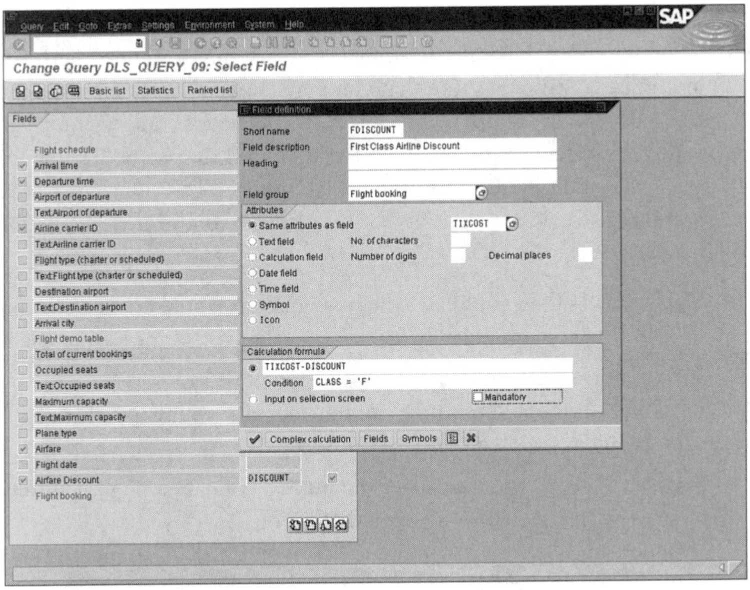

Figure 9.7
Instead of subtracting the initial Airfare (TIXCOST) value, you change it to subtract the amount entered on the selection screen in the Airfare Discount field (DISCOUNT).

7. Ensure that the First Class Discount field is selected on the Select Fields screen. Then navigate to the Basic List Line Structure screen by clicking the Basic List button on the Application toolbar. Confirm that it is set to be included in the report output by indicating a line and sequence number. (I listed mine as Line 1 and Sequence 8.) Click the Save button.

8. Execute your report by pressing F8. You are presented with the report's selection screen, which should contain an entry field labeled Airfare Discount (see Figure 9.8).

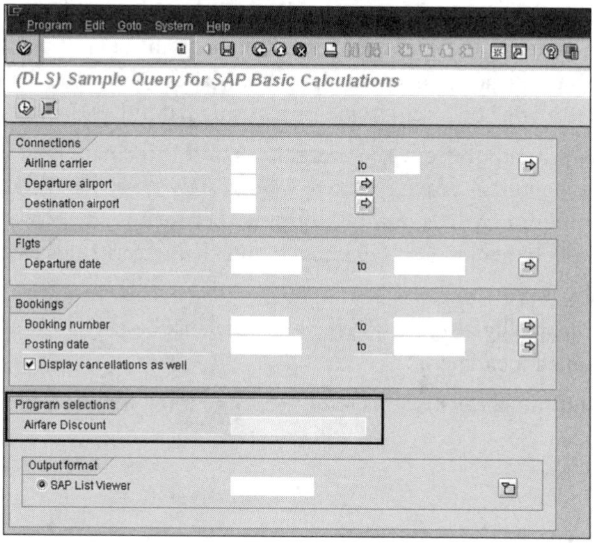

Figure 9.8
Any field indicated in the Field Definition dialog box as Input on the selection screen is automatically inserted on your report's selection screen.

9. Input a numeric value in the Airfare Discount field on the selection screen (for example, 250). Press F8 to see your updated SAP query, which now contains your newly added calculated field labeled First Class Airline Discount (see Figure 9.9).

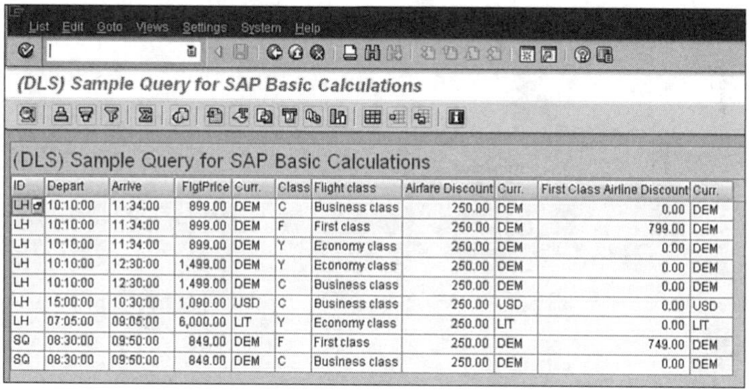

ID	Depart	Arrive	FlgtPrice	Curr.	Class	Flight class	Airfare Discount	Curr.	First Class Airline Discount	Curr.
LH	10:10:00	11:34:00	899.00	DEM	C	Business class	250.00	DEM	0.00	DEM
LH	10:10:00	11:34:00	899.00	DEM	F	First class	250.00	DEM	799.00	DEM
LH	10:10:00	11:34:00	899.00	DEM	Y	Economy class	250.00	DEM	0.00	DEM
LH	10:10:00	12:30:00	1,499.00	DEM	Y	Economy class	250.00	DEM	0.00	DEM
LH	10:10:00	12:30:00	1,499.00	DEM	C	Business class	250.00	DEM	0.00	DEM
LH	15:00:00	10:30:00	1,090.00	USD	C	Business class	250.00	USD	0.00	USD
LH	07:05:00	09:05:00	6,000.00	LIT	Y	Economy class	250.00	LIT	0.00	LIT
SQ	08:30:00	09:50:00	849.00	DEM	F	First class	250.00	DEM	749.00	DEM
SQ	08:30:00	09:50:00	849.00	DEM	C	Business class	250.00	DEM	0.00	DEM

Figure 9.9
The newly added column that contains the value of the Airfare field minus the value input on the selection screen displays only if the flight is first class.

10. You can return to the selection screen, modify the number inserted into the Airfare Discount field, and reexecute the report to cause a calculation to be performed dynamically each time.

THINGS TO REMEMBER

- You can use the SAP Query tool to perform basic calculations using local fields; no programming skills are required.

- The processing sequence of operands follows the usual precedence rules, where the one-character operators + and - take priority over the point operators *, /, DIV, and MOD, which in turn take priority over the operators + and - . You can change the processing sequence to suit your own requirements by using parentheses.

- Formulas can extend over one or several lines in free format. That is, the individual operands and operators can appear one immediately after the other in a consecutive sequence, or there may be a number of spaces between them. However, there can be no spaces within field names, and field names and character strings cannot extend over more than one line.

- You can automatically insert a system value, such as the current user's name, into a report by using a local field.

- Dynamic conditional calculations require a value to be input on the SAP Query tool's selection screen.

CHAPTER 10

CREATING ADVANCED CALCULATED FIELDS WITH THE SAP QUERY TOOL

In this chapter

Chapter 9, "Creating Basic Calculated Fields with the SAP Query Tool," discusses how you can create local fields to perform basic calculations without having any special technical training or security access. In this chapter, you will take those skills one step further and learn how to perform more advanced calculations.

Chapter 9 describes sample calculations, including basic mathematical operations and conditional operations. This chapter takes that information a step further by explaining how you can use the SAP Query tool to create more complex calculations. Not many SAP users are aware that basic calculations can be performed using the SAP Query tool reporting solution, and even fewer are aware of the advanced functions that are possible. In Chapter 9 you performed an if...then scenario. By using advanced calculations, you can perform an if...then scenario that has multiple conditions. Being able to perform these more complex types of calculations is a bonus that gives end users even greater access and flexibility in working with data within SAP.

The following are examples of advanced calculations you might want to perform by using the SAP Query tool:

- **HR/payroll**—You could create suggested specific salary increases for associates who are currently paid under the minimum for their pay grade.
- **Finance**—You could subtract the invoice date from the current date to determine the number of days that payment is past due and then determine late fees based on days-late increments (30 days, 45 days, and so on).
- **Logistics**—You could project future inventory levels based on projected sales figures and marketplace conditions.

CREATING A BASIC SAP QUERY FOR THIS CHAPTER

For the examples in this chapter, you need to follow along in your own SAP system. To do so, you need to create a basic SAP query that contains the fields shown in Table 10.1. (For a reminder of how to create a basic SAP query, see the instructions in Chapter 3, "Creating Basic Reports with the SAP Query Tool.") For my example, I named my report DLS_QUERY_10, where DLS is my initials.

TABLE 10.1   SAMPLE SAP QUERY IDES REPORT FOR USE IN CHAPTER 10 EXERCISES

Field Name	Line	Sequence
Airline carrier ID	1	1
Departure time	1	2
Arrival time	1	3
Airfare	1	4
Flight class	1	5

Field Name	Line	Sequence
Text: Flight class	1	6
Destination airport	1	7
Arrival city	1	8
Airport of departure	1	9

Figure 10.1 shows an example of the report output of this report.

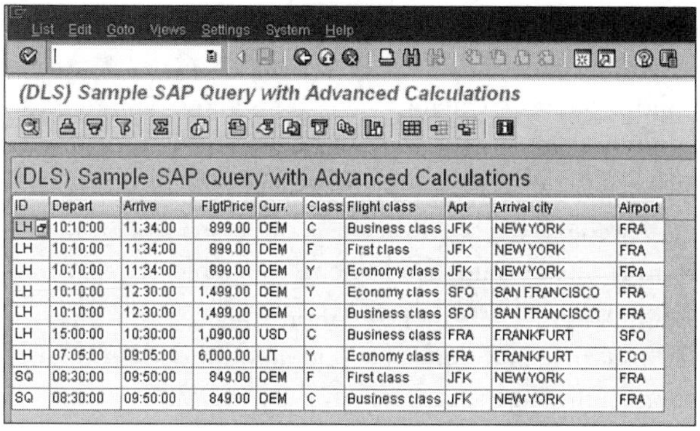

(DLS) Sample SAP Query with Advanced Calculations

ID	Depart	Arrive	FlgtPrice	Curr.	Class	Flight class	Apt	Arrival city	Airport
LH	10:10:00	11:34:00	899.00	DEM	C	Business class	JFK	NEW YORK	FRA
LH	10:10:00	11:34:00	899.00	DEM	F	First class	JFK	NEW YORK	FRA
LH	10:10:00	11:34:00	899.00	DEM	Y	Economy class	JFK	NEW YORK	FRA
LH	10:10:00	12:30:00	1,499.00	DEM	Y	Economy class	SFO	SAN FRANCISCO	FRA
LH	10:10:00	12:30:00	1,499.00	DEM	C	Business class	SFO	SAN FRANCISCO	FRA
LH	15:00:00	10:30:00	1,090.00	USD	C	Business class	FRA	FRANKFURT	SFO
LH	07:05:00	09:05:00	6,000.00	LIT	Y	Economy class	FRA	FRANKFURT	FCO
SQ	08:30:00	09:50:00	849.00	DEM	F	First class	JFK	NEW YORK	FRA
SQ	08:30:00	09:50:00	849.00	DEM	C	Business class	JFK	NEW YORK	FRA

Figure 10.1
Your report output may vary from what is shown here based on your system's data.

When your SAP query is complete and your report output appears in the same format as the example shown in Figure 10.1, you are ready to begin with the first exercise to insert an advanced mathematical formula in your SAP query report.

USING MULTIPLE CONDITIONS TO CREATE AN ADVANCED CALCULATED FIELD

In many cases, you want to see report output only if certain complex conditions are met. Chapter 9 provides an example of how to perform a calculation if a single condition is met. In that example, you added to Figure 9.6 a new calculated field that contains the value of the Airfare field minus 100, but only if the flight is first class. In this single-condition scenario, you performed a calculation only if the flight was first class. What if you wanted to perform different calculations depending on the flight class? For example, say that for first class, the Airfare field would be reduced by 100, for business class the Airfare field would be reduced by 50, and for coach class the Airfare field would be reduced by $25. As another example, you might need to base a condition on several variables, such as the wing of the airport used for each departure. There are several real-world applications for this type of calculation, including the following:

- **HR/payroll**—You could determine what security badge should be given to an employee based on the employee's location.

- **Finance**—You could determine the general ledger account number associated with a wage type.
- **Logistics**—For rebate processing, you could report on which accounts a rebate will be included with, based on certain account numbers.

To use local fields to perform complex calculations, you follow these steps:

1. Navigate to the main screen of the SAP Query tool by using transaction code **SQ01**, select the query you want to work with (for example, DLS_QUERY_10), and click the Change button.

2. Navigate to the Select Fields screen by clicking the Next Screen button on the application toolbar twice.

3. Select Edit, Short Names, Switch On/Off. This allows you to create short names for your existing query fields so that you can easily refer to them in calculations. Start by giving the Airline Carrier ID field the short name **Airline**.

4. Select Edit, Local Field, Create. Because your cursor was on the Airline field, a custom field is added to its field group (Flight Schedule Table).

5. When the Field Definition dialog box appears, input a short name (**GATE**) for your newly created local field and input the field description (**Gate name**), which will be the heading for the column in the report.

6. Define the attributes for the field, as shown in Figure 10.2. To output a potentially 10-digit gate code (for example, South gate), you could select the Text option and indicate that it will be 10 characters wide. However, you need to be sure that the column is wide enough to fit the column heading, which is set on the Field Definition dialog box (in this case, Gate Name—9 characters). Be sure to indicate that the character width will be able to accommodate the column heading and the largest entry (Gate Name) that could possibly be in that field.

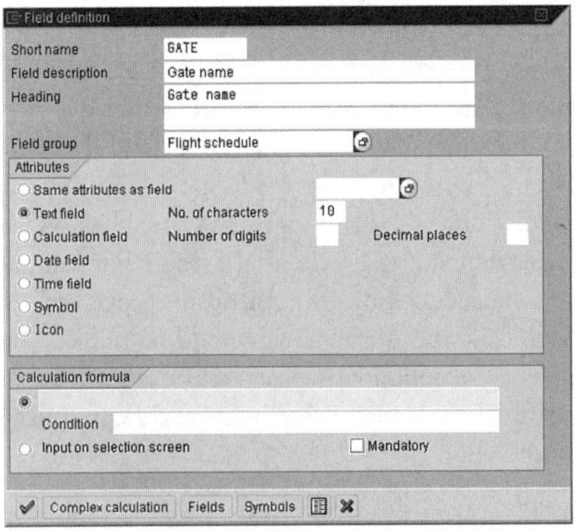

Figure 10.2
Setting the attributes to a text field with 10 characters permits the eventual output in the report of the largest gate name, North Gate.

7. Click the Complex Calculation button to bring up the Define Field: Complex Calculation dialog box, which allows you to input multiple conditions. As shown in Figure 10.3, you input of the conditions in the same order and mathematical format mentioned in Chapter 9.

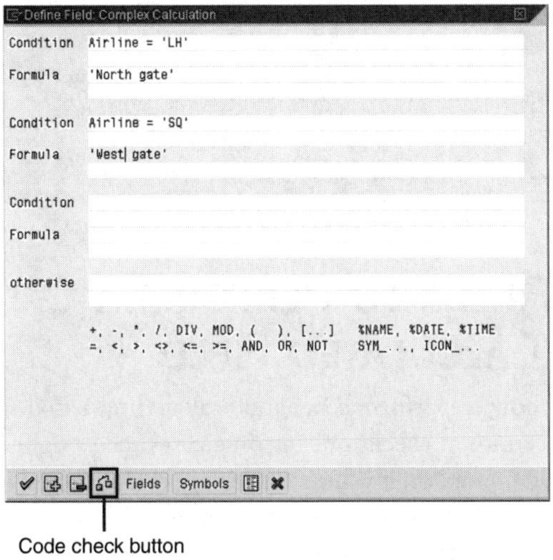

Figure 10.3
The Define Field: Complex Calculations dialog box permits the entry of three fixed conditions, although you are not required to use them all.

Code check button

8. Type the condition **AIRLINE = 'LH'** in the Condition line and then enter **'West Gate'** as the desired output if the condition is met in the Formula line. You can enter up to three different conditions on this screen. To ensure that you have typed correctly, click the Code Check button (or press Shift+F4). The SAP Query tool then checks your syntax to ensure that there are no typos.

9. To add the newly created field to your report output, confirm that the field is selected on the Select Fields screen by ensuring that the small box next to the Gate Name field at the bottom of the Flight Schedule field group is selected.

10. Navigate to the Basic List Line Structure screen by clicking the Basic List button on the application toolbar. You see your newly created field listed there, under the name you gave it in step 6. Add the new local field to your report output on the Basic List screen of the SAP query report by indicating a line and sequence number. (I listed mine as Line 1 and Sequence 10.) Click the Save button.

11. Execute your report by pressing F8. You are presented with the report's selection screen. Press F8 again to see your updated SAP query, which should now contain your newly added calculated field (see Figure 10.4).

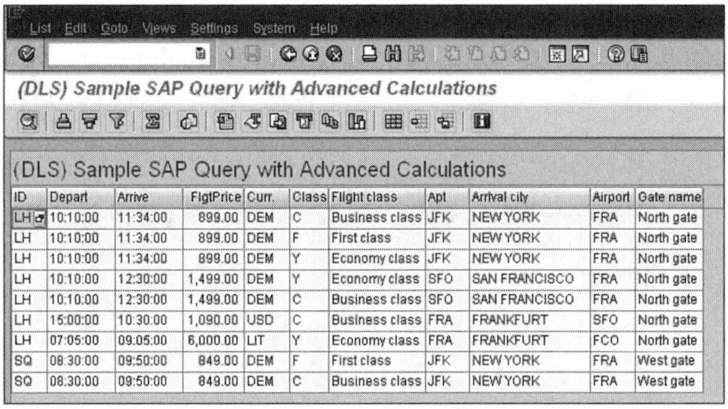

ID	Depart	Arrive	FlgtPrice	Curr.	Class	Flight class	Apt	Arrival city	Airport	Gate name
LH	10:10:00	11:34:00	899.00	DEM	C	Business class	JFK	NEW YORK	FRA	North gate
LH	10:10:00	11:34:00	899.00	DEM	F	First class	JFK	NEW YORK	FRA	North gate
LH	10:10:00	11:34:00	899.00	DEM	Y	Economy class	JFK	NEW YORK	FRA	North gate
LH	10:10:00	12:30:00	1,499.00	DEM	Y	Economy class	SFO	SAN FRANCISCO	FRA	North gate
LH	10:10:00	12:30:00	1,499.00	DEM	C	Business class	SFO	SAN FRANCISCO	FRA	North gate
LH	15:00:00	10:30:00	1,090.00	USD	C	Business class	FRA	FRANKFURT	SFO	North gate
LH	07:05:00	09:05:00	6,000.00	LIT	Y	Economy class	FRA	FRANKFURT	FCO	North gate
SQ	08:30:00	09:50:00	849.00	DEM	F	First class	JFK	NEW YORK	FRA	West gate
SQ	08:30:00	09:50:00	849.00	DEM	C	Business class	JFK	NEW YORK	FRA	West gate

Figure 10.4
The added calculated field appears in the report output, displaying data as requested in the Define Field: Complex Calculation dialog box.

USING MULTIPLE FIELDS TO PERFORM A CALCULATION IN AN ADVANCED CALCULATED FIELD

In Chapter 9 you learned how to perform a dynamic calculation based on the entry of data on a report's selection screen upon execution. In some cases, you might want to perform a calculation or output a value based on a value that is only calculated or input dynamically at report execution time. For example, you can use the same SAP query you have been working with in this chapter to create a calculated field to output the gate name based on the day the weather is entered on the selection screen (assuming for this example that the gate may vary based on the weather). There are several real-world applications for this type of conditional calculation, including the following:

- **HR/payroll**—You could analyze how much it would cost for an employee on the third shift to work on a holiday by calculating the cost of increasing the hourly rate by a conditional dollar amount that varies based on the year entered on the selection screen.
- **Finance**—You could monitor the impacts of accounts payable reports if an invoice were paid in a conditional time frame, based on whether the account was in good or poor standing, as indicated on the report's selection screen.
- **Logistics**—You could calculate the number of days a plant maintenance order has been open as of a conditional date entered on the selection screen and perform a calculation on a fee entered at runtime based on the date.

To create a calculated field that is based on another calculated field that uses dynamic selection screen input, you follow these steps:

1. Navigate to the main screen of the SAP Query tool by using transaction code **SQ01**, select the query you want to work with (for example, DLS_QUERY_10), and click the Change button.
2. Navigate to the Select Fields screen by clicking the Next Screen button on the application toolbar twice. If the short names are not already displayed, select Edit, Short Names, Switch On/Off to turn them on. You will create a new local field within the first field group (the Flight Schedule field group).

3. Position your cursor within any field in the Flight Schedule field group and then select Edit, Local Field, Create.

4. When the Define Field dialog box appears, input a short name (**WEATHER**) for your newly created local field and input the field description **Weather**, which will be the heading for the column in the report.

5. Define the attributes for the field by selecting the Text Field option and indicating that the width of the field will be seven characters. This is long enough to support the column heading and to accommodate the entries in the field that will be only one character.

6. Because the newly created field will simply store a value entered at runtime, select the Input on Selection Screen option button and the mandatory check box. Selecting the mandatory check box ensures that a value is entered on the selection screen upon report execution. Click the green Continue button to return to the Select Fields screen.

7. Create a calculated field that uses the Weather field's dynamic entry to affect the calculated field. In this case, you can reuse the Gate Name advanced calculated field from the previous example.

8. Position your cursor in the Gate Name field, on which you will base your calculated field.

9. Select Edit, Local Field, Change because, again, you are changing a field, not creating a new one. The Field Define Field dialog box appears. Click the Complex Calculation button to review the complex calculation created in the previous example (refer to Figure 10.3).

10. Modify the conditional statements to use the data entered in the new Weather field on the selection screen. You input these conditions, as shown in Figure 10.5, very similarly to how you entered them in the previous example, but this time, you are assuming that the value options for entry in the Weather field at runtime are limited to R (for rain), S (for snow), and F (for fog).

11. Type the condition **WEATHER = 'R'** in the Condition line and then enter the desired output **'West Gate'** if the condition is met in the Formula line. You can enter up to three conditions and an "all else/otherwise" option. This says that if an option other than the three listed occurs, the value listed should be output in the Otherwise section.

12. To ensure that you have typed correctly, click the Code Check button (or press Shift+F4). The SAP Query tool then checks your syntax to ensure that there are no typos.

13. To add the newly created field to your report output, confirm that the field is selected on the select fields screen by ensuring that the small box next to the Gate Name field at the bottom of the Flight Schedule field group is selected.

14. Navigate to the Basic List Line Structure screen by clicking the Basic List button on the application toolbar. You see your newly created field listed there, under the name you gave it in step 6. Add the new local field to your report output on the Basic List screen of the SAP query report by indicating a line and sequence number. (I listed mine as Line 1 and Sequence 11.) Click the Save button.

10

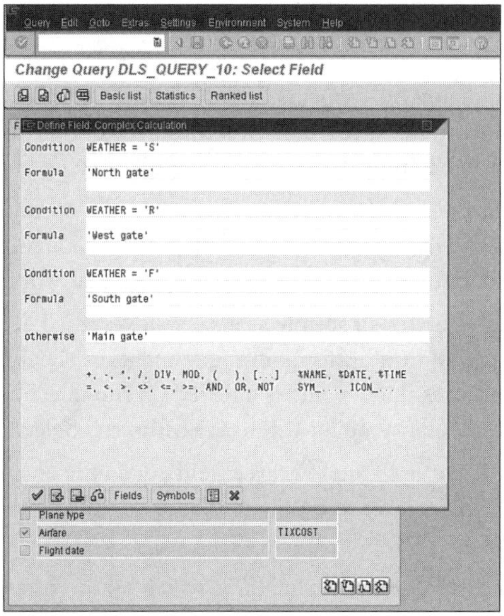

Figure 10.5
Three different conditional options and an otherwise condition are included.

15. Execute your report by pressing F8. You are presented with the report's selection screen, on which you are required to enter a value in the Weather field: R (for rain), S (for snow), or F (for fog), as shown in Figure 10.6.

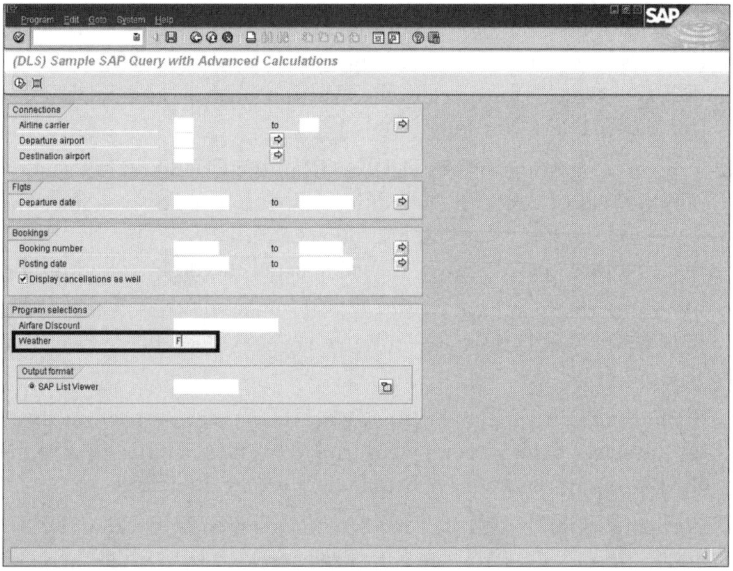

Figure 10.6
When not populated, the Weather field has a check mark in it to indicate that it is mandatory on the selection screen.

16. Input a value in the Weather field and then press F8 to see your updated SAP query. It should now contain your dynamically updated calculated field that varies the gate

number based on the weather (see Figure 10.7). Press F8 again to see the finished report (refer to Figure 10.6), which now includes the dynamically populated gate name. (In my example, I entered a weather condition of F.)

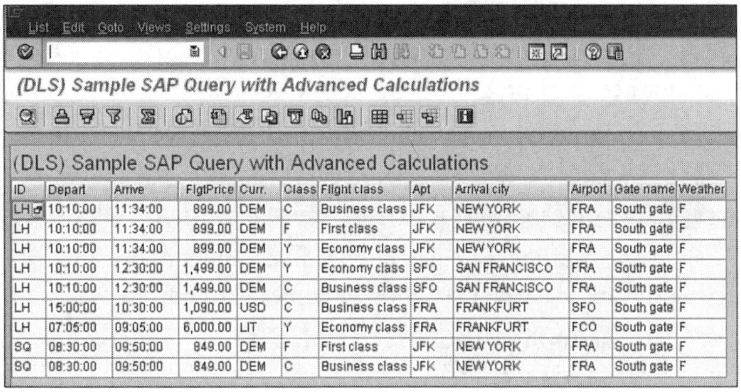

ID	Depart	Arrive	FlgtPrice	Curr.	Class	Flight class	Apt	Arrival city	Airport	Gate name	Weather
LH	10:10:00	11:34:00	899.00	DEM	C	Business class	JFK	NEW YORK	FRA	South gate	F
LH	10:10:00	11:34:00	899.00	DEM	F	First class	JFK	NEW YORK	FRA	South gate	F
LH	10:10:00	11:34:00	899.00	DEM	Y	Economy class	JFK	NEW YORK	FRA	South gate	F
LH	10:10:00	12:30:00	1,499.00	DEM	Y	Economy class	SFO	SAN FRANCISCO	FRA	South gate	F
LH	10:10:00	12:30:00	1,499.00	DEM	C	Business class	SFO	SAN FRANCISCO	FRA	South gate	F
LH	15:00:00	10:30:00	1,090.00	USD	C	Business class	FRA	FRANKFURT	SFO	South gate	F
LH	07:05:00	09:05:00	6,000.00	LIT	Y	Economy class	FRA	FRANKFURT	FCO	South gate	F
SQ	08:30:00	09:50:00	849.00	DEM	F	First class	JFK	NEW YORK	FRA	South gate	F
SQ	08:30:00	09:50:00	849.00	DEM	C	Business class	JFK	NEW YORK	FRA	South gate	F

Figure 10.7
Because an entry of F (fog) was indicated on the selection screen, the query reads the complex logic that says to output South Gate.

10

17. To test what other entries on the selection screen would do to the report output, click the Back Screen button and try various options, including weather conditions not listed, such as W, X, or Y. The SAP Query tool should appropriately read the complex calculation logic and output the otherwise condition, Main Gate.

Be sure to refer to Table 9.3 in Chapter 9 for assistance in properly performing complex calculations.

Helpful Hint
In the preceding example I used the Complex Calculation button to do three fixed conditions and an otherwise condition. Keep in mind that by maximizing the use of the operands AND, NOT, and OR, you can include even more conditions in your complex calculation logic.

USING A CALCULATED FIELD TO UPDATE A VARIANT IN A SCHEDULED SAP QUERY

In Chapter 6, "Using Reporting Selection Screens: Advanced Skills," you learned how to create variants to be saved with reports so that selection screens could be prepopulated with values, requiring no user interaction for report execution. As mentioned throughout this book, you can use a single SAP query report to satisfy multiple reporting needs simply by changing the values entered on the report's selection screen.

Having a variant saved with a report allows you to schedule the report as an SAP job to be run with no user interaction. To do this, you need to follow the steps outlined in any of the calculation examples provided in this chapter and Chapter 9. Then complete the steps outlined in Chapter 6, in the sections "How to Create a Variant for an SAP Query" and "Saving an SAP Query with a Variant."

THINGS TO REMEMBER

- You can perform advanced calculations in the SAP Query tool by using local fields, and you do not need any programming skills to do so.
- You can utilize multiple calculated fields that reference each other.
- You can automatically insert a system value, such as the date, into a report by using a local field, or you can insert it as a dynamic entry on the selection screen.
- You can utilize multiple calculated fields in conjunction with dynamic entry fields on the selection screen to create even more complex calculations.
- You can have up to three hard-set conditions (A, B, or C) plus an otherwise condition when using complex calculations.

CHAPTER **11**

INSERTING PICTURES AND GRAPHICS IN SAP QUERIES

In this chapter

Chapter 9, "Creating Basic Calculated Fields with the SAP Query Tool," discusses how you can create local fields to perform basic calculations without having any special technical training or security access. Chapter 10, "Creating Advanced Calculated Fields with the SAP Query Tool," discusses advanced calculations that also do not require you to have any advanced training. In this chapter, you'll use the skills you learned in the previous chapters to insert pictures and graphics. This chapter explains the calculations you can use to insert black-and-white pictures and color icons into SAP queries. A regular end user can perform these calculations in an SAP query without having any special ABAP training or security provisions.

USING SYMBOLS AND ICONS IN AN SAP QUERY

SAP has several dozen black-and-white pictures and color graphics that you can insert into reports. These symbols and icons are available to be used in any type of reporting, from SAP Query tool reporting to custom ABAP reporting.

Each symbol and icon in SAP has a technical name, which is stored in the SAP database. If you were writing a custom ABAP report, you would need to know these technical names and reference them in your code. For example, to reference the Carrier ID field from the SAP IDES Flight Scheduling test system in a report, you would reference its technical name, CARRID. With symbols and icons in SAP it works the same way, in that you need to reference the technical name of an object to include it in an SAP query report. Figure 11.1 lists the black-and-white symbols that are available in SAP.

CREATING THE BASIC SAP QUERY FOR THE EXAMPLES

For the examples in this chapter, it would be ideal if you could follow along in your own SAP system. To do so, you need to create a basic SAP query, using the instructions outlined in Chapter 3, "Creating Basic Reports with the SAP Query Tool." Your SAP query should contain the fields listed in Table 11.1.

TABLE 11.1   SPECIFICATION OF A SAMPLE SAP REPORT FROM THE IDES SYSTEM

Field Name	Line	Sequence
Airline carrier ID	1	1
Departure time	1	2
Arrival time	1	3
Airfare	1	4
Flight class	1	5
Text:Flight class	1	6
Airport of departure	1	7
Destination airport	1	8
Arrival city	1	9

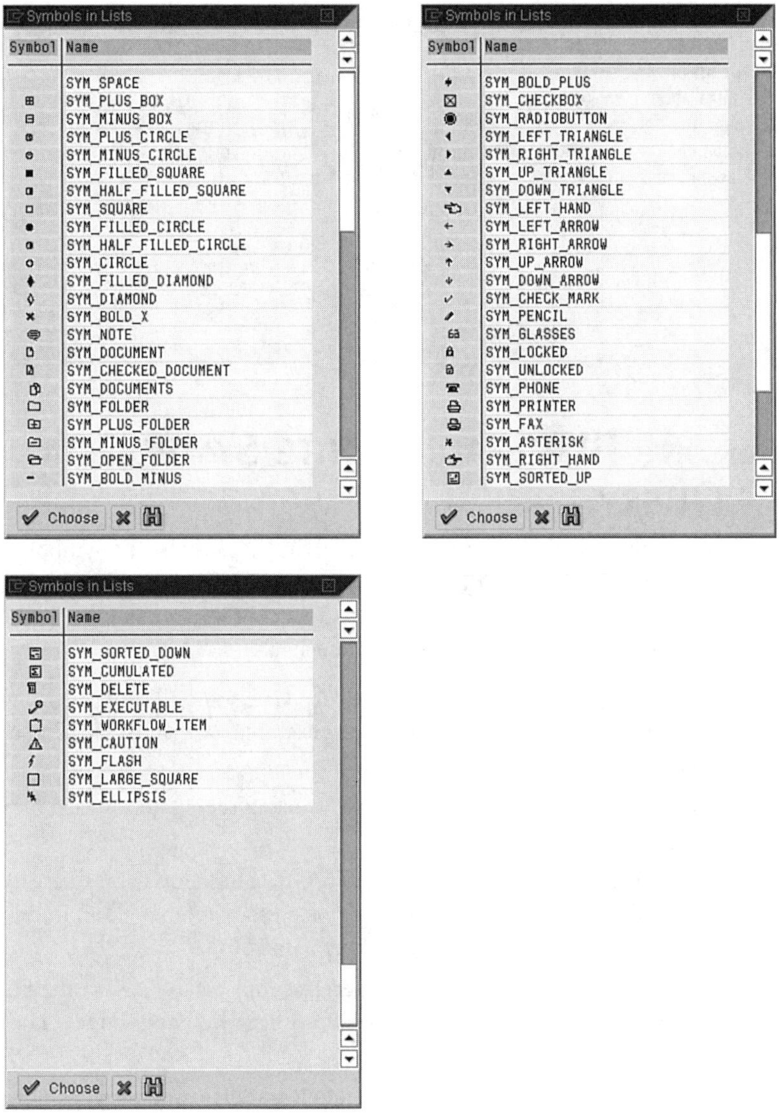

Figure 11.1
Symbols available in
SAP Version 4.6C.

Symbol	Name
	SYM_SPACE
⊞	SYM_PLUS_BOX
⊟	SYM_MINUS_BOX
⊕	SYM_PLUS_CIRCLE
⊖	SYM_MINUS_CIRCLE
■	SYM_FILLED_SQUARE
◪	SYM_HALF_FILLED_SQUARE
□	SYM_SQUARE
●	SYM_FILLED_CIRCLE
◐	SYM_HALF_FILLED_CIRCLE
○	SYM_CIRCLE
◆	SYM_FILLED_DIAMOND
◇	SYM_DIAMOND
✕	SYM_BOLD_X
✏	SYM_NOTE
▫	SYM_DOCUMENT
▣	SYM_CHECKED_DOCUMENT
⊞	SYM_DOCUMENTS
☐	SYM_FOLDER
⊞	SYM_PLUS_FOLDER
⊟	SYM_MINUS_FOLDER
⊟	SYM_OPEN_FOLDER
−	SYM_BOLD_MINUS

Symbol	Name
✦	SYM_BOLD_PLUS
⊠	SYM_CHECKBOX
◉	SYM_RADIOBUTTON
◀	SYM_LEFT_TRIANGLE
▶	SYM_RIGHT_TRIANGLE
▲	SYM_UP_TRIANGLE
▼	SYM_DOWN_TRIANGLE
✋	SYM_LEFT_HAND
←	SYM_LEFT_ARROW
→	SYM_RIGHT_ARROW
↑	SYM_UP_ARROW
↓	SYM_DOWN_ARROW
✓	SYM_CHECK_MARK
✎	SYM_PENCIL
👓	SYM_GLASSES
🔒	SYM_LOCKED
🔓	SYM_UNLOCKED
☎	SYM_PHONE
🖨	SYM_PRINTER
✉	SYM_FAX
✳	SYM_ASTERISK
☞	SYM_RIGHT_HAND
⊞	SYM_SORTED_UP

Symbol	Name
⊟	SYM_SORTED_DOWN
⊠	SYM_CUMULATED
🗑	SYM_DELETE
🔑	SYM_EXECUTABLE
◻	SYM_WORKFLOW_ITEM
△	SYM_CAUTION
⚡	SYM_FLASH
□	SYM_LARGE_SQUARE
⋯	SYM_ELLIPSIS

Figure 11.2 shows an example of the report output of this report.

11

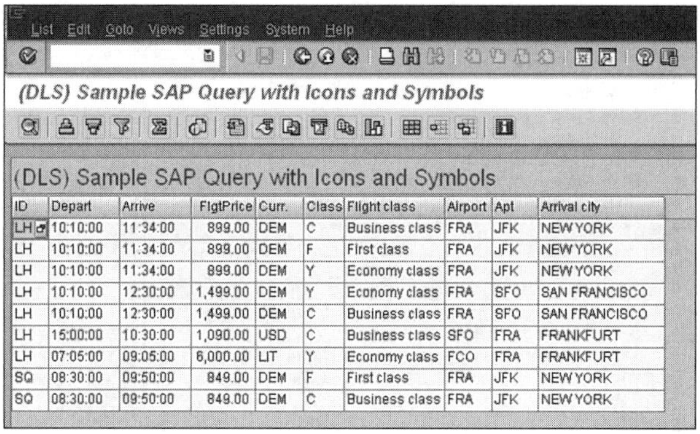

ID	Depart	Arrive	FlgtPrice	Curr.	Class	Flight class	Airport	Apt	Arrival city
LH	10:10:00	11:34:00	899.00	DEM	C	Business class	FRA	JFK	NEW YORK
LH	10:10:00	11:34:00	899.00	DEM	F	First class	FRA	JFK	NEW YORK
LH	10:10:00	11:34:00	899.00	DEM	Y	Economy class	FRA	JFK	NEW YORK
LH	10:10:00	12:30:00	1,499.00	DEM	Y	Economy class	FRA	SFO	SAN FRANCISCO
LH	10:10:00	12:30:00	1,499.00	DEM	C	Business class	FRA	SFO	SAN FRANCISCO
LH	15:00:00	10:30:00	1,090.00	USD	C	Business class	SFO	FRA	FRANKFURT
LH	07:05:00	09:05:00	6,000.00	LIT	Y	Economy class	FCO	FRA	FRANKFURT
SQ	08:30:00	09:50:00	849.00	DEM	F	First class	FRA	JFK	NEW YORK
SQ	08:30:00	09:50:00	849.00	DEM	C	Business class	FRA	JFK	NEW YORK

Figure 11.2
The output in the report depends on your SAP installation, but the column format should be the same as shown here.

INSERTING BLACK-AND-WHITE SYMBOLS IN AN SAP QUERY

There are many instances in which you might want to insert a symbol in a report. The most popular use of symbols is for the insertion of field-relevant pictures. For example, you could easily insert a picture of a telephone next to a column containing telephone numbers. To use local fields to insert a symbol, follow these steps:

1. Navigate to the main screen of the SAP Query tool, using transaction code **SQ01**. Select the query you want to work with (for example, DLS_QUERY_11) and then click the Change button.
2. Navigate to the Select Fields screen by using the white forward Next button on the Application toolbar.
3. Select Edit, Short Names, Switch On/Off. This allows you to create short names for your existing query fields so that you can easily refer to them in calculations. Start by giving the Flight Class field the short name **CLASS**.
4. Select Edit, Local Field, Create. Because your cursor was on the Flight Class field, a custom field is added to its field group (Flight Booking Table). The Field Definition dialog box appears.
5. In the Field Definition dialog box, input a short name for your newly created local field (for example, **SYMBOL**) and input a field description (for example, **Symbol**), which will be the heading for the column in the report.
6. Define the attributes for the field. To output a symbol, select the Symbol option (see Figure 11.3).
7. Click the Symbols button at the bottom of the Field Definition box to bring up a list of symbols and their names (refer to Figure 11.1). Note the name of the symbol you want to use, because you will need to type it in in the next step. For example, you could select SYM_UNLOCKED, a symbol representing an item that is unlocked.

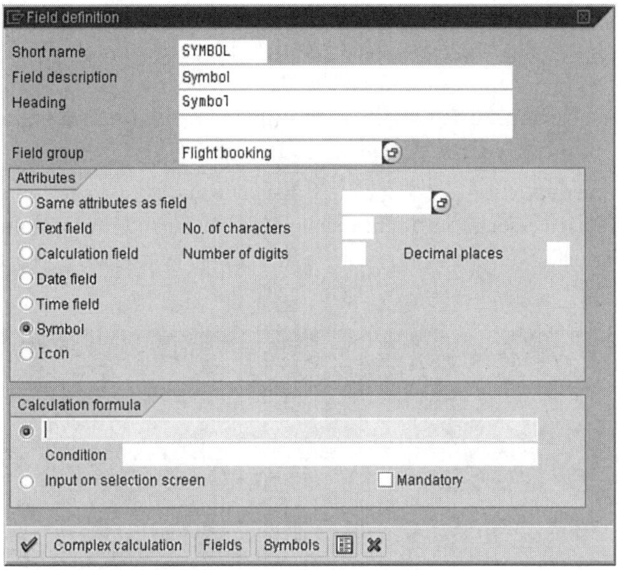

Figure 11.3
When you set the Attributes section to Symbol, SAP formats the field so that a black-and-white picture can be displayed.

8. Although the Symbols in Lists dialog box has a button labeled Choose, you actually have to click the green check mark Choose button to return to the Field Definition dialog box and type your symbol name in the Calculation field (see Figure 11.4). Press Enter to return to the SAP query.

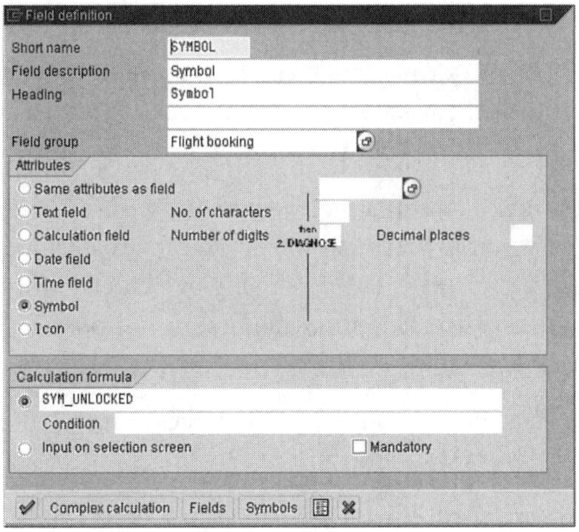

Figure 11.4
The SYM_UNLOCKED symbol typically represents an item that is unlocked.

9. To add the newly created field to your report output, confirm that the field is selected on the Select Field screen. In other words, the small box to the right of the Symbol field at the bottom of the Flight Booking field group should be selected.

11

10. Navigate to the Basic List Line Structure screen by clicking the Basic List button on the Application toolbar. You should see your newly created field listed there. Add the new local field to your report output on the Basic List screen of the SAP Query tool by using the skills you learned in Chapter 3 (indicating a line and sequence number). Click the Save button on your SAP query.

11. Execute your report by clicking the F8 Execute button; you are presented with the SAP query's standard selection screen. Click the F8 Execute button again to see your updated SAP query, which now contains your newly added symbol (see Figure 11.5).

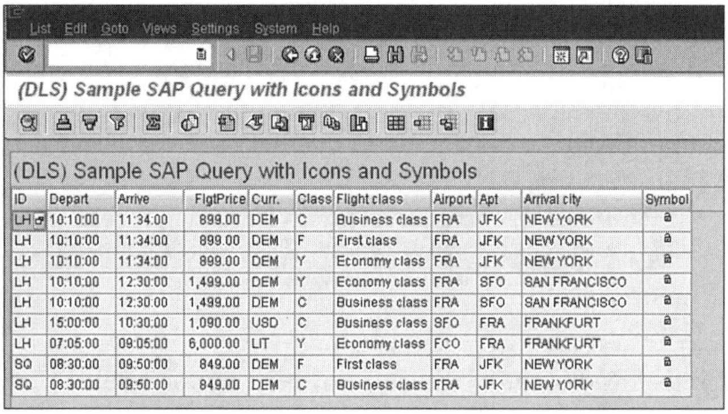

Figure 11.5
The added symbol field appears in the report output in the last column, as indicated on the Basic List Line screen.

INSERTING BLACK-AND-WHITE SYMBOLS IN AN SAP QUERY BY USING A SIMPLE CONDITION

You have inserted a picture in every row, which can be helpful if the picture is representative of all the data in the report. For this next example, however, let's use a condition to determine whether the picture should be output in each row.

In some cases, you might want to output a picture only if a certain condition exists. For an example using the SAP query you just worked with, you can create a local field that contains a symbol that appears if the passenger is listed as flying in first class. Best practice is to include the output of a symbol or icon in either the first or last position of your report data to call attention to that record.

To output a symbol based on a single condition, follow these steps:

1. Navigate to the main screen of the SAP Query tool, using transaction code **SQ01**. Select the query you want to work with (for example, DLS_QUERY_11) and then click the Change button.

2. Navigate to the Select Fields screen by using the white forward Next button on the Application toolbar. If the short names are not already displayed, select Edit, Short Names, Switch On/Off. This allows you to create short names for your existing query

fields so that you can easily refer to them in calculations. Enter the short name **CLASS** for the Flight Class field in the Flight Booking field group.

3. Place your cursor on the field name that you will base your calculated field on (for example, the Flight Class field).

4. Select Edit, Local Field, Create. Because your cursor was on the Flight Class field, a custom field is added to its field group (Flight Booking Table). The Field Definition dialog box appears.

5. In the Field Definition dialog box, input a short name for your newly created local field (for example, **FCLASS**) and input a field description (for example, **First Class Indicator**).

6. Define the attributes for the field. Indicate that the field will be a symbol.

7. Click the Symbols button at the bottom of the Field Definition box to bring up a list of symbols and their names (refer to Figure 11.1). Note the name of the symbol you want to use, because you will need to type it in in the next step. For example, you could select SYM_RIGHT_HAND, a symbol representing a hand pointing to the right.

8. Although the Symbols in Lists dialog box has a button labeled Choose, you actually have to click the green check mark Choose button to return to the Field Definition dialog box and type your symbol name in the Calculation field (see Figure 11.6).

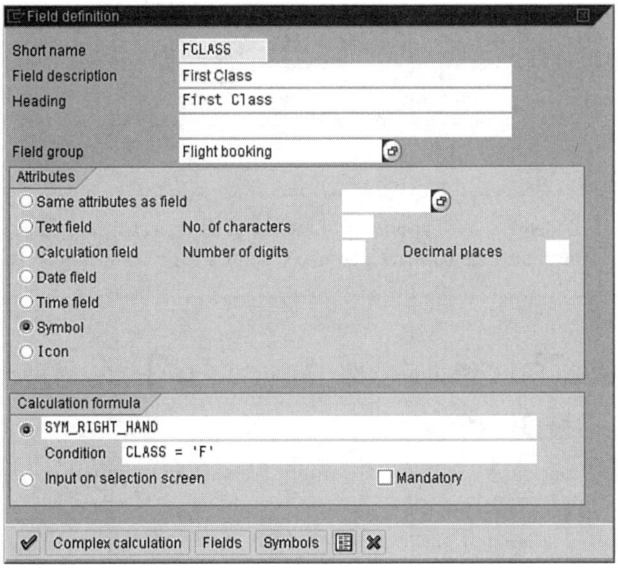

Figure 11.6
You can add a symbol to report based on a condition.

9. At the bottom of the Field Definition dialog, position your cursor in the text box to the right of the radio button labeled Condition, and then type the condition **CLASS = 'F'**. This translates to output the symbol if the class is first class. Press Enter to return to the SAP query.

10. To add the newly created field to your report output, confirm that the field is selected on the Select Field screen. In other words, the small box to the left of the First Class Indicator field at the bottom of the Flight Booking field group should be selected.
11. Navigate to the Basic List Line Structure screen by clicking the Basic List button on the Application toolbar. You should see your newly created field listed there. Add the new local field to your report output on the Basic List screen of the SAP Query tool by using the skills you learned in Chapter 3 (indicating a line and sequence number). Click the Save button on your SAP query.
12. Execute your report by clicking the F8 Execute button; you are presented with the SAP query's standard selection screen. Click the F8 Execute button again to see your updated SAP query, which now contains your new symbol for any line that contains data for a first-class passenger (see Figure 11.7).

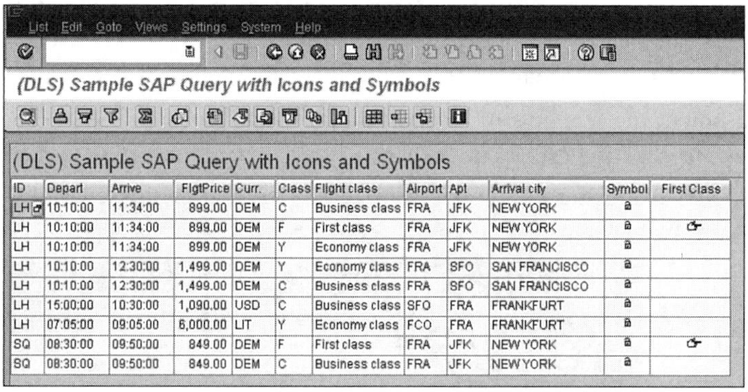

ID	Depart	Arrive	FlgtPrice	Curr.	Class	Flight class	Airport	Apt	Arrival city	Symbol	First Class
LH	10:10:00	11:34:00	899.00	DEM	C	Business class	FRA	JFK	NEW YORK		
LH	10:10:00	11:34:00	899.00	DEM	F	First class	FRA	JFK	NEW YORK		
LH	10:10:00	11:34:00	899.00	DEM	Y	Economy class	FRA	JFK	NEW YORK		
LH	10:10:00	12:30:00	1,499.00	DEM	Y	Economy class	FRA	SFO	SAN FRANCISCO		
LH	10:10:00	12:30:00	1,499.00	DEM	C	Business class	FRA	SFO	SAN FRANCISCO		
LH	15:00:00	10:30:00	1,090.00	USD	C	Business class	SFO	FRA	FRANKFURT		
LH	07:05:00	09:05:00	6,000.00	LIT	Y	Economy class	FCO	FRA	FRANKFURT		
SQ	08:30:00	09:50:00	849.00	DEM	F	First class	FRA	JFK	NEW YORK		
SQ	08:30:00	09:50:00	849.00	DEM	C	Business class	FRA	JFK	NEW YORK		

Figure 11.7
The newly added column contains a symbol for any record that meets the indicated condition.

NOTE

Depending on your printer settings, symbols may appear slightly different in the printed document than onscreen. Symbols do not transfer to Microsoft applications.

INSERTING A COLOR ICON IN AN SAP QUERY BY USING A SIMPLE CONDITION

There are many instances in which you might want to insert a color icon in a query report. The most popular use of icons is to identify certain records to make them stand out in electronic and printed reports. For example, you could easily insert a warning icon to indicate a line item in a report that requires special attention.

In this next example, you will insert an icon of a small car for any flight arriving in New York to indicate that those flights require shuttle transfers (via car) from the plane. To use local fields to insert an icon based on a single condition, follow these steps:

1. Navigate to the main screen of the SAP Query tool, using transaction code **SQ01**. Select the query you want to work with (for example, DLS_QUERY_11) and then click the Change button.

2. Navigate to the Select Fields screen by using the white forward Next button on the Application toolbar. If the short names are not already displayed, select Edit, Short Names, Switch On/Off. This allows you to create short names for your existing query fields so that you can easily refer to them in calculations. Enter the short name **ACITY** for the Arrival City field in the Flight Schedule field group.

3. Click the field name that you will base your calculated field on (for example, the ACITY field).

4. Select Edit, Local Field, Create. Because your cursor was on the Arrival City field, a custom field is added to its field group (Flight Schedule). The Field Definition dialog box appears.

5. In the Field Definition dialog box, input a short name for your newly created local field (for example, **SHUTTLE**) and input a field description (for example, **Shuttle**).

6. Define the attributes for the field. Indicate that the field will be an icon.

7. Click the Icons button at the bottom right of the Field Definition dialog box to bring up a list of icons and their names (see Figure 11.8). Use your cursor to select the name of the symbol you want to use. For example, you could select ICON_CAR, an icon representing a small car. Then click the Choose button. The Field Definition dialog box appears, with the icon name in the Calculation field (see Figure 11.9).

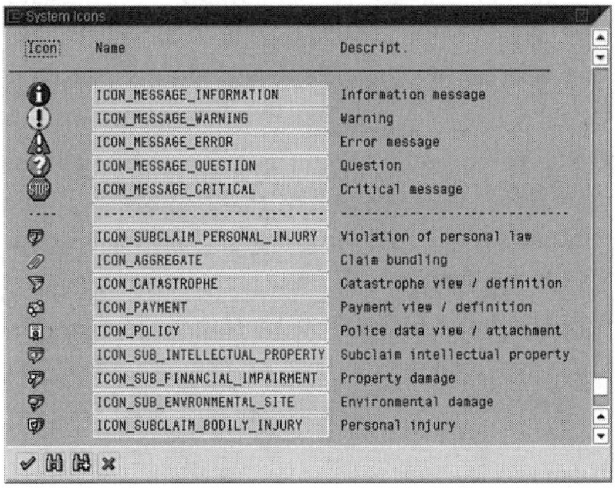

11

Figure 11.8
Icons, unlike symbols, are in color and are often larger.

Figure 11.9
As with a symbol, the addition of an icon to a report can be based on a condition.

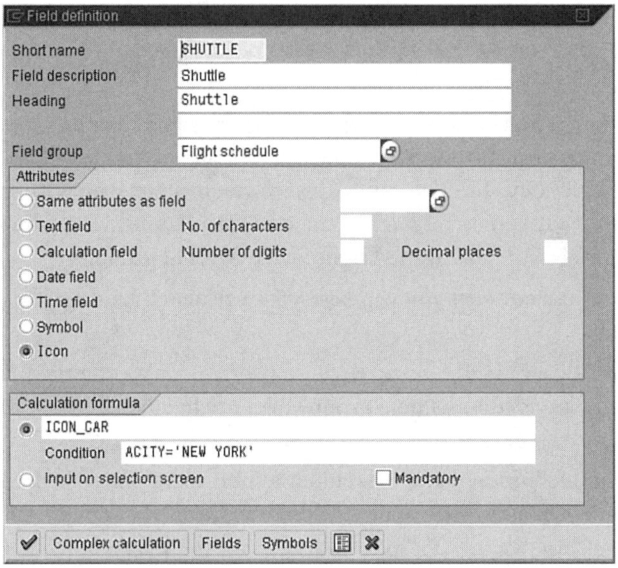

8. At the bottom of the Field Definition dialog, position your cursor in the text box to the right of the radio button labeled Condition and then type the condition `ACITY = 'NEW YORK'`. This translates to output the icon if the arrival city is New York. Press Enter to return to the SAP query.

9. To add the newly created field to your report output, confirm that the field is selected on the Select Field screen. In other words, the small box to the left of the Shuttle field at the bottom of the Flight Schedule field group should be selected.

10. Navigate to the Basic List Line Structure screen by clicking the Basic List button on the Application toolbar. You should see your newly created field listed there. Add the new local field to your report output on the Basic List screen of the SAP Query tool by using the skills you learned in Chapter 3 (indicating a line and sequence number). Click the Save button on your SAP query.

11. Execute your report by clicking the F8 Execute button; you are presented with the SAP query's standard selection screen. Click the F8 Execute button again to see your updated SAP query, which now contains your newly added symbol (see Figure 11.10).

NOTE

A color icon appears in an SAP List View (ALV) or in an ABAP list. Depending on your printer settings, icons may appear slightly different in a printed document than onscreen. Icons do not transfer to Microsoft applications.

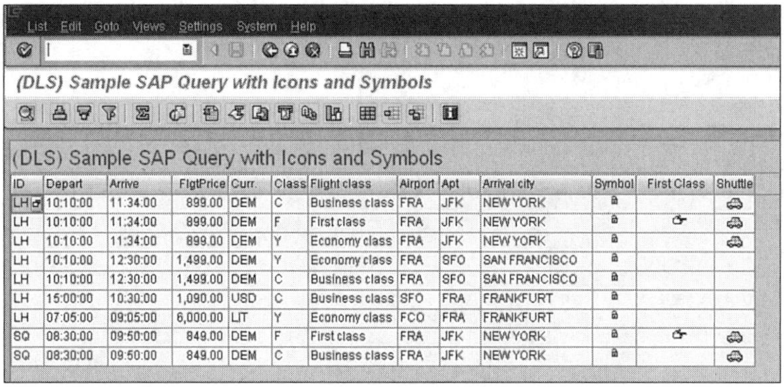

ID	Depart	Arrive	FlgtPrice	Curr.	Class	Flight class	Airport	Apt	Arrival city	Symbol	First Class	Shuttle
LH	10:10:00	11:34:00	899.00	DEM	C	Business class	FRA	JFK	NEW YORK			
LH	10:10:00	11:34:00	899.00	DEM	F	First class	FRA	JFK	NEW YORK			
LH	10:10:00	11:34:00	899.00	DEM	Y	Economy class	FRA	JFK	NEW YORK			
LH	10:10:00	12:30:00	1,499.00	DEM	Y	Economy class	FRA	SFO	SAN FRANCISCO			
LH	10:10:00	12:30:00	1,499.00	DEM	C	Business class	FRA	SFO	SAN FRANCISCO			
LH	15:00:00	10:30:00	1,090.00	USD	C	Business class	SFO	FRA	FRANKFURT			
LH	07:05:00	09:05:00	6,000.00	LIT	Y	Economy class	FCO	FRA	FRANKFURT			
SQ	08:30:00	09:50:00	849.00	DEM	F	First class	FRA	JFK	NEW YORK			
SQ	08:30:00	09:50:00	849.00	DEM	C	Business class	FRA	JFK	NEW YORK			

Figure 11.10
The newly added column contains an icon of a car for any record that meets the indicated condition.

INSERTING A COLOR ICON IN AN SAP QUERY USING MULTIPLE CONDITIONS WITH TWO OPERATORS

As discussed in Chapter 10, you can use a calculated field to evaluate multiple conditions to produce output.

To use local fields to perform complex calculations, follow these steps:

1. Navigate to the main screen of the SAP Query tool, using transaction code **SQ01**. Select the query you want to work with (for example, DLS_QUERY_11) and then click the Change button.
2. Navigate to the Select Fields screen by using the white forward Next button on the Application toolbar.
3. Select Edit, Short Names, Switch On/Off. Start by giving the Airfare field the short name **FARE**.
4. Select Edit, Local Field, Create. Because your cursor was on the Airfare field, a custom field is added to its field group (Flight Demo). The Field Definition dialog box appears.
5. In the Field Definition dialog box, input a short name for your newly created local field (for example, **POINT**) and input a field description (for example, **Price point**), which will be the heading for the column in the report.
6. Define the attributes for the field. To output an icon, select the Icon option.
7. Click the Complex Calculation button to bring up the Define Field: Complex Calculation dialog box, which allows you to input multiple conditions. You input the conditions, as shown in Figure 11.11, very similarly to the way you enter them for a basic calculation; however, in this case, you enter more than one condition.
8. Type a condition in the Condition line (for example, **FARE < 1000**) and type the desired output if the condition is met in the Formula line (for example, **ICON_INCOMING_OBJECT**).
9. Proceed to the next Condition line and insert your second condition, using multiple operators (for example, **FARE > 1000 AND FARE < 5000**) and type the desired output if the condition is met in the Formula line (for example, **ICON_OUTGOING_OBJECT**).

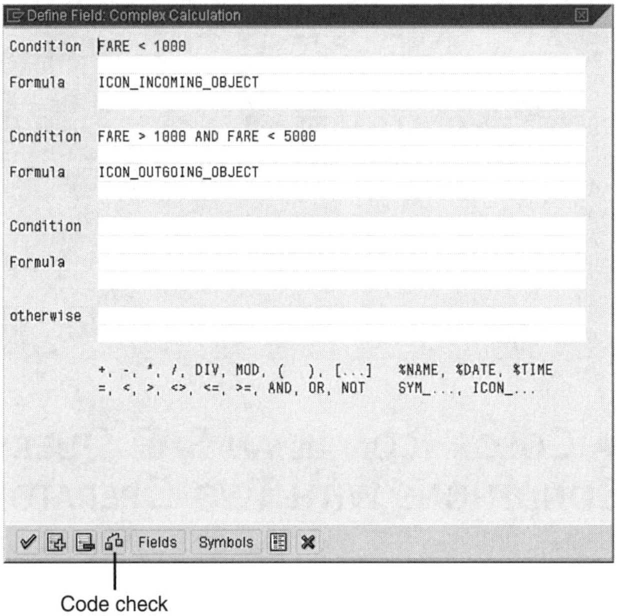

Figure 11.11
The Define Field:
Complex Calculation
dialog box lets you
enter three condi-
tions, although you
are not required to
use them all.

```
 Define Field: Complex Calculation                                  ⊠

Condition   FARE < 1000

Formula     ICON_INCOMING_OBJECT


Condition   FARE > 1000 AND FARE < 5000

Formula     ICON_OUTGOING_OBJECT


Condition


Formula


otherwise



        +, -, *, /, DIV, MOD, (   ), [...]   %NAME, %DATE, %TIME
        =, <, >, <>, <=, >=, AND, OR, NOT     SYM_..., ICON_...




    ✓ ▣ ▣ ᵍᵃ  Fields   Symbols  ▦ ✖
```

Code check

10. To check that you have typed correctly, click the Code Check button, shown in Figure 11.11 (or press Shift+F4). Code Check then checks your syntax to ensure that there are no typos.

11. Click the green check mark Enter button on the Field Attributes dialog box to return to the SAP query.

12. To add the newly created field to your report output, confirm that the field is selected on the Select Field screen. In other words, the small box to the left of the Price Point field at the bottom of the Flight Demo field group should be selected.

13. Navigate to the Basic List Line Structure screen by clicking the Basic List button on the Application toolbar. You should see your newly created field listed there. Add the new local field to your report output on the Basic List screen of the SAP Query tool by using the skills you learned in Chapter 3 (indicating a line and sequence number). Click the Save button on your SAP query.

14. Execute your report by clicking the F8 Execute button; you are presented with the SAP query's standard selection screen. Click the F8 Execute button again to see your updated SAP query, which now contains your newly added symbol (see Figure 11.12).

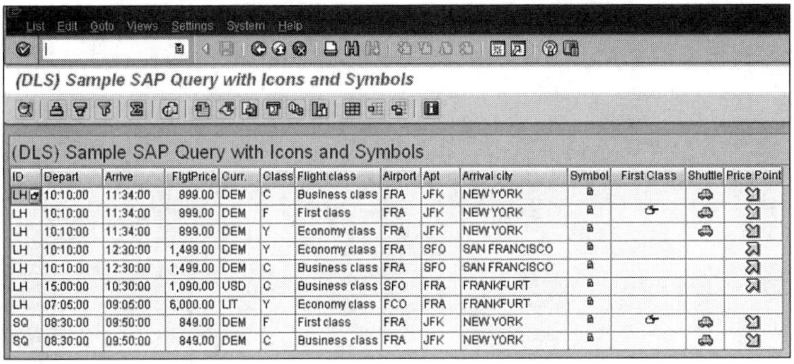

List Edit Goto Views Settings System Help

(DLS) Sample SAP Query with Icons and Symbols

(DLS) Sample SAP Query with Icons and Symbols

ID	Depart	Arrive	FlgtPrice	Curr.	Class	Flight class	Airport	Apt	Arrival city	Symbol	First Class	Shuttle	Price Point
LH	10:10:00	11:34:00	899.00	DEM	C	Business class	FRA	JFK	NEW YORK				
LH	10:10:00	11:34:00	899.00	DEM	F	First class	FRA	JFK	NEW YORK				
LH	10:10:00	11:34:00	899.00	DEM	Y	Economy class	FRA	JFK	NEW YORK				
LH	10:10:00	12:30:00	1,499.00	DEM	Y	Economy class	FRA	SFO	SAN FRANCISCO				
LH	10:10:00	12:30:00	1,499.00	DEM	C	Business class	FRA	SFO	SAN FRANCISCO				
LH	15:00:00	10:30:00	1,090.00	USD	C	Business class	SFO	FRA	FRANKFURT				
LH	07:05:00	09:05:00	6,000.00	LIT	Y	Economy class	FCO	FRA	FRANKFURT				
SQ	08:30:00	09:50:00	849.00	DEM	F	First class	FRA	JFK	NEW YORK				
SQ	08:30:00	09:50:00	849.00	DEM	C	Business class	FRA	JFK	NEW YORK				

Figure 11.12
The added icon appears as a down-pointing arrow for rows where the airfare is less than 1,000 and as an up-pointing arrow for those over 1,000 but under 5,000.

THINGS TO REMEMBER

- You can use black-and-white symbols for basic or advanced calculations.
- You can use color icons for basic or advanced calculations.
- A symbol or icon will appear in an SAP List View (ALV) or ABAP List SAP query report but will not carry over to Microsoft applications.
- The manner in which a symbol or icon appears on a printed report varies based on the printer.
- SAP offers several dozen symbols to choose from.
- SAP offers several hundred icons to choose from.
- In using symbols and icons when certain conditions are met, best practice is to output them in the first or last column of a report so that they call attention to that line in the report.

CHAPTER **12**

CREATING SIMPLE STATISTICS LISTS WITH THE SAP QUERY TOOL

In this chapter

Earlier chapters described how to maximize the use of the SAP Query tool to create basic lists (that is, simple column-based lists). This chapter discusses simple statistics lists.

You can create three types of reports by using the SAP Query tool: basic lists, statistics lists, and ranked lists. The most common type of SAP report is a basic list report. The data displayed in a basic list report has not been auto-summarized to display summary detail only. Generally speaking, the data is displayed as it appears in the R/3 database. In contrast to basic lists, the data in statistics and ranked lists is output in a compressed, summarized format.

You can create basic list query-based reports by using the steps covered in earlier chapters. When creating statistics list or ranked list reports, the main difference is that instead of selecting the Basic List button to proceed to the Basic List Line Structure screen, you select either the Statistics button or the Ranked List button on the Application toolbar (see Figure 12.1).

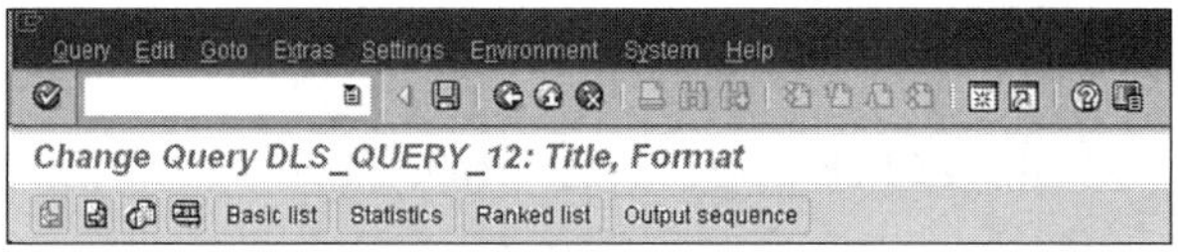

Figure 12.1
You navigate to the appropriate query screen by clicking the correct button on the Application toolbar.

STATISTICS LISTS IN THE SAP QUERY TOOL

Statistics lists allow you to produce summary analyses of data, including totals and averages. Statistics lists are similar to pivot tables in Microsoft Excel. To give you a better understanding of what a statistics list is all about, Table 12.1 shows an example of a basic list report from the HCM module that contains a report of some of the associates in the Mama Tricarico's company, used in earlier examples. This chapter compares this basic list to a statistics list to show the difference between the two.

TABLE 12.1   DAY SHIFT ASSOCIATES OF MAMA TRICARICO'S IN SAP HR MODULE IN BASIC REPORT LIST

Last Name	First Name	Employee Group	Employee Group Text	Position Title	Hourly Rate	Shift	Personnel Area
Beato	Nicholas	1	Active	Menu Designer	$8.50	1	3640
Lariosa	Michael	1	Active	Chef	$14.50	1	3011
Layden	Stephanie	2	Leave	Waitress	$4.25	1	3640
Whalen	Kristen	1	Active	Hostess	$6.50	2	3866
Kaupp	Nicole	1	Active	Waitress	$5.65	1	3640

Last Name	First Name	Employee Group	Employee Group Text	Position Title	Hourly Rate	Shift	Personnel Area
Hanna	Sherin	2	Leave	Pot Washer	$5.00	1	3640
Pearce	Brad	1	Active	Waitress	$5.65	1	3640
Brunsman	Kelly	1	Active	Waiter	$4.25	2	3591
Lewis	Nicolle	1	Leave	Chef	$16.50	2	3841
Whalen	Kylie	3	Terminated	Waitress	$4.25	2	3011
Count	= 10			Total	$75.05		

Using this report as an example, you can create a statistics list that summarizes the information. For example, you can create a statistics list that shows the average hourly rate for each personnel area (see Table 12.2).

TABLE 12.2 STATISTICS LIST EXAMPLE

Personnel Area	Count	Average Rate
3011	2	$9.38
3591	1	$4.25
3640	4	$4.68
3841	1	$16.50
3866	1	$6.50

CREATING A STATISTICS LIST WITH THE SAP QUERY TOOL

As discussed in Chapter 3, "Creating Basic Reports with the SAP Query Tool," creating basic lists with the SAP Query tool involves five basic screens. To create a statistics list, you follow the same steps, except that instead of clicking the Basic List button on the Selections screen, you click the Statistics button instead to bring up the Statistics Structure screen instead of the Basic List Structure screen.

To create a statistics list report by using the SAP Query tool, follow these steps:

1. Navigate to the Maintain Queries Initial screen by using transaction code /nSQ01.
2. Ensure that you are in the standard query area by selecting Environment, Query Areas and then choosing Standard Area (Client-Specific).
3. In the Query field, enter a name for the query you are creating (for example, *DLS*_Exercise_12, where *DLS* is your initials) and then click the Create button.

4. When the InfoSets of User Group ZTEST window appears, listing all the available InfoSets (that is, data sources) for your query group, select the ZTEST InfoSet and then press Enter. The Create Query Title Format screen appears, allowing you to save the basic formatting specifications for your query, including the name (title) and any notes you want to store for the query. The only required field is Title. Click the Save button on the toolbar.

5. Click the Next Screen button on the Application toolbar to navigate to the Select Field Group screen.

6. When the Select Field Group screen appears, listing all the field groups available in your InfoSet, place a check mark next to each field group whose fields you want to include in your report. (In my example, I selected all of them.) Click the Next Screen button on the Application toolbar.

7. When the Select Fields screen appears, giving you a list of all the available fields within the selected field groups, place a check mark next to each field that you want to include in your report. You can use the Page Up and Page Down buttons to navigate between all the fields. For this example, include the following fields:

    ■ Airline Carrier ID

    ■ Arrival City

    ■ Airfare

    ■ Text: Flight Class

8. Click the Next Screen button on the Application toolbar to continue. The Selections screen appears, listing all the fields you selected on the Select Fields screen, giving you the opportunity to add fields to your report's selection screen.

9. Add to your report's selection screen any fields you want by placing a check mark next to each field.

10. Click the Statistics button on the Application toolbar to create a statistics list in the SAP Query tool. The Statistics Line Structure screen appears, giving you an opportunity to define your compressed list report (see Figure 12.2).

11. Use the Statistics Line Structure screen to dictate how you want your report to appear, including sequence and summing specifications. You determine the statistics in this series of screens. Each statistic must have its own unique title, because you might generate several statistics. The details of the options for this screen are listed in the following section.

12

Figure 12.2
When creating statis-
tics lists, you use the
Statistics Line
Structure screen to
define the layout.

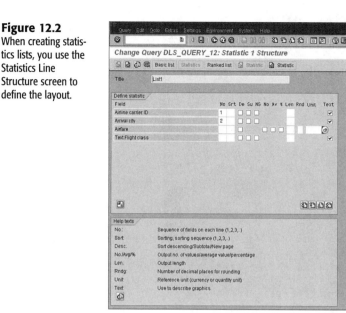

12. Specify the sequence in which you want to output the fields, and state whether you want them to be sorted in ascending or descending order, using Figure 12.3 as a reference. Totals are always calculated for numeric fields. You can therefore determine average values, the number of selected records, and the percentage share.

13. Press F8 to execute the report. As with almost all other reports in SAP, upon execution, you see the report's selection screen. The selection screen gives you an opportunity to specify any criteria for the output of your report. Notice that any fields indicated on the Selections screen are included on your selection screen, under the heading Program Selections.

14. Click the F8 Execute button on the Application toolbar to display your finished report. Your report output should look similar to that in Figure 12.4, but keep in mind that the actual values vary by organization.

12

Helpful Hint
You can use the Next Statistic button to create an additional statistic for the same query. You can define up to nine statistics for each query.

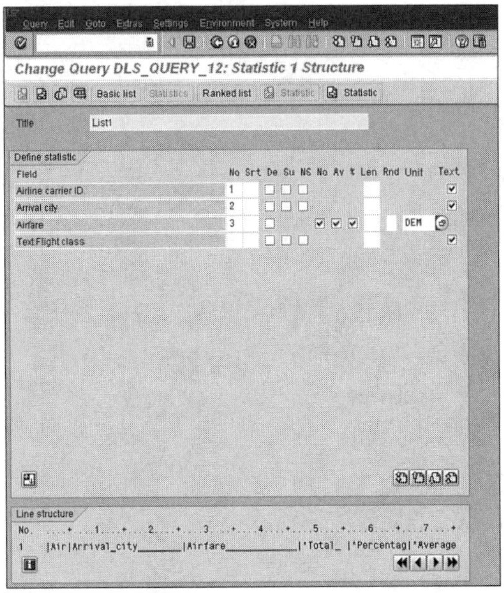

Figure 12.3
After you create a statistics list, the toolbar has a Next Statistic button that allows you to create multiple statistics.

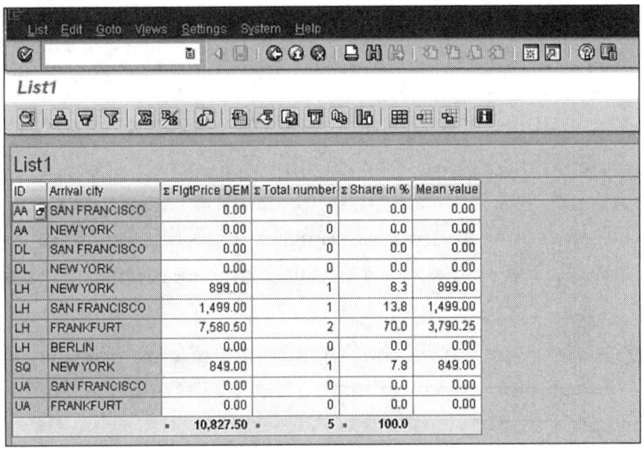

List1

ID	Arrival city	Σ FlgtPrice DEM	Σ Total number	Σ Share in %	Mean value
AA	SAN FRANCISCO	0.00	0	0.0	0.00
AA	NEW YORK	0.00	0	0.0	0.00
DL	SAN FRANCISCO	0.00	0	0.0	0.00
DL	NEW YORK	0.00	0	0.0	0.00
LH	NEW YORK	899.00	1	8.3	899.00
LH	SAN FRANCISCO	1,499.00	1	13.8	1,499.00
LH	FRANKFURT	7,580.50	2	70.0	3,790.25
LH	BERLIN	0.00	0	0.0	0.00
SQ	NEW YORK	849.00	1	7.8	849.00
UA	SAN FRANCISCO	0.00	0	0.0	0.00
UA	FRANKFURT	0.00	0	0.0	0.00
		• 10,827.50	• 5	• 100.0	

Figure 12.4
If you are using currency conversions, after the statistics, you see an overview that states which currency conversions were performed, as well as the date and exchange rate on which the conversions were based.

12

DETAILS OF THE OPTIONS AVAILABLE ON THE STATISTICS STRUCTURE SCREEN

The following sections describe the options that are available on the Statistics Line Structure screen (refer to Figure 12.2) of the SAP Query tool.

TITLE

This entry field allows you to enter a name for your first list. This title is used as the list header.

FIELD

All fields selected during the report creation process are listed here.

No (Sequence Number)

This column defines the sequence of fields within a statistic. You can assign sequence numbers between 1 and 98. When you define a statistic, the data is usually summarized (that is, several data records are processed to determine one line). With numeric fields, only the total is output.

NOTE

Statistics that do not contain numeric fields do not make sense, because there is no data summarization.

No (Sequence)

This column defines the sort sequence in the statistic. You assign a sequence number for sorting to every field on which you want to sort. The highest sort criterion must have the lowest sequence number, the next sort criterion a higher sequence number, and so on. It makes sense to assign the sequence numbers starting with 1 and in ascending order, without breaks (that is, the highest sort criterion should receive number 1), but this is not required.

De (Descending)

You can select this check box to sort the field in descending order.

Su (Subtotal)

If you select this field, ABAP/4 Query generates subtotals for the sort criterion in the statistic. (That is, whenever the sort criterion changes, a line containing the relevant subtotals is output.) If you want to calculate subtotals for a field (sort criterion) in a statistic, you should be aware of three conditions:

- You can only use sort fields.
- You must already have defined a sort for fields in the statistic, and the sort sequence must be in ascending order.
- The sort numbers of any fields following a field defined for sorting cannot be smaller than the sort number of the field itself.

Thus, if you want to generate a subtotal for the third field (Sequence Number 3), you must sort by this field and by both preceding fields. Because the sort sequence must also be in ascending order, the first field must have the sort number 1, the second field the sort number 2, and the third field the sort number 3. For example, you cannot calculate subtotals if the first field (Sequence Number 1) of a statistic has the sort number 2 and one of the following fields has the sort number 1. In that case, no subtotals can be calculated for any of the fields—not even the first.

12

NS (PAGE BREAK)

When you select this field, page breaks are inserted in your statistic for each sort string; that is, each time the sort string changes, a new page is displayed. To use this page break function for a particular field, three conditions must be met:

- Page breaks can only be generated for sort fields.
- Page breaks can only be created for a field if its preceding fields in the statistic are also sort fields and the sort order of these fields is ascending.
- No sort fields with sort numbers smaller than the sort number of the field in question may follow a field for which page breaks have been set.

For example, if you want to insert page breaks for Field Number 3 (Position 3 in the sort sequence), this field and both of the fields preceding it must be sort fields (that is, the system must sort according to them). Because the sort order must be ascending, the first field must have sort number 1, the second field sort number 2, and the third field sort number 3. In the example described in this chapter, you may not display with page breaks. If the first field contained in the statistic (Sequence Number 1) has sort number 2 and one of its subsequent fields has been assigned sort number 1, page breaks may not be displayed for any of these fields—not even for the first one.

No (DISPLAY)

This field is for retrieval of information about processed data records. This field appears only for fields in the database that are tied to numbers (for example, Currency is tied to a currency code such as USD. 1).

Suppose you want to create a country sales statistic, and you choose the fields Country UD and Sales. If you want to see the total sales for each country, you simply select the column Display for the field Sales.

Av (AVERAGE)

If you select this field, an average value is calculated for the field entered on the left for the individual summands.

% (PERCENTAGE)

If you select this field, the percentage of the field of the sum total is output.

LEN (LENGTH)

When you select this check box, the field is output in the list with its standard output length. You can alter the field width (length) in this field to improve the layout of a list.

RND (ROUNDING FACTOR)

You use this field to specify the number of decimal places to be used when rounding. For example, if you specify 3, the resulting amounts have three places before the decimal point (that is, round to the nearest thousand).

INIT (UNIT OF MEASUREMENT)

This field appears for any field tied to a unit of measurement (for example, currency, weight).

TEXT

If you select this field, the values of the field specified on the left are used to generate the text for SAP Business Graphics. If you select several fields, their values are used in the sequence in which they occur. SAP Business Graphics processes up to 30 characters of text per value.

CREATING A SUBTOTALED STATISTICS LIST WITH THE SAP QUERY TOOL

To create a subtotaled statistics list report with the SAP Query tool, follow these steps:

1. Navigate to the Maintain Queries Initial screen by using transaction code /nSQ01.

2. In the Query field, enter a name for the query you are creating (for example, *DLS_Exercise_12B*, where *DLS* is your initials) and then click the Create button.

3. When the InfoSets of User Group ZTEST window appears, listing all the available InfoSets (that is, data sources) for your query group, select the ZTEST InfoSet and then press Enter. The Create Query Title Format screen appears. Enter a title and then click the Save button on the toolbar.

4. To navigate to the next screen in the SAP query creation process, click the Next Screen (white navigational arrow) button on the Application toolbar. The Select Field Groups screen appears, listing all the field groups available within the InfoSet. Place a check mark next to each field group from which you want to include fields in your report (I selected them all). Click the Next Screen button on the Application toolbar.

5. When the Select Fields screen appears, listing all the available fields within the selected field groups, place a check mark next to each field that you want to include in your report. You can use the Page Up and Page Down arrows to navigate between all the fields. For this example, include the following fields:
   - Airline Carrier ID
   - Arrival City
   - Airfare
   - Text: Flight Class

6. Click the Next Screen button on the application toolbar to continue.

7. When the Selections screen appears, listing all the fields you selected on the Select Fields screen, add any of the fields to the selection screen that will be presented when you execute your report. You can add any fields you want to the selection screen by placing a check mark next to each field. For this example I have not added any.

8. Click the Statistics button on the application toolbar to create a statistics list in the SAP Query tool.

9. When the Statistics Line Structure screen appears, define your compressed list report, as shown in Figure 12.5. Specify the sequence in which you want to output the fields, and state whether you want them to be sorted in ascending or descending order. Indicate the Text option for each of the fields. Indicate a subtotal for the Airline Carrier ID field (refer to Figure 12.5).

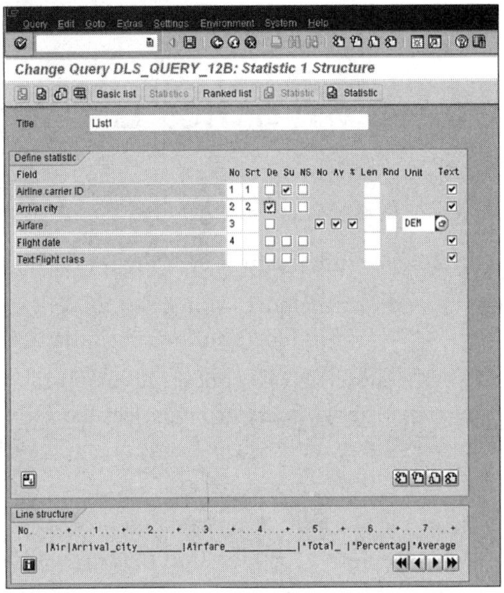

Figure 12.5
By activating the Su checkbox on the Statistics Line Structure screen, you can display the subtotals row as well as displaying the total.

10. Press the F8 button on your keyboard to execute the report. As with almost all other reports in SAP, upon execution, you are presented with the report's selection screen.

11. Click the F8 Execute button on the Application toolbar to display your finished report. Your report output should appear similar to that shown in Figure 12.6, but keep in mind that the actual values vary by organization.

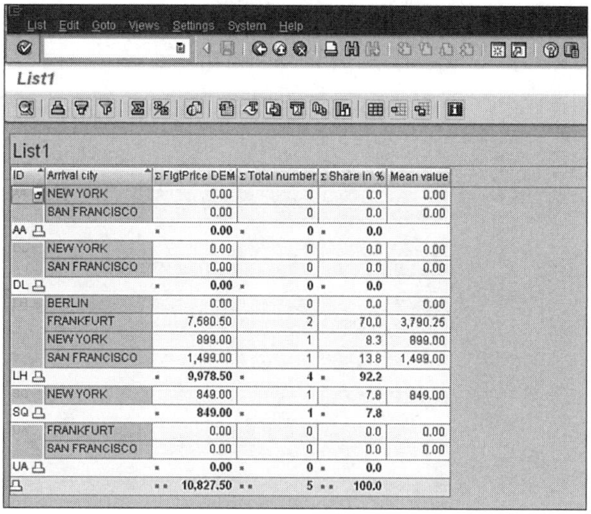

ID	Arrival city	Σ FlgtPrice DEM	Σ Total number	Σ Share in %	Mean value
	NEW YORK	0.00	0	0.0	0.00
	SAN FRANCISCO	0.00	0	0.0	0.00
AA		0.00	0	0.0	
	NEW YORK	0.00	0	0.0	0.00
	SAN FRANCISCO	0.00	0	0.0	0.00
DL		0.00	0	0.0	
	BERLIN	0.00	0	0.0	0.00
	FRANKFURT	7,580.50	2	70.0	3,790.25
	NEW YORK	899.00	1	8.3	899.00
	SAN FRANCISCO	1,499.00	1	13.8	1,499.00
LH		9,978.50	4	92.2	
	NEW YORK	849.00	1	7.8	849.00
SQ		849.00	1	7.8	
	FRANKFURT	0.00	0	0.0	0.00
	SAN FRANCISCO	0.00	0	0.0	0.00
UA		0.00	0	0.0	
		10,827.50	5	100.0	

Figure 12.6
If you are using currency conversions, after the statistics, you see an overview that states which currency conversions were performed, as well as the date and exchange rate on which the conversions were based.

THINGS TO REMEMBER

- You can use the SAP Query tool to create three types of reports: basic lists, statistics lists, and ranked lists.
- Statistics lists allow you to show summarized data in a format that is not possible with basic lists.
- Totals are always calculated for numeric fields. You can therefore determine average values, the number of selected records, and the percentage share.
- By activating the Su check box on the Statistics Line Structure screen, you can display the subtotals row as well as the total.
- If your report output includes currency conversions, after the statistics is an overview that states which currency conversions were performed, as well as the date and exchange rate on which the conversions were based.

CHAPTER 13

CREATING ADVANCED STATISTICS LISTS WITH THE SAP QUERY TOOL

In this chapter

Chapter 12, "Creating Simple Statistics Lists with the SAP Query Tool," covers how to create very basic statistical lists by using the SAP Query tool. This chapter takes that information to the next level, explaining how to create advanced statistical lists, which combine the functionality of calculated fields and statistical lists. If you are not comfortable with creating a basic list or a basic statistical list, you should practice the skills described in earlier chapters before proceeding.

Very often in report writing, it is most meaningful to view summarized data to make business decisions. This chapter uses the SAP IDES flight scheduling system as an example. Line item details, such as a basic list report displaying a list of scheduled flights for each day, are helpful for planning and being prepared for the day's schedule. However, sometimes it is helpful to analyze the average number of flights by each day of the week or to look at how many flights one airline had in each month of the year compared to another airline. Advanced statistics are ideal for this type of summarized data.

The following sections show the syntax to use within calculated fields and also show how you can use calculated fields in conjunction with statistics to provide a summarized statistics report. You will begin by creating a basic list report (as discussed in Chapter 3, "Creating Basic Reports with the SAP Query Tool"). This report will serve as detail data and will be used for reference only. Next, you will create an advanced statistics report that summarizes the detail data in four quarterly views, using calculated fields plus statistics.

CREATING A BASIC LIST FOR REFERENCE BY USING THE SAP QUERY TOOL

To create a basic list report by using the SAP Query tool, you follow these steps:

1. Navigate to the Maintain Queries Initial screen by using transaction code /nSQ01.

2. Ensure that you are in the standard query area by selecting Environment, Query Areas and then choosing Standard Area (Client-Specific).

3. In the Query field, enter **DLS_Exercise_13** (where *DLS* is your initials) as the name for the query you are creating, and then click the Create button.

4. When the InfoSets of User Group ZTEST window appears, listing all the available InfoSets (that is, data sources) for your Query Group, select the ZTEST InfoSet and then click Enter. The Create Query Title Format screen appears, allowing you to save the basic formatting specifications for your query, including the name (title) and any notes you want to store for the query. The only required field is Title (for example, Sample Advanced Statistics Report). Click the Save button on the toolbar.

5. To navigate to the Select Field Groups screen, click the Next Screen button on the Application toolbar.

6. When the Select Field Groups screen appears, listing all the field groups available in your InfoSet, place a check mark next to each field group whose fields you want to include in your report. (In my example, I selected all three.) Click the Next Screen button on the Application toolbar.

7. When the Select Fields screen appears, giving you a list of all the available fields within the selected field groups, place a check mark next to each field that you want to include in your report. You can use the Page Up and Page Down buttons to navigate between all the fields. For this example, include the following fields in the following order:

- Flight Date
- Airline Carrier ID
- Departure Time
- Arrival Time
- Airfare
- Text: Flight Class
- Airport of Departure
- Destination Airport
- Arrival City

8. Click the Next Screen button on the Application toolbar to continue. The Selections Screen appears, listing all the fields you selected on the Select Fields screen, giving you the opportunity to add fields to your report's selection screen.

9. You can add to your report's selection screen any fields you want by placing a check mark next to each field. (In my example, I did not add any.)

10. Click the Basic List button on the Application toolbar to create a basic list in the SAP Query tool. The Basic List Line Structure screen appears, showing a list of the fields you selected to include in your report.

11. For each field, specify the line and sequence number as you want them to appear on your report (see Figure 13.1). You can also use the Basic List Line Structure screen to indicate sort order, totals, and counts, if needed.

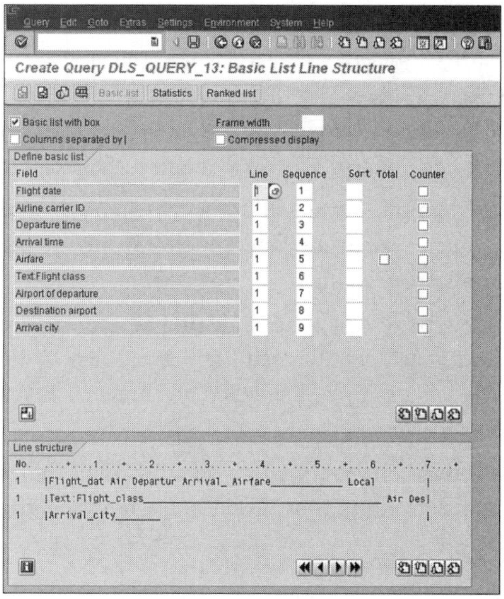

Figure 13.1
Unlike the Statistics screen, the Basic List Line Structure screen requires only line and sequence numbers.

12. Proceed directly to the report's selection screen by pressing F8. The report's selection screen gives you an opportunity to specify any criteria for the output of your report.
13. Press F8 to execute your finished report. Your report output should look similar to that in Figure 13.2, but keep in mind that the actual values vary by organization.

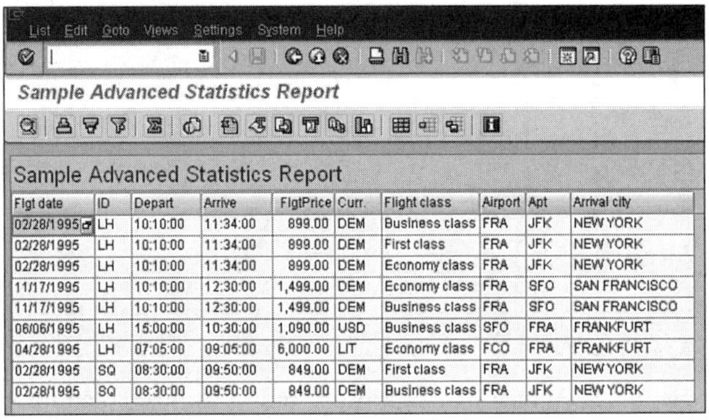

Flgt date	ID	Depart	Arrive	FlgtPrice	Curr.	Flight class	Airport	Apt	Arrival city
02/28/1995	LH	10:10:00	11:34:00	899.00	DEM	Business class	FRA	JFK	NEW YORK
02/28/1995	LH	10:10:00	11:34:00	899.00	DEM	First class	FRA	JFK	NEW YORK
02/28/1995	LH	10:10:00	11:34:00	899.00	DEM	Economy class	FRA	JFK	NEW YORK
11/17/1995	LH	10:10:00	12:30:00	1,499.00	DEM	Economy class	FRA	SFO	SAN FRANCISCO
11/17/1995	LH	10:10:00	12:30:00	1,499.00	DEM	Business class	FRA	SFO	SAN FRANCISCO
06/06/1995	LH	15:00:00	10:30:00	1,090.00	USD	Business class	SFO	FRA	FRANKFURT
04/28/1995	LH	07:05:00	09:05:00	6,000.00	LIT	Economy class	FCO	FRA	FRANKFURT
02/28/1995	SQ	08:30:00	09:50:00	849.00	DEM	First class	FRA	JFK	NEW YORK
02/28/1995	SQ	08:30:00	09:50:00	849.00	DEM	Business class	FRA	JFK	NEW YORK

Figure 13.2
This report displays all the line item details of scheduled flights in your IDES test database.

CREATING AN ADVANCED STATISTICS LIST BY USING THE SAP QUERY TOOL

To create an advanced statistics list that summarizes the data displayed in the basic list you created in the preceding section, you use calculated fields and advanced statistics by following these steps:

1. Navigate to the Maintain Queries Initial screen by using transaction code **/nSQ01**.
2. In the Query field, enter ***DLS*_Exercise_13A** (where *DLS* is your initials) as the name for the query you are creating, and then click the Create button.
3. When the InfoSets of User Group ZTEST window appears, listing all the available InfoSets (that is, data sources) for your Query Group, select the ZTEST InfoSet and then click Enter. The Create Query Title Format screen appears, allowing you to save the basic formatting specifications for your query, including the name (title) and any notes you want to store for the query. The only required field is Title.
4. Enter a title (for example, Sample Advanced Statistics Query A) and then click the Save button on the toolbar. To navigate to the Select Field Groups screen, click the Next Screen button on the Application toolbar.
5. When the Select Field Groups screen appears, listing all the Field groups available in your InfoSet, place a check mark next to each Field group whose fields you want to include in your report. (In my example, I selected all three.) Click the Next Screen button on the Application toolbar.
6. When the Select Fields screen appears, giving you a list of all the available fields within the selected field groups, select Edit, Short Names, Switch On/Off. Create short names

13

for your existing query fields so that you can easily refer to them in calculations. Enter **TOTAL** as the short name for the Total of Current Bookings field and enter **FDATE** for the Flight Date field. The Flight Date field specifies the date of the flight, and the Total Current Bookings field tells the amount of money spent on the flight. By using a combination of calculated fields and statistics, you can calculate the total of current bookings by airline for each quarter of a year, as determined by a year input at report execution time.

7. To create a local field to store the date (which will be input on the report's selection screen at runtime), place your cursor on the Flight Date field and then select Edit, Local Field, Create. The Define Field dialog box appears.

8. Input **Year** as the short name for your newly created local field Year, and input **Year** again as a field description (see Figure 13.3).

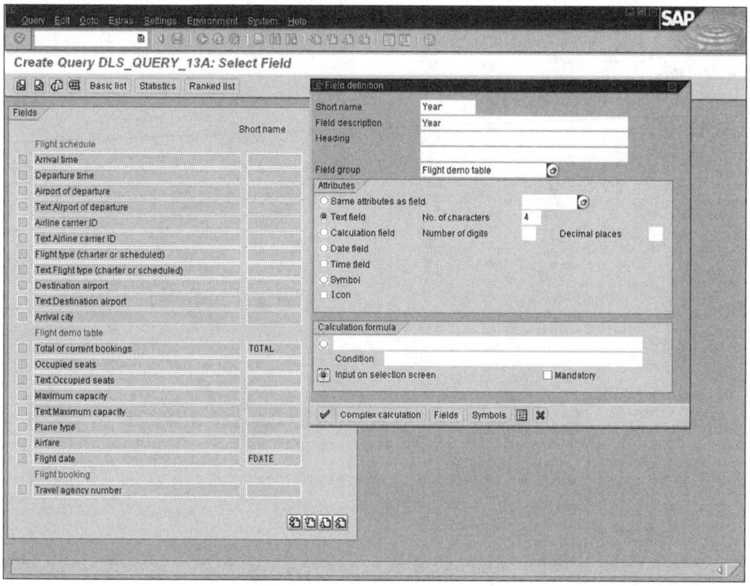

Figure 13.3
For this example, you input a short name and indicate that you want the field to be a text field with four characters (for example, 2007).

9. Define the attributes for the field by selecting the Text option button and indicating that you want it to be four characters wide (which is wide enough to accommodate the column heading and the output year, for example).

10. Select the option button labeled Input on Selection Screen to include the Year field on the report's selection screen so that you can input a value at report runtime. Click the Continue button to close the Define Field dialog box and return to the Select Field Group screen.

11. Create calculated fields that read the Year field and deduce the appropriate quarter of the year (that is, Quarter 1, 2, 3, or 4) to determine where the summarized data should

be output in the report. To do so, position your cursor in the Year field to base your calculated field on it, and then select Edit, Local Field, Create to create a new field. The Define Field dialog box appears.

12. Input **Q1** as the short name for your newly created local field and input **Quarter 1** as the field description.

13. Define the attributes for the field. Because this field will output a summarized version of the Total of Current Bookings field, you can select that the field have the same attributes as the Total field. (Both are currency fields.)

14. Click the Complex Calculation button. Enter the calculation formula with the condition **FDATE [YEAR] = YEAR AND 1 <= FDATE [MONTH] AND FDATE [MONTH] <= 3** and the formula **TOTAL** (see Figure 13.4).

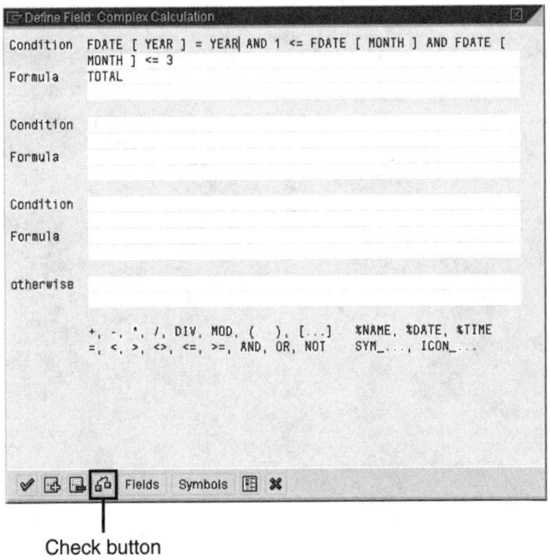

Figure 13.4
With long formulas, you can use the Complex Calculation button so that your formula can extend beyond a single line.

Check button

15. Click the Check button (highlighted in Figure 13.4) to ensure that you have typed the mathematical formula correctly. Click the Continue button to return to the Define Field dialog box, and then click the Continue button to return to the Select Field Group screen.

Helpful Hint
You can create a new column in your report called Quarter 1 to review the Flight Date field and determine what quarter it falls under. For example, January through March would be Quarter 1, and October through December would be Quarter 4. The complex formula used in this example and shown in Figure 13.4 is based on using the various operands and operators covered in Chapter 9, "Creating Basic Calculated Fields with the SAP Query Tool," and Chapter 10, "Creating Advanced Calculated Fields with the SAP Query Tool."

Now that the new Quarter 1 field has been created, you need to repeat those steps to create three more calculated fields to accommodate Quarters 2, 3, and 4, which will review the Flight Date field and extrapolate what quarter each total booking falls into. The formula you input translates to output in the appropriate quarter column (1, 2, 3, or 4) to display the total of the Total of Current Bookings field for any flight that is within each quarter.

16. Position your cursor in the Q1 field to base your calculated field on it, and then select Edit, Local Field, Create. The Define Field dialog box appears.

17. Input the short name **Q2** for your newly created local field, and then input **Quarter 2** as the field description.

18. Define the attributes for the field. Because this field will output a summarized version of the Total of Current Bookings field, you can select that the field have the same attributes as the Total field. (Both are currency fields.)

19. Click the Complex Calculation button. Enter the calculation formula with the condition **FDATE [YEAR] = YEAR AND 4 <= FDATE [MONTH] AND FDATE [MONTH] <= 6** and the formula **TOTAL**. This translates to output in the Quarter 2 column the total of the Total of Current Bookings field for any flight that is within Quarter 2 (Months 4, 5, and 6).

20. Click the Check button (highlighted in Figure 13.4) to ensure that you have typed the mathematical formula correctly. Click the Continue button to return to the Define Field dialog box, and then click the Continue button to return to the Select Field Group screen.

21. Position your cursor in the Q1 field to base your next calculated field on it, and then select Edit, Local Field, Create. The Field Definition dialog box appears.

22. Input the short name **Q3** for your newly created local field, and then input **Quarter 3** as the field description.

23. Define the attributes for the field. Because this field will output a summarized version of the Total of Current Bookings field, you can select that the field have the same attributes as the Total field. (Both are currency fields.)

24. Click the Complex Calculation button. Enter the calculation formula with the condition **FDATE [YEAR] = YEAR AND 7 <= FDATE [MONTH] AND FDATE [MONTH] <= 9** and the formula **TOTAL**. This translates to output in the Quarter 3 column the total of the Total of Current Bookings field for any flight that is within Quarter 3 (Months 7, 8, and 9).

25. Click the Check button (highlighted in Figure 13.4) to ensure that you have typed the mathematical formula correctly. Click the Continue button to return to the Define Field dialog box, and then click the Continue button to return to the Select Field Group screen.

26. Position your cursor in the Q1 field to base your next calculated field on it, and then select Edit, Local Field, Create. The Define Field dialog box appears.

27. Input the short name **Q4** for your newly created local field, and then input **Quarter 4** as the field description.

13

28. Define the attributes for the field. Because this field will output a summarized version of the Total of Current Bookings field, you can select that the field have the same attributes as the Total field. (Both are currency fields.)

29. Click the Complex Calculation button. Enter the calculation formula with the condition **FDATE [YEAR] = YEAR AND 10 <= FDATE [MONTH] AND FDATE [MONTH] <= 12** and the formula **TOTAL**. This translates to output in the Quarter 4 column the total of the Total of Current Bookings field for any flight that is within Quarter 4 (Months 10, 11, and 12).

30. Click the Check button (highlighted in Figure 13.4) to ensure that you have typed the mathematical formula correctly. Click the Continue button to return to the Define Field dialog box, and then click the Continue button to return to the Select Field Group screen.

31. To proceed with the statistics, click the Statistics button on the Application toolbar to create a statistics list in the SAP Query tool. The Statistics Line Structure screen appears.

32. Name your compressed list report **LIST_1** (see Figure 13.5).

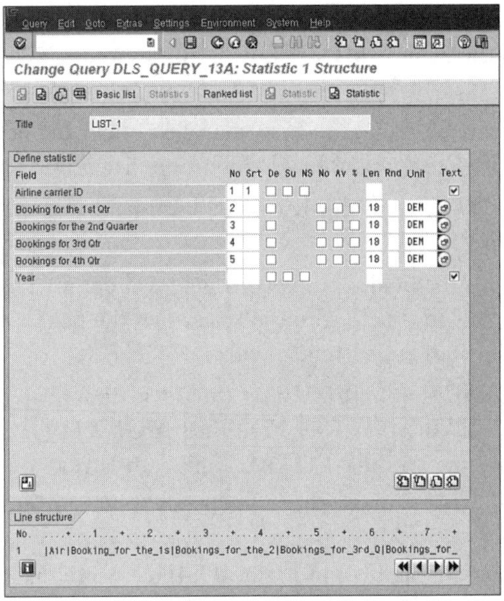

Figure 13.5
Unless currency conversions are used, you need to select the unit of measurement. For demonstration purposes, this figure shows DEM selected instead of USD because most entries in the SAP test database use German currency DEM.

33. Specify the sequence in which you want to output the fields, and state whether you want them to be sorted in ascending or descending order. Totals are always calculated for numeric fields. You can therefore determine average values, the number of selected records, and the percentage share. Indicate lengths and unit numbers for the calculated fields, as shown in Figure 13.5.

34. Press F8 to execute the report. As with almost all other reports in SAP, when you execute this report, you are presented with the report's selection screen.

35. Because in step 8 you created a calculated field to be input on the report's selection screen for the year, called Year, you need to enter a four-character year, such as **1995**, before continuing.

36. Press F8 to display the finished report. Your report output should appear similar to that in Figure 13.6, but keep in mind that the actual values vary by organization.

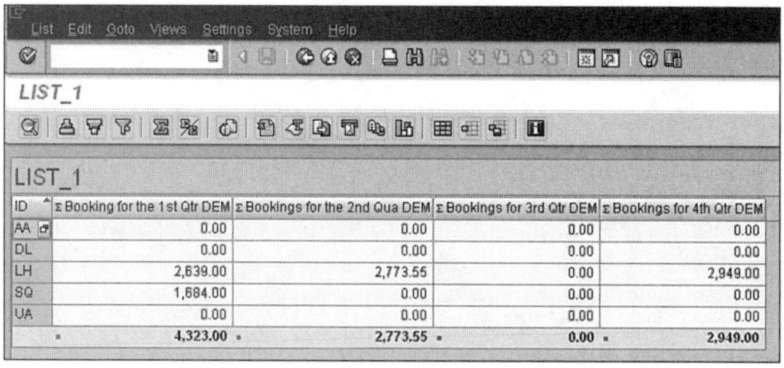

Figure 13.6
If you are using currency conversions, after the statistics, you see an overview that states which currency conversions were performed, as well as the date and exchange rate on which the conversions were based.

ID	Σ Booking for the 1st Qtr DEM	Σ Bookings for the 2nd Qua DEM	Σ Bookings for 3rd Qtr DEM	Σ Bookings for 4th Qtr DEM
AA	0.00	0.00	0.00	0.00
DL	0.00	0.00	0.00	0.00
LH	2,639.00	2,773.55	0.00	2,949.00
SQ	1,684.00	0.00	0.00	0.00
UA	0.00	0.00	0.00	0.00
*	4,323.00 *	2,773.55 *	0.00 *	2,949.00

Helpful Hint
Creating the detail report at the beginning of this chapter allows you to not only reconcile your calculated report output but also to see which year you should input on your report's selection screen to produce output. This example has flight data only for 1995, so that is the year indicated on the selection screen upon execution.

Having the ability to create your own reports with summarized, averaged, and calculated SAP report data is empowering, because it means you no longer need to extract data and report from it by using a third-party tool such as Microsoft Access or Excel. It also saves you from having to rely on a technical ABAP programmer to create detailed, advanced statistical reports in SAP Query.

THINGS TO REMEMBER

- You use statistics lists to produce summarized information.
- You can be creative with the use of operands and operators in determining quarters within a year.
- If you are using a multi-currency client, your currency conversions are displayed after your report output.
- Creating advanced statistics is easy when you have mastered the skills taught in this chapter.

13

CHAPTER 14

CREATING RANKED LISTS WITH THE SAP QUERY TOOL

In this chapter

The previous chapters covered how to create basic and advanced statistical lists by using the SAP Query tool. This chapter teaches the skills necessary to create ranked lists using the SAP Query tool. Ranked lists are helpful in statistical rank reporting, where you want not only summarized compressed data but data in ranked order (either ascending or descending). If you are not comfortable creating a basic list or creating a basic statistical list, you should practice the skills described in earlier chapters before proceeding with this one.

WHAT ARE RANKED LISTS?

If you were to review the SAP help documentation's definition of *ranked lists* in the standard SAP glossary at http://help.SAP.com, you might end up scratching your head for days, trying to determine what a ranked list is:

> With statistics, numerical values (for example, sales) belonging to particular key terms (for example, an airline carrier or a charter flight) are added together. The result is displayed in a table that gives you an overview of how the numeric values are distributed across the individual key terms. Ranked lists are special types of statistics. Here too, numeric values for key terms are added together and displayed in a table. However, a numerical value is always used to sort the data. This value is called a ranked list criterion. Only a certain number of items are displayed. Ranked lists are therefore useful for asking questions such as: "Which 10 flight connections have the highest sales?" When you choose a numeric value as the only sort criterion in a statistic, the result is practically a ranked list. With statistics, however, you cannot restrict the number of items that are displayed.

The easiest way to think of a ranked list is to think of putting items in order and then ranking them in terms of highest to lowest or vice versa. For example, let's look at a real-world example involving some fictional associates from Mama Tricarico's restaurant, which was used in earlier examples (see Table 14.1).

TABLE 14.1   FICTIONAL ASSOCIATES OF MAMA TRICARICO'S

Last Name	First Name	Employee Group	Employee Group Text	Position Title	Hourly Rate	Shift
Smith	Nicholas	1	Active	Menu Designer	$8.50	1
Stone	Michelle	1	Active	Chef	$14.50	1
Black	Nicole	2	Leave	Waitress	$4.25	1
Murphy	Janeen	1	Active	Hostess	$6.50	2
Lancer	Patricia	1	Active	Waitress	$5.65	1
Cane	Casey	2	Leave	Pot Washer	$5.00	1
Whalen	Irene	1	Active	Waitress	$5.65	1
Yankee	Kevin	1	Active	Waiter	$4.25	2

14

Last Name	First Name	Employee Group	Employee Group Text	Position Title	Hourly Rate	Shift
Lawrence	William	1	Leave	Chef	$16.50	2
Caldwell	Cindy	3	Terminated	Waitress	$4.25	2
Count =	10			Total	$75.05	

You could quite easily rank the three highest-paid associates from the list in Table 14.1 by manually reviewing the list:

1. Lawrence, William ($16.50)
2. Stone, Michelle ($14.50)
3. Smith, Nicholas ($8.50)

However, for a very large list, you might want to create a report that automatically ranks everyone in order. That is exactly what ranked lists do: They rank lists in either ascending or descending order.

CREATING A RANKED LIST BY USING THE SAP QUERY TOOL

In this section you will create a ranked list report by using the SAP Query tool, and you will base the ranked list on a calculated field. So this exercise will allow you to practice two skills. The exercises in this chapter use the SAP IDES Test Flight Scheduling system. You will begin by creating an SAP ranked list that ranks the airlines that have the greatest number of available seats left on their current flights. To do so, follow these steps:

1. Navigate to the main screen of the SAP Query tool by using transaction code **SQ01**, select the query you want to work with (for example, DLS_QUERY_14, where DLS is my initials), and click the Change button.

2. Navigate to the Select Field Groups screen and select the field group names that contain the fields you want to include in your report. (In my example, I selected all three.) Click the Next Screen button on the Application toolbar to access the Select Fields screen.

3. Select the fields you want to include in your report: Airline Carrier ID, Flight Date, Maximum Capacity, and Total of Current Bookings.

4. If the short names are not already displayed, select Edit, Short Names, Switch on/off to turn them on. Enter the short name **MAX** for the Maximum Capacity field and the short name **OCC** for the Occupied Seats field.

5. Create a calculated field that determines how many seats are free on each flight by taking the number of available seats (Maximum Capacity field) and subtracting the number of seats taken (Occupied Seats field). Position your cursor in the Occupied Seats field to base your calculated field on it.

14

6. Select Edit, Local Field, Create. Because your cursor was on the Occupied Seats field, a custom field is added to its field group (Flight Demo Table).

7. Select Edit, Local Field, Create. The Define Field dialog box appears. Input **Free** as the short name for your newly created local field, and input the field description **Free Seats**, which will be the heading for the column in the report.

8. Define the attributes for the new field. It should have the same attributes as the Occupied Seats field (OCC).

9. Select the Calculation Formula option button at the bottom of the dialog box (it should be selected by default) and then enter the basic mathematical formula **MAX – OCC** in the box to the right of it (see Figure 14.1). This formula will start with the total maximum capacity for the flight and will subtract the number of seats currently occupied to yield the number of available or free seats left over.

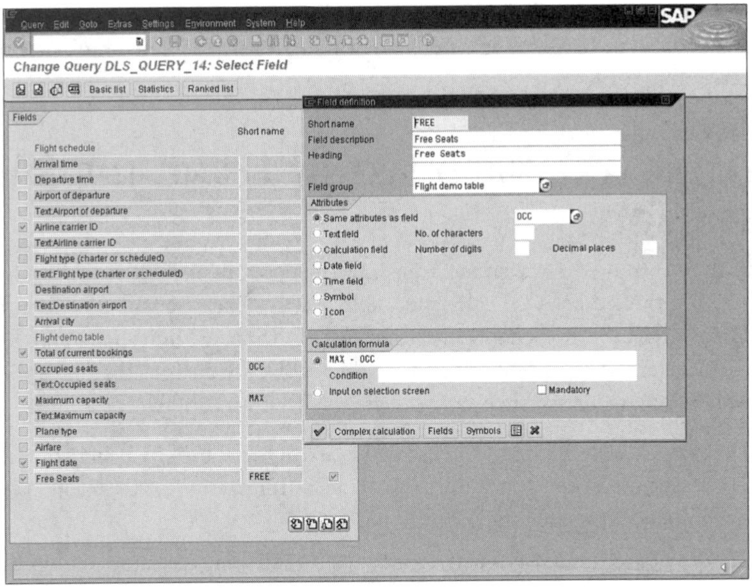

Figure 14.1
The basic mathematical formula is performed to populate the Free Seats column of the report.

10. Click the Continue button to close the Define Field dialog box and return to the Select Field Groups screen.

11. Navigate to the Ranked List Structure screen by clicking the Ranked List button on the Application toolbar. The Ranked List Structure screen appears, allowing you to define your report output. Name your compressed list report `Ranked_List_1`.

12. Use the Ranked List Structure screen to dictate how you want your report to appear, including rank number specifications. Assign a sequence number to each field that appears in the ranked list to determine the sequence in which they are output. Review the nine options available on this screen (see Table 14.2).

14

NOTE

When you define a ranked list, the data is summarized; that is, several data records are processed to determine one line. With numeric fields, the total is always output. Every ranked list must contain at least one numeric field.

TABLE 14.2   THE OPTIONS ON THE RANKED LIST STRUCTURE SCREEN

Option	Description
Title	This entry field allows you to enter a name for your first list. This title is used as the list header.
Field	All fields selected during the report creation process are listed here.
No	You use these boxes to define the sequence of fields within a ranked list. You can assign sequence numbers between 1 and 98.
Crit	If you select this option button, the field specified on the left is included in the ranked list, and the ranked list is sorted by the ranked list criterion.
Asc	If you select this check box, the fields are sorted in ascending order (low numeric value to high); if you do not select the box, the fields are sorted in descending order (high numeric value to low).
Len	You can choose an output length other than the standard output length. You can make a specification here to improve the layout of your list. Be aware that if the output length you choose is shorter than the standard output length, the field values output in the list will be incomplete.
Rnd	You select this option to specify the number of decimal places to be used when rounding. For example, if you specify 3, the resulting amounts have three places before the decimal point (that is, rounding to the nearest thousand).
Unit	This field appears for any field tied to a unit of measurement (for example, a currency or weight).
Text	If you select this check box, the values of the field specified on the left are used to generate the texts for SAP Business Graphics. If you select several fields, their values are used in the sequence in which they occur. SAP Business Graphics processes up to 30 characters of text per value.

13. Assign the sequence numbers, starting with 1 and in ascending order, without breaks. Indicate that you want to output the fields Airline Carrier ID, Flight Date, Free Seats, and Maximum Capacity. Specify the sequence in which you want to output the fields, and state whether you want them to be sorted in ascending or descending order, as shown in Figure 14.2.

14. Indicate that you want to rank on free seats (refer to Figure 14.2).

15. To execute the report and view the selection screen, press F8.

16. Press F8 to display your finished report. Your report output should appear similar to that in Figure 14.3, but keep in mind that the actual values vary by organization.

14

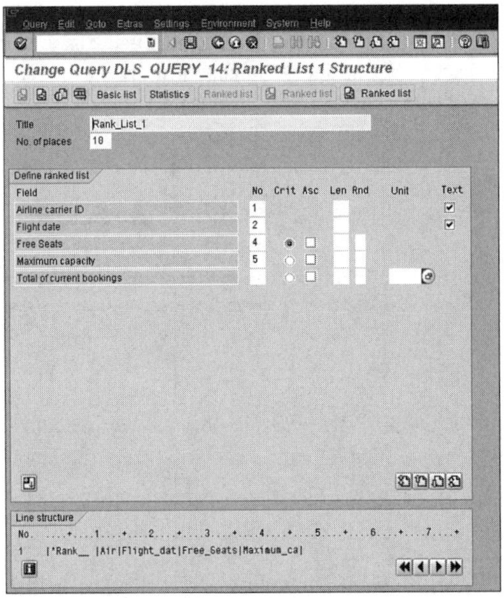

Figure 14.2
All ranked lists contain lead columns that are determined by the query itself. When you scroll horizontally, these fields always remain visible onscreen.

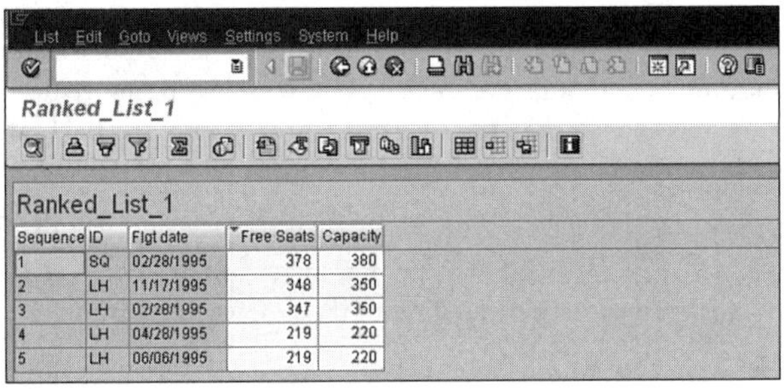

Figure 14.3
This ranked list displays the flights and carrier IDs of the five flights that have the greatest number of available seats.

Helpful Hint
On the Ranked List screen, you can click the Next Ranked List button on the Application toolbar if you want to define another ranked list.

SAMPLE USES OF RANKED LISTS IN SAP R/3

When I think of ranked lists, I often think of high school class rankings. For example, if your graduating class had 1,000 students, and you were Number 1, you were the valedictorian. Other rankings were important, too, for college admissions (and bragging rights). Ranking is useful in many different ways, including those listed here:

- **Purchasing information system**—You could create a ranked list of the 10 vendors that have the highest purchase order values.

- **Sales information system**—You could create a ranked list of the 50 customers with the highest incoming orders.

- **Inventory control**—You could create a ranked list of the 50 materials with the highest purchase order values.

- **Shop floor information system**—You could create a ranked list of the 20 work centers with the shortest lead times.

- **Plant maintenance information system**—You could create a ranked list of the 10 functional locations with the highest number of breakdowns.

- **Quality management information system**—You could create a ranked list of the 10 vendors with the highest number of returned lots.

- **Human capital management**—You could create a ranked list of the 100 departments with the largest numbers of active associates.

THINGS TO REMEMBER

- Using ranked lists is helpful for statistical analysis of data when you want the data ranked in order.

- You can create calculated fields within an SAP Query tool ranked list.

- The ranked number column in a report is frozen in place if you scroll horizontally, making it easy for you to review the ranked list.

14

CHAPTER **15**

HR AND PAYROLL REPORTING OPTIONS IN THE HCM MODULE

In this chapter

This chapter describes the various reporting options available for human resources and payroll reporting in the SAP Human Capital Management (HCM) module. Reporting in the HCM module is often referred to as human resources (HR) and payroll reporting. HR and payroll reporting used to be challenging in SAP. This chapter describes the tools that are now available and which are the best for effectively and easily reporting SAP R/3 HCM data. If you have no intention of working with the HCM module, you can skip this chapter.

THE REPORTING TOOLS IN THE HCM MODULE

Within SAP R/3 are five different options for reporting in the HCM module:

- Standard SAP-delivered reports
- The HR Information System (HIS) tool
- The InfoSet (Ad Hoc) Query tool
- The SAP Query and QuickViewer tools
- Custom ABAP reports

Outside the SAP R/3 environment, there are also options for reporting in the HCM module, including the following:

- SAP NetWeaver Business Intelligence (formerly known as Business Warehouse)
- Third-party tools, such as Crystal Reports, Microsoft Access, and so on

This chapter explains each of the reporting options available in SAP R/3 and provides detailed instructions on how to maximize your reporting capabilities for the HCM module.

STANDARD SAP-DELIVERED REPORTS

A standard SAP R/3 environment has more than 4,000 standard reports installed for all application areas within SAP. Approximately 200 of them are specific to the HCM module, including reports for payroll, personnel administration, personnel management, time management, training and event management, organizational management, and travel management. Navigating through and investigating these reports to ensure that a report is what you expect it to be is the key to successful reporting.

Standard reports are designed to satisfy many basic HCM requirements, including generic employee lists, birthday lists, and new hire and separation reports. In addition, a standard SAP R/3 installation comes with reports to satisfy country-specific requirements. For example, standard U.S. government reports, such as the EE0-1, ERISA, OSHA, and AAP report, are available, as is the Japanese Social Insurance premium check report. You can view the standard reports delivered with your SAP R/3 installation on the Easy Access page by selecting Human Resources, Information System, Reports. Several suboptions are available for each of the different types of reports for each of the application submodules (see Figure 15.1).

Figure 15.1
Reports are listed in the Reports node of the Easy Access menu for each application area within SAP.

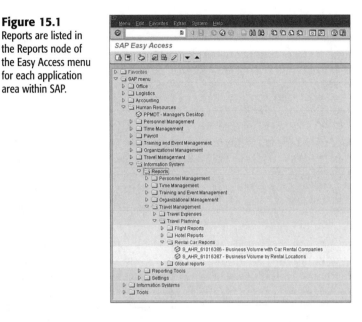

To learn more about any of these reports, you can select the report name, right-click, and select the Display Documentation option. Your configured Help solution appears, and you can read more about the report, including any required configuration and prerequisites.

NOTE

> When standard reports were initially developed in earlier versions of SAP, programmers built them in the custom language ABAP. However, beginning with SAP version 4.6, many standard reports have been converted from custom ABAP reports and changed into global SAP queries (for example, the birthday list report).

There are three important guidelines to follow when executing standard SAP-delivered reports:

- You must be properly trained before you begin to do reporting.
- You need to understand the configuration of the data specific to your installation and organization.
- You need to understand the company decisions specific to your installation and organization as to where data was loaded.

The following sections discuss these guidelines in more detail.

RECEIVING TRAINING BEFORE REPORTING

It is critical that users be properly trained before they begin reporting. As discussed in Chapter 5, "Basics of Using Reporting Selection Screens," a user needs to be able to use

Selection screens for SAP reporting to successfully produce reports and to ensure that you do not have a resource impact on your database. If a selection screen is not properly completed, the report will retrieve the incorrect records. A skipped or incorrectly completed selection screen can have an impact on the database resource engines that support the application.

UNDERSTANDING THE CONFIGURATION OF DATA

It is important that users understand the configuration of data specific to their particular installations and organizations. SAP has standard fields that all organizations use in the same fashion. For example, the Last Name field stores an associate's last name, and the Date of Birth field stores the associate's date of birth. However, there are also several fields within the R/3 database that different organizations use differently. For example, when a company builds its enterprise structure (for example, company code, personnel area, subarea), its personnel structure (for example, employee group, subgroup), and its organizational structure (for example, organizational unit, position, job), it does so based on its own business-specific needs. For example, two different organizations, Company ABC and Company DEF, may use different values in the personnel structure to define an associate's status within the organization. Company ABC might use the following employee groups:

1 = Active Associate

2 = Paid Leave Associate

3 = Terminated Former Associate

4 = Temporary Worker

Company DEF, on the other hand, might use these employee groups:

1 = On Call

2 = Temp

3 = Active

4 = Terminated

5 = On Leave

UNDERSTANDING THE COMPANY LOAD PLACEMENT DECISIONS

Users need to understand the company data load and configuration decisions specific to their installations and organizations. As mentioned earlier, there are some fields that every company can configure to its liking. In addition to these configurable fields, SAP customers tend to make decisions about where data will be loaded. For example, there are several places where an associate's start date can be stored. A fairly common option is to place an associate's date of hire in an Infotype 41 Date Specifications record for all associates.

If Company ABC implemented SAP and loaded each associate's hire date on Infotype 41 (in the Date for Data Type field), as is a popular best practice, the company would not have a correct start date value in any standard SAP-delivered reports. This is because many of the

SAP standard reports use a different field to store what SAP refers to as the entry date, which is not on Infotype 41; rather, it is tied to the date on which the first event occurred for the associate, as recorded in the Start Date field on Infotype 0. Sample standard SAP-delivered reports that use this entry date include the Birthday List report and the Flexible Employee Data report, among others.

How to Search the SAP R/3 Database for Reports

In addition to the general name of a report (for example, Birthday List), every SAP report also has a technical program name, which the database recognizes as the behind-the-scenes program name. RVSPERAU is an example of a program (technical) name of a report. Generally, the first two letters of a technical program name are a code for the module name. You can search for reports by area by following these steps:

1. Use transaction code SA38 (or SE38).

2. Type in the appropriate two-letter prefix and a *. The following are the possible two-letter prefixes:

Module	Prefix
Controlling	J1, J5, or J6
Financials	RF
Human Capital Management	RP
Materials Management	RM
Plant Maintenance	PP
Quality Management	RQ
Sales and Distribution	RL or RV

3. Press F4 to view a result list of reports within the specified module. Note that not every program listed with the appropriate prefix is a report; some may be transactions, behind-the-scenes programs, and so on.

4. When you see the name of a program and its description and you want to learn more about it to see if it would be a helpful report, place your cursor on the report name and then click the Accept button on the dialog box to return to the previous screen.

5. Select the Documentation option button (as shown in Figure 15.2) and then click the Display button to view a detailed description of the report and the requirements for its use.

HR INFORMATION SYSTEM (HIS)

The HR Information System (HIS) is a tool that allows you to execute standard SAP reports from a graphical interface. The best way to describe the difference between standard SAP-delivered reports and HIS is that HIS reports do not produce a selection screen upon execution. That is because when you select an object from a pictorial graphical view, you have already defined your selections. In other words, HIS uses a structural method of requesting reports by letting you start them directly from a picture of your structure (or data). This picture is displayed via SAP Structural Graphics. Structural Graphics allows you to view hierarchically based data in a pictorial view. How you access Structural Graphics determines the type of objects you can work with. For example, if you access Structural Graphics through the position report options, you can work with only positions and employees.

Figure 15.2
Transaction code
SE38 is tied to the
ABAP Editor, where
you can view the
documentation for
any SAP program.

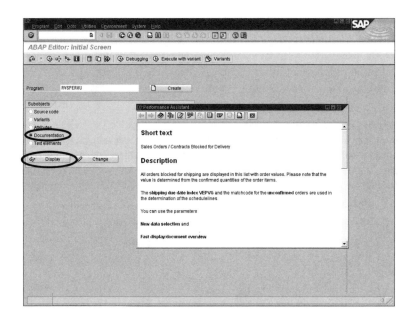

When you execute HIS, two SAP environments are open. The first window is the SAP Structural Graphics window, from which you are required to select an object. The second window lists available reports for the object selected. You use the second window to start a report for the selected object. What makes this type of reporting unique is that because you are starting with an object and proceeding from there, you are not required to enter data in a report selection screen, because HIS sets the required selection parameters automatically whenever possible.

Helpful Hint

The default parameters that HIS uses correspond to the selection parameters that are most commonly used when reports are run. Using these parameters is a helpful and efficient method of presetting reports. You can check and change these settings at any time by using the Change/Display Standard Settings function in the HIS menu.

The most popular challenge with reporting using HIS is that you are often unable to print data or have difficulty doing so. The Structural Graphics window is designed primarily for viewing and navigating the report data online and not necessarily for printing. Executing a pictorial view of the organizational structure onscreen would automatically vary the display onscreen. It does not, as most applications do, automatically fit to the screen so that it can easily be printed. Rather, it expands the screen so that you have to scroll in several directions to see all the report data. When you attempt to print that data, it does not automatically fit to designated page sizes, so it looks like several pages of unconnected graphics.

To investigate the reports available within HIS, you begin at the Easy Access menu and select Human Resources, Information System, Reporting Tools, HIS (or use transaction code **PPIS**). The window shown in Figure 15.3 appears.

Figure 15.3
The options in the HIS graphical display group box enable you to determine the objects that are displayed in Structural Graphics and the objects that you can use as root objects for reporting.

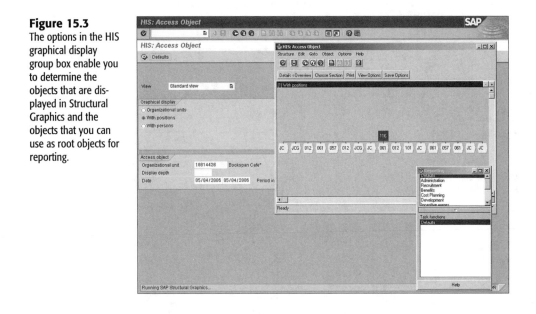

Helpful Hint
As with SAP standard reports, for reports available within HIS, you can review documentation. To do so, you select any object on the screen as the object you want to report on. A small Reporting dialog box appears, displaying two smaller windows: Reporting and Task Functions (see Figure 15.3). Your previous selection determines which reporting options are available under Task Functions. You can select any item in the Reporting section of the box. Under Task Functions, you select a report. Then you click the Help button at the bottom of the dialog box, and a description of the selected report is displayed.

THE INFOSET (AD HOC) QUERY TOOL

In the earliest versions of SAP, a bolt-on reporting tool was available for HR and payroll reporting, but it was very cumbersome to work with. As SAP evolved, it launched a solution embedded within the R/3 environment called the Ad Hoc Query tool. In its earliest form, the Ad Hoc Query tool was designed for use only in the HR module, and it was designed to give users quick-and-easy one-time data lookup. Since that time, the HR and Payroll modules have been renamed the HCM module, and the Ad Hoc Query tool has been combined with the functionality of the more advanced SAP Query tool, to form what is now referred to as the InfoSet Query tool. (However, in the HCM module and in some SAP Help documentation, it is still referred to as the Ad Hoc Query tool.) The InfoSet (Ad Hoc) Query tool is designed for simple one-time data retrievals from the SAP R/3 database.

The InfoSet (Ad Hoc) Query tool was designed to provide fast and easy access to basic data. Unlike the SAP Query tool, the InfoSet (Ad Hoc) Query tool is a WYSIWYG (what you see is what you get) resource that gives users quick-and-dirty access to counts and simple basic lists, as shown in Figure 15.4. You can access this tool by using transaction code **SQ01** and then clicking the InfoSet Query button.

Figure 15.4
The InfoSet (Ad Hoc) Query is a tool within the SAP Query tool that you can use as an alternative to component queries.

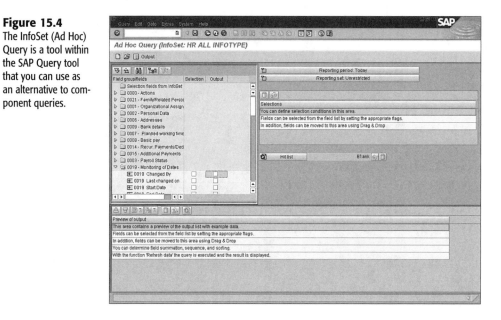

Chapter 19, "Creating Basic Reports with the InfoSet (Ad Hoc) Query Tool," addresses the use of the InfoSet (Ad Hoc) Query tool for reporting in the HCM module. At this point, it is important to note that although the HR Ad Hoc tool was the only end-user tool available for reporting in the HCM module, it is not the preferred tool for HR and payroll reporting in SAP R/3; rather, you should use the SAP Query tool for that use.

THE SAP QUERY AND QUICKVIEWER TOOLS

Bar none, the most robust SAP R/3 end-user reporting tool for HCM reporting is the SAP Query tool. Earlier chapters of this book explained the SAP Query tool in great detail. By using the SAP Query tool, an organization can satisfy virtually all its end-user reporting needs for all application modules, especially HCM.

The QuickViewer is a single-screen version of the SAP Query tool that you can use for one-time data lookups. The use of the QuickViewer tool is covered in detail in Chapter 20, "Creating QuickViews by Using QuickViewer."

CUSTOM ABAP REPORTS

In addition to the three main reporting avenues for HCM reporting described so far in this chapter, an organization inevitably requires at least a handful of custom ABAP reports.

You can create custom reports by using code and logic developed by ABAP programmers in SAP's ABAP Editor. This is sometimes referred to as creating a report from scratch. Figure 15.5 shows an example of the code written to create an ABAP report.

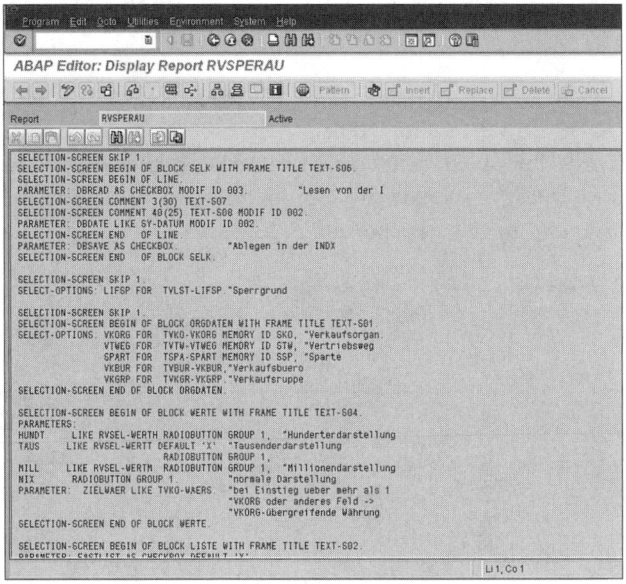

Figure 15.5
Programmers skilled in the language of ABAP and dialog processing can use the ABAP Editor to create custom reports.

Creating a custom report from scratch by using ABAP code has both benefits and challenges. Some of the main benefits are that a report can be created for any application area within the SAP R/3 environment and that the programmer has complete control over the formatting, spacing, security, output, and logic used. Negatives include the required staffing of skilled ABAP programmers who are familiar with each specific application landscape (for example, the HCM module). Custom programs require additional support and testing and are isolated from SAP patches, updates, and upgrades. When SAP provides upgrades and patches to your system, it does so only to the database and programs that SAP supplies, so if you use the ABAP language to create your own programs, SAP will not know to update your custom programs. Therefore, any custom ABAP report requires more strenuous testing than a traditional query or standard SAP report, which will have all the necessary accommodations from any upgrade or patch.

It is important to create custom ABAP reports only where it is impossible to develop them via other means (for example, using standard reports, HIS, or the SAP Query tool).

One popular method of making a custom report without having to build it from scratch is to review the standard SAP-delivered reports. If they do not completely meet your needs, you can make a copy of the original and then modify it by using the SAP Modification Assistant. The SAP Modification Assistant is a cool utility that you can use to make modifications to programs by using the ABAP Editor. The Modification Assistant tracks and records those changes to assist in upgrades. The tool assigns each modification you make to its corresponding unit and logs it for both the modification overview and upgrade.

REPORTING OPTIONS IN SAP R/3 FOR THE HCM MODULE

If you look through the table of contents for this book, you see that the bulk of the chapters are dedicated to the SAP Query tool. That is because it is a very comprehensive, easy-to-use tool with a great deal of functionality compared to the other available tools (for example, the InfoSet (Ad Hoc) Query tool). Table 15.1 compares the SAP reporting tools to assist you in weighing your options for HCM reporting in SAP R/3.

TABLE 15.1	A COMPARISON OF THE AVAILABLE REPORTING OPTIONS IN SAP R/3			
Reporting Option	**Description**	**Pros**	**Cons**	**Examples**
Standard SAP-delivered reports	Predelivered SAP reports in multiple country formats to assist with generic HCM reporting	■ Available for immediate use ■ No development or design requirements ■ Automatically updated in upgrade, Legal Change Packet (LCP), or patch release cycles	■ Limited flexibility ■ Cannot alter content or output format	OSHA, EEO-1, AAP, and government regulatory reports
HIS	An adequate solution for providing a pictorial view of HCM data in a structural graphic format	■ Available for immediate use ■ Hierarchical data is viewable in a graphical form with relationships	■ Limited flexibility ■ Cannot alter content or output format ■ Cannot easily print graphics	An organizational structure of positions within a department
InfoSet (Ad Hoc) Query tool	A quick lookup tool for one-time inquiries of SAP HR (Ad Hoc) or SAP application (InfoSet) data	■ Fast retrieval of a single unformatted list ■ User-friendly ■ Requires no programming ■ Can be converted to SAP Query	■ Limited flexibility ■ Cannot format or generate multiple-line lists ■ Not connected to ABAP Workbench	A quick count of the number of associates within a particular department

Reporting Option	Description	Pros	Cons	Examples
SAP Query tool	A detailed, friendly end-user report-writing tool designed for every application area within SAP R/3, including HCM	■ Fast access ■ User-friendly ■ No programming required ■ Permits multiple-line lists, graphics, colors, calculations, subtotaling, and so on ■ Connected to ABAP Workbench	■ Before this book, no training materials were on the market to teach end users how to use it	A detailed summary of associate benefit enrollment participation grouped by plan, with coverage percentages
Custom ABAP reports	Reports that can be written in the ABAP Editor by trained SAP programmers	■ Complete flexibility in design, retrieval, and output of report data	■ Requires hard coding ■ Requires a separate test cycle ■ Does not receive upgrades, patches, or LCPs ■ Requires a learning curve	A detailed analysis of associate turnover by department compared to the average cost per associate, as calculated in the Finance module

USING THE HCM MODULE AT YOUR ORGANIZATION

Chapter 1, "Getting Started with the SAP R/3 Query Reporting Tools," includes a section titled "Comparing the Query Tools to Decide Which to Use." That brief section says that the best business practice is to configure and use one main Query tool at your organization to ease support and training considerations and to ensure that your report data is consistent. That section also mentions that the most robust of the SAP query-based reporting solutions is the SAP Query tool. This recommendation that the best end-user reporting solution is the SAP Query tool also holds true for HCM reporting. Your SAP R/3 system comes pre-delivered with three data sources (logical databases) that can be used for reporting on HR and payroll data from the HCM module. These three logical databases are called PnP, PcH, and PaP.

As mentioned earlier, because the SAP Query tool has such robust and comprehensive capabilities, organizations often permit its use by super users or power users—users who are the savviest of the functional/business experts who utilize the solution. Casual users are often given only transaction codes or shortcuts to execute reports already created by others within

15

the SAP Query tool. I have heard the argument that savvy, trained business folk should use SAP Query, and casual users should use the InfoSet (Ad Hoc) Query tool or the QuickViewer. However, I recommend that an organization select a tool for primary use and train its end users on it. That way, the organization avoids any possible data inconsistencies due to different tool use. I always recommend the use of the SAP Query tool above all other tools because it has the most features and flexibility.

THINGS TO REMEMBER

- There are five reporting options in the R/3 landscape for HCM reporting.
- Investigating the SAP-delivered reports to see where they do and do not meet your needs is critical.
- Printing from the SAP HIS Structural Graphics component is challenging.
- The Ad Hoc Query tool was initially designed only for the HR module but is now available to all modules as the InfoSet Query tool.
- The SAP Query tool is a robust end-user reporting tool for HCM reporting.

CHAPTER 16

SPECIAL CONSIDERATIONS FOR CONFIGURING HR AND PAYROLL REPORTING IN THE HCM MODULE

In this chapter

In Chapter 15, "HR and Payroll Reporting Options in SAP for the HCM Module," you learned about the various reporting options available in the Human Capital Management (HCM) module. This chapter goes a step further, detailing the important considerations, tricks, and special configurations required for SAP reporting for HR and payroll reporting in the HCM module. If you have no intention of working with the HCM module, you can skip this chapter.

CONFIGURING INFOSETS FOR THE HCM MODULE

The configuration steps outlined in Chapter 2, "One-Time Configuration for Query Tool Use," describe how easy it is to configure the SAP Query tool for use. As you learned in Chapter 2, you can complete the one-time configuration in four quick and easy steps:

1. Create query groups.
2. Assign users to query groups.
3. Create InfoSets.
4. Assign your InfoSet to your query group.

The basic need for creating query groups and InfoSets (the data sources) for use in SAP HCM reporting is the same for any type of reporting. You need query groups to segregate your users into meaningful working groups such that only the appropriate users access, create, and change reports within their areas of expertise. For example, in a typical large organization, you might have query groups for payroll, benefits, savings, rewards, and so on—basically, a query group for every relevant area within the HR department. There is really only one primary difference between the general configuration steps and the steps specific to the HCM module, and it has to do with InfoSet configuration (step 3). The four steps just listed are covered in great detail in Chapter 2, in the section "Steps in Configuring the Query Tools." Step 1 (create query groups) and step 2 (assign users to query groups) should be performed according to the instructions outlined in Chapter 2. To create a new InfoSet specific to reporting in the HCM module, you need to follow these steps:

1. Log in to the area of your SAP client where your InfoSets will be maintained. (Best practice dictates that you maintain InfoSets in your development client.)
2. Navigate to the screen InfoSet: Initial Screen, shown in Figure 16.1, by using the transaction code /nSQ02.
3. Ensure that you are in the appropriate query area by selecting Environment, Query Areas and then selecting Standard Area. (Best practice dictates that you maintain your queries in the standard area.)
4. Type in the InfoSet name you will be creating (for example, ZTEST_HR) and click the Create button. A dialog box labeled InfoSet: Title and Database appears.
5. Type the InfoSet description (for example, HCM Test InfoSet) in the Name field.
6. Select the logical database you want to use as a source. As mentioned earlier, you can create InfoSets by using a variety of sources, the most common of which is the logical database. Three logical databases are available for the HCM module, as detailed in

Table 16.1. Select the Logical Database radio button, select or input PnP in the field to its right, and then click the green check mark Continue button. A dialog box like the one shown in Figure 16.2 appears.

NOTE

There are no published translations for the three-character logical database names used in SAP. Earlier chapters use the SAP-delivered Training Flight Scheduling logical database, which is called F1S, presumably for Flight Scheduling 1, but there is no documentation to support this. With regard to the HCM logical databases, PnP refers to the Personnel Administration submodule, PcH refers to the Personnel Development submodule, and PaP refers to the Recruitment submodule.

16

TABLE 16.1 LOGICAL DATABASES AVAILABLE FOR HCM REPORTING

	Logical Database		
Characteristic	**PnP**	**PcH**	**PaP**
Selection of:	Persons	Objects from personnel development submodule	Applicants
Infotypes	Infotypes for: ■ Personnel Administration (0000–0999) ■ Time Management (2000–2999) ■ Payroll result infotypes ■ Infotypes for Personnel Planning objects that can be related to persons ■ Custom infotypes (9000 series)	If the object type is specified: ■ Infotypes for the object type ■ Infotypes for objects that can be related to the specified object type If the object type is not specified: ■ All infotypes	Infotypes for: ■ Recruitment (4000–4999) ■ Some infotypes for Personnel Administration (such as 0001 and 0002)
Considerations	Use the logical database PnP to report on human resources (HR) master data. It is possible to use the logical database PcH to access this data, but PnP meets such reporting requirements more quickly because it is best suited to the task of electing persons. The logical database PnP enables you to access HR master data and infotypes from Personnel Planning.	This logical database generally enables you to report on all HR infotypes. However, SAP advises not using this logical database unless you want to report on Personnel Planning data.	The logical database PaP enables you to access data from Recruitment.

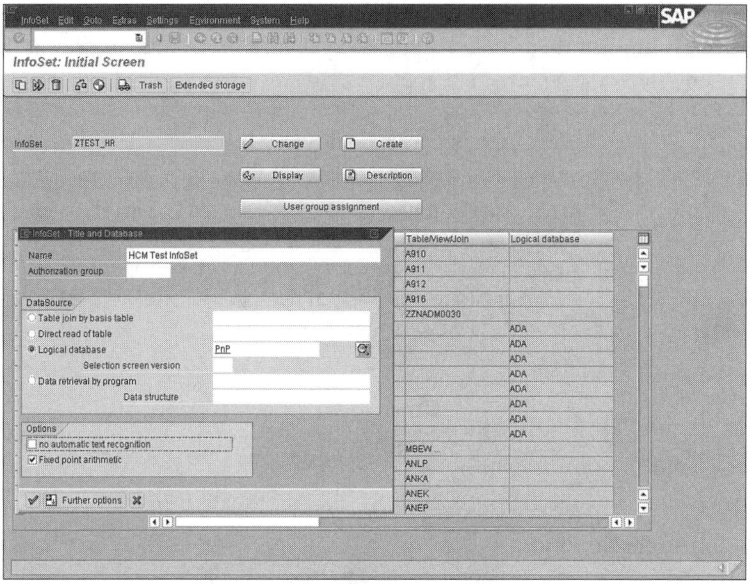

Figure 16.1
You create and modify InfoSets for all modules in SAP R/3 by using the InfoSet: Initial Screen.

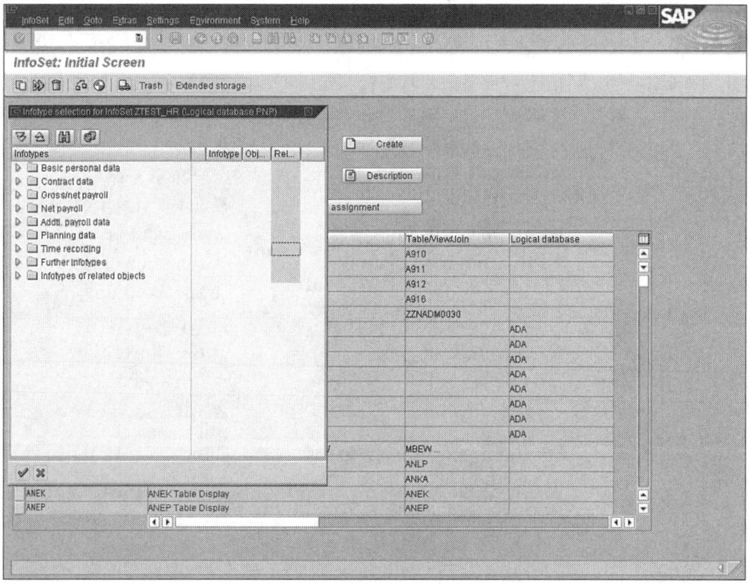

Figure 16.2
The Infotype Selection dialog box lists the primary infotype categories within the Personnel Administration submodule of HCM.

7. In the Infotype Selection dialog, use the small arrows to the left of each infotype category to see a list of all the infotypes included in each. Then select the small box to the right of each infotype that you want to be available within your data source (see Figure 16.3).

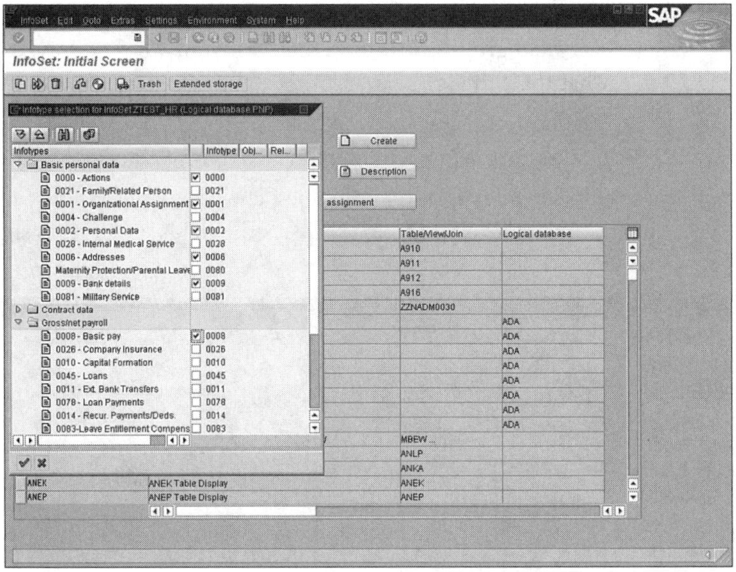

Figure 16.3
You should indicate only the infotypes that you currently use because you will always be able to return to the Infotype Selection dialog to add more.

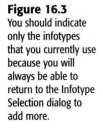

8. Click the green check mark Continue button. A Change InfoSet screen similar to the one shown in Figure 16.4 appears, listing all the infotypes you previously indicated that you wanted to include in your InfoSet. The Change InfoSet screen is divided into three sections:

   ■ The top-left section of the Change InfoSet screen displays a list of all previously selected infotypes, with two indicators under each. The first is a small blue box indicating the table that stores this infotype's fields. The second is related additional fields for that infotype.

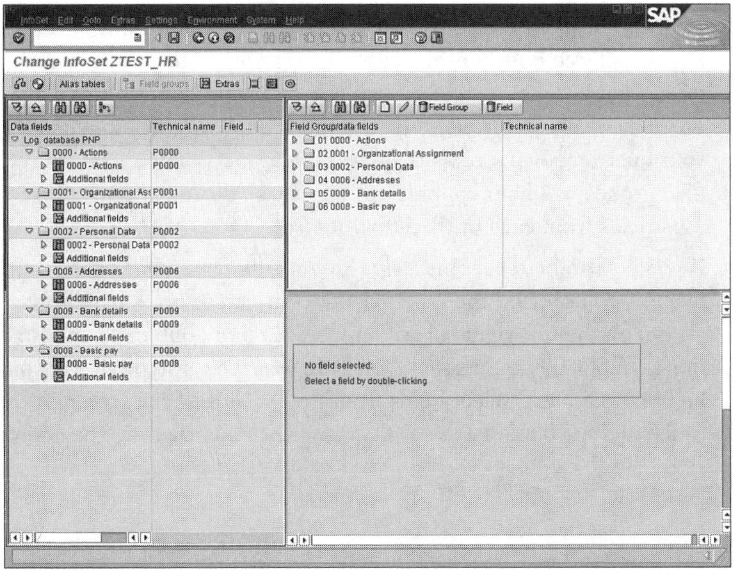

Figure 16.4
The Change InfoSet screen is divided into three sections.

16

- The top-right section of the screen, labeled Field Groups, lists all the necessary field groups, already created for you. These infotypes (field groups) are what the end user sees when creating reports using the SAP Query tools.

- The bottom-right section of the screen is populated with options and information only when a field from a table is selected on the left (see Figure 16.5).

9. To view the fields in each of the infotypes, click the expand subtree button next to each table name. The table expands and displays the fields under it, as shown in Figure 16.5.

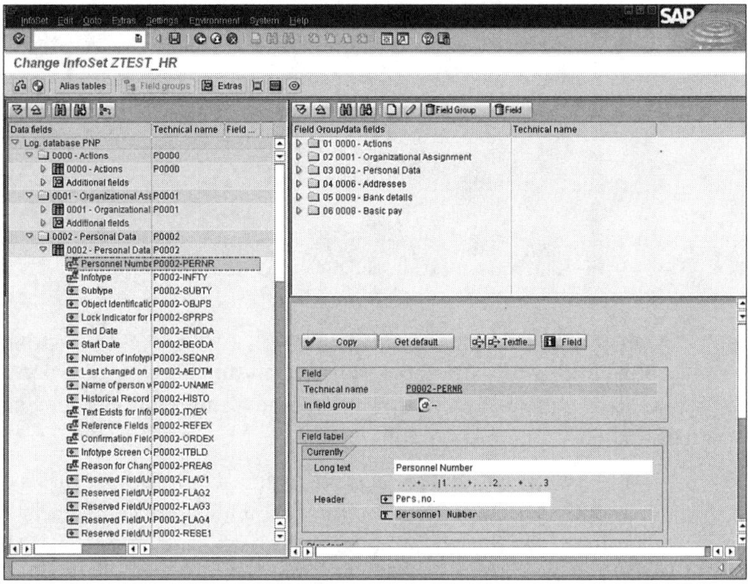

Figure 16.5
You see some fields listed that you do not recognize because the Change InfoSet screen displays every available field for the infotype, regardless of whether it is one used by your organization.

10. View the fields in each of the field groups on the top right of the screen by clicking the expand subtree button next to each field group. The field group expands, displaying the fields under it. These field groups will display in your query tools while reporting; only the fields that you include in your field groups will be available for field selection in your query reporting tools that use this InfoSet as their data source. By default, these field groups will be prepopulated for you, by default containing the most commonly used fields from each of the infotypes (see Figure 16.6).

11. If you determine that some fields are missing from your field groups that you want to include, you can add them by placing your cursor on the appropriate infotype (field group) on the top-right side of your screen and double-clicking to make that infotype (for example, 0002: Personal Data) the selected infotype (field group); it will appear highlighted. Next, select fields from the left side of the screen in the appropriate table from Infotype 0002: Personal Data and then add them to the appropriate infotype (field

group) at the top-right of the screen. You do this by placing your cursor on a field on the left side of the screen, right-clicking, and selecting the option Add Field to Field Group (see Figure 16.7).

Figure 16.6
The most commonly used fields for each infotype are already included in its respective field group.

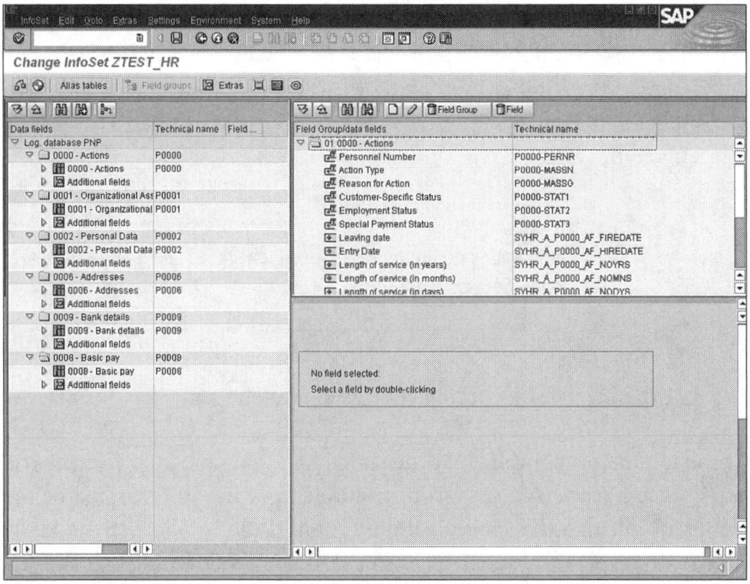

Figure 16.7
You should only add a field to its corresponding infotype's field group (for example, fields from Infotype 0002 to field group Infotype 0002: Personal Data).

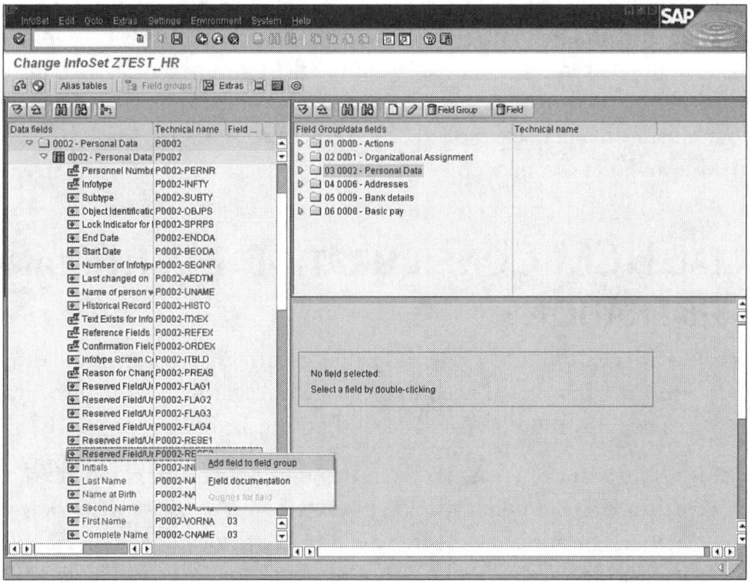

The field you just added to the indicated infotype (field group) now appears at the top right of the screen. You can continue to add fields using the same procedure. Be sure to add fields to the appropriate field group. For example, fields from Infotype 0001 should only be added to the field group for Infotype 0001: Organizational Assignment.

12. When each field group contains the fields you want, click the Save button on the toolbar. A message appears in the status bar, saying that your InfoSet was saved.

13. Generate the InfoSet by clicking the Generate (red beach ball) button on the Application toolbar. A message appears in the status bar, saying that your InfoSet was generated.

NOTE

> When you generate an InfoSet, SAP checks to see if any errors are present in the logic of the InfoSet's configuration.

14. Exit the InfoSet by clicking the green Back button.

Of the four steps mentioned at the start of this section, step 1 (create query groups) and step 2 (assign users to query groups) should have been performed before you began this exercise. Now that the special configuration of the InfoSet for the HCM module is complete, you simply need to perform step 4 (assign your InfoSet to your query group), which is covered in great detail in Chapter 2, in the section "Steps in Configuring the Query Tools."

You can also easily remove fields from infotype field groups that you are not using. For example, if your organization does not use some of the fields that are listed in a field group by default, you can remove them from the field group to reduce confusion. Removing fields from field groups involves virtually the same process as just described: You simply place your cursor on a field on the left side of the screen, right-click, and select the option Delete Field from Field Group.

SPECIAL HCM CONFIGURATION MAINTENANCE CONSIDERATIONS

Because the HCM module is designed differently than many of the other SAP modules, there are some things you need to be aware of regarding your configuration. It is important to note a couple cautions related to configuring an InfoSet in the HCM module:

- It is important to create as few InfoSets as possible to eliminate redundancy. You should create a master InfoSet specific to each logical database that you will use. For example, many organizations have three main InfoSets for HCM reporting: one for each logical database depicted in Table 16.1. Each time you make a change to an InfoSet, you have to propagate the changes to all others. Having a master source for each is ideal.

- Just because you can add tables to an existing InfoSet based on a logical database does not mean you should do so. For example, Chapter 17, "Special Considerations for HR and Payroll Reporting in the HCM Module," discusses data sources and how you can add extra tables. Unless you are trained in programming ABAP within the HCM module and have a firmly established understanding of the hierarchy of relational data within the HCM database, plus a distinct understanding of the effective dating relationships, you should not add tables to an existing InfoSet.

- You should not place fields in field groups other than those for their infotypes. For example, as mentioned earlier in this chapter, field groups are already created for HCM reporting, with fields already in them. You should not move the fields into other field groups. For example, you should not move the Last Name field from Field Group 0002: Personal Data to Field Group 0008: Basic Pay, because doing so would confuse the indexing of the database engine that is annexing the report data for retrieval and presentation.

ADDING INFOTYPES TO AN INFOSET

After you create an InfoSet, you can return to it at any time to add infotypes. To do so, you follow these steps:

1. Log in to the area of your SAP client where your InfoSets are maintained.

2. Navigate to the InfoSet: Initial screen by using the transaction code /nSQ02.

3. Ensure that you are in the appropriate query area by selecting Environment, Query Areas and selecting Standard Area. (Best practice dictates that you maintain query areas in the standard area.)

4. Type in the InfoSet name you will be creating (for example, ZTEST_HR) and click the Change button. Your InfoSet should look similar to the one shown earlier, in Figure 16.4.

5. Select Edit, Change Infotype Selection. A dialog box like the one shown during the InfoSet creation process (refer to Figure 16.3) appears, listing all the infotypes.

6. In the Infotype Selection dialog, use the small arrows to the left of each infotype category to see a list of all the infotypes included in each. Then select the small box to the right of each infotype that you want to be available within your data source.

7. Click the green check mark Continue button to return to the main screen of the InfoSet, which should now include your added infotype(s) in the Field Group list on the top-right side of the screen.

8. By default, these field groups are prepopulated with the most popular fields from each of the infotypes. Ensure that the fields you want are included in the new field groups on the top-right side of the screen. Keep in mind that only the fields you include in your field groups will be available for field selection in your query reporting tools that use this InfoSet as their data source.

9. Click the Save button on the toolbar. A message appears in the status bar, saying that the InfoSet was saved.

10. Generate the InfoSet by clicking the Generate (red beach ball) button on the Application toolbar. A message appears in the status bar, saying that the InfoSet was generated.

Adding Custom Infotypes to an InfoSet

As just mentioned, after an InfoSet is created, you may return to it at any time to add infotypes. SAP provides infotypes that can be activated for custom company-specific use. These Personnel Administration infotypes are in the 9000 namespace. Adding these infotypes to an existing InfoSet based on a logical database is easy. You add them by using the process just detailed, although the infotypes will likely be listed at the bottom of the group in the dialog box labeled Further Infotypes.

REPORTING ON DATA FROM TWO MODULES IN THE SAME QUERY

To report based on any data from the Personnel Development module, you must perform evaluations according to your company's organizational structure. In other words, the Personnel Development submodule of the SAP HCM module evaluates objects in a hierarchy. So, unlike with basic reporting using the PnP Personnel Administration submodule logical database, you need to define a report based on a hierarchical structure. To be able to create an SAP query that contains data from infotypes within SAP's Personnel Administration submodule plus data from the Personnel Development submodule, you need to evaluate persons, not objects. You need to be able to include only data that functionally can be reported along a hierarchical line. Being able to report on data from the Personnel Development and Personnel Administration submodules within a single query-based report is one of the most popular challenges for users creating reports in the SAP HCM module, regardless of the tool used. With regard to query-based reporting, SAP describes two possible solutions, as described in the following sections.

USING AN INFOSET BASED ON THE PNP LOGICAL DATABASE

The logical database PnP enables you to access HR master data infotypes from the Personnel Administration submodule of HCM. Specifically, it includes infotypes 0000–0999 and 2000–2999, payroll result and custom 9000-series infotypes, and infotypes for personnel planning objects that can be related to persons. In other words, you can report on data from the Personnel Development submodule of HCM that is traditionally stored in the PcH logical database within your InfoSet based on the PnP logical database only if that data is related to a person. From a technical perspective, this means you can use the logical database PnP to report on all the infotypes that exist for objects (Infotype 1000) that have a direct relationship (Infotype 1001) with the Person object.

For example, if you wanted to use an InfoSet based on logical database PnP to include Personnel Development data such as a list of organizational units and the default cost centers associated with each, you couldn't, because none of the fields mentioned (organizational unit or cost center) includes the Person object. They do not tie back to a person, so trying to use an InfoSet based on PnP with additional fields from PcH for this scenario would be unsuccessful.

However, you could create an InfoSet using PnP and include fields from PcH if you were running a report to evaluate the costs, number of attendees booked, and instructor for a business event on which an employee is booked. In this scenario, you have data that is related to a person, so it would work.

You activate the Personnel Development infotypes from within an InfoSet based on logical database PnP by using the same method outlined earlier in this chapter, in the section "Adding Infotypes to an InfoSet." The Personnel Development infotypes are listed at the very bottom of the list of infotypes in the Infotype Selection dialog box (refer to Figure 16.2).

16

USING AN INFOSET BASED ON THE PcH LOGICAL DATABASE

The preceding section discussed creating an InfoSet based on logical database PnP from the Personnel Administration submodule of HCM and then adding to it fields from the PcH logical database to include fields from the Personnel Development submodule of HCM. Now let's think about the opposite: creating an InfoSet based on logical database PcH and then adding fields from the PnP logical database.

The inclusion of the Personnel Administration infotypes in the PcH logical database was not in place until SAP version 4.0. You activate the Personnel Administration infotypes from within an InfoSet based on logical database PcH by using the same method outlined in the section "Adding Infotypes to an InfoSet." The Personnel Administration infotypes are listed at the very bottom of the list of infotypes in the Infotype Selection dialog box.

Now here is the difficult part: When you create a report that is based on an InfoSet that was built using logical database PcH but that includes fields from the Personnel Administration submodule, you are presented with a traditional Personnel Development–based selection screen. Traditional Personnel Development selection screens work differently than almost all other selection screens in that they are object-based. They require you to specify an object type (because Personnel Development is based on objects such as organizational units, positions, and so on) and enter an evaluation path to execute a report. An evaluation path represents the hierarchical relationship between objects (for example, path O-S-P represents the relationships between organizational units, positions, and persons). When you select persons and infotype records, the conditions of the underlying logical database apply. The time period selection refers only to the validity period of the infotype records. If the beginning or end of the validity period falls within the selected period, the length of the validity period is given when you output the data. Otherwise, the time interval of the selection is displayed.

In other words, you have to be savvy about what you are trying to report. In Personnel Development object-based reporting, you are evaluating an object, such as an organizational unit. You can run a report of all associates and their race and gender based on the organizational units. The report will list each organizational unit and then the Personnel Administration information under each.

Helpful Hint
You can find step-by-step instructions on how to use evaluation paths in SAP Personnel Development reporting at http://sap.help.com, in the library under Evaluations According to a Company's Organizational Structure.

THINGS TO REMEMBER

- The configuration of the SAP R/3 Query tools specific to the HCM module is not significantly different from the configuration for other SAP modules.

- Three logical databases are designed for reporting in the HCM module: PnP, PcH, and PaP. PnP is the most common; it includes all infotypes from the Personnel Administration submodule.

- You should create as few InfoSets as possible to eliminate redundancy. You should create one master InfoSet for each logical database.

- The ability to access infotypes from the Personnel Administration submodule by using the logical database PnP is a special feature made available in SAP version 4.0.

- When reporting based on Personnel Administration and Personnel Development data within the same SAP query, on the selection screen, you specify an object type and enter an evaluation path.

CHAPTER 17

SPECIAL CONSIDERATIONS FOR HR AND PAYROLL REPORTING IN THE HCM MODULE

In this chapter

Chapter 16, "Special Considerations for Configuring HR and Payroll Reporting in the HCM Module," provided a good deal of information on the special considerations required in the one-time configuration of the SAP Query tool for reporting in the Human Capital Management (HCM) module. This chapter provides tips and tricks on how best to design and execute human resources (HR) and payroll reports within the HCM module to maximize your success. If you are not using the HCM module of SAP, you can skip this chapter.

PAYROLL RESULT REPORTING WITH THE SAP QUERY TOOL

The data that is reported when you use the SAP Query tool is primarily stored/displayed in infotypes. The traditional challenge with reporting on payroll results is that they are not stored in infotypes; rather, they are stored in payroll clusters. However, SAP recognizes this challenge and makes it possible for you to report on payroll results by using the SAP Query tool. You do so by having the data from the payroll clusters update infotypes that are designed to store the payroll results such that you can simply pick and choose the infotypes and fields you want to include in your reports to easily evaluate payroll results.

SAP R/3 provides a handful of predefined infotypes for this purpose. The wage types required for the evaluation can be entered in the infotypes listed in Table 17.1.

TABLE 17.1 PAYROLL RESULTS INFOTYPES

Infotype Number	Infotype Name
0402	Payroll Results: Period Values
0403	Payroll Results: Period Values (not required at present)
0458	Payroll Results: Monthly Accumulation
0459	Payroll Results: Quarterly Accumulation
0460	Payroll Results: Annual Accumulation

You can either activate these predefined infotypes via the Implementation Guide or create your own infotypes by using the same structures. You can enhance these infotypes by using additional wage types and then activating the infotypes. Turning on these infotypes for use makes the necessary data from the payroll result clusters available in the Personnel Administration submodule PnP logical database for reporting.

NOTE

A number of tables are used to populate the infotypes used for payroll result reporting. Trained ABAP programmers who will likely be involved in the decision about whether to turn on these payroll results infotypes will be curious about which tables to use. It is safe to say that the decision about what and where to store varies by organization. However, the following notes are can guide trained payroll-specific ABAP programmers through the configuration:

- Infotype 0402 needs the RT data for the current period results.
- Infotypes 0458, 0459, and 0460 need a combination of CRT and TCRT.
- You should use TCRT for any tax-related information (for example, /401, /403–/406 (FICA), and so on).
- You should use CRT for any company-specific wage types, but any wage types that are used for W-2 purposes should be stored in the TCRT table as well.

ELIMINATING DUPLICATE-LINE REPORTING IN THE HCM MODULE

Upon execution of virtually any report in SAP, an end user sees a selection screen that provides the opportunity to further clarify selections. (See Chapter 5, "Basics of Using Reporting Selection Screens," and Chapter 6, "Using Reporting Selection Screens: Advanced Skills," for more information on selection screens.)

The most common date parameter for reporting in the SAP HCM module on the selection screen is the date selection period Today. Selecting Today ensures that the data you have retrieved from the database is valid as of today. One thing to note here is that if you have any future-dated records (for example, for increases or organizational changes), they will not be included in your report output because technically they do not exist yet. Many users wonder why they sometimes retrieve multiple (or duplicate) line items when selecting Today for an HCM report. This happens only with certain infotypes that have multiple values in a single or table-based storage space. This might sound pretty technical, but basically it means that the database pulls all the records that meet the specified criteria.

Most users complain of duplicate record results when selecting the Other or Person Selection Period date parameters because multiple records may exist for that employee during the date range specified.

An example of an infotype that does not produce multiple lines in an SAP Query is Infotype 0002: Personal Data. This is because Infotype 0002 stores each piece of information in a single identifiable field; for example, it stores an associate's first name in the field labeled First Name onscreen. Behind the scenes, the data entered in this field is stored in the SAP database in the P002-VORNA structure, where P002 identifies the infotype number (in this case Infotype 2). P002-VORNA is referred to as the field's technical details. To view a field's technical details, you need to place your cursor in a field (for example, the Birth Date field on Infotype 0002) and then press F1. The Performance Assistant dialog box appears (see Figure 17.1), providing a definition of the specified field. The Performance Assistant dialog box provides a Technical Information button that you can click to view the field's technical details (see Figure 17.1). Figure 17.2 shows the Technical Information dialog box that appears.

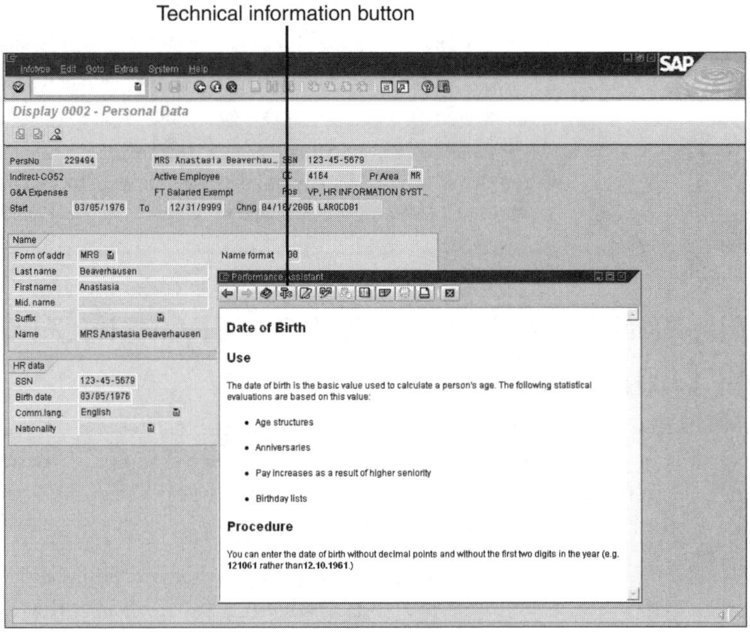

Technical information button

Figure 17.1
The Performance Assistant dialog box provides a definition of the selected field and, in some cases, examples of its usage.

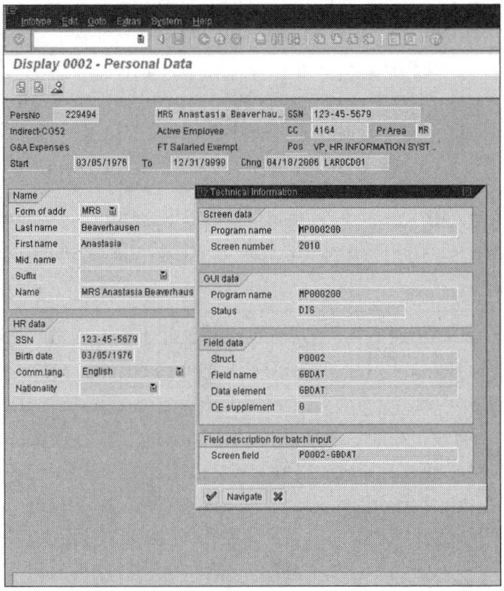

Figure 17.2
The Technical Information dialog box displays the behind-the-scenes database information about the selected field.

The associate's date of birth is the only information that should be stored in the designated Birth Date (P0002-GBDAT) field, because the Birth Date field on Infotype 0002 is designed exclusively for that purpose. In comparison, Figure 17.3 shows Infotype 0041: Date Specifications, which is often known to produce duplicate records when its fields are included in an HCM report.

Figure 17.3
Infotype 0041: Date Specifications allows an organization to save multiple date types for an associate in a single place.

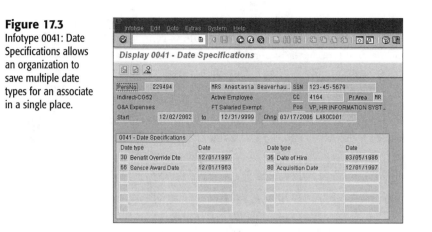

For Infotype 0041, there is not a single field identified for only a single piece of data; rather, the data that can be stored in each field is variable. Infotype 0041 is designed to permit storage of customer-specific dates. During configuration, you determine the date types that you want to use for your organization. For example, in Figure 17.3, the fictional associate has four different date types, stored as Date Types 30, 36, 66, and 80, listed in numeric order. Unlike with Infotype 0002, with Infotype 0041, the fields on this screen can store variable data. If you were to look at the technical details of the Date Type 30 date field (for example, the first date field listed, labeled Benefit Override Dte), you would see the value P0041 - DAT01. If you were to look at the details of the next date field immediately to its right (for example, the field labeled Date of Hire), you would see the value P0041 - DAT02.

In the first example, the value DAT01 is assigned because that date is stored in the first position on that screen. Similarly, in the second example, the value DAT02 is assigned because that date is stored in the second position on that screen. If you added a new date type for the associate (for example, Date Type 23), that would then become assigned to the technical field P0041 - DAT01 because it would then be in the first numeric position (because 23 is numerically before 30). If you created a query-based report, run as of today, to include the First Name and Last Name fields from Infotype 0002, the report output would appear in a single line across the page for each associate. However, if you ran a report and listed the Date Type and Date for Date Type fields in the output, you would display multiple lines in the report for each associate for each date stored on their Infotype 41, which includes the technical fields P0041 - DAT01 through P0041 - DAT12. Using the sample shown in Figure 17.3, you would display four line items for the associate, one for each date type.

There are two possible solutions for single-line reporting based on infotypes, including Infotype 41: a basic solution and an advanced solution.

THE QUICK-AND-DIRTY SOLUTION FOR SINGLE-LINE REPORTING BASED ON INFOTYPES

With the quick-and-dirty, limited solution for single-line reporting based on infotypes, if you wanted to create a basic list query report that would include an associate's hire date (for example, Date Type 36), you would simply need to include the Date Type field on your report's selection screen. Using that method, you could, upon report execution, specify that you want only that one date type in the report output, thus ensuring that you get only a single line of data per associate in your report output. This same method works on Infotype 0006: Addresses, where multiple subtypes of addresses are available. This is a limited workaround because of the way a selection screen works. It includes in your report only data that meets the criteria entered on the selection screen. So, for example, if you were to produce a report of everyone and their hire date on a single line, as just mentioned, the single-line report output would include only those associates who have the specified date type. If some folks were missing it, for example, they would be excluded from the report output.

This quick-and-dirty workaround is helpful when you are sure all associates meet the criteria entered on the selection screen (so you get complete output) or when you want your report output to include only those associates. A downside of this method is that you are limited to reporting based on only one item in a single report. So, for example, if you wanted to include hire date (Date Type 30) and service award date (Date Type 66) from the preceding example, you would still get two lines for each associate. The same would be true if you were to run a list of employee addresses from Infotype 0006: Addresses. You would only have the option to specify a particular subtype of address (01 - Mailing, 02 – Permanent Residence, and so on), as specified in the Address Subtype field on the report's selection screen, or you would display both and have multiple lines per associate.

THE ADVANCED SOLUTION FOR SINGLE-LINE REPORTING BASED ON INFOTYPES

The second and more technical solution for single-line reporting based on infotypes is designed for ABAP programmers. The premise is that you can insert into the InfoSet (your report's data source) code that evaluates each of the fields for you and creates fields in the InfoSet that store each specific field. Using the Infotype 41 example, you could add code to your InfoSet that evaluates each of the date types specific to your company's configuration (for example, Date Types 30, 36, 66, and 80) and creates fields in the InfoSet for each specific date type, allowing you to simply select which dates you want to include in your report output (regardless of the number you want to include), and all will appear on one line.

This advanced solution enables you to simply select which fields you want to include in your report output. Adding code to an InfoSet is a subject geared toward trained ABAP programmers and is beyond the scope of this book. However, because this is one of the most popular challenges for HCM reporting, this section includes some quick notes on it.

Listing 17.1 shows an example of ABAP program code developed by a trained HR ABAP programmer that you can include in a SAP Query tool InfoSet to assist with the challenge of reporting based on an infotype that stores variable data. For example, you can add this code to the InfoSet, to create new fields in your InfoSet that store each Date field from Infotype 0041 in a single designated field. That way, you can include any or all dates in a report from your Infotype 0041 (regardless of whether the associate has values for the date types), all on a single line in the SAP Query tool.

LISTING 17.1   SAMPLE CODE TO ADD TO INFOSET FOR INFOTYPE 41 REPORTING

```
REPORT ZHR_DATES .
INFOTYPES: 0041 NAME I0041.
TABLES: PA0167.
DATA: DAR LIKE PA0041-DAR01,
 DAT LIKE PA0041-DAT01,
 HIREDATE LIKE PA0041-DAT01,
 REHIREDATE LIKE PA0041-DAT01,
 LASTHIREDATE LIKE PA0041-DAT01,
 ADJSVCDATE LIKE PA0041-DAT01,
 TERMDATE LIKE PA0041-DAT01,
 SEPARATIONDATE LIKE PA0041-DAT01,
 BENTERMDATE LIKE PA0041-DAT01,
 KEY_DATE1 TYPE D.

FORM GET_DATE USING VALUE(PERNR)
 VALUE(DATUM)
 VALUE(TYPE)
 CHANGING RESULT.

 CLEAR RESULT.
 PERFORM READ_INFOTYPE(SAPFP50P) USING
 PERNR '0041' SPACE SPACE SPACE DATUM DATUM '0' 'NOP' I0041.
 IF SY-SUBRC EQ 0.
 DO 20 TIMES
 VARYING dar FROM I0041-dar01 NEXT I0041-dar02
 VARYING dat FROM I0041-dat01 NEXT I0041-dat02.
 IF dar IS INITIAL.
 EXIT.
 ENDIF.
 IF DAR EQ TYPE.
 RESULT = DAT.
 exit.
 ENDIF.
 ENDDO.
 ENDIF.
ENDFORM.
```

The data types referenced in this code are specific to the way a sample organization has them configured, so you need to substitute for them the names and numbers that you use at your organization. The code reads through all the different table values and assigns each date to a specific field for use in reporting. You can use this code as a helpful reference to set up your own custom fields for reporting on things like date types and wage types.

UNDERSTANDING SELECTION PERIOD FIELDS ON THE SELECTION SCREENS OF HCM REPORTS

Many people have difficulty determining how the period fields function on HCM module report selection screens, as shown in Figure 17.4. As a result, their reports include data they did not intend to include.

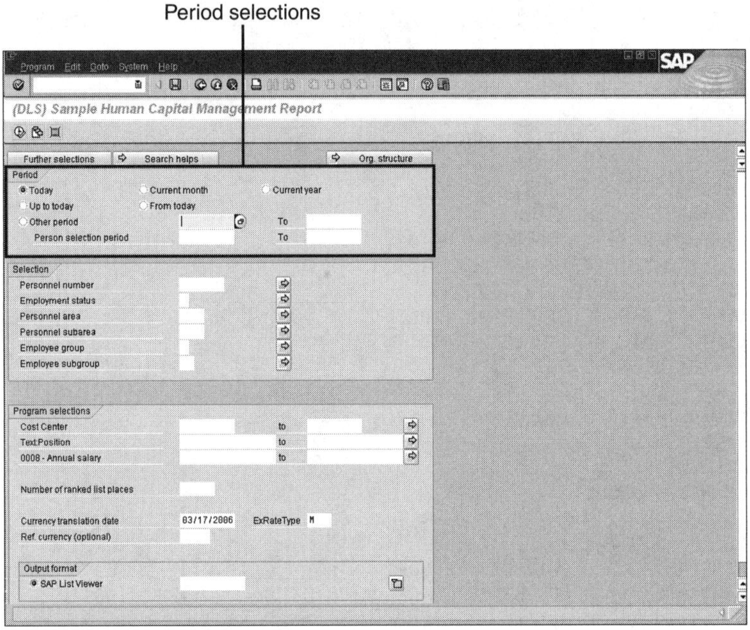

Period selections

Figure 17.4
The top of the selection screen labeled Period has several options.

In SAP, whenever a report is executed (that is, based on a logical database, as queries are) and no variant exists for it as a default, the SAP system default is the Period labeled Other. If you leave that Other selection in place, and if you do not enter a specific date range to the right of it, your report will begin to pull every record from the HCM database. Needless to say, this is not a good idea. The following sections describe the various selection period options and how you use each of them.

THE TODAY OPTION

The Today selection is the most popular and the most commonly used in SAP Query tool reporting. As discussed earlier in this chapter, selecting Today ensures that the data you have retrieved from the database is valid as of today. An important consideration is that if any future-dated records exist (for example, future-dated increases or organizational changes), they will not be included in the report output because, technically, they do not exist yet. If you select the Today period indicator for your report, the system date is used as the key date for the Person selection period.

THE CURRENT MONTH OPTION

If you select the Current Month option, the first and last days of the current month (as determined by the system date) are used as the start and end dates for the Person selection period.

THE CURRENT YEAR OPTION

If you select the Current Year option, the first and last days of the current year (as determined by the system date) are used as the start and end dates of the Person selection period.

THE UP TO TODAY OPTION

If you select the Up to Today field, the beginning of time (defined as 01/01/1800) and the system date are used as the start and end dates of the Person selection period. This is the opposite of the From Today selection period.

THE FROM TODAY OPTION

If you select the From Today option, the end of time (defined as 12/31/9999) and the current system date are used as the start and end dates of the Person selection period. This is the opposite of the Up to Today selection period.

THE OTHER PERIOD AND PERSON SELECTION PERIOD OPTIONS

Other Period is the system default. As discussed earlier in this chapter, if you select Other Period and leave the dates next to it blank, SAP pulls every record in the database from the beginning of time (defined as 01/01/1800) to the end of time (defined as 12/31/9999). Therefore, if you really want to select Other Period, you need to enter a date range on the screen.

The Person Selection Period enables you to specify the period in which employee data records are read. Only records that overlap with the specified period by at least one day are selected. To define an interval, you enter the start date in the left column and the end date in the right column.

You can select Other Period, enter dates in the range boxes to its right, and input dates in the Person Selection Period fields below it to ensure that the system selects only employees who are members of the company on at least one day in the specified period. These are persons with valid organizational assignment (Infotype 0001) records. You can specify an interval by entering the start and end dates in the left and right columns.

AUDITING QUERY EXECUTION

The HCM module usually has an increased level of security considerations because of the nature of the data (for example, Social Security numbers, annual salary, benefits). Although this task is usually performed by your administration/security/basis team, you can follow these steps to audit when a query report has last been run and by whom:

1. Enter transaction code **ST03** (Workload Analysis of SAP System).
2. Select the server you want to analyze.
3. Choose the time frame you want to analyze.
4. Choose Transaction Profile.

5. Sort the list by program/transaction code and look for the query you want to find.

6. Double-click the program/transaction code to see who ran it and when it was run.

7. Repeat steps 2 through 6 for each server you want to audit.

CONFIGURING HR ACTIONS/EVENTS TO IMPROVE REPORTING CAPABILITIES

You can customize the configuration of personnel actions, such as hiring, terminations, and organizational assignments within your SAP R/3 HCM module. You can customize the SAP R/3-delivered actions, also known as *personnel events*, to your company's needs so that you can collect necessary data and assign specific employment statuses. You can then classify the employee data collected during your actions with reason codes to provide better employee groupings for reporting. Before you configure new actions, however, you need to answer three questions:

- What data do I need to collect?
- What statuses do I want to assign?
- What are my reporting goals related to these actions?

The following sections explain why these questions are so important and then show you how to create your own HR actions.

WHAT TO COLLECT

You determine which infotypes to include in each event based on what data you want to collect. Take organizational actions, for example. For a simple promotion, you could start with Infotype 0000 (to record the action and its reason code), Infotype 0001 (to record the organizational change), and Infotype 0008 (to record the change in salary). Those are the basics, but you need to think a step further. For example, do you want to collect any other pertinent information along with the promotion? The following is a sample checklist to stimulate your thought process about what infotypes to include in an action:

Question	Infotype to Add
Does this action require a change to any dates collected for the employee?	0041: Date Specifications
Does this action require any reminder dates to be updated for the employee?	0019: Date Monitoring
Does the change in status (part time to full time or vice versa) have an impact on the person's benefits eligibility?	0171: General Benefits Information (and other benefits-related infotypes)
Does the employee life event require update or delimitation of the spouse or dependent information?	0021: Family/Related Person

Question	Infotype to Add
If you are processing an employee's address change, does that person also have a bank change that would affect his or her direct deposit?	0009: Bank Details
Does a leave event require a change to the employee's travel privileges while on leave?	0017: Travel Privileges

After you determine what data you want to collect, you need to determine what statuses to assign.

It is possible to create an action without using Infotype 0000. For example, if you are creating an action to update an address, you can decide whether you want Infotype 0000 to be recorded for the address change. The system already date-delimits the old address, so history is properly preserved. Therefore, based on your company's administrative guidelines, you may or may not want Infotype 0000 created for every event.

WHAT STATUSES TO ASSIGN

You can use events to change an employee's status (for example, new-hire actions make them active, and terminations make them withdrawn). You have three options for the status to assign for each event:

- Basic Employment Status
- Special Payment Status
- Customer Specific Status

You use Basic Employment Status to set the status to which you want the employee to be changed. This appears on Infotype 0000 in the Employment Status field. The standard SAP-delivered options are as follows:

- 0: Employee not with Company (used for termination actions)
- 1: Employee with Company, but Inactive (used for unpaid leaves)
- 2: Employee with Company, but as Retiree (used for retiree actions)
- 3: Employee Active in Company (hire/rehire and non-status change organizational actions)

For the Special Payment Status, three options can update Infotype 000:

- 0: Special Payment: No Entitlement
- 1: Special Payment: Standard Wage Type
- 2: Special Payment: Special Wage Type

Customer Specific Status is optional. You can use Customer Specific Status to determine your own custom statuses to be assigned during the actions. By using Customer Specific Status, you can really maximize your reporting options.

17

THE REPORTING GOALS RELATED TO ACTIONS

HR actions not only collect information and assign statuses but also provide groupings of employees for reporting purposes. Having reason codes associated with actions is the only way to ensure that you can classify employees into the appropriate groups so that you can obtain the data you need. For example, if you have a termination action without reason codes, you might be able to determine that you had 100 terminations in the past month, but you would have no idea why. Creating reason codes that allow you to distinguish between avoidable (quit for better pay) and unavoidable (death) reasons helps you get a comprehensive look at your workforce.

One action for which a reason code is very important is a pay-change–related action. Employees can have changes in pay for a variety of reasons, the most common being promotions and demotions. Many states require companies to report promotions and demotions. Assigning reason codes to your pay-change–related actions for promotions and demotions is a good way to ensure that you are collecting the appropriate information.

MAXIMIZING THE USE OF EVENT REASON CODES

Using reason codes can really make or break you when it is time to evaluate the employees who have undergone events. The termination example mentioned in the preceding section is a good indicator of this. Without a record of *why* someone was terminated, the actual record of a termination action does not provide much information. A best practice is to determine the reasons you want to track and evaluate your turnover reports to see what your needs really are. After making a list of termination reasons, you can determine whether you want to group them to make them more useful. Table 17.2 provides a list of reason code examples.

TABLE 17.2   SAMPLE TERMINATION REASON CODES FOR TERMINATION EVENT

Reason Code	Reason Name
A1	Death
A2	Military duty
A3	Medical
B1	Better Opportunity – More Money
B2	Better Opportunity – Better Benefits
B3	Better Opportunity – Commute-Related
C3	Gross Misconduct
D1	Dissatisfaction with Job
D2	Dissatisfaction with Supervisor
D3	Dissatisfaction with Pay

These sample codes would allow you to classify termination reason codes into four categories: Unavoidable Termination (A), Employees Who Took Positions at Another Company (B), Employees Who Were Terminated for Cause (C), and Employees Who Quit Because They Were Dissatisfied with the Company (D). Using codes A, B, C, and D enables you to group the codes as needed and simplifies reporting later.

You can also maximize the use of the reason codes for pay-change–related actions. An employee's pay could change for at least a dozen reasons. Only by properly grouping these pay changes into categories can you address your reporting needs. For example, distinguishing which employees were promoted and demoted in a certain period of time is a frequent reporting need to satisfy governmental regulatory reporting, such as affirmative action plan reporting. Creating actions specific to promotions or demotions or having multiple specific reason codes for a single pay-change action is a way to meet that requirement.

Creating actions in SAP is an easy task. After you have thought through the three questions presented earlier in this chapter, you can complete the configuration by using the SAP Implementation Guide. The configuration of actions and reason codes is most often performed by the functional person responsible for system configuration. It is important to note that the HR/business side of the organization should dictate what the event and reason codes are. They should not be driven by other departments, such as the Payroll department or the IT organization.

THINGS TO REMEMBER

- You can report on payroll results if you activate infotypes to store the resulting data.
- You can eliminate duplicate line reporting quickly and easily by using the indicator or subtype on your report's selection screen.
- Understanding the differences between the selection periods on your report's selection screen ensures that you always retrieve the correct information in your reports.
- You can report based on all Infotype 0041 dates on a single line by adding some custom fields to your InfoSet.
- The manner in which your actions are configured should be based on business decisions to appropriately assign statuses and to maximize reporting options.

CHAPTER **18**

SECURITY CONCEPTS IN SAP R/3 QUERY-BASED REPORTING TOOLS

In this chapter

This chapter addresses how you can configure the SAP environment to permit varying levels of use of the SAP Query tools to users. It does not have to do with what a person can see when executing a SAP query. Recall from Chapter 2, "One-Time Configuration for Query Tool Use," that SAP standard logical databases are used whenever InfoSets are created. As noted in Chapter 2, you should always use logical databases as the data source within InfoSets that are used for query-based reporting. Using a logical database as your data source guarantees that the SAP solution is smart enough to know which areas of the data a user is allowed to see so that only the appropriate data will show in an SAP query report. Regardless of what type of security access the person who created the report has, the system is smart enough to display only the appropriate data for the user executing the report. (Note that this is the case only when logical databases are used as the data source if a SAP query is created using an InfoSet that is based on anything other than a logical database (for example, a table, a table join, a program). It is fair to say that no security whatsoever is in place when the query is run because all records within the tables are displayed in the report output.)

NOTE

Dedicated professionals in each organization are responsible for security. It is recommended that the security decisions, configuration, and administration described in this chapter be performed by those dedicated security professionals. The basics of how security works for SAP queries are described here so that you have a full picture of the reporting solution. I recommend that you follow your company's established guidelines for modifying security roles and that you make the information in this chapter available to your designated security professionals. A system administrator can control access rights to the InfoSet (Ad Hoc) Query tool by using roles or query groups. Exactly one SAP query group must be assigned to a role (an InfoSet must be associated with the query group), although the user does not need to be listed in the query group. If users want to save their reports, they need authorization object S_QUERY, field ACTVT, value 02; otherwise, they can only create and execute reports.

SECURITY FOR THE SAP QUERY TOOL

You can use two methods to ensure security for the SAP Query tool: query groups and authorizations. The following sections describe these two methods.

USING QUERY GROUPS TO PROVIDE SECURITY FOR THE SAP QUERY TOOL

Chapter 2 mentions that a query group (known as a user group in versions of SAP prior to version 4.6) is a collection of SAP users who are grouped. A user's assignment to a query group determines which queries he or she can execute or maintain. It also designates which InfoSets (that is, data sources) the user can access. Basically, query groups permit users to create, modify, and execute reports in a certain area within SAP R/3.

Using query groups is an easy way to group and segregate report users and reports. You can also use query groups as an avenue for security. For example, if a user is not placed in any query group, he or she cannot create or maintain queries. If you decide a user should not have access to SAP queries (via the Query tool's initial entry screen, which you reach by using transaction code SQ01), you should simply not assign that user to any query groups. A user who is not assigned to any query groups cannot create, execute, or change any queries, because he or she is unable to access the screen to do so by using transaction code SQ01.

SAP Query reports can also be assigned to transaction codes so that users who do not belong to a query group and/or do not have access to transaction code SQ01 can access them.

USING AUTHORIZATIONS TO PROVIDE SECURITY FOR THE SAP QUERY TOOL

The specific authorization object for the SAP Query tool is S_QUERY. The security administrator can set the field ACTVT for the authorization object to designate that a user can create, configure, or translate (for multiple language configurations) SAP queries. A security administrator can use the information shown in Table 18.1 to assign authorizations specific to the ACTVT authorization object. These authorizations are valid within both standard and global query areas. (See Chapter 1, "Getting Started with the SAP R/3 Query Reporting Tools," for more information on application areas.)

TABLE 18.1   ASSIGNING AUTHORIZATIONS SPECIFIC TO THE ACTVT OBJECT

ACTVT Field Value	Description
02	Create or change queries
23	Maintain configuration of the SAP Query tool (query groups and InfoSets)
67	Language translation

AUTHORIZATIONS FOR CREATING OR CHANGING QUERIES (ACTVT = 02)

Users need the ACTVT value set to 02 to create new SAP queries and/or modify existing queries via the main SAP Query tool screen found via transaction code SQ01.

AUTHORIZATIONS FOR MAINTAINING CONFIGURATION OF SAP QUERY (QUERY GROUPS AND INFOSETS) (ACTVT = 23)

As discussed in Chapters 1 and 2, the process of configuring the SAP Query tool, including the creation of query groups and InfoSets, is very easy to do but should be done only by a trained technical person within the development environment of a SAP solution. A user who will be responsible for this configuration needs to have the ACTVT value set to 23.

If a technical developer will be expanding the use of the logical database to include any custom programs or ABAP, he or she needs to have authorization for maintaining the authorization object S_DEVELOP with the value PROG for field OBJTYPE and the value AQ* for the field OBJNAME. This authorization should be given only to trained ABAP programmers in the development environment. It is the same authorization that a user needs to access the ABAP Editor (via transaction code SE38) to create or change programs whose names begin with AQ. Users who can create and maintain InfoSets without this special designation can only select fields, connect additional tables or structures, and define parameters and selection criteria.

AUTHORIZATIONS FOR LANGUAGE COMPARISON

SAP's language translation capabilities make it possible for end users to customize the text elements (named objects) within their SAP solution for multiple languages. When a user creates an SAP query, he or she begins by inputting a title in the language the user logged in with. As with all other named objects entered by the user, these objects exist in SAP in the user's logon language. Language translation is possible such that a user can enter the equivalent named object text in another language to accommodate a user who will be logging on to the solution in a different language. Users need the ACTVT value set to 67 to utilize the language comparison utility.

Users who have authorization for the authorization object S_QUERY with both the values 02 and 23 have authorization to access all queries of all query groups without being explicitly entered in each query group.

18

Helpful Hint

If a query accesses a certain table when it is run, the user needs display authorization for authorization object S_TABU_DIS. The field DICBERCLS must contain the table's authorization groups. This sophisticated authorization object protects SAP tables from unauthorized access. It is important to note that this is the same authorization that you need to be able to display tables using either the Data Browser (transaction SE16) or the initial table maintenance screen (transaction SM31).

SECURITY FOR THE INFOSET (AD HOC) QUERY AND QUICKVIEWER TOOLS

You can use two methods to ensure security for the InfoSet (Ad Hoc) Query tool and the QuickViewer tool: query groups and roles. The following sections describe these two methods.

USING QUERY GROUPS TO PROVIDE SECURITY FOR THE INFOSET (AD HOC) QUERY AND QUICKVIEWER TOOLS

You control access rights to the InfoSet (Ad Hoc) Query and QuickViewer tools by using query groups exactly the same way as you do with the SAP Query tool, as described earlier in this chapter, in the section "Using Query Groups to Provide Security for the SAP Query Tool."

USING ROLES TO PROVIDE SECURITY FOR THE INFOSET (AD HOC) QUERY AND QUICKVIEWER TOOLS

Exactly one query group (with InfoSets assigned) must be assigned to a role. It is not required to enter or select individual usernames in the query group, because they are assigned in the role assignment. This means that a user who is assigned to a role is automatically copied into the query group assigned to the role. This assignment functions only when the user uses the role to navigate to (that is, call) the InfoSet (Ad Hoc) Query or QuickViewer tools. If the InfoSet (Ad Hoc) Query or QuickViewer tools are accessed via another method, the traditional access authorization implemented using SAP query groups is applicable. For a user to be able to save InfoSet queries or QuickViews, he or she needs authorization object S_QUERY, with the field ACTVT set to 02. If the user does not have this authorization, he or she can execute the available InfoSets and queries within the role, but he or she cannot save queries.

THINGS TO REMEMBER

- The configuration of security for any area within SAP should be performed by a trained SAP security administrator.
- Options for SAP Query tool authorizations are based on query groups and authorizations.
- Restricting users based on query groups is an easy way of limiting their access.
- Options for InfoSet (Ad Hoc) Query tool and QuickViewer tool authorizations are based on query groups and roles.
- A special security authorization is required for users to be able to use the language translation facility.

18

CHAPTER 19

CREATING BASIC REPORTS WITH THE INFOSET (AD HOC) QUERY TOOL

In this chapter

This chapter outlines how to create basic queries by using the InfoSet (Ad Hoc) Query tool. If you are looking to use the InfoSet (Ad Hoc) Query tool for reporting in the Human Capital Management (HCM) module only, you should review Chapter 15, "HR and Payroll Reporting Options in the HCM Module," before proceeding with this chapter.

Helpful Hint

Although it is recommended that you create SAP query reports live in your production environment, it is important while you are learning and training to practice in your test or quality assurance client so as not to have any impact on production while you are learning.

Unlike the SAP Query tool, covered in earlier chapters, the InfoSet (Ad Hoc) Query tool is a reporting utility that users can use to retrieve simple single-use lists of SAP R/3 data. The InfoSet (Ad Hoc) Query tool is a reporting tool delivered with SAP version 4.6 and above that is based on the functionality of the SAP Query tool and the Ad Hoc Query tool from earlier versions of SAP R/3.

NOTE

The Ad Hoc Query tool was a simple reporting utility designed for the HCM module in SAP's earliest versions. The Ad Hoc Query tool was renamed the InfoSet Query tool in version 4.6, and it was expanded for use in all modules (although when it is executed from within the HCM module, it is still referred to as the Ad Hoc Query tool). I refer to the tool throughout as the InfoSet (Ad Hoc) Query tool.

Unlike the SAP Query tool (which has multiple screens), with the InfoSet (Ad Hoc) Query tool, all query information, including the selection criteria for InfoSet (Ad Hoc) Query reporting, is available on a single screen. The InfoSet (Ad Hoc) Query tool is designed so that you can pose questions to the SAP system and receive real-time answers.

CREATING A BASIC QUERY WITH THE INFOSET (AD HOC) QUERY TOOL

To create a basic report with the InfoSet (Ad Hoc) Query tool, follow these steps:

1. Log in to the area of your SAP client where your query reports will be created. (Best practice dictates that you maintain query reports in your live production client.)

2. You can access the InfoSet (Ad Hoc) Query tool in three ways:

   - Through an application-specific role, using the Easy Access menu
   - Via the SAP Query tool, by using transaction code SQ01 and then clicking the InfoSet Query button
   - Via transaction code /nPQAH

When you navigate to the InfoSet (Ad Hoc) Query tool main screen using any of these methods, you see a dialog box that prompts you to select your InfoSet (data source) from the designated environment (QUERY group).

3. Select your InfoSet and then press Enter. The main screen of the InfoSet (Ad Hoc) Query tool appears, as shown in Figure 19.1.

Figure 19.1
The fields listed in the Field Groups section of the selected InfoSet appear on the top left of the InfoSet (Ad Hoc) Query screen.

The main screen of the InfoSet (Ad Hoc) Query tool has three sections:

- The actual InfoSet from which you select and choose your fields (top left)
- A Selections section (top right)
- A sample report display (bottom)

4. To create an InfoSet (Ad Hoc) Query report, select the check box in the Output column next to each field you want to include in the output of your report. For example, Figure 19.2 shows a few fields selected.

5. Notice that any field selected for layout is now displayed at the bottom of the screen (with bogus data) to assist you in seeing what your report will look like.

6. Add fields to your Selections section (which functions as the report's selection screen) by selecting the appropriate check box in the Selection column next to each field you want to be able to select on (that is, specify) when executing your report. For example, Figure 19.3 shows one field selected.

19

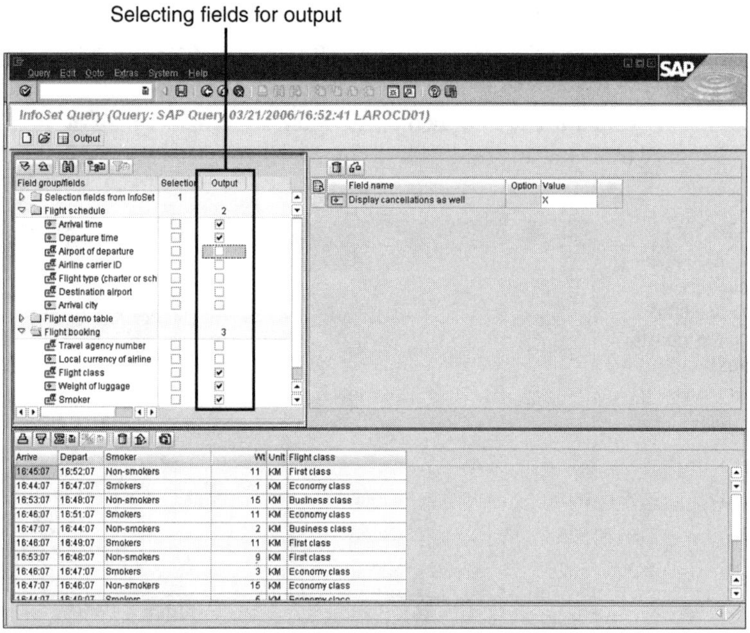

Selecting fields for output

Figure 19.2
You will recognize the field groups from those created during configuration of the InfoSet.

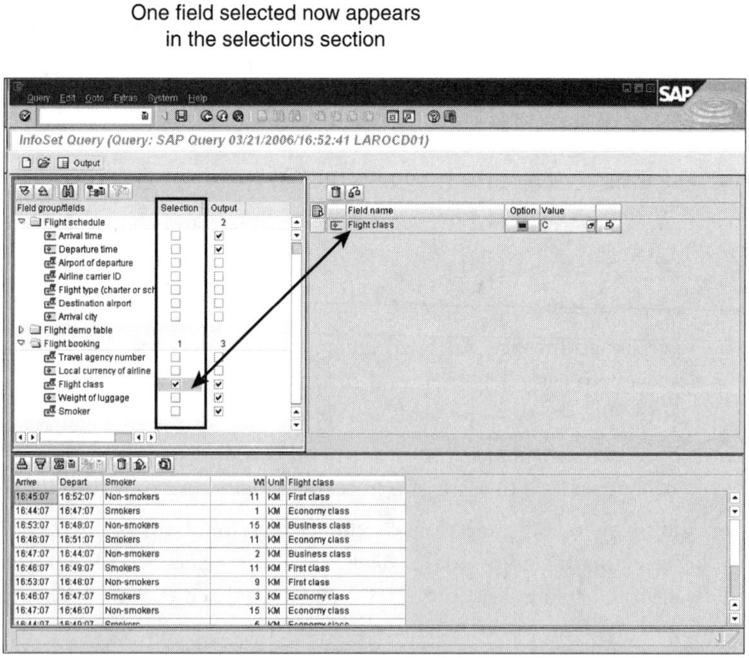

One field selected now appears in the selections section

Figure 19.3
The Selections section in InfoSet (Ad Hoc) Query tool reporting appears at the top right of the screen.

Any field(s) indicated for selection now appear on the top-right side of the screen. The Selections section works just as a standard selection screen works, allowing you to input values before execution to further specify your reporting output. (For example, you could specify to include only business class (Type C) flights in a report.)

7. To proceed to your InfoSet (Ad Hoc) Query report output, click the Start Output button on the Application toolbar (or press the F8 key on your keyboard) to execute the report. By default, your report displays in the SAP List Viewer (previously known as the ABAP List Viewer [ALV]), from which you can easily drag and drop the columns and/or manipulate the look of the output (see Figure 19.4).

Figure 19.4
The SAP List Viewer view of the InfoSet (Ad Hoc) Query report is similar to the default report output shown for SAP Query tool reports.

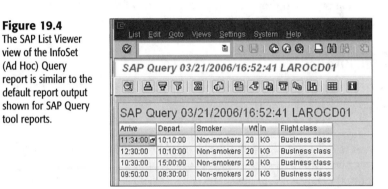

THE OPTIONS AVAILABLE ON THE INFOSET (AD HOC) QUERY TOOL SCREEN

The following sections describe the options that are available on the InfoSet (Ad Hoc) Query Tool screen.

THE APPLICATION TOOLBAR

The Application toolbar on the main screen of the InfoSet (Ad Hoc) Query tool has three buttons:

- **Create**—This button allows you to create new InfoSet (Ad Hoc) queries.
- **Open**—This button allows you to open existing InfoSet (Ad Hoc) queries.
- **Output List**—This button executes a query and displays the report output.

THE FIELD GROUPS SECTION TOOLBAR

The top-left window of the InfoSet (Ad Hoc) Query tool screen is where you select the fields that you want to include in the Selections section and in your report output via the two designated columns labeled Selection and Output. Five buttons are available on the field groups section toolbar:

- **Expand and Collapse**—These buttons expand or collapse the selected field group.
- **Find**—This button allows you to search for a field of interest. You click the Find button, type in the appropriate keyword, and then click the check mark Enter button to

go directly to the first instance in which that keyword exists within the expanded field groups.

■ **Field Groups**—This button allows you to vary the way in which you view the fields within the data source. The default option is to display them in field groups, as shown in Figure 19.3. However, you can click this button to see options for displaying the data in a logical database structure or in a field catalog structure.

■ **Fields for a Field Group**—This button is available only if you had previously clicked the Field Groups button and the option to view your fields in a field catalog structure. Clicking this button returns your list of fields to be segregated by field group.

THE SELECTIONS SECTION TOOLBAR

Only two buttons exist in the Selections section of the InfoSet (Ad Hoc) Query tool screen:

■ **Delete**—This button allows you to delete any entries entered in the selection fields in the Selections section.

■ **Check**—This button allows you to validate the entries made within the selection fields to check whether they are valid entries. For example, if the Flight Class field is listed in the Selections section, the only appropriate values for that field are C, Y, and F (for Business Class, Economy Class, and First Class, respectively). If another character is entered and the Check button is clicked, you are alerted that an invalid value has been entered.

THE OUTPUT SAMPLE SECTION TOOLBAR

The seven options available at the bottom of the InfoSet (Ad Hoc) Query tool screen are designed to allow you to work with your sample output:

■ **Ascending Sort and Descending Sort**—These buttons allow you to select any column in the sample output and sort it in either ascending or descending order.

■ **Sum**—This button allows you to select any numeric column within your sample output and request that the data be summarized, as shown in Figure 19.5.

Attached to the Sum button is a drop-down arrow that provides additional mathematical functions for calculating the mean, minimum, and maximum values for any selected column in the report.

■ **Subtotals**—This button allows you to select any meaningful column within your sample output and request that the data be subtotaled, as shown in Figure 19.6.

■ **Delete**—This button allows you to select any column in the sample output section of the InfoSet (Ad Hoc) Query tool screen and prevent that column from being displayed in your report output.

■ **Initialize Formatting**—This button resets any output formatting you inserted to its original state. You can use this function if you no longer need to create subtotals or totals.

■ **Refresh Data**—If you change the output list in such a way that a new selection must take place (when you add a new field, for example), you see the bogus data in the output list again. You need to click the Refresh Data button so that the query is executed again and real data is displayed in the output section of the screen.

Figure 19.5
The Weight of Luggage field was totaled by selecting the Weight of Luggage column and then clicking the Sum button on the output sample section toolbar.

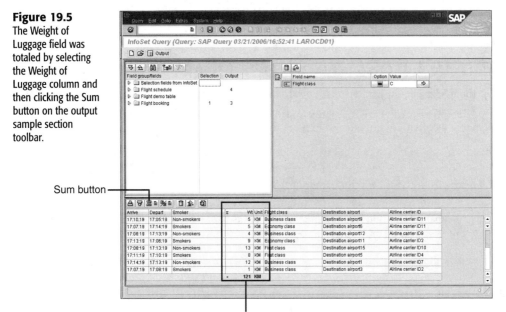

Sum button

Summarized data

Figure 19.6
The report was subtotaled by selecting the Smoker field and then clicking the Subtotals button on the output sample section toolbar.

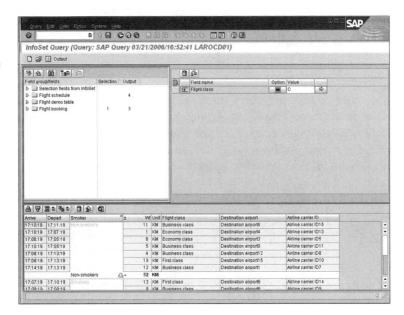

19

MODIFYING AN INFOSET (AD HOC) QUERY

After you create an InfoSet (Ad Hoc) Query, you might want to return to the design screen to make changes and modifications. You can click the green Back button to return to the design screen from the SAP List Viewer display of your report output. In addition, you can change the format of your report from the SAP List Viewer output screen by selecting Settings, Layout, Change.

SAVING AN INFOSET (AD HOC) QUERY

On the design screen in the InfoSet (Ad Hoc) Query tool, you can click the Save button on the Application toolbar to save a query. After designing an InfoSet (Ad Hoc) query, you can change it as often as you like and execute the updated query.

If and where you can save a query depends on your authorizations and on the reporting you are authorized to carry out. (See Chapter 18, "Security Concepts in SAP R/3 Query-Based Reporting Tools," for more information.) If you are authorized to save queries (authorization object S_QUERY with the value 02 for the field ACTVT), you can save from either the Application toolbar or the File menu. The way these functions work depends on your previous work with the InfoSet (Ad Hoc) Query tool.

The following sections describe the various options for saving InfoSet (Ad Hoc) queries.

SAVE (FIRST USAGE)

The first time you use the Save function, SAP takes you to a dialog box where you can enter a short name and description for your InfoSet (Ad Hoc) query. This dialog box is a bit confusing. The system proposes a new name if the template you call up is an InfoSet; if it is a query, the system proposes a query name. If you save a query under the same name again (that is, if you overwrite it), the query is locked for other users. That is, other users of the InfoSet (Ad Hoc) Query tool can continue to use the locked query as a template, but they cannot overwrite it.

If you are a member of a query group and your configuration follows the recommendations in Chapter 2, "One-Time Configuration for Query Tool Use," you can also select from the dialog box a query group to which you want to assign the query to easily group your saved queries as recommended. As with the SAP Query tool, with the InfoSet (Ad Hoc) Query tool you can belong to multiple query groups.

SAVE (NOT FIRST USAGE)

If you use the Save function again with a changed query during a session with the InfoSet (Ad Hoc) Query tool, the query you saved before is overwritten. The dialog box is not shown again. Locks that already exist remain valid.

SAVE AS

As with the Microsoft family of products, using the Save As function allows you to save an open item under a new name to distinguish it from the original item. This function primarily exists so that you can copy queries and edit them afterward. With this function, the dialog box is always shown so you can enter the query name and a description. The system proposes the name of the query that you used as template. The query is saved and locked under the name entered. If you have already saved and therefore locked the template, this lock is removed.

If you are configured to be a member of a query group, you can also select from the dialog box a query group to which you want to assign the query. At this point, you can switch between query groups to which you are assigned and that have access to the current InfoSet. Again, as with the SAP Query tool, with the InfoSet (Ad Hoc) Query tool you can belong to multiple query groups. It is important to note that if you select an existing query from the list of available InfoSet (Ad Hoc) queries, that query is overwritten when you confirm.

NOTE

> The query is locked when you save it. In other words, other users can continue working on the query at the same time as you, but they end up using the old (unchanged) version as a template in the current session with the InfoSet (Ad Hoc) Query tool. It is important to note that they can no longer save the query under its original name. This also means that you can save a query under a certain name only if the query is not locked by another user. If you have locked a query by saving it and then you select a new template for your InfoSet (Ad Hoc) Query tool, the lock on the query used before is removed, and another user can save the query in a changed version.

RESTRICTIONS WITH THE INFOSET (AD HOC) QUERY TOOL

19

The InfoSet (Ad Hoc) Query tool uses the SAP List Viewer as its default output. Unlike the SAP Query tool, where up to nine ranked lists and up to nine statistics per query are possible, with the InfoSet (Ad Hoc) Query tool, every query can output only one list, and you cannot distribute output fields over several lines. Recall from earlier chapters that advanced functions are available with the SAP Query tool, including the ability to create calculations (local fields) and insert graphics, icons, colors, custom headers and footers, and so on. These functions are not possible with the InfoSet (Ad Hoc) Query tool.

Because the InfoSet (Ad Hoc) Query tool can output only one list and cannot distribute output fields over several lines, you should not process an available query with the InfoSet (Ad Hoc) Query tool if it contains multiple lists, a basic list with line groups, or calculated fields.

If you use a query with one of these properties in the InfoSet (Ad Hoc) Query tool, the parts of the output are shown as follows:

- **Multiple lists**—Only the first list is displayed.
- **A basic list with line groups**—Only the first line of each is displayed.
- **Calculated fields**—Local fields are not displayed.

These properties are lost if you overwrite the query. However, they are not lost as long as you do not save the query, and you can continue to call and execute the query with all properties by using the SAP Query tool via transaction code SQ01 and clicking the SAP Query button.

SECURITY CONSIDERATIONS FOR USING THE INFOSET (AD HOC) QUERY TOOL

The information in the following sections is designed for trained SAP security/administration professionals. To call the InfoSet (Ad Hoc) Query tool, your SAP R/3 system provides you with four reports and function modules (of the same name), which implement the InfoSet (Ad Hoc) Query tool call and determine access rights and reporting type for the InfoSet (Ad Hoc) Query tool. The following sections describe the reports/function modules that are available.

THE SAP_QUERY_DEVELOPMENT_ROLE MODULE

You use the SAP_QUERY_DEVELOPMENT_ROLE module for access using role development.

The following are the parameters for this module:

- Role (input necessary)
- InfoSet (optional)
- Query (optional)

A query group from the global area has to be assigned to the role. If you specify an InfoSet, it has to be assigned to the query group. If you specify a query, it has to be assigned to the query group.

THE SAP_QUERY_AD_HOC_ROLE MODULE

You use the SAP_QUERY_AD_HOC_ROLE module for access using role and ad hoc reporting.

The following are the parameters for this module:

- Role (input necessary)
- InfoSet (optional)
- Query (optional)

A query group from either the global or standard area has to be assigned to the role. If you specify an InfoSet, it has to be assigned to the query group. If you specify a query, it has to be assigned to the query group.

THE SAP_QUERY_DEVELOPMENT MODULE

You use the SAP_QUERY_DEVELOPMENT module for access using query group and development.

The following are the parameters for this module:

- Query group (optional)
- InfoSet (optional)
- Query (optional)

The query group has to come from the global application area. If you specify more than one parameter, the parameters must match, meaning that the InfoSet has to be assigned to the query group, and the query must be based on the specified InfoSet.

THE SAP_QUERY_AD_HOC MODULE

You use the SAP_QUERY_AD_HOC module to access using query group and ad hoc reporting.

The following are the parameters for this module:

- Query area (standard setting: Standard area)
- Query group (optional)
- InfoSet (optional)
- Query (optional)

First, you need to decide which query area (standard or global) you want to work in with the InfoSet (Ad Hoc) Query tool. (The standard area is recommended.) To work in the global area, you select the global area indicator. Then you enter the remaining parameters. It is important to note that if you specify more than one parameter, the parameters must match: The InfoSet has to be assigned to the query group, and the query must be based on the specified InfoSet.

The InfoSet (Ad Hoc) Query tool has default values in the specified query area and query group parameters, and only ad hoc–style reporting can take place. In other words, a user who accesses the InfoSet (Ad Hoc) Query tool from the HCM module or menu path either goes straight to the initial screen of the InfoSet (Ad Hoc) Query tool, where the assigned InfoSet is displayed, or can choose between several assigned InfoSets (as described in the step-by-step instructions earlier in this chapter, in the section "Creating a Basic Query with the InfoSet (Ad Hoc) Query Tool"). In this type of call in the HCM module, the InfoSet Query tool is referred to as the Ad Hoc Query tool.

19

THINGS TO REMEMBER

- Creating a report by using the InfoSet (Ad Hoc) Query tool is very easy.

- The InfoSet Query tool is called the Ad Hoc Query tool when executed from within the HCM module.

- The InfoSet (Ad Hoc) Query tool does not contain the advanced options that the SAP Query tool contains.

- When you use the InfoSet (Ad Hoc) Query tool, each query can output only one list, and you cannot distribute output fields over several lines.

- Understanding how to save queries created with the InfoSet (Ad Hoc) Query tool is critical to ensuring that you do not overwrite other work.

19

CHAPTER **20**

CREATING QUICKVIEWS BY USING QUICKVIEWER

In this chapter

Creating reports by using the QuickViewer tool is easy. This chapter outlines how to create basic reports, called QuickViews, by using the QuickViewer tool.

Helpful Hint

Although it is recommended that you create SAP query reports live in your production environment, it is important while you are learning and training to practice in your test quality assurance client so as not to have any impact on production while you are learning.

UNDERSTANDING QUICKVIEWER

Unlike the SAP Query tool, which is a complete reporting solution tool, the SAP QuickViewer tool, delivered with SAP version 4.6 and above, is a WYSIWYG (what you see is what you get) utility for quickly collecting data from an R/3 system. To define a report by using the QuickViewer, you simply enter texts (titles) and select fields and options to define the QuickView. With this tool, you create QuickViews, not reports. Users cannot share QuickViews as they can reports, but they can convert QuickViews to reports to use them with the SAP Query tool.

Like the other Query tools, the QuickViewer allows you to define reports without having any technical or programming knowledge. The QuickViewer is especially useful for new users and occasional system users. The QuickViewer is basically a single-screen version of the SAP Query tool. Although QuickViews are user dependent, you can convert a QuickView into a SAP Query report to make the information available to others.

QuickViews have the same functional attributes as queries. However, there are a number of differences between QuickViews and queries created using the SAP Query tool:

- **Basic lists**—QuickViews can define only basic lists, as opposed to the multiple-line queries and ranked or statistical lists that the SAP Query tool can create.

- **Security**—Security initial setup is simpler in the QuickViewer than in the SAP Query tool because no query group assignment is necessary with QuickViews.

- **User dependency**—Each user has his or her own personal list of QuickViews, and unless they are converted to SAP queries, QuickViews cannot be shared or exchanged among users.

- **Data source**—Unlike with the SAP Query tool, with the QuickViewer, you are not required to use an InfoSet. When you define a QuickView, you can specify its data source dynamically. You can use tables, database views, table joins, logical databases, and even InfoSets as the data sources for QuickViews.

- **Modes**—A similarity between the SAP Query tool and the QuickViewer is that each provides two modes for designing reports: a standard mode (called Basis mode) and a graphical mode (called Layout mode).

The QuickViewer emulates the SAP Query reporting tool on a single screen. It is divided into three major sections:

- The top left lists the tables and data fields contained in the data source.
- The bottom left is the Help application.
- The right side of the screen is the QuickViewer main screen, where you design a QuickView. The main screen section has three tabbed sections that you use to specify a QuickView.

CREATING A QUICKVIEW BY USING QUICKVIEWER

Creating a QuickView by using the QuickViewer tool is simple. You just follow these steps:

NOTE

> Like the SAP Query tool, QuickViewer can be run in two modes: Basis (standard) and Layout (graphical) mode. In Basis mode, the system automatically renders the report from specified parameters, and in Layout mode, a user can tweak the report's interface via a visual tool that allows dragging and dropping. As with the SAP Query tool, it is easier to work with the QuickViewer in Basis mode.

1. Navigate to the main screen of the SAP R/3 QuickViewer by using transaction **SQVI** (see Figure 20.1). (You can also open the QuickViewer's main screen by clicking the QuickViewer button on the main screen of the SAP Query tool or by choosing an application-specific role from the Easy Access menu.)

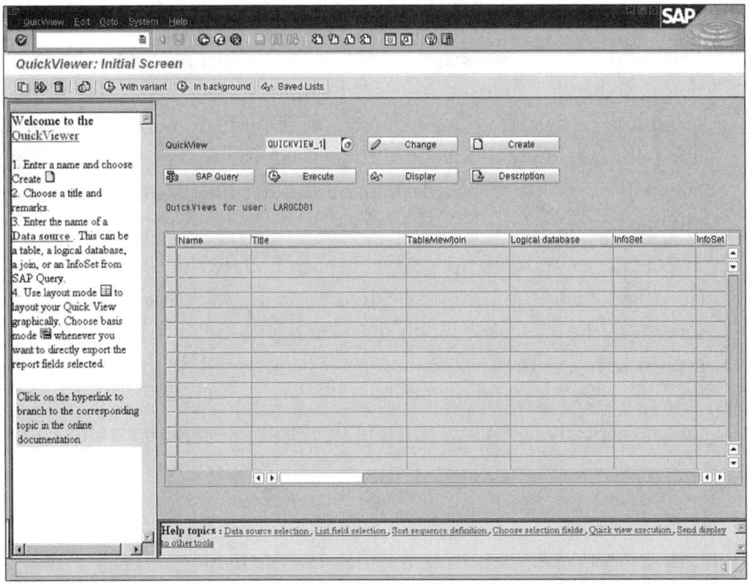

Figure 20.1
The main screen of the QuickViewer reporting tool looks very similar to the main screen of the SAP Query tool.

2. On the main screen, enter a name for your QuickView (for example, **QUICKVIEW_1**) and then click the Create button. A dialog box appears, asking you to select your data source (see Figure 20.2).

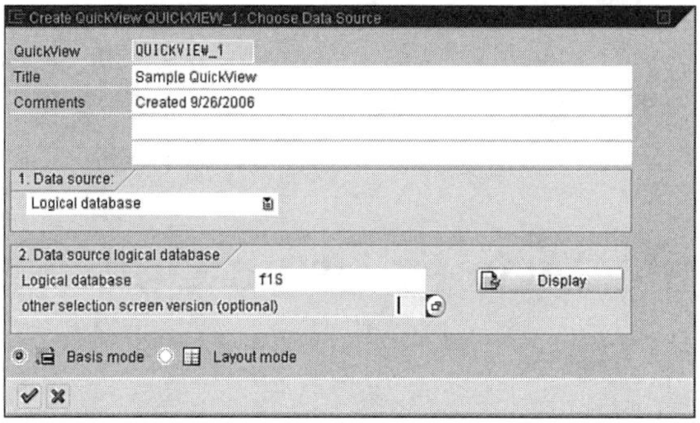

Figure 20.2
The selection of a data source at design time mirrors the process of creating a data source during configuration.

3. On the Create QuickView: Choose Data Source dialog box, insert a title (for example, **Sample QuickView**) and, if desired, insert comments (for example, the date it was created).

4. Identify where your data is coming from by selecting an option in the Data Source field (for example, a logical database). When you select a data source, the bottom of the screen changes to show suboptions specific to the data source (for example, a specific logical database). For this example, enter the logical database Flight Scheduling System (f1S).

5. At the bottom of the dialog box, choose to create the QuickView in Basis mode. When you are done making entries and selections in this dialog, click the green arrow Enter button.

6. Select the first tab on the main screen, the List Fld. Select tab, which lists the output fields. Select any fields on the right side of the screen, listed in the Available Fields grouping, by selecting the gray keys to the left of the field names, and then click the left-pointing single-arrow button between the two groupings. To move all fields in the data source so that they will be included in your report output, click the left-pointing double-arrow button (see Figure 20.3).

7. Select the second tab, Sort Sequence, to dictate the sort order for the selected fields (see Figure 20.4). Indicate a desired order by selecting fields on the right side of the screen, in the Available Fields grouping, and then click the left-pointing single-arrow button between the two groupings. The selected fields appear in the Fields in List column, in the order in which they were selected. Use the radio buttons to the left of the fields to specify that you want the field to be sorted in ascending or descending order.

20

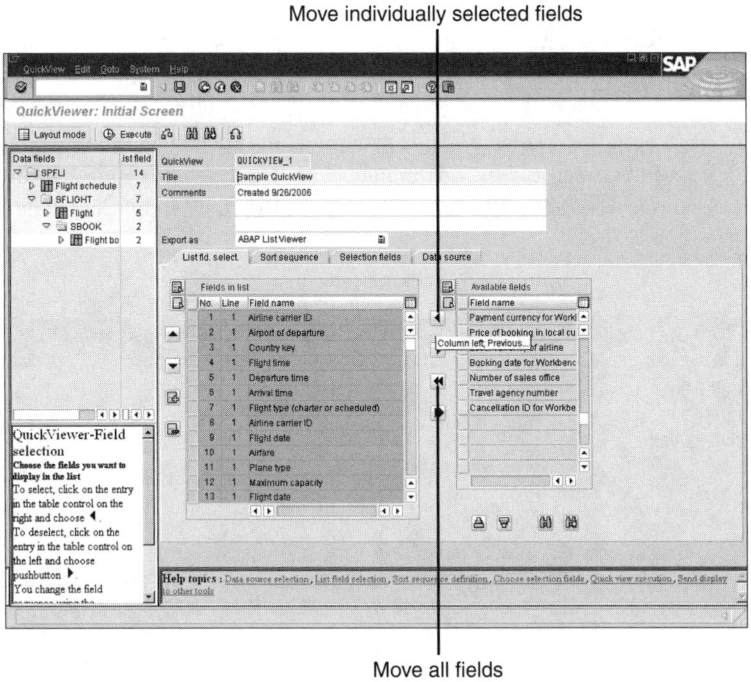

Move individually selected fields

Figure 20.3
You indicate what fields you want to be output in your QuickView by using the Fields in List column section of the main screen.

Move all fields

Ascending   Descending

Figure 20.4
You can sort in ascending or descending order.

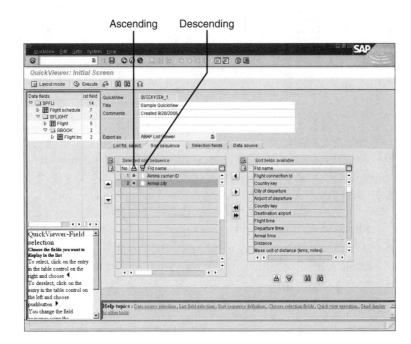

8. Select the third tab, Selection Fields, to indicate what fields to include on the QuickView's selection screen upon execution (see Figure 20.5). (Note that some fields already exist, as indicated by a lock icon, based on designations in the logical database—f1S in this case—selected for the QuickView.) Select fields on the right side of the screen, in the Available Fields grouping, and then click the left-pointing single-arrow button between the two groupings. The selected fields appear in the Selection Fields column. For example, Figure 20.5 shows that the Flight Class field has been added.

Lock indicator

Figure 20.5
You can add fields to the selection screen to specify particular data upon execution.

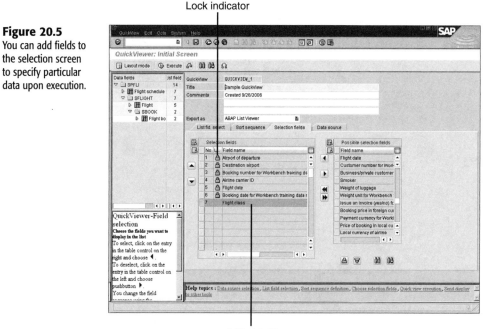

Added field

9. Select the fourth tab, Data Source, to confirm that the QuickViewer is using the correct data source for this QuickView (see Figure 20.6).

10. Note in the middle of the screen that you have different export options for the QuickView. SAP List Viewer is the default, but you can select a different option from the Export As drop-down box.

11. Click the Execute button on the Application toolbar to view the report's selection screen. If needed, further specify your selections on the selection screen.

12. Click the Execute button to see your completed QuickView, which should look similar to the QuickView shown in Figure 20.7.

20

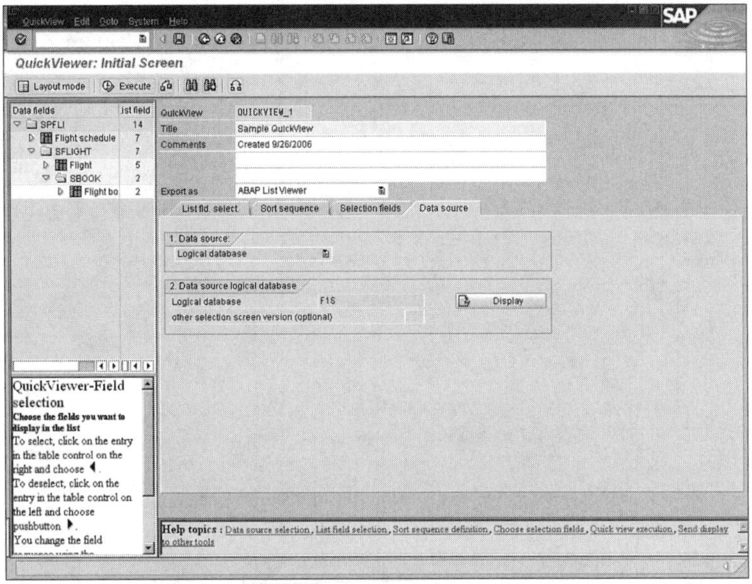

Figure 20.6
You can display the details of your data source by clicking the Display button.

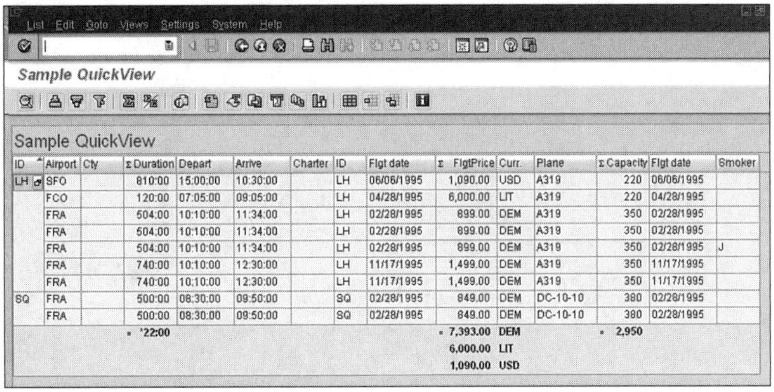

Figure 20.7
The QuickView output looks similar to the output of an SAP query.

THE OPTIONS AVAILABLE ON THE QUICKVIEWER SCREEN

The QuickViewer reporting tool provides a number of options on its four tabs.

The first tab in the QuickViewer, Output Fields, lists all the fields that will be included in your QuickView output. This tab has 10 buttons; their functions are described in Table 20.1.

20

TABLE 20.1   BUTTONS ON THE OUTPUT FIELDS TAB OF THE QUICKVIEWER

Button	Button Name	Description
	Select All	Selects all fields within the section
	Deselect All	Unselects all fields within the section
	Next Value	Moves the selected field up, in order
	Previous Value	Moves the selected field down, in order
	Insert line	Inserts a line at the selected field
	Delete Line	Deletes the inserted line
	Ascending Sort	Sorts the data listed in alphabetical ascending order
	Descending Sort	Sorts the data listed in alphabetical descending order
	Find	Searches through the Available Fields column for any data indicated in the search dialog box
	Find Next	Searches through the Available Fields column for the next instance of data indicated in the search dialog box

MODIFYING A QUICKVIEW

After you create a QuickView, only you have access to it, because it is user-dependent (unless you convert it to an SAP query). However, you can return to an existing QuickView and make changes by following these steps:

1. Navigate to the main screen of the SAP R/3 QuickViewer by using transaction **SQVI**. (You can also open the QuickViewer's main screen by clicking the QuickViewer button on the main screen of the SAP Query tool or by choosing an application-specific role from the Easy Access menu.)

2. Select an existing QuickView from the list (or type in its name) and then click the Change button. The QuickViewer: Initial screen appears.

3. Make any required changes to the QuickView.

4. Save your changes by clicking the Save button on the Application toolbar.

USING QUICKVIEWER IN LAYOUT MODE

As mentioned earlier in this chapter, you can use the QuickViewer in Basis or Layout mode. Layout mode provides a graphical representation of the QuickView. To see a QuickView in Layout mode, follow these steps:

1. Navigate to the main screen of the SAP R/3 QuickViewer by using transaction **SQVI**. (You can also open the QuickViewer's main screen by clicking the QuickViewer button on the main screen of the SAP Query tool or by choosing an application-specific role from the Easy Access menu.)

2. Select an existing QuickView from the list (or type in its name) and then click the Change button. The QuickView main screen appears.

3. Select Goto, Layout Mode (or press F5). The screen displays graphically, as shown in Figure 20.8.

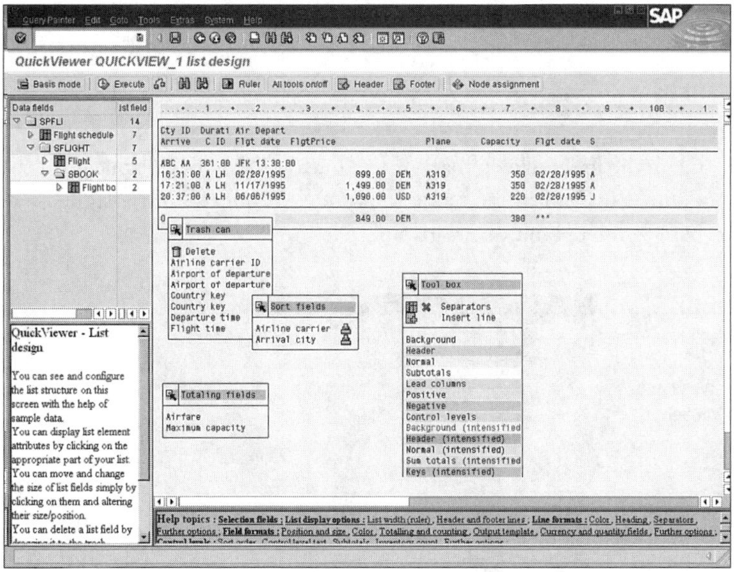

Figure 20.8
The QuickView output looks similar to the output of the SAP Query tool when displayed in Layout mode.

CONVERTING A QUICKVIEW TO A SAP QUERY

As mentioned earlier in this chapter, QuickViews are user-dependent, and other users cannot use them. If you have created a QuickView and you want to share it with others or add to it functionality that is not supported by QuickView, you can convert the QuickView to an SAP query. To do so, follow these steps:

NOTE

> To convert a QuickView into an SAP query, you first choose a query group that you are assigned to and that you will want to assign your query to. If the QuickView you want to convert is based on an InfoSet, that InfoSet must be assigned to your query group. See Chapter 2, "One-Time Configuration for Query Tool Use," for more information.

1. Navigate to the main screen of the SAP R/3 Query tool by using transaction **SQ01**.
2. Select Query, Convert QuickView. A Convert QuickView dialog box, like the one shown in Figure 20.9, appears. The very first alphabetical QuickView you have created appears in this dialog, as does your username.

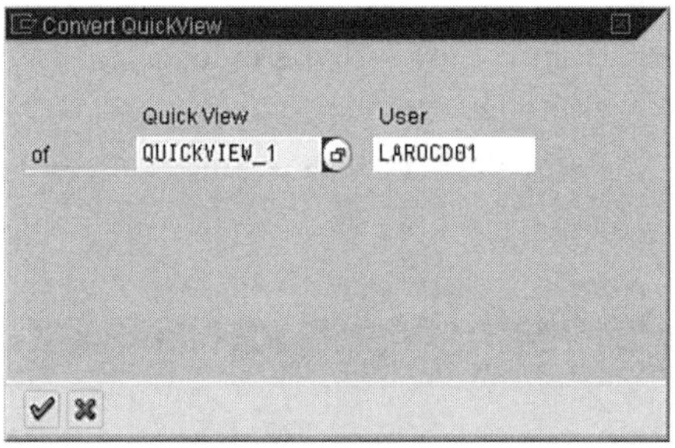

Figure 20.9
All the QuickViews you have created are listed in the QuickView drop-down box.

3. Click the green check mark Enter button. New fields appear on the dialog box (see Figure 20.10). Enter a name for your SAP query. Your assigned query group is listed here as the default query group.

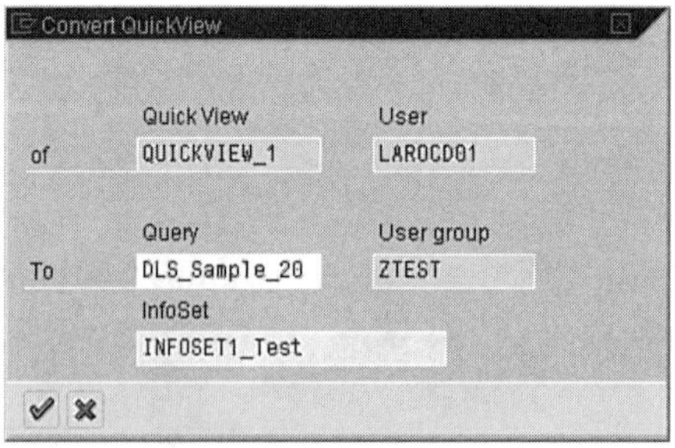

Figure 20.10
You must input a name for your converted QuickView and declare an InfoSet.

20

4. If the QuickView you want to convert was created using a logical database, a table, or a table join, input your choice for the InfoSet. The InfoSet is then generated automatically. Recall from Chapter 2 that the SAP Query tool's functionality is based on InfoSets. To be able to proceed in the SAP Query tool, you must define an InfoSet (data source) for this query.

5. Click the green check mark Enter button. Your QuickView is now in your list of SAP queries.

QUICKVIEWER SECURITY CONSIDERATIONS

An important security distinction that applies to the QuickViewer does not apply to the InfoSet (Ad Hoc) Query tool or the SAP Query tool: the dynamic declaration of the data source.

If you think about the recommended strategies for deploying and configuring the data source with the SAP Query tool and the InfoSet (Ad Hoc) Query tool, you will recall that the configuration of the data source happens only in the development environment. A technical professional trained in your development environment must configure the InfoSet (data source) for reporting with the InfoSet (Ad Hoc) Query tool and the SAP Query tool. Furthermore, when creating InfoSets (data sources) with those tools, you should use logical databases to provide security. When a logical database is used within a data source and a user writes a query-based report by using that data source, the SAP solution is smart enough to determine who the user is and what the user has access to; it then restricts the user's reporting results accordingly.

A QuickView's data source is declared when the QuickView is built. So, for example, you can say you want to create a QuickView that uses a table. Doing so ensures that every field and every record in the table is available to you. This raises a security concern, however. With the ability to directly read tables, you can bypass traditional security concepts and have access to all data.

Let's look at a real-world example from the Human Capital Management (HCM) module. In the HCM module, users commonly have access to different things. One level of access can be based on location. For example, some users would have access to all associates in New York, and others would have access to associates in California. When any SAP Query report is created that uses a logical database within its data source, the security settings specify which users can see which locations. For example, if Jim had access only to New York, his executed report would contain only New York associates, and if Dan had access only to California associates, upon execution of the same report, Dan would see only the California associates.

If a user created a QuickView by using the QuickViewer tool and specified the employee table directly (rather than the logical database that includes it), the user would see all associates (from New York, California, North Carolina, and so on) in his or her report output, bypassing security.

It is a best practice to choose one reporting solution and use it exclusively. Considering the security limitations of the QuickViewer, best practice dictates that it should not be the tool of choice.

THINGS TO REMEMBER

- Creating QuickViews is quick and easy.
- You must declare a data source when creating a QuickView.
- You can convert QuickViews to SAP queries.
- QuickViews are available only in SAP 4.6C and later.
- There are security implications for allowing end users to use the QuickViewer reporting tool.

CHAPTER 21

SAP REPORTING WITH MICROSOFT EXCEL

In this chapter

This chapter describes how to maximize the use of the Microsoft Excel application in query reporting. This chapter is designed for those who are currently using some form of reporting that they wish to transmit and share with Microsoft Excel for further charting or pivot table analysis. You can use this chapter even if you do not create any SAP reports but can execute reports in SAP and have access to Microsoft Excel.

USING SAP REPORTING WITH MICROSOFT OFFICE

In SAP versions 4.6 and later, the integration between SAP and Microsoft Office gives you the capability to make a report's output look like a Microsoft Office document, in either Excel or Word. The Microsoft Office application runs as a control within the SAP R/3 environment. Virtually all R/3 functions are available on the worksheet of the Office application. If you are running a PC that has Microsoft Office applications and SAP R/3 installed, you can view report output via Microsoft. If Microsoft Office applications are not installed on your PC, the default report format, a normal list format, is used.

Project Duet is a revolutionary enterprise software collaboration between SAP and Microsoft that was announced in 2005. Duet is the first joint product created by Microsoft and SAP, and it revolutionizes how information workers access enterprise applications. SAP and Microsoft claim that by using Duet, companies will be able to enjoy time and cost savings, increases in process compliance, improvements in decision making, and decreases in redundancy and data errors. Company employees will also have improved and more flexible SAP access and greater productivity and efficiency. Duet is to be sold and supported by both SAP and Microsoft. To learn more about this unique partnership and what will be available in Duet, visit http://www.duet.com, www.sap.com/duet, and www.microsoft.com/office/sap.

MAXIMIZING SAP REPORTS BY USING MICROSOFT EXCEL

Microsoft Excel is a popular software solution used for all kinds of reporting. Microsoft Excel, like other Microsoft products, including Word, Access, and Outlook, serves as a great complement to SAP R/3 reporting solutions. Chapter 7, "Creating Advanced Reports with the SAP Query Tool," explains how you can use the SAP Query tool to create graphical reports such as polar diagrams, bar charts, pie charts, and so on. It also mentions that although you can create these graphical reports using SAP's Business Graphics, it is sometimes preferable to use Excel to produce colorful charts, graphs, and diagrams. This chapter explains how to use Excel in conjunction with SAP.

THE FICTIONAL SAP REPORT FOR A BASIC MICROSOFT EXCEL COLUMNAR CHART

This chapter uses simple data sources based on SAP reports. It uses a fictional company that sells dog treats, called MyDoggieTreats.com. The company wants to analyze some SAP report data pictorially (in graphic form).

The sample data source used for the first example in this chapter is a list of sales orders for the company. The assumption is that MyDoggieTreats.com uses SAP and that this sample data (in any form, whether a SAP query, a custom ABAP report, or something else) is from an SAP report that has been executed and is shown in Figure 21.1. The fictional report data in this example contains basic information about the sales made by each salesperson. To follow along in your own SAP system, you can use any report that contains any data. However, it will be most meaningful if your report output has a single line for each record you want to include in the chart.

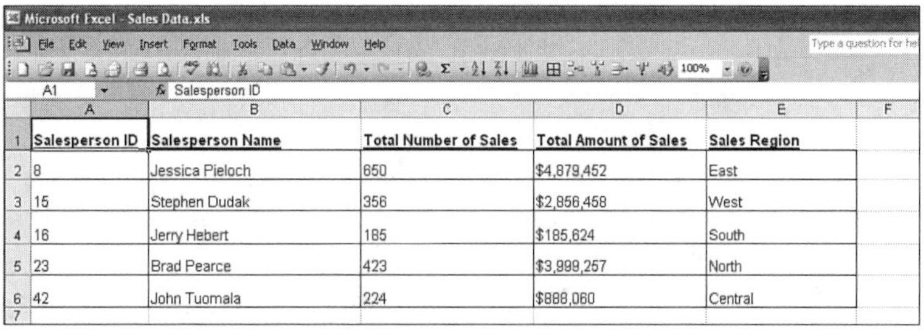

Salesperson ID	Salesperson Name	Total Number of Sales	Total Amount of Sales	Sales Region
8	Jessica Pieloch	650	$4,879,452	East
15	Stephen Dudak	356	$2,856,458	West
16	Jerry Hebert	185	$185,624	South
23	Brad Pearce	423	$3,999,257	North
42	John Tuomala	224	$888,060	Central

Figure 21.1
The fictional data source to be used in the example is a list of sales volume by salesperson.

CREATING A BASIC COLUMNAR CHART WITH MICROSOFT EXCEL

To create a basic columnar Excel chart from SAP data, you follow these steps:

1. Open any report output screen that displays an SAP report. It can be an SAP query, a custom ABAP report, an SAP standard-delivered report, or any other format.
2. You have multiple options for how to get your SAP data into Excel, each of which varies depending on your installation version of SAP R/3 and your installation version of Excel. Because there are multiple options for different versions, the menu path and buttons vary for each. It is a good idea to save your SAP report output into an Excel worksheet, which you will use as your mail merge data file. The most popular way to do this is to click the Excel button on your report output toolbar. Excel launches and displays the SAP report in an Excel worksheet. Next, save the report in Excel (for example, as c:\Sales Data.xls). Close and exit SAP and Excel.

NOTE

> It is not required that you exit Excel to continue, but it is recommended that you do so from a resource perspective (how much memory your PC is using to run SAP and Excel simultaneously) and because, depending on your versions of SAP and Microsoft Office, it may be easier.

3. Launch Excel and open your saved data source file (for example, c:\Sales Data.xls). For this example, create a graph that lists the number of sales by salesperson. Use your mouse to highlight the appropriate columns (for example, Salesperson and Number of Sales). With the columns selected, click the Chart Wizard button on the Application toolbar. A Chart Wizard dialog box appears, enabling you to create pictorial graphs of your SAP data.

NOTE

> If you are unable to locate the Chart Wizard button, you can search for it in SAP Help, which then provides the menu path specific to your version of Excel. A popular menu path is Insert, Chart.

4. On the Chart Wizard - Step 1 of 4 dialog, select the Standard Types tab, which lists all of the different types of charts you can select (see Figure 21.2). From the Chart Type list, select Column and then click the Next button.

Figure 21.2
The Chart Wizard dialog box helps you create a chart by allowing you to simply pick and choose the information required in the wizard.

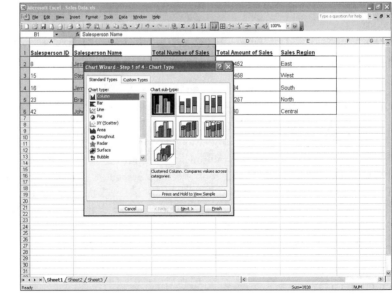

5. On the Chart Wizard - Step 2 of 4 dialog, select the Data Range tab, which displays a list of the columns and rows you highlighted in step 3 (see Figure 21.3). It allows you to decide which series you want to chart—the columns or the rows—and it gives you the option to use radio buttons to toggle between the two to see the differences. For this example, select the Columns radio button and then click the Next button.

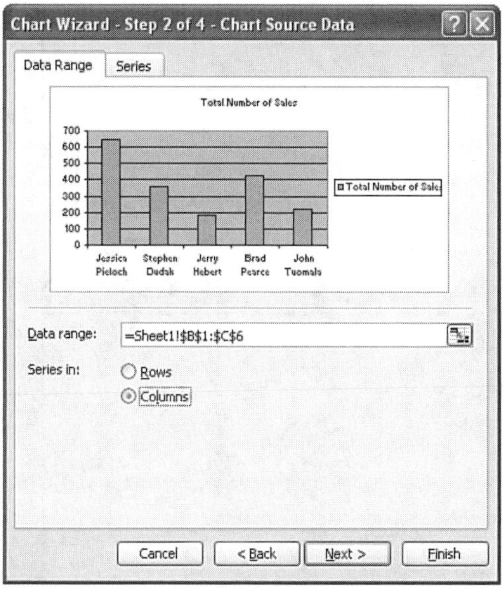

Figure 21.3
The popular option is to chart your data in columns, although charting in rows is sometimes meaningful, depending on the report type.

6. On the Chart Wizard - Step 2 of 4 dialog, select the Series tab, which shows how the options you select will affect your chart. The box on the left, labeled Series, lists your existing data series name(s). You can make data modifications here on the data series from the chart without affecting the data on your worksheet. For basic charts, no activity is required on this tab. Click the Next button to continue.

7. Examine the Chart Wizard - Step 3 of 4 dialog, which displays a sample preview of your chart on the right side of each tab. You can make changes on the left side of each tab and preview them on the right. This dialog box contains the following tabs:

   ■ **Titles**—On this tab, shown in Figure 21.4, you click in a box and then type the text you want for a chart or axis title. To insert a line break in a chart or axis title, you click the text in the chart, click where you want to insert the line break, and then press Enter.

   ■ **Axes**—This tab, shown in Figure 21.5, displays or hides the chart's primary axes. The Category (X) Axis option displays or hides the category (X) axis, and the Category (Y) Axis option displays or hides the category (Y) axis.

21

Figure 21.4
You can use the Titles tab to customize the chart title and axis labels for a chart.

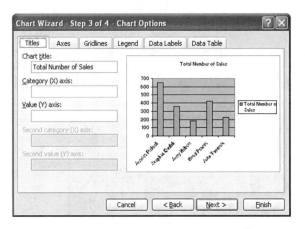

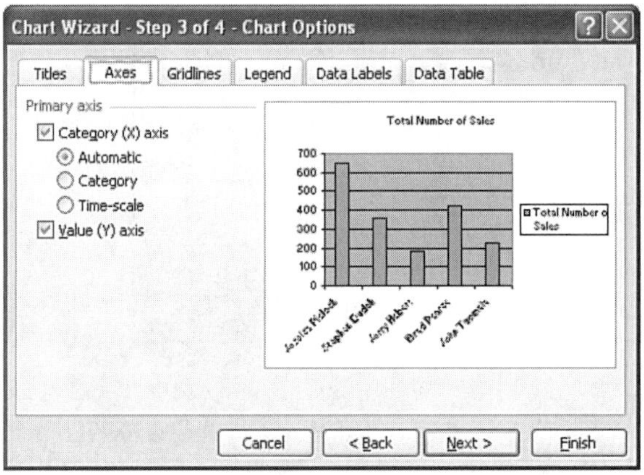

Figure 21.5
You can use the Axes tab to customize the axis label formats for a chart.

■ **Gridlines**—This tab, shown in Figure 21.6, allows you to select whether to display gridlines for each of the different categories and axes.

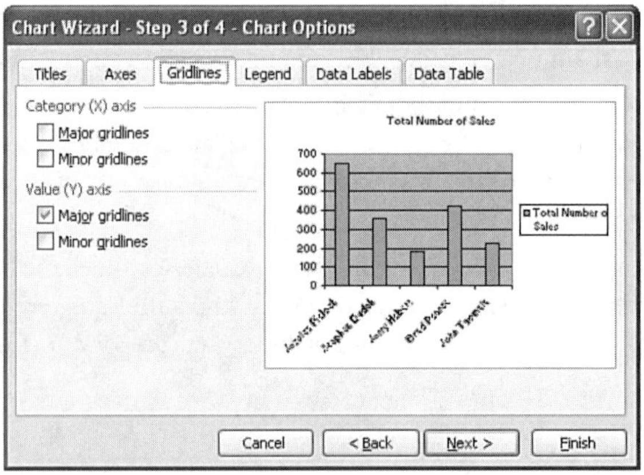

Figure 21.6
On the Gridlines tab you indicate whether to include gridline markers in a graph.

- **Legend**—This tab, shown in Figure 21.7, allows you to include or omit the report's legend and allows you to alter where it is placed within the graph.

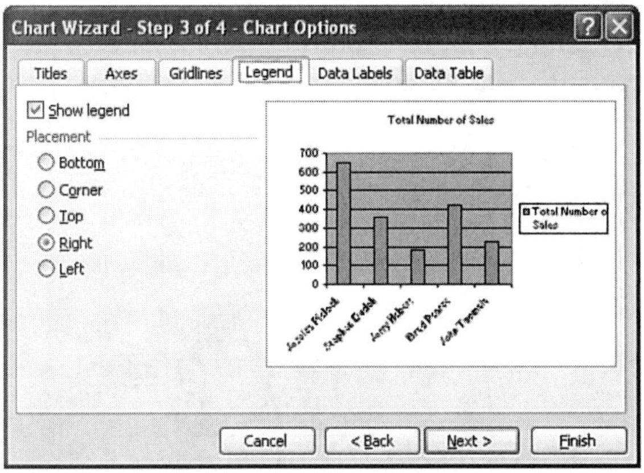

Figure 21.7
On the Legend tab you indicate the desired placement of the graph's legend within the graph output.

- **Data Labels**—A handful of options are available on this tab (see Figure 21.8). The Label Contains options display data on the selected axis as the default category (X) axis, even if data is date-formatted. The Series Name option displays data on the selected axis as the default category (X) axis, even if data is date-formatted. The Category Name option displays the category name assigned to all data points (for scatter and bubble charts, the X value is displayed). The Value option displays the value represented for all data points. The Percentage option, available for pie- and doughnut-style charts, displays the percentage of the whole for all data points. The Bubble Size option displays the sizes for each bubble in a bubble chart, based on the values of the third data series. The Separator drop-down allows you to choose how the contents of the data label are separated. Legend Key places the legend keys with the assigned format and color next to the data labels in the chart.

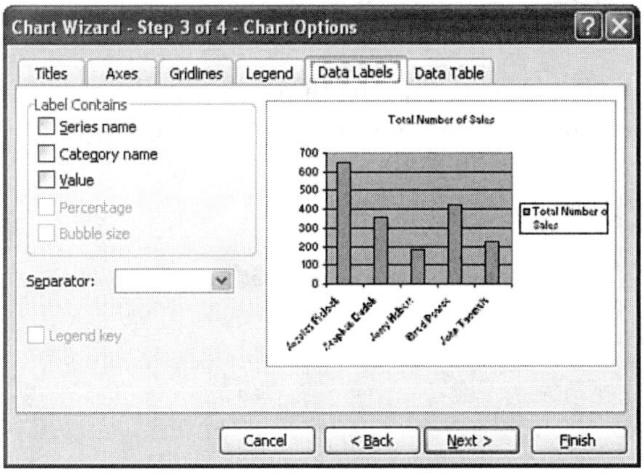

Figure 21.8
The Data Labels tab provides multiple options for formatted output of a graph.

21

■ **Data Table**—Only two options are available on this final tab, shown in Figure 21.9. The first is Show Data Table, which displays the values for each data series in a grid below the chart. This option is not available for pie, scatter, doughnut, bubble, radar, or surface charts. The second option, Show Legend Keys, displays legend keys, with the assigned format and color for each plotted series next to the series label in the data table.

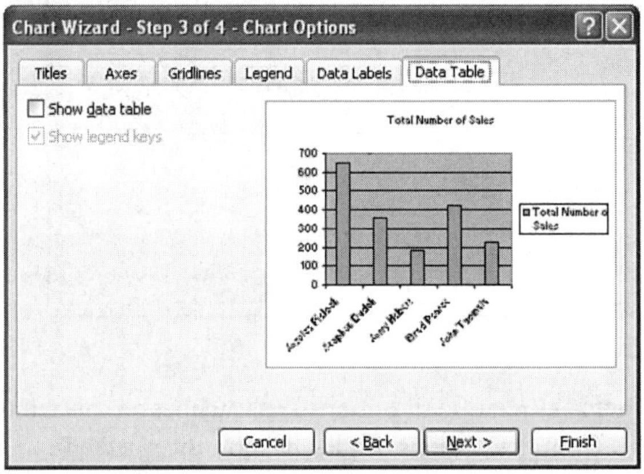

Figure 21.9
The Data Table tab allows you to indicate that you would like to include a data table or legend key in a graph.

No data input is required in any of these tabs for this example. When you are finished examining them, click the Next button to proceed to the final step.

8. The Chart Wizard - Step 4 of 4 dialog asks if you want to create a new worksheet with the chart or if you want to include it in your current worksheet. For this example, leave the default selected and click the Finish button to see your chart inserted into the Microsoft Excel document (see Figure 21.10).

Helpful Hint

You do not need to select any data on any of the fields or tabs in the Chart Wizard for it to work. You can simply click the Next button to create a chart of your report data.

When you complete your Excel chart, you can edit or print it. To learn more about these operations, visit www.support.microsoft.com and search for "Microsoft Excel Chart Wizard."

Figure 21.10
The chart is embedded as a graphic into a Microsoft Excel workbook, and you can edit its size and placement by using your mouse.

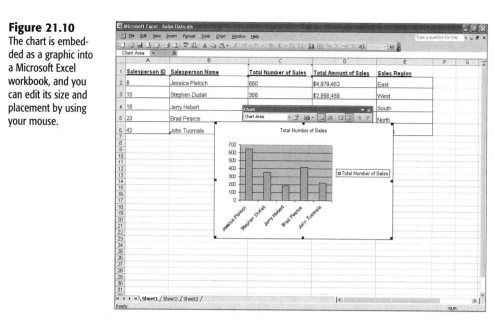

THE FICTIONAL SAP REPORT FOR A BASIC MICROSOFT EXCEL PIE CHART

This example uses a simple data source based on a Human Capital Management (HCM) module employee list report. The fictional company uses SAP, and this sample report (in any form, whether a SAP query, a custom ABAP report, or something else) from SAP has been executed and is shown in Figure 21.11. The fictional report in this example contains basic information about associates and their annual pay. To follow along in your own SAP system, you can use any report that contains any data. However, it will be most meaningful if your report output has a single line for each record you want to include in the chart.

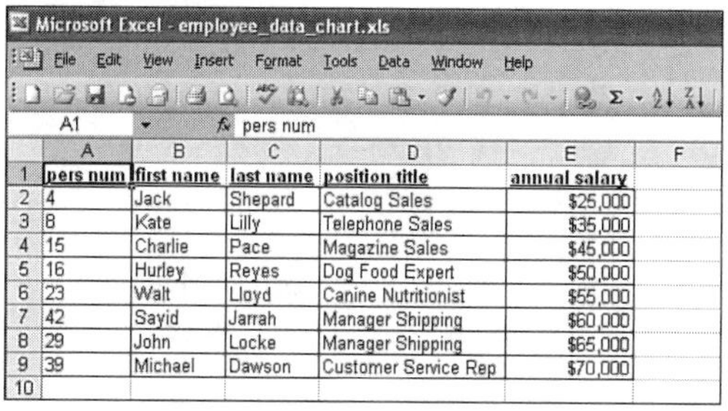

Figure 21.11
The fictional data source to be used in the example is a list of associate names, titles, and salaries.

Microsoft Excel - employee_data_chart.xls

	pers num	first name	last name	position title	annual salary
1	pers num	first name	last name	position title	annual salary
2	4	Jack	Shepard	Catalog Sales	$25,000
3	8	Kate	Lilly	Telephone Sales	$35,000
4	15	Charlie	Pace	Magazine Sales	$45,000
5	16	Hurley	Reyes	Dog Food Expert	$50,000
6	23	Walt	Lloyd	Canine Nutritionist	$55,000
7	42	Sayid	Jarrah	Manager Shipping	$60,000
8	29	John	Locke	Manager Shipping	$65,000
9	39	Michael	Dawson	Customer Service Rep	$70,000
10					

21

CREATING A BASIC GRAPHICAL PIE CHART WITH MICROSOFT EXCEL

To create a basic Excel pie chart from SAP data, you follow these steps:

1. Open any report output screen that displays an SAP report. It can be an SAP query, a custom ABAP report, an SAP standard-delivered report, or any other format.

2. You have multiple options for how to get your SAP data into Excel, each of which varies depending on your installation version of SAP R/3 and your installation version of Excel. Because there are multiple options for different versions, the menu path and buttons vary for each. It is a good idea to save your SAP report output into an Excel worksheet, which you will use as your mail merge data file. The most popular way to do this is to click the Excel button on your report output toolbar. Excel launches and displays the SAP report in an Excel worksheet. Next, save the report in Excel (for example, as c:\employee_data_chart.xls). Close and exit SAP and Excel.

NOTE

> It is not required that you exit Excel to continue, but it is recommended that you do so from a resource perspective (how much memory your PC is using to run SAP and Excel simultaneously) and because, depending on your versions of SAP and Microsoft Office, it may be easier.

3. Launch Excel and open your saved data source file (for example, c:\employee_data_chart.xls). For this example, create a custom pie chart that charts each position and the annual salary associated with it. Use your mouse to highlight the appropriate columns (for example, Position and Annual Salary). With the columns selected, click the Chart Wizard button on the Application toolbar. A Chart Wizard dialog box appears, enabling you to create pictorial graphs of your SAP data.

4. On the Chart Wizard - Step 1 of 4 dialog, select the Custom Types tab, and then select Pie Explosion from the Chart Type list (see Figure 21.12). Click Next.

5. Click the Next button on each of the next two wizard dialogs without making any changes.

6. In the Chart Wizard - Step 4 of 4 dialog, select the In a New Sheet option, and then click the Finish button. A new Microsoft worksheet is created, with your pie chart inserted in it (see Figure 21.13).

When you finish your Excel chart, you can edit or print it. To learn more about these operations, visit www.support.microsoft.com and search for "Microsoft Excel Chart Wizard."

21

Figure 21.12
This tab displays the user-defined and built-in custom chart types that Microsoft Excel provides.

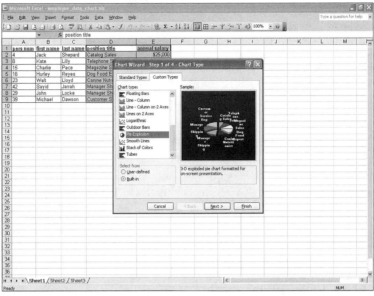

Figure 21.13
The chart is as large as the worksheet, and you can save it as a separate workbook.

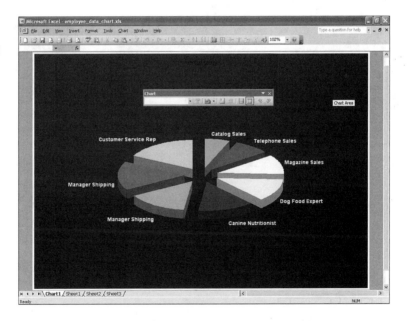

MAKING MICROSOFT EXCEL PIVOT TABLES USING SAP REPORT DATA

One of the best options in SAP reporting is the ability to have your SAP data automatically converted to an Excel pivot table report. A pivot table report allows you to slice and dice your data and analyze it multiple ways, without having to use a database or code logic. As Microsoft likes to say, using a pivot table can help you see the big picture by summarizing and analyzing your data in a simple table format.

You have the option of downloading any relevant report to a pivot table via any basic report output screen in SAP. That is, the ability to download to Excel pivot tables is not specific to a particular SAP reporting tool; it can be done via any of them, including custom ABAP reports.

You have multiple options for how to get your SAP data into Excel, each of which varies depending on your installation version of SAP R/3 and your installation version of Excel. Because there are multiple options for different versions, the menu path and buttons vary for each. A popular way to do so is to click the Excel button on your Report Output toolbar (see Figure 21.14). Microsoft Excel launches, displaying your SAP report in a Microsoft Excel worksheet that has multiple tabs, one of which is labeled Pivot (see Figure 21.15). Working with your SAP report data in a pivot table gives you additional options in analyzing your report output. To learn more, visit www.support.microsoft.com and search for "PivotTable reports 101."

Figure 21.14
This sample SAP report contains data from the SAP Flight Scheduling Test system.

Microsoft Excel button

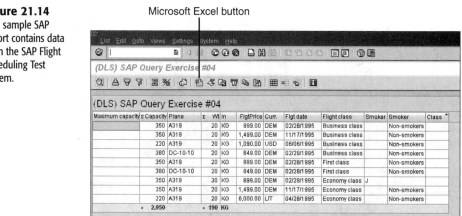

Figure 21.15
When a report is converted to a pivot table in Excel, the column headings change to drop-down boxes to make it easier to work with the data.

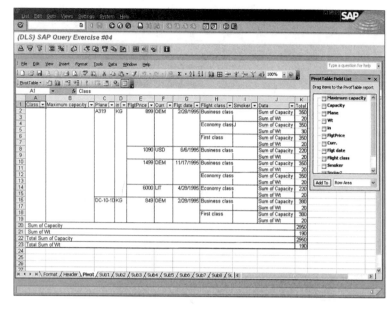

THINGS TO REMEMBER

- Microsoft Excel complements your existing reporting solutions.

- The menu paths within SAP vary based on your graphical user interface and installation versions. However, the ability to download an SAP report from SAP to an Excel file is available in all versions.

- Creating basic charts and graphs in Microsoft Excel is easy using the Chart Wizard.

- The Chart Wizard has several options, including a tab that allows you to select from built-in and custom charts.

- Working with your SAP report data in pivot table form is an ideal way to analyze complicated data.

CHAPTER **22**

SAP QUERY REPORTING WITH MICROSOFT WORD AND OUTLOOK

In this chapter

22

This chapter describes how you can maximize the use of the Microsoft Word application in reporting. This chapter is designed for those who are currently using some form of reporting that they wish to transmit and share with Word for further processing or analysis. You can use this chapter even if you do not create any SAP reports but can execute reports in SAP and have access to Word.

MAXIMIZING SAP REPORTS BY USING WORD

As discussed throughout this book, SAP has a variety of reporting solutions to assist you in extracting meaningful data from your SAP database. The decision of whether to use Word as part of a reporting arsenal is often based on the reporting need. You can use Word as a complement to the existing SAP reporting solutions.

The two most common reasons users share SAP data with Word are to create mailing labels/envelopes and to create mail merges for letters or other communications. Suppose that you need to send to each of your vendors a letter that contains information specific to your account with that vendor, including the vendor number, payment terms, and so on. Manually creating each letter individually would take an exhaustive amount of time. That's where the mail merge concept comes in. By using Word's mail merge functionality, all you have to do is create one document that contains the information that is the same in each copy and then add some placeholders for the information that is unique to each copy. The mail merge functionality automatically produces all the letters for you, and it automatically inserts the relevant data that is unique to each.

THE FICTIONAL SAP REPORT FOR A WORD FORM LETTER

Mail merging allows you to take data from a data source (such as an SAP report) and insert it into a template letter. For this example, you will create a form letter from a simple data source (an Excel worksheet). This fictional example involves a company that sells dog treats, MyDoggieTreats.com. It wants to send a thank-you letter to each of its vendors.

The assumption is that MyDoggieTreats.com uses SAP, and each vendor is stored in the MyDoggieTreats.com SAP R/3 database. Sample data (which can be in any form, whether an SAP query, a custom ABAP report, or something else) is shown in Figure 22.1. The fictional report data in this example contains basic information about the vendor. To follow along in your own SAP system, you can use any report that contains any data. However, it will be most meaningful if your report output has a single line for each record you want to include in the mail merge. For example, if it is a list of vendors, each vendor should be output on a single line.

NOTE

For my examples, I use Microsoft Word 2003, Service Pack 2, although I indicate version differences where applicable.

Vendor #	Vendor Name	Category	Contact Name 1	Street Address 1	Street Address 2	City	State	Zip	Years as Preferred Vendor
10291	Savant Consulting	IT Consulting	Clay Molinari	113 Smith St.	Apt. 16 F	Wantagh	NY	11793	22
10292	Doggie Food	Ingredients	Kelly Brunsman	1906 Main Ave.		Massapega	NY	11758	29
10293	Office Stuff	Office Supplies	Brad Pearce	6 Willow Way		Charlotte	NC	28217	18
10294	Clean Care	Cleaning	Jim Signorile	9612 Clearwater Ave.		Indian Trail	NC	28612	4
10295	Health Works	Ingredients	Pat Smith	123 86th St.	Apt. 15	Brooklyn	NY	11209	53
10296	Luxury Limo	Transportation	Bob Kovacs	9 Yorkmont Lane	2nd Floor	New York	NY	11692	2
10297	Easy Cab	Transportation	Raj Pragasam	1816 Resource Way		Parsippany	NJ	2061	18

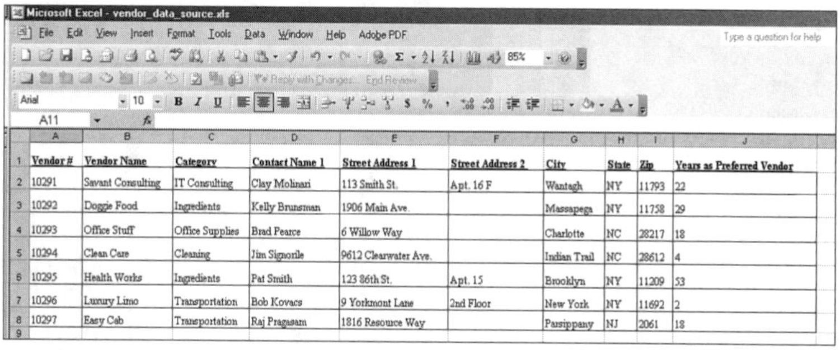

Figure 22.1
The fictional data source to be used in the examples in this chapter is a list of vendors in SAP.

CREATING A MAIL MERGE FORM LETTER BY USING WORD

To create a Word mail merge, follow these steps:

1. Open any report output screen that displays an SAP report. It can be an SAP query, a custom ABAP report, a standard SAP-delivered report, or any other format.
2. You have multiple options for how to get your SAP data into Microsoft Word for use in a mail merge; the options vary, depending on your installation version of SAP R/3 and your installation version of Word. Because there are multiple options for different versions, the menu path and buttons vary for each. It is a good idea to save your SAP report output into an Excel worksheet, which you will use as your mail merge data file. The most popular way to do this is to click the Excel button on your report output toolbar. Excel launches and displays the SAP report in an Excel worksheet. Next, save the report in Excel (for example, as `c:\vendor_data_source.xls`). Close and exit SAP and Excel.
3. You have multiple options for how to get your SAP data into Word; the options vary, depending on your installation version of SAP R/3 and your installation version of Word. Because there are multiple options for different versions, the menu path and buttons vary for each. It is a good idea to save your SAP report output into an Excel worksheet, which you will use as your mail merge data file. The most popular way to do this is to click the Excel button on your report output toolbar. Excel launches and displays the SAP report in an Excel worksheet. Next, save the report in Excel (for example, as `c:\vendor_data_source.xls`). Close and exit SAP and Excel.
4. Launch Word. The menu path to create a mail merge varies, depending on your installed version of Word. If you are unable to locate the mail merge option, you can search for it in Microsoft Help to find the menu path. One possible menu path is Tools, Letters and Mailings, Mail Merge Wizard (see Figure 22.2). Selecting this option brings up a dialog box or navigation menu that walks you through the process of creating a mail merge letter. The objective is to have the mail merge options displayed and your data source open behind the scenes (see Figure 22.3).

Figure 22.2
The wizard alerts you to the steps in the process, including what step you are currently on.

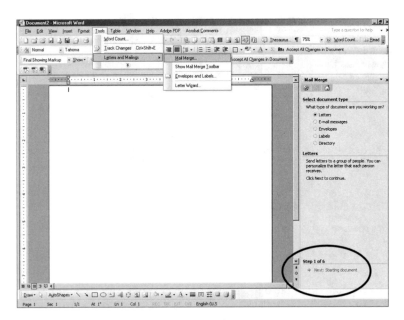

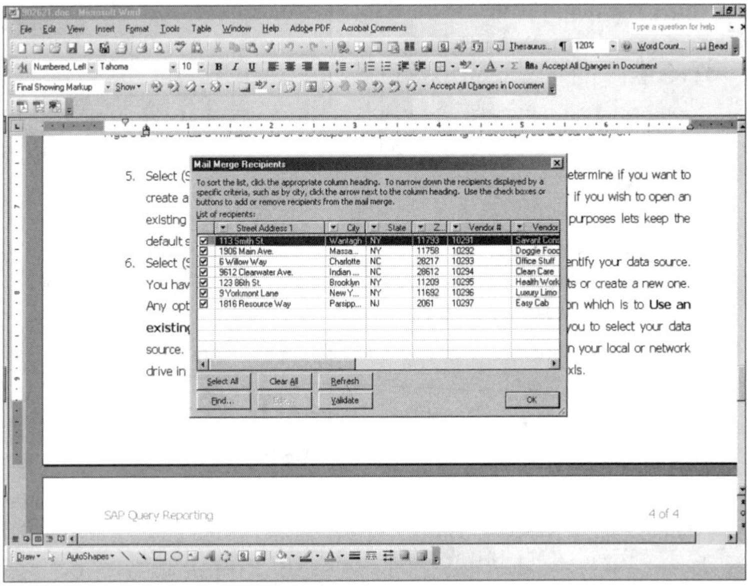

Figure 22.3
The wizard may appear differently in various versions of Word, but the steps to continue are the same.

5. On the bottom-right side of your screen (refer to Figure 22.2), select (Step 1 of 6) Next: Starting Document; this is the section of the wizard that walks you through the creation of the mail merge. After you select this option, the wizard section of the screen updates, allowing you to decide whether to create a new Word template, use the current one open onscreen, or open an existing Word document. Any option is okay, but for demonstration purposes, keep the default selection, which is Use the Current Document.

6. In the wizard, select (Step 2 of 6) Next: Select Recipients; you are prompted to identify your data source. You have three options: use an existing file, select from Outlook contacts, or create a new one. Any option is okay, but for demonstration purposes, keep the default selection, which is Use an Existing List. Use the Browse link to select the Excel worksheet that you saved on your local or network drive in step 1 (for example, c:\vendor_data_source.xls). A dialog box appears, asking you to indicate whether your data source has column headings.

7. For this example, select Yes. (Note that the sample report shown in Figure 22.1 has a heading for each column.) A dialog box like the one shown in Figure 22.3 appears, displaying your data source.

8. In the wizard, select (Step 3 of 6) Next: Write Your Letter. A blank document appears on the main screen, and options appear on the Application toolbar or on the navigation pane on the right (see Figure 22.4).

Figure 22.4
In earlier versions of Word, the fields are located in the Insert Merge Fields drop-down menu on the Application toolbar.

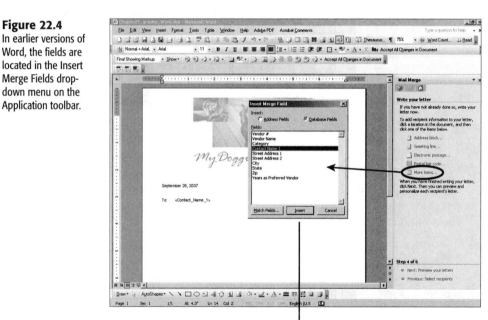

Selecting More items... will launch this dialog box

9. Begin to type your form letter directly into the document. You can include pictures or use only text. When you are ready to begin inserting fields from your data source into the document, you can select the appropriate option on your screen; the available options vary by version. In the Word 2003 version displayed in Figure 22.4, you can select the More Items link to open the Insert Merge Field dialog box, which displays each of your fields (see Figure 22.4).

10. In the Insert Merge Field dialog box, select the fields you want to include and then click the Insert button. When a field is inserted, it appears as a placeholder surrounded

22

by double brackets. Data from your data source will be inserted into this placeholder when you are finished with your letter. Continue typing your letter and inserting fields as necessary (see Figure 22.5).

Figure 22.5
The inserted place-holders for the fields are shown in boldface in this figure only to assist you in viewing them; they do not normally appear in boldface.

11. When you are finished writing your letter, select the link (Step 4 of 6) Next: Preview Your Letters. The document displays your letter with the first row of your data source report inserted. To preview the other letters, you can select the forward directional arrow button (see Figure 22.6).

12. After you preview your letter, select the link (Step 5 of 6) Next: Complete the Merge. The wizard proceeds to Step 6 of 6, where you have the option to print or save the merged document. Select the appropriate option. Your individual customized letters are sent to your designated printer, one for each record in the data source file, or saved as a Word document.

Helpful Hint

There is a distinction between the mail merge letter "template" you created during the steps outlined here and the finished product that you are asked to save. Saving the template document gives you the ability to update the data source (the Excel worksheet) in the future, and your template will be available with the new data each time it is opened. That is different from the saved merged version. If you elect to save the merged version, a fixed (that is, with no dynamic data) copy of a Word document will be saved. If that document is opened again, it will not read from the data source file.

Figure 22.6
Each record in your data source will be a separate page in your mail merge document.

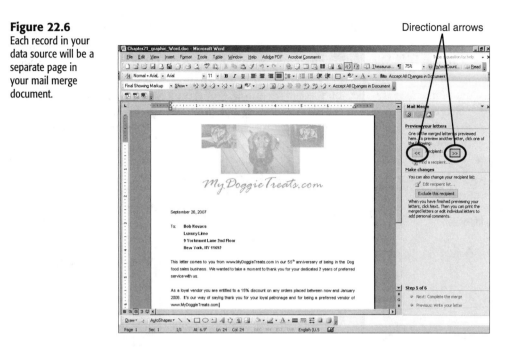

Directional arrows

When you complete your mail merge to Word, you can edit individual letters, make changes, and so on by using the Microsoft solution options. To learn more, visit www.support.microsoft.com and search for "Microsoft Word mail merge letter."

Creating Mail Merge Mailing Labels by Using Word

As shown in the previous example, mail merging allows you to take data from a data source (such as an SAP report) and insert it into a template letter. On some occasions, you might want to use Word to produce mailing labels or envelopes. For this example, you will create mailing labels from the same data source used in the previous example and shown in Figure 22.1. In this fictional example, you need to create the mailing labels to go on the envelopes of the letters created in the previous example.

To create a Word mail merge document of mailing labels, follow these steps:

1. Open any report output screen that displays an SAP report. It can be an SAP query, a custom ABAP report, a standard SAP-delivered report, or any other format.

2. You have multiple options for how to get your SAP data into Microsoft Word for use in a mail merge; the options vary, depending on your installation version of SAP R/3 and your installation version of Word. Because there are multiple options for different versions, the menu path and buttons vary for each. It is a good idea to save your SAP report output into an Excel worksheet, which you will use as your mail merge data file. The most popular way to do this is to click the Excel button on your report output toolbar. Excel launches and displays the SAP report in an Excel worksheet. Next, save the report in Excel (for example, as c:\vendor_data_source.xls). Close and exit SAP and Excel.

3. Launch Word. The menu path to create a mail merge varies, depending on your installed version of Word. If you are unable to locate the mail merge option, you can search for it in Microsoft Help to find the menu path. One possible menu path is Tools, Letters and Mailings, Mail Merge. Selecting this option brings up a dialog box or navigation menu that walks you through the process of creating mail merge labels. The objective is to have the mail merge options displayed and your data source open behind the scenes. Figure 22.7 shows the first screen of the wizard, shown on the right side of the screen.

Figure 22.7
The different types of merges are listed, including the option for labels.

4. Select the link (Step 1 of 6) Next: Starting Document and then select the Label Options link. Word is compatible with a variety of label programs, including Avery. To format your document to make labels, select the appropriate label type by number, size, or description from the dialog box shown in Figure 22.8. Click the OK button. Your document should now look like a sheet of labels.

5. Select (Step 2 of 6) Next: Select Recipients; you are prompted to identify your data source. You have three options: use an existing file, select from Outlook contacts, or create a new one. Any option is okay, but for demonstration purposes, keep the default selection, which is Use an Existing List. Use the Browse link to select the Excel worksheet that you saved on your local or network drive in step 1 (for example, c:\vendor_data_source.xls). A dialog box appears, asking you to indicate whether your data source has column headings.

6. For this example, select Yes. (Note that the sample report shown in Figure 22.1 has a heading for each column.) A dialog box appears, displaying your data source.

7. Select (Step 3 of 6) Next: Arrange Your Labels. A blank sheet of labels appears on the main screen, and options appear on the Application toolbar or on the navigation pane on the right (as shown in Figure 22.9). Select More Items to open the Insert Merge Field dialog box, which displays each of your fields.

Figure 22.8
Boxes of labels are coded with numbers that correspond to the numbers listed in this dialog box.

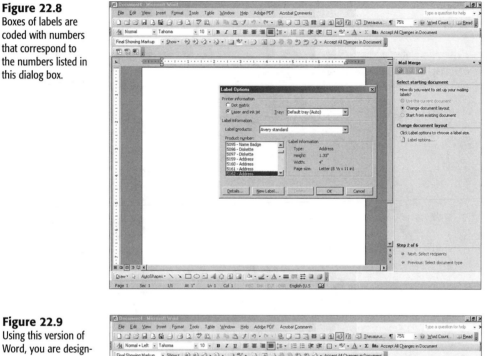

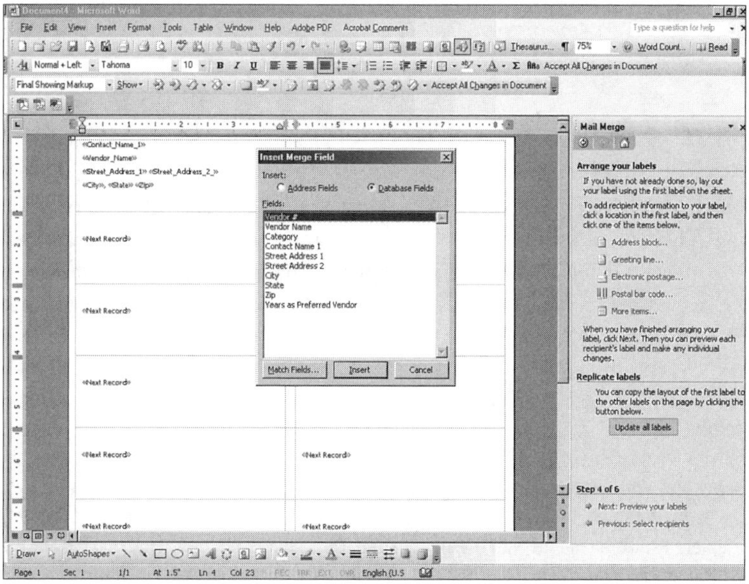

Figure 22.9
Using this version of Word, you are designing only the first label on the sheet.

8. In the Insert Merge Field dialog box, select the fields you want to include and then click the Insert button. When a field is inserted, it appears as a placeholder surrounded by double brackets. Data from your data source will be inserted in this placeholder when you are finished creating your labels.

9. After completing the design of a single label, click the Update All Labels button (see Figure 22.10). Your entire sheet of labels is updated with placeholder fields, one in each label on the sheet.

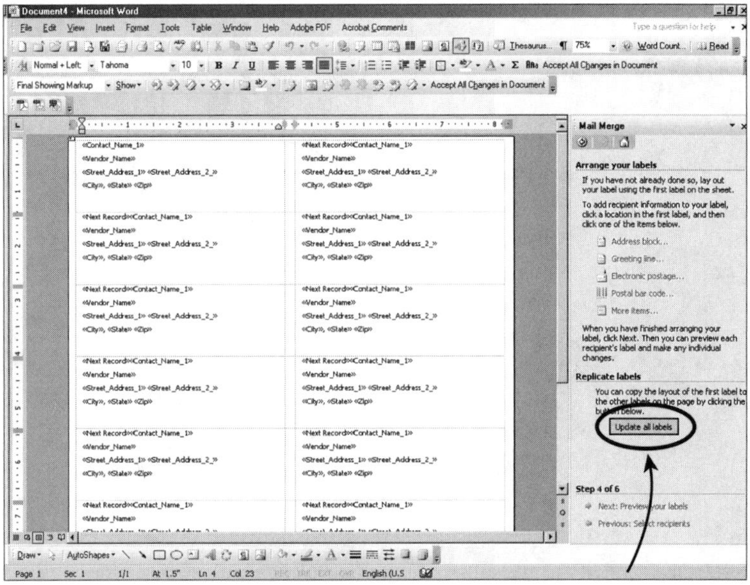

Figure 22.10
The placeholder that Word inserts automatically, <<Next Record>>, determines where a new record should be inserted.

10. Select the link (Step 4 of 6) Next: Preview Your Labels. Your sheet is populated with the fields in your data source (see Figure 22.11).

11. Preview your labels and then select the link (Step 5 of 6) Next: Complete the Merge. The wizard proceeds to Step 6 of 6, and you have the option to print or save the merged labels. Select the appropriate option. Your mailing labels are sent to your designated printer (be sure to insert the label paper according to the instructions) or saved as a Word document.

Helpful Hint

As with form letter templates in the previous example, there is a distinction between the mail merge labels "template" you created during the steps outlined here and the finished product that you are asked to save. Saving the template labels enables you to update the data source (the Excel worksheet) in the future, and your template will be available with the new data each time it is opened. That is different from the saved merged version. If you elect to save the merged version, a fixed (that is, with no dynamic data) copy of a Word document will be saved. If that document is opened again, it will not read from the data source file, and the labels will not be updated.

Figure 22.11
The address labels are updated from the data in the Excel file.

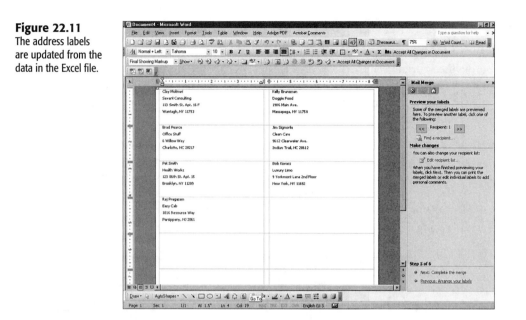

When you complete your mail merge to Word, you can edit individual labels, make changes, and so on by using the Microsoft solution options. To learn more, visit www.support. microsoft.com and search for "Microsoft Word mail merge labels."

CREATING MAIL MERGE ENVELOPES BY USING WORD

The steps to create mail merge envelopes using your SAP data and Word are almost identical to the steps for creating mailing labels. However, in step 3 in the preceding section and shown in Figure 22.7, you select the option Envelopes instead of Labels.

To learn more, visit www.support.microsoft.com and search for "Microsoft Word mail merge envelopes."

MAXIMIZING REPORTING OPTIONS BY USING WORD AND OUTLOOK

Did you know that you can create automated email messages by using the mail merge process? Here is a fictional example of how this would be helpful. Every so often, you receive a paycheck (or remuneration statement showing wages earned). Your company is responsible for getting that to you each pay period. Some companies distribute it via the mail. In order for it to successfully get to you, your address record in the SAP Human Capital Management (HCM) system has to be accurate.

The Fictional SAP Report (Data Source) for a Word-to-Outlook Automatic Email

You can use Word to send an individual email to each associate that contains his or her own unique personal information (that is, address) for the associate to review and validate/respond. The method described in the following section is not unique to SAP but can be based on data in an SAP solution.

In the HCM module of SAP, records of associate data are stored on screens called infotypes. Each area of data is stored on a separate screen. For example, an associate's name and birth date are stored on Infotype 0002, and that person's rate of pay is stored on Infotype 0008. An associate's email address can be stored on Infotype 0105. The fictional report used in this example contains the basic information about an associate, including that person's email address. A sample of the data source used in this example is shown in Figure 22.12.

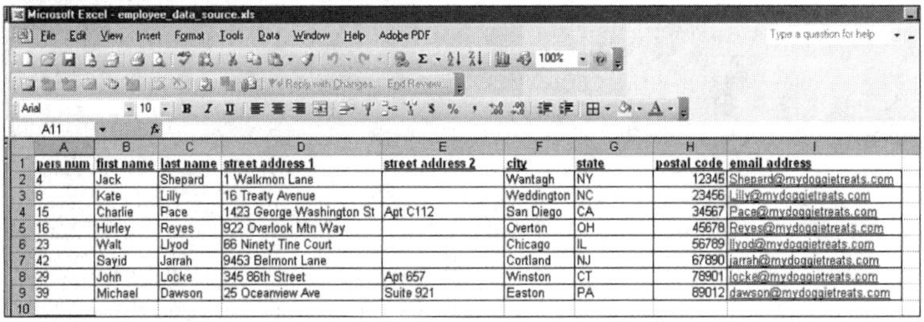

pers num	first name	last name	street address 1	street address 2	city	state	postal code	email address
4	Jack	Shepard	1 Walkmon Lane		Wantagh	NY	12345	Shepard@mydoggietreats.com
8	Kate	Lilly	16 Treaty Avenue		Weddington	NC	23456	Lilly@mydoggietreats.com
15	Charlie	Pace	1423 George Washington St	Apt C112	San Diego	CA	34567	Pace@mydoggietreats.com
16	Hurley	Reyes	922 Overlook Mtn Way		Overton	OH	45678	Reyes@mydoggietreats.com
23	Walt	Llyod	66 Ninety Tine Court		Chicago	IL	56789	llyod@mydoggietreats.com
42	Sayid	Jarrah	9453 Belmont Lane		Cortland	NJ	67890	jarrah@mydoggietreats.com
29	John	Locke	345 86th Street	Apt 657	Winston	CT	78901	locke@mydoggietreats.com
39	Michael	Dawson	25 Oceanview Ave	Suite 921	Easton	PA	89012	dawson@mydoggietreats.com

Figure 22.12
A list of associates from the SAP HCM module of a fictional company.

Creating Mail Merge Outlook Emails with Word

To create a Word mail merge for emails, follow these steps:

1. Open any report output screen that displays an SAP report. It can be an SAP query, a custom ABAP report, a standard SAP-delivered report, or any other format.
2. You have multiple options for how to get your SAP data into Word; the options vary, depending on your installation version of SAP R/3 and your installation version of Word. Because there are multiple options for different versions, the menu path and buttons vary for each. It is a good idea to save your SAP report output into an Excel worksheet, which you will use as your Word mail merge data file. The most popular way to do this is to click the Excel button on your report output toolbar. Excel launches and displays the SAP report in an Excel worksheet. Next, save the report in Excel (for example, as `c:\employee_data_source.xls`). Close and exit SAP and Excel.
3. Launch Word. The menu path to create a mail merge varies, depending on your installed version of Word. If you are unable to locate the mail merge option, you can search for it in Microsoft Help to find the menu path. One possible menu path is Tools, Letters and Mailings, Mail Merge Wizard. Selecting this option brings up a dialog box or navigation menu that walks you through the process of creating a mail merge letter. The objective is to have the mail merge options displayed and your data source open

behind the scenes. Figure 22.13 shows the first step of the wizard on the right side of the screen.

4. Select the E-mail Messages option button and then select the link (Step 1 of 6) Next: Starting Document. You are prompted to determine whether to create a new Word template, use the current one, or open an existing Word document. Any option is okay, but for demonstration purposes, keep the default selection, which is Use the Current Document.

Figure 22.13
The option to create mail merges with email is not available in all versions of Word.

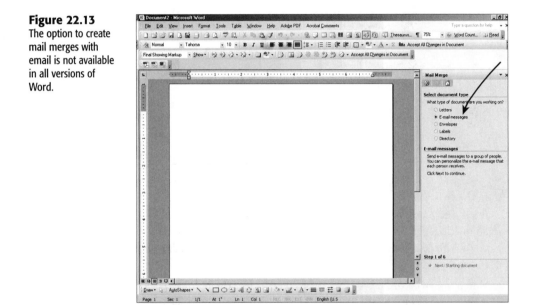

5. Select (Step 2 of 6) Next: Select Recipients; you are prompted to identify your data source. You have three options: use an existing file, select from Outlook contacts, or create a new one. Any option is okay, but for demonstration purposes, keep the default selection, which is Use an Existing List. Use the Browse link to select the Excel worksheet that you saved on your local or network drive in step 1 (for example, c:\employee_data_source.xls). A dialog box appears, asking you to indicate whether your data source has column headings.

6. For this example, select Yes. (Note that the sample report shown in Figure 22.1 has a heading for each column.)

7. Select (Step 3 of 6) Next: Write Your Letter. Begin typing your email text into the blank document. When you are ready to begin inserting fields from your data source into the document, you can select the appropriate option on your screen; the available options vary by version. In the 2003 version displayed in Figure 22.14, you can select the More Items link to open the Insert Merge Field dialog box, which displays each of your fields.

Figure 22.14
The merge fields are shown in boldface in this figure for illustration purposes only; they do not normally appear in boldface.

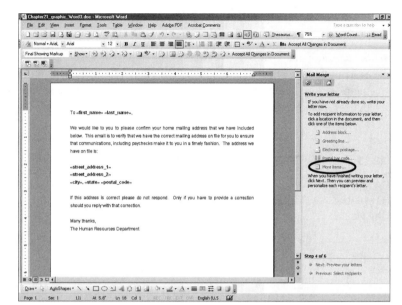

8. In the Insert Merge Field dialog box, select the fields you want to include and then click the Insert button. When a field is inserted, it appears as a placeholder surrounded by double brackets. Data from your data source will be inserted into this placeholder when you are finished with your email. Continue typing your email text and inserting fields as necessary.

9. When you are finished writing your email, select the link (Step 4 of 6) Next: Preview Your Letters. The text is populated with the fields in your data source.

10. After you preview your letter, select the link (Step 5 of 6) Next: Complete the Merge. The wizard proceeds to Step 6 of 6. Select the link Merge to Electronic Mail. A dialog box like the one shown in Figure 22.15 appears.

11. In the To: box in the Merge to E-mail dialog, select the field name in your data source that contains the email addresses (for example, the field labeled Email Address). Input a subject line that will be used for all the emails, and select a mail format. You can also indicate if you want to send the email to all or only some records. When you are done selecting options in this dialog, click the OK button.

12. Outlook immediately begins sending each of your emails, each of which contains unique information to the individual email addresses from the original report.

13. Save the mail merge by clicking the Save button on the Application toolbar.

To learn more, visit www.support.microsoft.com and search for "Microsoft Word mail merge e-mail."

Figure 22.15
This box allows you to determine matching fields and specify whether to merge all records.

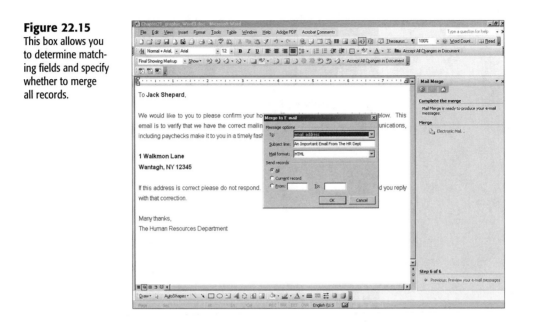

THINGS TO REMEMBER

- Microsoft Word is a good complement to SAP reporting solutions.
- The menu paths in SAP vary based on your installation versions. However, the ability to download an SAP report from SAP to an Excel file is available in all versions.
- Creating form letters by using SAP report data is an easy way to automate a communication so that you do not have to type the same letter over and over.
- Using the mail merge features to create mailing labels and envelopes is a helpful and fast way to do mailings that contain SAP report data.
- Creating automated email communications from a data source that contains email addresses is an ideal way to reach out to people and share unique data.

CHAPTER **23**

SAP REPORTING WITH MICROSOFT ACCESS

In this chapter

This chapter describes how you can maximize the use of the Microsoft Access application in reporting. This chapter is designed for those who are currently using some form of reporting that they wish to transmit and share with Access for further analysis. You can use this chapter even if you do not create any SAP reports but can execute reports in SAP and have access to Access.

This chapter explains how to use the Access Report Wizard to import and create reports and how to create reports that contain data from SAP combined and merged with data from a third-party solution.

MAXIMIZING SAP REPORTS BY USING ACCESS

Access is a popular software solution used for all kinds of reporting. Access, like other Microsoft products, including Word, Excel, and Outlook, serves as a great complement to SAP R/3 reporting solutions. Access is a common solution used by many organizations that do not know how to create reports using the tools outlined in this book. Because Access is a standard software solution installed on many company computers, and because it is very easy for an end user who has no technical skills to use, it is commonly used for SAP reporting.

I have heard of organizations that run a daily or weekly download of information from their SAP solution, which they import into Access. They then do most of their reporting from Access. Although this may be helpful for organizations that do not know how to create reports in SAP, it does require some considerations, as outlined in the next section.

There are three general reasons why companies use Access in addition to their existing SAP reporting. The first is because Access and its wizards are very user-friendly; any user can follow along and create reports and so on. The second reason has to do with the volume of data: When working with data that is particularly large and cumbersome, it may be more time-efficient to work with that data outside the SAP environment, in Access. Finally, Access gives you the ability to cross-reference data from multiple systems and sources into a single report. An example of this is provided later in this chapter. All in all, Access can be a great complement to your existing SAP reporting solutions.

CONSIDERATIONS WHEN USING ACCESS FOR SAP REPORTING

The dramatic difference between reporting directly within SAP and reporting using Access is based on two factors: security and timeliness. One of the most important considerations when using Access for reporting on SAP data is the appreciation that the data, once in Access, has no security limitations. I know this one sounds like a no-brainer, but sometimes a company does not realize the implications until the solution is in place. When the SAP reporting tools described in this book (and configured using the recommended guidelines) are used, security is not a concern. SAP security identifies who the user is and permits that user to see only the data that he or she is allowed to see (regardless of what type of access the person who created the report had). The concern with extracting your SAP data and placing it in Microsoft Access is that all data is downloaded, and any user can access it when it is outside the SAP R/3 environment.

The second consideration when using Access for SAP reporting is timeliness. This concern is the same with any non–SAP R/3 reporting solution, including Crystal Reports and SAP's Business Information Warehouse (BIW), where the reporting is first fed to a repository and then reported from. Reporting in this manner, as opposed to online reporting in the SAP Query tool, for example, does not occur in real time. In some cases, reporting does not need to be real-time, so a solution such as Crystal Reports, BIW, or Access would be a good fit.

Where tools such as BIW and Access are really useful is when you want to evaluate data from multiple sources. By using the SAP reporting tools described in this book, you can easily create thorough, detailed reports of data from your SAP R/3 system. However, if you want to report on data from your SAP R/3 solution plus data from an additional system (such as your distribution database), you can do so easily by using Access.

THE FICTIONAL SAP REPORT FOR A BASIC ACCESS REPORT

This fictional example uses a basic Human Capital Management (HCM) module report from SAP that contains information about associates, including their names, personnel numbers, and home mailing addresses. Table 23.1 shows a sample of the data in the fictional report.

TABLE 23.1	SAMPLE SAP HCM REPORT OF ASSOCIATE INFORMATION					
pers num	first name	last name	street address 1	city	state	postal code
1254587	Jack	Shepard	1 Walkmon Lane	Wantagh	NY	12345
1254591	Kate	Lilly	16 Treaty Avenue	Weddington	NC	23456
1254595	Charlie	Pace	1423 George Washington St	San Diego	CA	34567
1254599	Hurley	Reyes	922 Overlook Mtn Way	Poplin Oats	OH	45678
1254603	Walt	Llyod	66 Ninety Tine Court	Chicago	IL	56789
1254607	Sayid	Jarrah	9453 Belmont Lane	Cortland	NJ	67890
1254611	John	Locke	345 86th Street	Winston	CT	78901
1254615	Michael	Dawson	25 Oceanview Ave	Easton	PA	89012

GETTING YOUR SAP REPORT DATA INTO ACCESS

To get SAP report data into Access, follow these steps:

1. Open any report output screen that displays an SAP report. It can be an SAP query, a custom ABAP report, a standard SAP-delivered report, or any other format.

2. You have multiple options for how to get your SAP data into Access, each of which varies depending on your installation version of SAP R/3 and your installation version

of Access. Because there are multiple options for different versions, the menu path and buttons vary for each. It is a good idea to save your SAP report output in an Excel worksheet, which you will use as your mail merge data file. The most popular way to do this is to click the Excel button on your report output toolbar. Excel launches and displays the SAP report in an Excel worksheet. Next, save the report in Excel (for example, as `c:\employee-data_file.xls`). Close and exit SAP and Excel.

3. Launch Access and create a new Access database by selecting the white page Create button on the Application toolbar and then selecting the link Create a Blank Database. A dialog box appears, asking you to name and save your database. Name and save your database, using a name such as `c:\my documents\database1.mdb`. Click OK to continue to the main screen of your newly created empty Access database.

4. Import the SAP data into the empty Access database. To do so, select File, Get External Data, Import. A dialog box appears, giving you the opportunity to locate the file you saved in step 2.

5. Select the file (for example, `c:\employee-data_file.xls`) and then click the Import button. The Import Spreadsheet Wizard appears, to walk you through the import of your SAP data into Access (see Figure 23.1).

Helpful Hint

By default, the Import dialog box looks for Access database files only. You need to change the File As Type box at the bottom of the dialog box to Excel Files in order for your file to appear.

Figure 23.1
The Import Spreadsheet Wizard helps you import a data file by allowing you to simply pick and choose the information required.

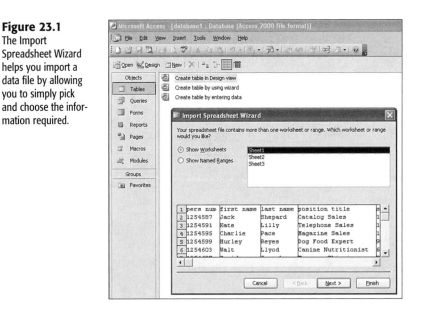

6. Look at the list of worksheets on the wizard (for example, Sheet 1, Sheet 2, and so on), and select the worksheet that contains your SAP data (depending on your installed

version of SAP and your SAPGUI settings, it may be the last sheet in the list labeled Raw Data). Then click the Next button.

7. In the next screen, select the check box to indicate that your data source contains column headers, and then click the Next button.

8. The next screen has two options: You can either merge the data into an existing table or create a new table. Because this is an empty database that you created from scratch, select the option In a New Table and then click the Next button.

9. On the next screen, specify information about each of the fields you are importing. For example, you can alter the column heading names and select to exclude some columns if you wish. Click the Next button to proceed.

10. When the wizard prompts you to assign or select a primary key, do so. A primary key is a unique record in your data file that distinguishes all the records from each other. For basic SAP reporting, it is sufficient to allow Microsoft to create one for you, which is the default option (see Figure 23.2). Click the Next button to proceed.

23

Figure 23.2
The Import Spreadsheet Wizard inserts a primary key at the start of your data file that contains a unique number that can be used to make a record in the report unique.

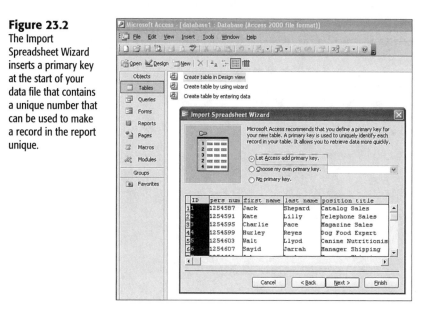

11. Name your table (for example, `Employee Address Table`) and then click the Finish button. A dialog box appears, indicating that your table was successfully imported.

12. Click OK. If you had any errors in importing the data, you are alerted of that at this time. Your database now contains one table called Employee Address Table, which you can view by double-clicking the table name listed on the screen. The table opens on the screen; it looks a good deal like an Excel worksheet, as shown in Figure 23.3.

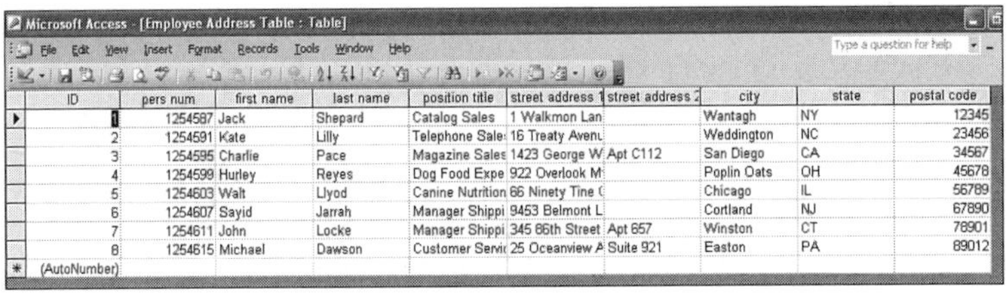

Figure 23.3

This Access table and the one defined in Table 23.1 at the beginning of this chapter contain the same information.

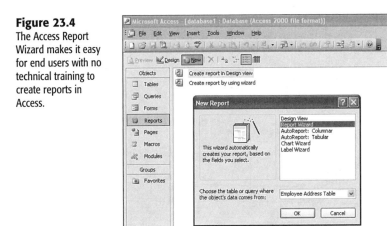

USING THE ACCESS REPORT WIZARD TO CREATE A REPORT OF SAP DATA

One of the primary reasons that Access is a popular reporting complement to SAP is its availability to be used by casual users who have no technical skills. Access includes step-by-step wizards that can be used to easily create a variety of reports. To use the Access Report Wizard to create a report with your imported SAP data, follow these steps:

1. Select the link Reports from the menu on the left side of the screen, and then click the New button on the Application toolbar. A New Report dialog box appears.

2. In the New Report dialog box, select the option Report Wizard, and then select your table from the drop-down box at the bottom of the screen (see Figure 23.4). Then click the OK button.

Figure 23.4

The Access Report Wizard makes it easy for end users with no technical training to create reports in Access.

3. The first screen of the Access Report Wizard lists all the fields available in your table and gives you the option of adding some or all of these fields to your report by using the single selection (>) or all selections (>>) field indicators in the middle of the screen. Select all fields and then click the Next button.

4. On the next screen, select grouping levels, if desired, and then click Next.

5. On the next screen (see Figure 23.5), indicate your sorting (ascending or descending) preference. For this example, sort on the unique ID key (ascending) followed by the last name field (ascending). Then click the Next button.

Figure 23.5
You have the option
to sort in either
ascending or
descending order
for up to four fields
in this step of the
wizard.

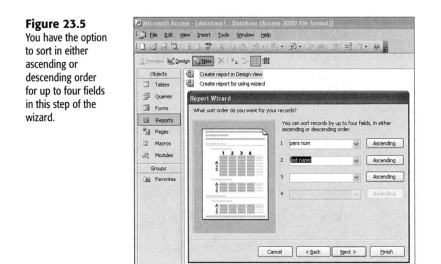

23

6. On the next screen, specify the layout for your report. In this case, indicate that you want it to appear in landscape orientation and in tabular layout. Then click the Next button.

7. The next screen displays at least six different predefined styles for you to choose from for your report. By default, the Corporate format is selected, but you can preview each by selecting it. Click the Next button, change the title of the report, and then click the Finish button to see the finished report (see Figure 23.6).

Figure 23.6
The selected format-
ting option enhances
the look of the report
with colors and fonts.

Employee Address Table

rs num	last name	ID	first name	position title	street address	street address	city	state	postal code
1254587	Shepard	1	Jack	Catalog Sales	1 Wallmon Lane		Wantagh	NY	12345
1254591	Lilly	2	Kate	Telephone Sales	16 Treaty Avenue		Weddington	NC	23456
1254595	Pace	3	Charlie	Magazine Sales	1423 George Washi	Apt C112	San Diego	CA	34567
1254599	Reyes	4	Hurley	Dog Food Expert	922 Overlook Mtn		Poplin Oaks	OH	45678
1254603	Lloyd	5	Walt	Canine Nutritionist	66 Ninety Tine Cour		Chicago	IL	56789
1254607	Jarrah	6	Sayid	Manager Shipping	9453 Belmont Lane		Cortland	NJ	67890
1254611	Locke	7	John	Manager Shipping	345 86th Street	Apt 657	Winston	CT	78901
1254615	Dawson	8	Michael	Customer Service R	25 Oceanview Ave	Suite 921	Easton	PA	89012

Besides the Report Wizard, Access also has wizards for creating charts, graphs, mailing labels, and so on. To see what other options are available for easy reporting, select the Reports link from the left side of the screen and then click the New button on the Application toolbar. The New Report dialog box appears, listing the various wizards.

MAXIMIZING SAP AND THIRD-PARTY SOLUTION REPORTS BY USING ACCESS

Creating basic reports, charts, graphs, labels, and so on is easy, thanks to the Access Report Wizard. Using Access with SAP is especially helpful when you want to report on data from two different computer systems. Table 23.1, earlier in this chapter, includes sample data from an SAP HCM system. What if you wanted to create a report with data from SAP plus data from a separate third-party system, such as a building's security access system? You could do so if both systems shared a common key. The following sections explain how.

THE FICTIONAL DATA SOURCE FOR A THIRD-PARTY DATABASE

Table 23.1, earlier in this chapter, showed the SAP HCM module report data used in the earlier example. Table 23.2 shows a report run from non-SAP third-party building security software, UCGI Access System. To create a report that contains data from SAP (for example, name and address) plus data from the security system (for example, access level and schedule access), you could use Access.

TABLE 23.2 UCGI ACCESS SYSTEM DATA (NON-SAP THIRD-PARTY TECHNOLOGY)			
pers num	**access level**	**schedule access**	**date accesses approved**
1254587	Level 1	Weekday	June 20, 1967
1254591	Level 2	Weekend	August 25, 1969
1254595	Level 3	Weekday	June 9, 2006
1254599	Level 1	Weekday	August 9, 1999
1254603	Level 3	Weekday	September 26, 1997
1254607	Level 4	Anytime	January 11, 2005
1254611	Level 1	Weekday	February 1, 2006
1254615	Level 2	Weekday	December 5, 2004

The key requirement for being able to create a report that contains fields from each of these separate databases within the same integrated report is that you have to have a unique common field between the two. You need a field that exists in both data sources, such as pers num, that you can use to link the two sources together. The following sections describe how to create a single Access report that contains integrated data from these two different computer systems.

GETTING THIRD-PARTY COMPUTER SYSTEM REPORT DATA INTO ACCESS

Earlier in this chapter, I explained how to import SAP report data into Access. This example builds on that earlier one. You will be adding additional data to your existing Access database so that you can report on both within the same report. To get your third-party computer solution report data into your existing Access database, follow these steps:

1. Open your third-party computer solution (whatever it may be) and download your report to an Excel file on your computer. Save the file (for example, as `c:\UCGI_security_file.xls`). After saving your report in Excel, close and exit your third-party solution.

2. Launch Access and open the existing Access database you created earlier (that is, `c:\my documents\database1.mdb`). Click OK to continue to the main screen of your Access database, which should now contain at least one table (Employee Address Table, from your SAP system).

3. To bring in your third-party computer system (for example, UCGI) report data that you saved in step 1, select File, Get External Data, Import.

4. In the dialog box that appears, locate the file you saved in step 1 (for example, `c:\UCGI_security_file.xls`). Then click the Import button. The Import Spreadsheet Wizard appears, to walk you through the import of your third-party database data into Access.

Helpful Hint

By default, the Import dialog box looks for Access database files only. You need to change the File As Type box at the bottom of the dialog box to Excel Files in order for your file to appear. The Import Spreadsheet Wizard appears, to walk you through the import of your SAP data into Access.

---

5. Look at the list of worksheets on the wizard (for example, Sheet 1, Sheet 2, and so on). Select the worksheet that contains your third-party report data, and then click the Next button.

6. In the next screen, select the check box to indicate that your data source contains column headers, and then click the Next button.

7. The next screen has two options: You can either merge the data into an existing table or create a new table. Select the option Place It in a New Table, and then click the Next button.

8. On the next screen, specify information about each of the fields you are importing. For example, you can alter the column heading names and select to exclude some columns if you wish. Click the Next button to proceed.

9. When the wizard prompts you to assign or select a primary key, do so. A primary key is a unique record in your data file that distinguishes all the records from each other. For this basic example, allow Microsoft to create one for you, which is the default option. Click the Next button to proceed.

10. Give your table a name (for example, UCGI Security Access Table) and then click the Finish button. A dialog box appears, indicating that your table was successfully imported.

11. Click OK. If you had any errors in importing the data, you are alerted of that at this time. Your database now contains two separate tables: one called Employee Address Table and another called UCGI Security Access Table.

CREATING AN ACCESS QUERY TO LINK DATA FROM TWO DIFFERENT COMPUTER SYSTEMS

This section explains how to combine data from two different tables (from two different database computer sources) into a single report. Using the fictional data sources in Tables 23.1 and 23.2 earlier in this chapter, you need to now create a single report that includes data from both, as shown in Table 23.3.

TABLE 23.3   SAMPLE COMBINED REPORT: SAP HR REPORT OF ASSOCIATE ADDRESSES AND UCGI ACCESS SYSTEM REPORT OF ASSOCIATE ACCESS LEVELS

pers num	first name	last name	street address 1	city	state	postal code	access level	schedule access
1254587	Jack	Shepard	1 Walkmon Lane	Wantagh	NY	12345	Level 1	Weekday
1254591	Kate	Lilly	16 Treaty Avenue	Weddington	NC	23456	Level 2	Weekend
1254595	Charlie	Pace	1423 George Washington St	San Diego	CA	34567	Level 3	Weekday
1254599	Hurley	Reyes	922 Overlook Mtn Way	Poplin Oats	OH	45678	Level 1	Weekday
1254603	Walt	Llyod	66 Ninety Tine Court	Chicago	IL	56789	Level 3	Weekday
1254607	Sayid	Jarrah	9453 Belmont Lane	Cortland	NJ	67890	Level 4	Anytime
1254611	John	Locke	345 86th Street	Winston	CT	78901	Level 1	Weekday
1254615	Michael	Dawson	25 Oceanview Ave	Easton	PA	89012	Level 2	Weekday

To create an Access query that links data from the two existing tables, follow these steps:

1. Launch Access and open the Access database you created earlier (that is, c:\my documents\database1.mdb). Click OK to continue to the main screen of your Access database, which should now contain two tables (Employee Address Table, from your SAP system, and UCGI Security Access Table, from the third-party computer solution).

2. Select the Query navigation tab on the left side of the window, and then click the New button on the Application toolbar.

3. When the New Query dialog box appears, click OK. The dialog box changes to a box labeled Show Table that lists all the tables that exist in the database.

4. Select each table and insert it into your query by clicking the table name and then clicking the Add button. After adding both tables, click the Close button. The screen should now look like the one shown in Figure 23.7.

Figure 23.7

Access links the two tables by the ID field because it has the same name in both tables.

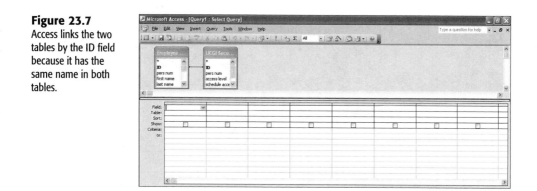

5. Notice that the two tables are linked with a line. Access assumes that because the two tables contain a field called ID, the data in them is the same. As in this situation, that may not always be the case. Select the line between the two fields and then press Delete to delete it.

6. One field in the two tables contains the same data: the pers num field (refer to Tables 23.1 and 23.2). Therefore, you want to create a relationship between the two tables based on the pers num field. To do so, place your cursor on the pers num field in the first table and drag it to the pers num field in the second table. A line linking the two appears.

7. Double-click the linking line to see the properties of the join, as shown in Figure 23.8. The default option on the Join Properties screen is the one you want, so click OK.

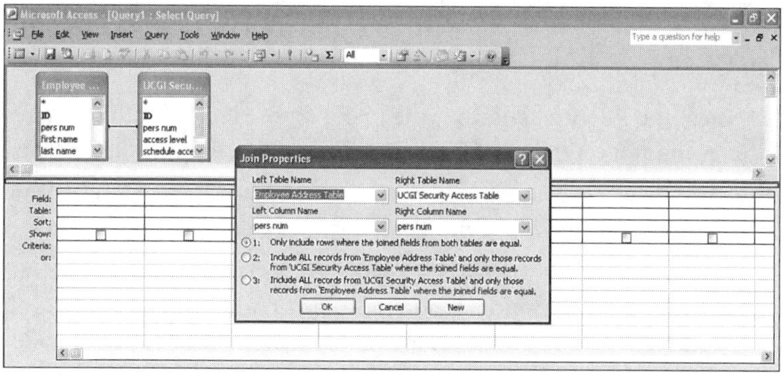

Figure 23.8

Two tables that contain the same unique value (in this case, pers num) can be joined.

8. Now that the two tables are joined, select the individual fields from the specific tables you want to include in your query (report). You do so by selecting a field from a table at the top of the screen and dragging it to the bottom of the screen.

9. To see the finished, combined data source, click the View button (see Figure 23.9). The finished query is shown in Figure 23.10. Click the Save button on the Application toolbar and then give your new query a name (for example, Query 1).

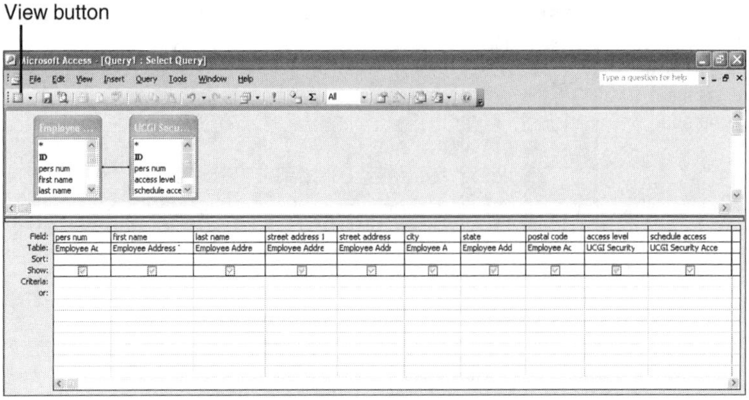

View button

Figure 23.9
The Query Design view in Access lists each table and field name.

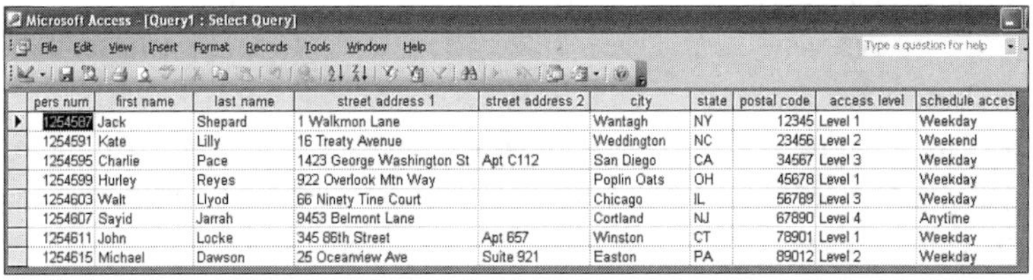

Figure 23.10
The Query Preview view of Access looks the same as a table view in Access.

USING THE ACCESS REPORT WIZARD TO CREATE A REPORT OF SAP AND THIRD-PARTY QUERY DATA

To use a Microsoft Access wizard to create a report with your newly created query that contains data from your two imported tables (from SAP and from the third-party computer system, UCGI), follow these steps:

1. Select the Reports link from the menu on the left side of the screen and then click the New button on the Application toolbar. A New Report dialog box appears.

2. In the New Report dialog box, select the option Report Wizard, and then select your query from the drop-down box at the bottom of the screen. Then click the OK button.

3. The first screen of the Access Report Wizard lists all the fields available in your table and gives you the option of adding some or all of these fields to your report by using the single selection (>) or all selections (>>) field indicators in the middle of the screen. Select the pers num, first name, last name, access level, and schedule access fields, and then click the Next button.

4. On the next screen, select a grouping level, if desired, and then click Next.

5. On the next screen, indicate your sorting (ascending or descending) preference. For this example, sort on the pers num field (ascending) followed by the last name field (ascending). Then click the Next button.

6. On the next screen, specify the layout for your report. In this case, indicate that you want it to appear in landscape orientation and in tabular layout. Then click the Next button.

7. The next screen displays at least six different styles for you to choose from for your report. By default, the Corporate format is selected, but you can preview each by selecting it. Select the Casual option and then click the Next button to change the title of the report. Then click the Finish button to see the finished report (see Figure 23.11).

Figure 23.11
Access reports created with the Report Wizard have special formatting and design based on the template selected (in this example, the Casual template).

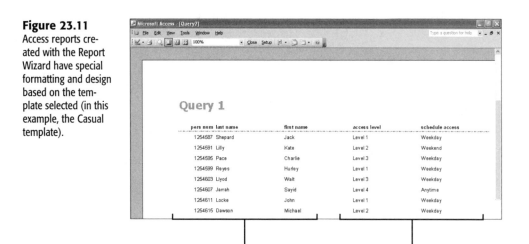

THINGS TO REMEMBER

- Microsoft Access is a good complement to SAP reporting solutions.
- The menu paths in SAP vary based on your installation versions. However, the ability to download an SAP report from SAP to an Excel file is available in all versions.
- Access is great for combining data from multiple systems into a single report.
- Access can produce mailing labels and charts via the helpful Report Wizard.
- There is no security on data placed in Access, so be sure that any databases that store confidential information are stored on a secure drive.

QUICK REFERENCE GUIDE

In this appendix

This appendix is designed to be an easy, quick-reference guide of the material that is covered in this book, and it should prove helpful for your organization with regard to SAP Query-based reporting, administration, and deployment.

BASICS OF SAP R/3 QUERY-BASED REPORTING

The following SAP R/3 query reporting options are delivered with a standard SAP installation:

- The SAP Query tool
- The InfoSet (Ad Hoc) Query tool
- The QuickViewer tool

The Query tools in SAP have four technical aspects:

- Query areas
- Query groups
- InfoSets
- Administrative decisions (company-specific)

CONFIGURING THE SAP QUERY TOOLS

Configuring the SAP Query tools involves four steps:

- Step 1: Create query groups.
- Step 2: Assign users to query groups.
- Step 3: Create InfoSets.
- Step 4: Assign InfoSets to query groups.

STEP 1 OF 4: CREATE QUERY GROUPS

To do the one-time configuration required for using the SAP Query tool, follow these steps:

1. Log in to the area of your SAP client where your query groups will be maintained.
2. Navigate to the User Groups: Initial screen by using the transaction code /nSQ03.
3. Ensure that you are in the appropriate query area by following the menu path Environment, Query Areas and selecting Standard Area.
4. Type the name for your query group in the User Group field (for example, ZTEST). Then click the Create button.
5. When a dialog box appears, asking you to provide a description for your query group, type Test Query Group 1 and then click the green checkmark Save button.

STEP 2 OF 4: ASSIGN USERS TO YOUR QUERY GROUPS

To assign users to a query group, perform the following steps:

1. Click the Assign Users and InfoSets button.

2. Type in the SAP user IDs of any users you wish to include in your query group, making sure to include your own user ID.

3. Click the Save button on the toolbar. A message appears in your SAPGUI status bar, saying "User group ZTEST saved."

STEP 3 OF 4: CREATE INFOSET

To create a new InfoSet, you perform the following steps:

1. Log in to the area of your SAP client where your InfoSets will be maintained.

2. Navigate to the InfoSet: Initial screen by using the transaction code /nSQ02.

3. Ensure that you are in the appropriate query area by selecting Environment, Query Areas and then selecting Standard Area.

4. Type in a name for your InfoSet (for example, ZTEST). Then click the Create button.

5. On the InfoSet: Title and Database screen, type an InfoSet description in the Name field (for example, Test InfoSet 1).

6. On the InfoSet: Title and Database screen, select the Logical Database radio button, select or input logical database f1s in the field to its right, and then press Enter. A Change InfoSet screen appears, displaying a list of all tables available in the selected logical database for your InfoSet. The logical database selected, f1S, contains three test tables, called SPFLI, SBOOK, and SFLIGHT, which correspond to the three field groups listed at the top right. The field groups are what the end users will actually see when they are creating reports using the SAP Query reporting tool.

7. To view the fields in each of the three tables, use the expand subtree button next to each table name. The table selected expands and displays the fields underneath.

8. Assign fields to the field groups (shown on the top right of the screen) within the InfoSet. These field groups will display in the SAP Query tool during reporting. Only the fields that you include in your field groups will be available for field selection in the SAP Query tool that uses this InfoSet as its data source. By default, these field groups will be empty.

9. Place your cursor on the first field group, Flight Schedule, and double-click to highlight that field group as the selected field group. Next, select fields from the left side of the screen from the Flight Schedule table and add them to the Flight Schedule field group by placing your cursor on a field on the left side of the screen, right-clicking, and selecting the option Add Field to Field Group.

10. When the field you just added to the Flight Schedule field group appears at the top right of the screen, add fields to your selected functional group by following the procedure outlined in step 9. Be sure to add fields to the appropriate field groups.

A

For example, fields in the Flight Schedule table should be added to the Flight Schedule field group, and fields from the Flight Booking table should be added to the Flight Booking field group.

11. After you have added a series of fields to your field groups, click the Save button on the toolbar. A message appears in the status bar, saying that your InfoSet was saved.

12. Generate the InfoSet by clicking the Generate button (the red beach ball) from the Application toolbar. A message appears in the status bar, saying that the InfoSet was generated.

13. Exit the Change InfoSet screen by clicking the green Back button.

STEP 4 OF 4: ASSIGN INFOSET TO QUERY GROUP

To assign an InfoSet to a query group, you follow these steps:

1. On the InfoSet: Initial screen (which you reach by entering transaction code /n**SQ02**), make sure your InfoSet name (for example, ZTEST) is present in the InfoSet text box, and click the User Group Assignment button.

2. In the InfoSet: Assign to User Groups screen that appears, highlight your query group (for example, ZTEST) by selecting the gray button to the left of it, and then click the Save button. A message appears in the status bar, saying that the assignment of InfoSet has been saved.

3. Exit the InfoSet: Assign to User Groups screen by clicking the green Back button.

QUERY CONFIGURATION MAINTENANCE FUNCTIONS

To return to a data source and make changes to it, you follow these steps:

RETURNING TO AN INFOSET TO ADD FIELDS

To add an additional field to your InfoSet, follow these steps:

1. Log in to the area of your SAP client where your InfoSets are maintained.

2. Navigate to the InfoSet: Initial Screen by using the transaction code /n**SQ02**.

3. Ensure that you are in the appropriate query area by selecting Environment, Query Areas and then selecting Standard Area.

4. Type the name of the InfoSet that you want to make changes to and then click the Change button.

5. Review the fields that are currently present in the field groups (shown on the top right of your screen) in your InfoSet.

6. When you initially created the InfoSet, it is likely that you did not add all fields in the logical database to your field groups. Determine which field group is the appropriate one to add a field to. Place your cursor on that field group and double-click it to highlight it as the selected field group. Then select fields from the left side of the screen

from the corresponding table and add them to the highlighted field group by placing your cursor on a field on the left side of the screen, right-clicking, and selecting the option Add Field to Field Group Remember to ensure that you add fields to the appropriate field group. Your newly added fields now appear in your selected field group.

7. When you have finished adding fields, click the Save button on the toolbar. A message appears in the status bar, saying that the InfoSet was saved.

8. Generate the InfoSet by clicking the Generate button on the Application toolbar. A message appears in the status bar, saying that the InfoSet has been generated.

RETURNING TO AN INFOSET TO DELETE FIELDS

To delete a field from your InfoSet, follow these steps:

1. Log in to the area of the SAP client where your InfoSets are maintained.

2. Navigate to the InfoSet: Initial screen by using the transaction code /nSQ02.

3. Ensure that you are in the appropriate query area by following the menu path Environment, Query Areas and selecting Standard Area.

4. Type in the InfoSet name and then click the Change button. The Change InfoSet screen appears, displaying a list of all the tables available in your InfoSet. The logical database f1S that is selected contains three test tables, called SPFLI, SBOOK, and SFLIGHT, which correspond to the three field groups listed at the top right.

5. To view the fields in each of the three tables, use the expand subtree button next to each table name. The table selected expands and displays the fields underneath.

6. Review the fields that are currently present in the field groups (shown on the top right of your screen) in your InfoSet.

7. Determine which field group you want to delete fields from and place your cursor on it. Double-click the field group to highlight it as the selected field group. Next, place your cursor on a field in the field group on the top-right side of the screen, right-click, and select the option Delete Field from Field Group. The deleted fields no longer appear in your selected field group.

8. When you have finished deleting fields, click the Save button on the toolbar. A message appears in the status bar, saying that the InfoSet was saved.

9. Generate the InfoSet by clicking the Generate button on the Application toolbar. A message appears in the status bar, saying that the InfoSet has been generated.

CHANGING THE NAME OF A FIELD OR COLUMN HEADER

You can alter the name of a field and its column heading when it appears in a query-based report by simply following these steps:

1. Select a field by double-clicking it in the top-right side of the screen. The details of that field appear on the bottom-right side of the screen.

2. Alter the field name by editing the text in the Long Text field, and edit the column heading of the field as it will appear in reports by editing the text in the second line of the Header field at the bottom right.

3. Click the Save button on the toolbar. A message appears in the status bar, saying that the InfoSet was saved.

4. Generate the InfoSet by clicking the Generate button on the Application toolbar. A message appears in the status bar, saying that the InfoSet has been generated.

REVERTING THE NAME OF A FIELD OR COLUMN HEADER TO ITS ORIGINAL NAME

If you have altered the name of a field or column heading, you can revert it to the standard SAP-delivered text by following these steps:

1. Select a field by double-clicking it in the top-right side of the screen. The details of that field appear on the bottom-right side of the screen.

2. Click the Get Default button. The field and column names revert to their original names.

3. Click the Save button on the toolbar. A message appears in the status bar, saying that the InfoSet was saved.

4. Generate the InfoSet by clicking the Generate button on the Application toolbar. A message appears in the status bar, saying that the InfoSet has been generated.

CREATING A BASIC LIST QUERY BY USING THE SAP QUERY TOOL

To create a basic list query by using the SAP Query tool, follow these steps:

1. Log in to your SAP client where your query reports will be created.

2. Navigate to the Maintain Queries Initial screen by using the transaction code /nSQ01. SAP offers a graphical version of the SAP Query tool, called the Graphical Query Painter; if you have not used the SAP Query tool, the Graphical Query Painter is set as your default. To turn off the Graphical Query Painter and learn to create easy step-by-step reports by using the SAP Query tool, select Settings, Settings and then deselect the Graphical Query Painter check box.

3. The title bar lists the query group you are currently in. For example, your title bar might read Query from User Group ZTEST: Initial Screen. If you are assigned to multiple query groups, press F7 to see a list of them all.

4. As discussed in Chapter 1, "Getting Started with the SAP R/3 Query Reporting Tools," it is recommended that you create your queries in the standard query area. Ensure that you are in the standard query area by selecting Environment, Query Areas and then selecting Standard Area.

5. In the Query field, type **DLS_QUERY_01** where **DLS** is your initials) as the name for the query you are creating and then click the Create button.

6. The InfoSets of User Group ZTEST window appears, listing all the available InfoSets (that is, data sources) for your query group. Because you created only one (in my example, ZTEST) in Chapter 2, "One-Time Configuration for Query Tool Use," it is the only one listed. Select the InfoSet you created (ZTEST, in my example) and then click the green check mark button.

7. The Create Query Title Format screen appears. This screen allows you to save the basic formatting specifications for your query, including the name (title) and any notes you want to store for the query. The only required field is Title (long report description). For this example, fill in only the Title field and then click Save. (For my example, I used the title (DLS) SAP Query Exercise #01.)

8. Navigate to the next screen in the SAP query creation process by selecting the Next Screen (white navigational arrow) button on the Application toolbar. (You can use the navigational arrows to navigate between the different screens of the SAP Query tool.) The Select Field Group screen appears, listing all the Field groups available within your InfoSet. (In my example, the field groups Flight Schedule [SPFLI], Flight Demo Table [SFLIGHT], and Flight Booking [SBOOK] are listed.)

9. Place a check mark next to each field group from which you want to include fields in your report. Navigate to the next screen in the SAP query creation process by selecting the Next Screen (white navigational arrow) button on the Application toolbar. The Select Field screen appears, showing a list of all the available fields in the selected field groups.

10. Place a check mark next to each field that you want to include in your report. You can use the Page Up and Page Down keys to navigate between all the fields. Select the Next Screen (white navigational arrow) button on the Application toolbar to open the Selections screen, which lists all the fields you have selected.

11. If desired, add any of the fields to the selection screen that will be presented when you execute your report. You can add a field to the Selections screen by placing a check mark next to each one.

12. Click the Basic List button on the Application toolbar to create an SAP basic list query. The Basic List Line Structure screen appears, showing a list of the fields that you selected to include in your report.

13. For each field, specify the line and sequence number, as you want them to appear on your report. Also use this screen to indicate sort order, totals, and counts, if needed. Start by entering the line and sequence numbers.

14. For this example, proceed directly to the report by pressing F8, which causes the report to execute.

15. As with almost all other reports in SAP, when you execute this report, you see the report's selection screen. Specify any criteria for the output of your report. Notice that any fields indicated on the Selections screen are included on your selection screen, under the heading Program Selections.

A

16. Select the F8 Execute button on your Application toolbar (it looks like a clock) to display your finished report. Your report output appears. (Keep in mind that the actual values vary by organization: The output of the report corresponds to the specification entered on the Basic List Line Structure screen.)

QUERY MAINTENANCE FUNCTIONS

Table A.1 provides detailed descriptions of each of the output format options.

TABLE A.1   SAP QUERY REPORTING OUTPUT OPTIONS

Option	Description
SAP List Viewer	When you select this option, your list is not displayed onscreen in the normal form when the query is processed. Instead, the first sublist is transferred to the SAP List Viewer directly. You must be able to transfer this first sublist (it must be either a single-line basic list, a statistic, or a ranked list). This is the default selection.
ABAP List	When you select this option, the report appears in SAP as a basic list, without any formatting or fancy Microsoft Excel–looking features. This was the format of all standard SAP Query tool reports in versions earlier than SAP 4.6C.
Graphic	This function allows you to display the information from your list by using SAP Business Graphics. In contrast to the other functions described in this table, the Graphic function can handle an extract from only one column of your sublist, and the column must contain numeric values. In addition, your SAP system has to have Business Graphics enabled.
ABC Analysis	You can use the ABC Analysis function for any single-line basic list, all statistics, and any ranked list that contains at least one numeric field.
Executive Information System (EIS)	This function provides a link to the Executive Information System (EIS). It transfers the data in your query to the EIS database via an interface so that you can perform further analyses. When you activate this function, you specify various options or storing the data in a dialog box.
File Store	When you select this option, the list is not displayed onscreen when you execute the query, but the first sublist is passed directly to the download interface and stored as a file. The first sublist must be a single-line basic list, a statistic, or a ranked list. When you select the field, a parameter is predefined on the selection screen.
Display as Table	When you select this option, your report output is displayed in an SAP Table Control object that looks similar to the SAP List Viewer but offers less functionality. The first sublist must be a one-line basic list, a statistic, or a ranked list. When you select this option, a parameter is predefined on the selection screen.

Option	Description
Word Processing	When you select this option, the word processing functions can be called from the list display and from the table display. You can use this option to create Microsoft Word form letters.
Spreadsheet	When you select this option, the spreadsheet functions can be called from the list display and from the table display. You can use this option to create Microsoft Excel spreadsheets.
Private File	When you select this option, the list is not displayed onscreen when you execute the query, but the sublist is passed directly to a function module. This is an SAP enhancement and must be implemented by the customer.

COPYING EXISTING SAP QUERIES (SAME CLIENT, SAME QUERY GROUP)

Follow these steps to copy a query:

1. Navigate to the main screen of the SAP Query tool by using transaction code **SQ01** and select from the list the query you want to copy (or type the query's name in the Query box at the top of the screen).

2. Click the white copy button on the Application toolbar. The Copy a Query dialog box appears.

3. Type in a new name for your copied SAP query in the To Query Name box and then press Enter. Be sure to follow the naming rules discussed earlier in this appendix when naming the copied query.

4. When your copied SAP query appears in the same user group as the original, change the long report title (description) of the copied query to distinguish it from the original.

COPYING OR MOVING EXISTING SAP QUERIES (SAME CLIENT, DIFFERENT QUERY GROUP)

Follow these steps to copy a query to a new query group:

1. Navigate to the main screen of the SAP Query tool by using transaction code **SQ01** and select from the list the query you want to copy (or type the query's name in the Query box at the top of the screen).

2. On a scrap of paper, write down the name of the query and the name of the query group in which it currently resides.

3. Press Shift+F7 to view a list of all query groups to which you are assigned.

4. Double-click the query group you want to move the query to. You are now on the main screen of the SAP Query tool, and the query group is listed on the top left of the screen.

5. Click the white Copy button on the Application toolbar.

6. When a dialog box appears, take a look at your scrap of paper and type the query and query group names into the form.

7. Type a new name for your copied SAP query in the To Query Name box, ensuring that the Query (User) Group lists the new query group name to which you are moving the query.

8. Press Enter. Your copied SAP query, with its new name, appears in the new query group, along with the original query group.

9. Be sure to change the long report title (description) of the copied query to distinguish it from the original (as needed), and be sure to follow the naming rules discussed earlier in this chapter when naming the copied query.

DELETING SAP QUERIES

To delete an SAP query, follow these steps:

1. Navigate to the main screen of the SAP Query tool by using transaction code **SQ01** and select from the list the query you want to delete (or type the query's name in the Query box at the top of the screen).

2. Select the trash can Delete button on the Application toolbar.

3. When the Delete Query dialog box appears, confirm that you want to delete the query by pressing Enter. A message appears in the bottom left of the screen, letting you know that the query has been successfully deleted.

CREATING A VARIANT FOR AN SAP QUERY

You can create a variant in several different ways. The following instructions work for any version of SAP, beginning with version 4.0:

1. Begin at the main screen of the SAP Query tool, which you reach by using transaction code **SQ01**. Select the query for which you would like to create a variant by selecting (highlighting) the gray bar to the left of the table or by typing the query name in the box at the top of the screen.

2. Select Goto, Maintain Variants. The screen ABAP Variants - Initial Screen appears.

3. Type a name for your variant and then click the Create button. You are presented with the selection screen for the report for which you decided to create a variant in step 1. This screen gives you the opportunity to input selections that will be saved as a variant.

4. Input values on the selection screen that you want to save and then click the Save button on the Application toolbar. The first time you save the variant, the Save Attributes screen appears. When you modify an existing variant, you can click the Variant Attributes button to access this screen.

5. The only required field for entry on the Save Attributes screen is the Description field. Enter a description for your variant in this field and then click the Save button to complete the variant creation process. It is a good idea to use a description that describes the variant.

6. Click the green Back button to return to the Maintain Variants screen.

7. Click the green Back button again to return to the main SAP Query tool screen.

EXECUTING A REPORT WITH A VARIANT (EXECUTE WITH VARIANT)

Multiple variants can exist for a report, and you can decide which one to use prior to report execution by following these steps:

1. Begin at the main screen of the SAP Query tool, which you reach by using transaction code **SQ01**. Select your report and then click the Execute with Variant button on the Application toolbar. A dialog box that contains a drop-down field of all the variants for the selected report appears.

2. Select the variant you want to use and then press Enter.

3. Click the Execute button. The report executes, displaying the saved variant.

EXECUTING A REPORT WITH A VARIANT (EXECUTE)

Multiple variants can exist for a report, and you can decide which one to use upon report execution by following these steps:

1. Begin at the main screen of the SAP Query tool, which you reach by using transaction code **SQ01**. Select your report and then press F8 or click the Execute button. The report's selection screen appears.

2. On the selection screen's Application toolbar, click the Get Variant button (immediately to the right of the Execute button). A dialog box containing a drop-down field of all variants for the selected report appears.

3. Select the variant you want to use and then press Enter.

4. Click the Execute button. The report executes, displaying the selected variant.

SAVING AN SAP QUERY WITH A VARIANT

In addition to selecting a variant prior to or upon report execution, you can save a variant with a query as a default, such that when the report is executed, that variant is automatically used to populate the report's selection screen:

1. Begin at the main screen of the SAP Query tool, which you reach by using transaction code **SQ01**. Select your report and then click the Change button. The Title, Format screen of the SAP Query tool appears.

2. In the Special Attributes section of the Title, Format screen, select the Variant drop-down box to see a list of all variants that exist for the selected report.

3. Select the variant you want to use and then press Enter.

4. Check the Execute Only with Variant check box.

5. Click the Save button and then press F8 or click Execute.

6. Click the Execute button. The report executes, displaying the saved variant. Because it was saved with the query, every time it is executed, the saved default variant will be used. The variant can be overwritten with new values, or a new variant can be selected after execution; however, it will always be presented as the default.

EDITING A VARIANT FOR AN SAP QUERY DIRECTLY FROM THE SELECTION SCREEN

After a variant is created, you can modify it on the selection screen by following these steps:

1. On the selection screen, change the values as desired and then click the Save button on the Application toolbar. A confirmation box appears, asking if you want to overwrite the existing variant.

2. Click Yes. The changes to your variant are saved.

EDITING A VARIANT FOR AN SAP QUERY FROM THE ABAP VARIANTS - INITIAL SCREEN

After a variant is created, you can modify it on the screen ABAP Variants - Initial Screen by following these steps:

1. Begin at the main screen of the SAP Query tool, which you reach by using transaction code **SQ01**. Select the query for which you would like to modify the variant by selecting (highlighting) the gray bar to the left of the table or by typing the query name in the box at the top of the screen.

2. Select Goto, Maintain Variants. The screen ABAP Variants - Initial Screen appears.

3. Select your variant from the drop-down box and then click the Change button. You are presented with the selection screen for the report.

4. Modify the values on the selection screen as you like and then click the Save button on the Application toolbar.

5. To modify the attributes, click the Variant Attributes button and make the desired changes.

6. Make any other modifications desired on this screen and then click the Save button to complete the variant modification process.

CREATING A STATISTICS LIST WITH THE SAP QUERY TOOL

To create a statistics list report by using the SAP Query tool, you follow these steps:

1. Navigate to the Maintain Queries Initial screen by using transaction code **/nSQ01**.

2. Ensure that you are in the standard query area by selecting Environment, Query Areas and then choosing Standard Area (Client-Specific).

3. In the Query field, enter a name for the query you are creating (for example, **DLS_Exercise_12**, where *DLS* is your initials) and then click the Create button.

4. When the InfoSets of User Group ZTEST window appears, listing all the available InfoSets (that is, data sources) for your query group, select the ZTEST InfoSet and then press Enter. The Create Query Title Format screen appears, allowing you to save the basic formatting specifications for your query, including the name (title) and any notes you want to store for the query. The only required field is Title. Click the Save button on the toolbar.

5. Click the Next Screen button on the Application toolbar to navigate to the Select Field Group screen.

6. When the Select Field Group screen appears, listing all the field groups available in your InfoSet, place a check mark next to each field group whose fields you want to include in your report. (In my example, I selected all of them.) Click the Next Screen button on the Application toolbar.

7. When the Select Fields screen appears, giving you a list of all the available fields within the selected field groups, place a check mark next to each field that you want to include in your report. You can use the Page Up and Page Down buttons to navigate between all the fields. For this example, include the following fields:

   ■ Airline Carrier ID

   ■ Arrival City

   ■ Airfare

   ■ Text: Flight Class

8. Click the Next Screen button on the Application toolbar to continue. The Selections screen appears, listing all the fields you selected on the Select Fields screen, giving you the opportunity to add fields to your report's selection screen.

9. Add to your report's selection screen any fields you want by placing a check mark next to each field.

10. Click the Statistics button on the Application toolbar to create a statistics list in the SAP Query tool. The Statistics Line Structure screen appears, giving you an opportunity to define your compressed list report.

11. Use the Statistics Line Structure screen to dictate how you want your report to appear, including sequence and summing specifications. You determine the statistics in this series of screens. Each statistic must have its own unique title, because you might generate several statistics. Specify the sequence in which you want to output the fields and state whether you want them to be sorted in ascending or descending order. Totals are always calculated for numeric fields. You can therefore determine average values, the number of selected records, and the percentage share.

12. Press F8 to execute the report. As with almost all other reports in SAP, upon execution, you see the report's selection screen. The selection screen gives you an opportunity to specify any criteria for the output of your report. Notice that any fields indicated on the Selections screen are included on your selection screen, under the heading Program Selections.

13. Click the F8 Execute button on the Application toolbar to display your finished report.

A

CREATING A SUBTOTALED STATISTICS LIST WITH THE SAP QUERY TOOL

To create a subtotaled statistics list report with the SAP Query tool, follow these steps:

1. Navigate to the Maintain Queries Initial screen by using transaction code /nSQ01.

2. In the Query field, enter a name for the query you are creating (for example, DLS_Exercise_12B, where DLS is your initials) and then click the Create button.

3. When the InfoSets of User Group ZTEST window appears, listing all the available InfoSets (that is, data sources) for your query group, select the ZTEST InfoSet and then press Enter. The Create Query Title Format screen appears. Enter a title and then click the Save button on the toolbar.

4. To navigate to the next screen in the SAP query creation process, click the Next Screen (white navigational arrow) button on the Application toolbar. The Select Field Groups screen appears, listing all the field groups available within the InfoSet. Place a check mark next to each field group from which you want to include fields in your report (I selected them all). Click the Next Screen button on the Application toolbar.

5. When the Select Fields screen appears, listing all the available fields within the selected field groups, place a check mark next to each field that you want to include in your report. You can use the Page Up and Page Down arrows to navigate between all the fields. For this example, include the following fields:

   - Airline Carrier ID
   - Arrival City
   - Airfare
   - Text: Flight Class

6. Click the Next Screen button on the application toolbar to continue.

7. When the Selections screen appears, listing all the fields you selected on the Select Fields screen, add any of the fields to the selection screen that will be presented when you execute your report. You can add any fields you want to the selection screen by placing a check mark next to each field. For this example I have not added any.

8. Click the Statistics button on the application toolbar to create a statistics list in the SAP Query tool.

9. When the Statistics Line Structure screen appears, define your compressed list report. Specify the sequence in which you want to output the fields, and state whether you want them to be sorted in ascending or descending order. Indicate the Text option for each of the fields. Indicate a subtotal for the Airline Carrier ID field.

10. Press the F8 button on your keyboard to execute the report. As with almost all other reports in SAP, upon execution, you are presented with the report's selection screen.

11. Click the F8 Execute button on the Application toolbar to display your finished report. Your report output appears.

CREATING A RANKED LIST BY USING THE SAP QUERY TOOL

To create a ranked list by using the SAP Query tool, follow these steps:

1. Navigate to the main screen of the SAP Query tool by using transaction code **SQ01**, select the query you want to work with (for example, *DLS*_QUERY_14, where *DLS* is your initials), and click the Change button.

2. Navigate to the Select Field Groups screen and select the field group names that contain the fields you want to include in your report. (In my example, I selected all three.) Click the Next Screen button on the Application toolbar to access the Select Fields screen.

3. Select the fields you want to include in your report: Airline Carrier ID, Flight Date, Maximum Capacity, and Total of Current Bookings.

4. If the short names are not already displayed, select Edit, Short Names, Switch On/Off to turn them on. Enter the short name **MAX** for the Maximum Capacity field and the short name **OCC** for the Occupied Seats field.

5. Create a calculated field that determines how many seats are free on each flight by taking the number of available seats (Maximum Capacity field) and subtracting the number of seats taken (Occupied Seats field). Position your cursor in the Occupied Seats field to base your calculated field on it.

6. Select Edit, Local Field, Create. The Define Field dialog box appears. Input **Free** as the short name for your newly created local field and input the field description **Free Seats**, which will be the heading for the column in the report.

7. Define the attributes for the new field. It should have the same attributes as the Occupied Seats field (OCC).

8. Select the Calculation Formula option button at the bottom of the dialog box (it should be selected by default) and then enter the basic mathematical formula **MAX – OCC** in the box to the right of it. This formula will start with the total maximum capacity for the flight and subtract the number of seats currently occupied to yield the number of available or free seats left over.

9. Click the Continue button to close the Define Field dialog box and return to the Select Field Groups screen.

10. Navigate to the Ranked List Structure screen by clicking the Ranked List button on the Application toolbar. The Ranked List Structure screen appears, allowing you to define your report output. Name your compressed list report `Ranked_List_1`.

11. Use the Ranked List Structure screen to dictate how you want your report to appear, including rank number specifications. Assign a sequence number to each field that appears in the ranked list to determine the sequence in which they are output. Review the nine options available on this screen.

A

12. Assign the sequence numbers, starting with 1 and in ascending order, without breaks. Indicate that you want to output the fields Airline Carrier ID, Flight Date, Free Seats, and Maximum Capacity. Specify the sequence in which you want to output the fields, and state whether you want them to be sorted in ascending or descending order.

13. Indicate that you want to rank on free seats.

14. To execute the report and view the selection screen, press F8.

15. Press F8 to display your finished report. Your report output should appear. Keep in mind that the actual values vary by organization.

CREATING A BASIC QUERY WITH THE INFOSET (AD HOC) QUERY TOOL

To create a basic report with the InfoSet (Ad Hoc) Query tool, follow these steps:

1. Log in to the area of your SAP client where your query reports will be created.

2. Access the InfoSet (Ad Hoc) Query tool in one of the three possible ways:

   ■ Through an application-specific role, using the Easy Access menu

   ■ Via the SAP Query tool, by using transaction code `SQ01` and then clicking the InfoSet Query button

   ■ Via transaction code `/nPQAH`

   When you navigate to the InfoSet (Ad Hoc) Query tool main screen using any of these methods, you see a dialog box that prompts you to select your InfoSet (data source) from the designated environment (QUERY group).

3. Select your InfoSet and then press Enter. The main screen of the InfoSet (Ad Hoc) Query tool appears. The main screen of the InfoSet (Ad Hoc) Query tool has three sections:

   ■ The actual InfoSet from which you select and choose your fields (top left)

   ■ A Selections section (top right)

   ■ A sample report display (bottom)

4. To create an InfoSet (Ad Hoc) Query report, select the check box in the Output column next to each field you want to include in the output of your report.

5. Notice that any field selected for layout is now displayed at the bottom of the screen (with bogus data) to assist you in seeing what your report will look like.

6. Add fields to your Selections section (which functions as the report's selection screen) by selecting the appropriate check box in the Selection column next to each field you want to be able to select on (that is, specify) when executing your report. Any field(s) indicated for selection now appear on the top-right side of the screen. The Selections section works just as a standard selection screen works, allowing you to input values before execution to further specify your reporting output. (For example, you could specify to include only business class (Type C) flights in a report.)

7. To proceed to your InfoSet (Ad Hoc) Query report output, click the Start Output button on the Application toolbar (or press the F8 key on your keyboard) to execute the report. By default, your report displays in the SAP List Viewer (previously known as the ABAP List Viewer [ALV]), from which you can easily drag and drop the columns and/or manipulate the look of the output.

CREATING A QUICKVIEW WITH QUICKVIEWER

Creating a QuickView by using the QuickViewer tool is simple. You just follow these steps:

1. Navigate to the main screen of the SAP R/3 QuickViewer by using transaction **SQVI**. (You can also open the QuickViewer's main screen by clicking the QuickViewer button on the main screen of the SAP Query tool or by choosing an application-specific role from the Easy Access menu.)

2. On the main screen, enter a name for your QuickView (for example, **QUICKVIEW_1**) and then click the Create button. A dialog box appears, asking you to select your data source.

3. On the Create QuickView: Choose Data Source dialog box, insert a title (for example, **Sample QuickView**) and, if desired, insert comments (for example, the date it was created).

4. Identify where your data is coming from by selecting an option in the Data Source field (for example, a logical database). When you select a data source, the bottom of the screen changes to show suboptions specific to the data source (for example, a specific logical database). For this example, enter the logical database Flight Scheduling System (f1S).

5. At the bottom of the dialog box, indicate to create the QuickView in Basic mode. When you are done making entries and selections in this dialog, click the green arrow Enter button.

6. Select the first tab on the main screen, the List Fld. Select tab, which lists the output fields. Select any fields on the right side of the screen, listed in the Available Fields grouping, by selecting the gray keys to the left of the field names, and then click the left-pointing single-arrow button between the two groupings. To move all fields in the data source so that they will be included in your report output, click the left-pointing double-arrow button.

7. Select the second tab, Sort Sequence, to dictate the sort order for the selected fields. Indicate a desired order by selecting fields on the right side of the screen, in the Available Fields grouping, and then click the left-pointing single-arrow button between the two groupings. The selected fields appear in the Fields in List column, in the order in which they were selected. Use the radio buttons to the left of the fields to specify that you want the field to be sorted in ascending or descending order.

A

8. Select the third tab, Selection Fields, to indicate what fields to include on the QuickView's selection screen upon execution. (Note that some fields already exist, as indicated by a lock icon, based on designations in the logical database—f1S in this case—selected for the QuickView.) Select fields on the right side of the screen, in the Available Fields grouping, and then click the left-pointing single-arrow button between the two groupings. The selected fields (for example, the Flight Class field) appear in the Selection Fields column.

9. Select the fourth tab, Data Source, to confirm that the QuickViewer is using the correct data source for this QuickView.

10. Note in the middle of the screen that you have different export options for the QuickView. SAP List Viewer is the default, but you can select a different option from the Export As drop-down box.

11. Click the Execute button on the Application toolbar to view the report's selection screen. If needed, further specify your selections on the selection screen.

12. Click the Execute button to see your completed QuickView.

REPORT DISTRIBUTION STRATEGIES

You have multiple options for distributing SAP R/3 query-based reports:

- Adding queries to transaction codes (and subsequently to Favorites menus)
- Adding queries to menu paths
- Scheduling reports to run as jobs with automatic distribution to an email address in various forms (PDF, XLS, TXT, and so on.)
- Creating a report tree

INDEX